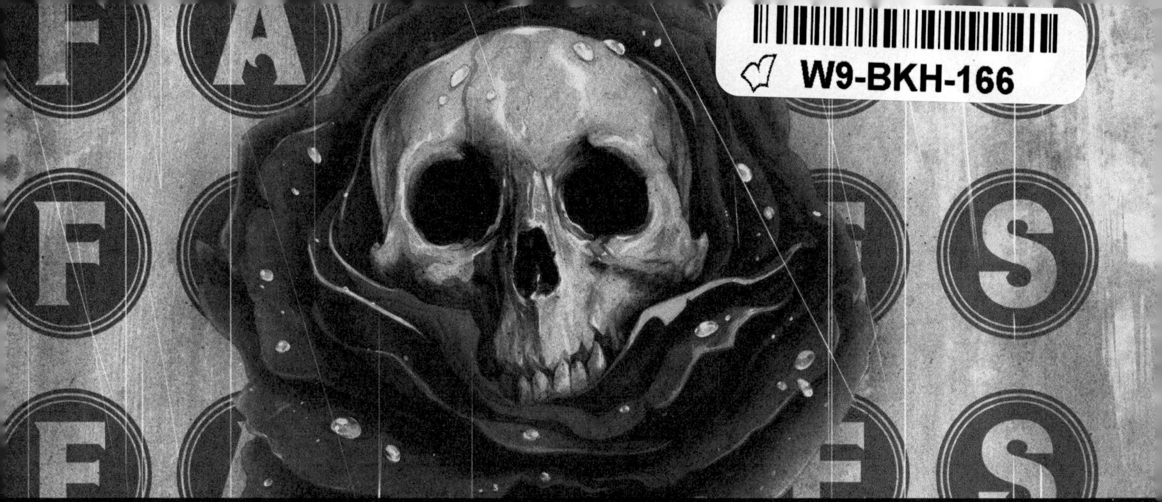

FABLES: HAPPILY EVER AFTER

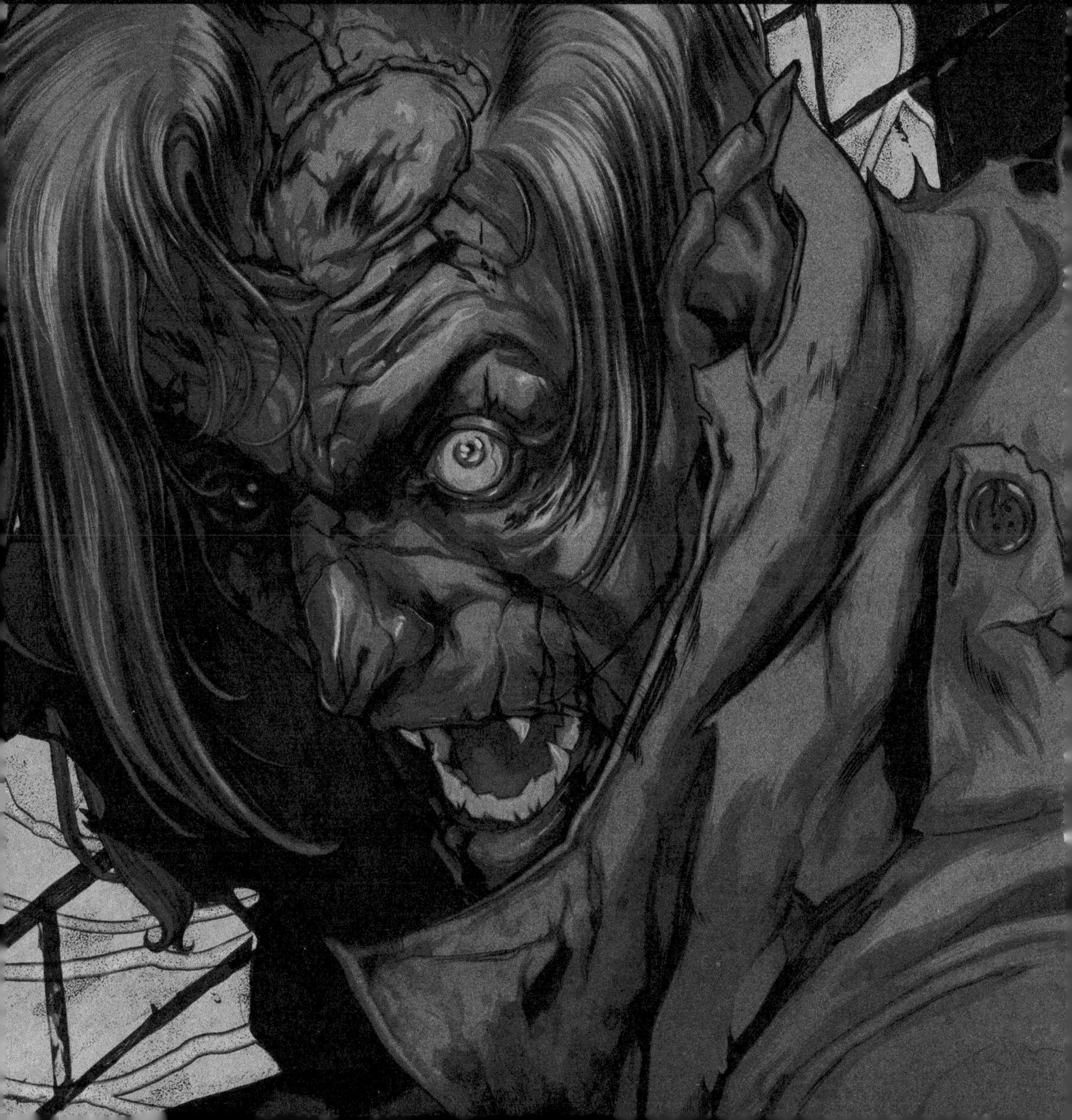

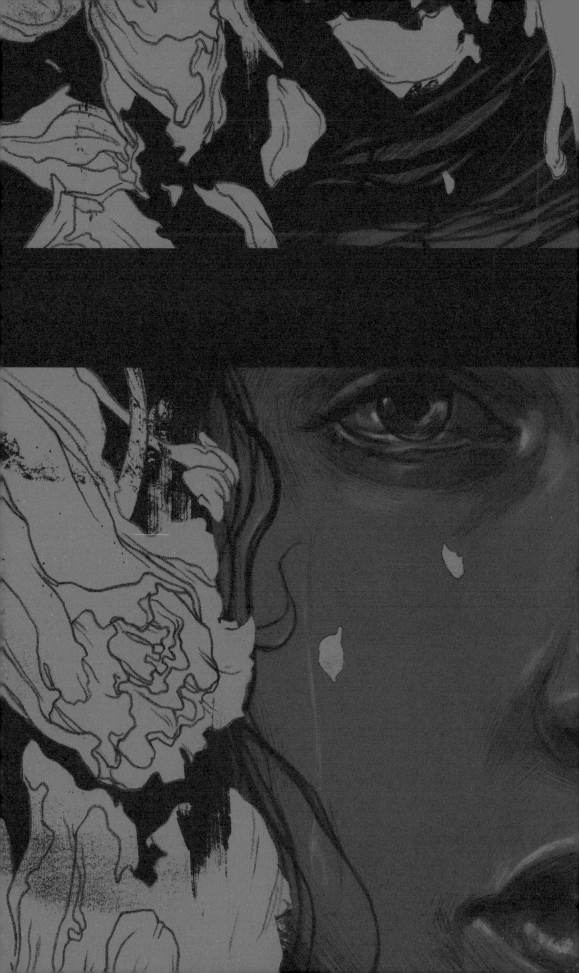

FABLES: HAPPILY EVER AFTER

FABLES CREATED BY BILL WILLINGHAM

Bill Willingham
Matthew Sturges
Writers

Mark Buckingham
Steve Leialoha
Andrew Pepoy
Dan Green
Eric Shanower
Tony Akins
Shawn McManus
Nimit Malavia
Jae Lee
Terry Moore
Russ Braun
Chrissie Zullo
Artists

Lee Loughridge
June Chung
Andrew Dalhouse
Colorists

Todd Klein
Letterer

Nimit Malavia
Cover Art and Original Series Covers

SHELLY BOND
Executive Editor – Vertigo and Editor – Original Series

ROWENA YOW
Associate Editor – Original Series

SCOTT NYBAKKEN
Editor

ROBBIN BROSTERMAN
Design Director – Books

HANK KANALZ
Senior VP – Vertigo and Integrated Publishing

DIANE NELSON
President

DAN DIDIO and **JIM LEE**
Co-Publishers

GEOFF JOHNS
Chief Creative Officer

AMIT DESAI
Senior VP – Marketing and Franchise Management

AMY GENKINS
Senior VP – Business and Legal Affairs

NAIRI GARDINER
Senior VP – Finance

JEFF BOISON
VP – Publishing Planning

MARK CHIARELLO
VP – Art Direction and Design

JOHN CUNNINGHAM
VP – Marketing

TERRI CUNNINGHAM
VP – Editorial Administration

LARRY GANEM
VP – Talent Relations and Services

ALISON GILL
Senior VP – Manufacturing and Operations

JAY KOGAN
VP – Business and Legal Affairs, Publishing

JACK MAHAN
VP – Business Affairs, Talent

NICK NAPOLITANO
VP – Manufacturing Administration

SUE POHJA
VP – Book Sales

FRED RUIZ
VP – Manufacturing Operations

COURTNEY SIMMONS
Senior VP – Publicity

BOB WAYNE
Senior VP – Sales

This volume of final planning, penultimate schemes and fatal farewells is dedicated with respect and gratitude to the comic shop retailers who took FABLES immediately to heart and hand-sold issues in multitudes to readers of all stripes, creating returning customers of remarkable loyalty. Forgive me for thanking you collectively, but thanks are owed and hereby tendered.
— *Bill Willingham*

In memory of Ashley Salter and Jeremy Dale.
— *Mark Buckingham*

Logo design by Brainchild Studios/NYC

FABLES: HAPPILY EVER AFTER

Published by DC Comics. Compilation Copyright © 2015 Bill Willingham and DC Comics. All Rights Reserved.

Originally published in single magazine form as FABLES 141-149. Copyright © 2014, 2015 Bill Willingham and DC Comics. All Rights Reserved. All characters, their distinctive likenesses and related elements featured in this publication are trademarks of Bill Willingham. VERTIGO is a trademark of DC Comics. The stories, characters and incidents featured in this publication are entirely fictional. DC Comics does not read or accept unsolicited submissions of ideas, stories or artwork.

DC Comics, 1700 Broadway, New York, NY 10019
A Warner Bros. Entertainment Company.
Printed in the USA. First Printing.
ISBN: 978-1-4012-5132-1

Library of Congress Cataloging-in-Publication Data

Willingham, Bill, author.
  Fables. Volume 21, / Bill Willingham, Mark Buckingham.
    pages cm
    ISBN 978-1-4012-5132-1 (paperback)
  1. Fairy tales--Comic books, strips, etc. 2. Legends—Comic books, strips, etc. 3. Graphic novels. I. Buckingham, Mark, illustrator. II. Title.
  PN6727.W52F434 2014
  741.5'973—dc23
                            2014010271

SUSTAINABLE FORESTRY INITIATIVE   Certified Sourcing
www.sfiprogram.org
SFI-01042
APPLIES TO TEXT STOCK ONLY

Table of Contents

WHO'S WHO IN FABLETOWN

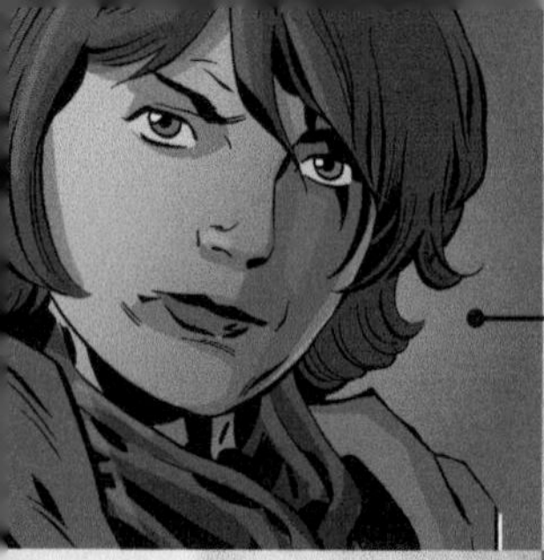

Rose Red

Snow White's sister, and the newest incarnation of the timeless King Arthur archetype.

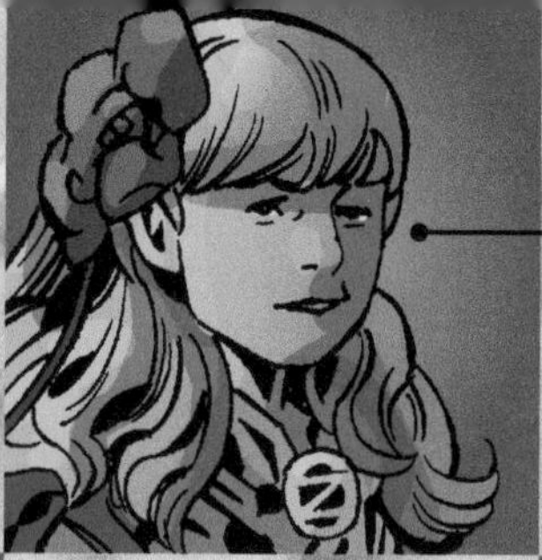

OZMA

The misleadingly youthful-looking leader of Fabletown wizards and witches.

MADDY

Also known as the Invisible Walker, her feline stealthiness is unmatched in this or any other world.

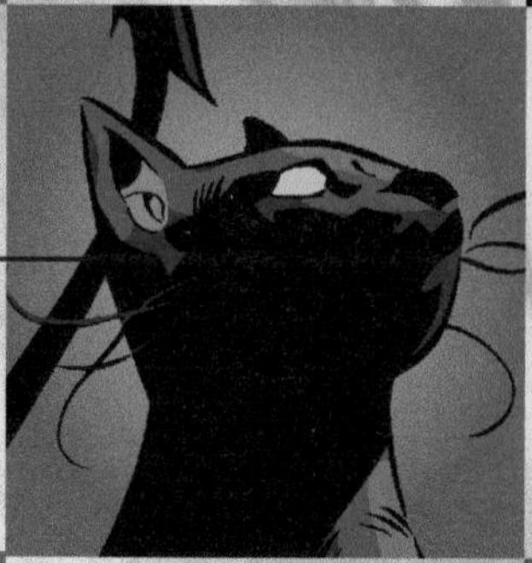

CINDERELLA

An off-the-books spy and general clandestine badass.

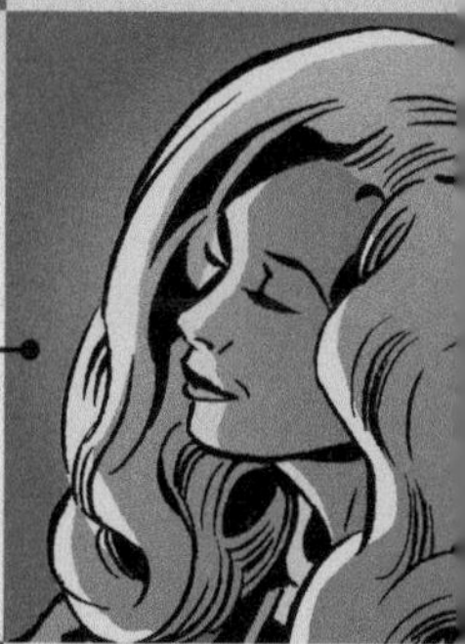

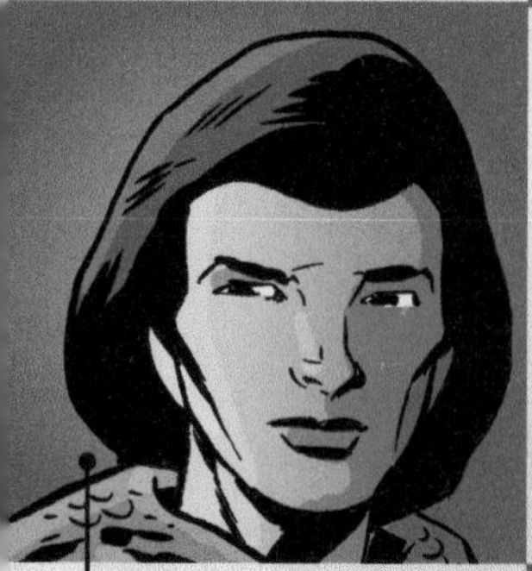

BLOSSOM WOLF

One of Snow and Bigby's six surviving children.

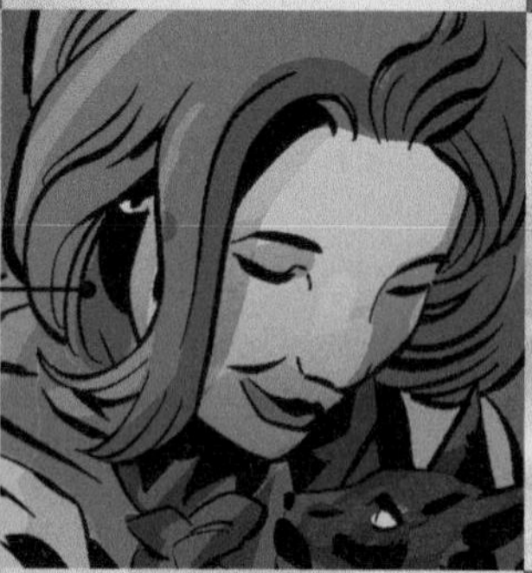

WINTER WOLF

Another child of Snow and Bigby, she has taken up th mantle of her late grandfa to serve as the new North

LANCELOT DU LAC

After a long exile spent in the armor of the Forsworn Knight, this rehabilitated paladin has assumed a new position in Rose Red's court.

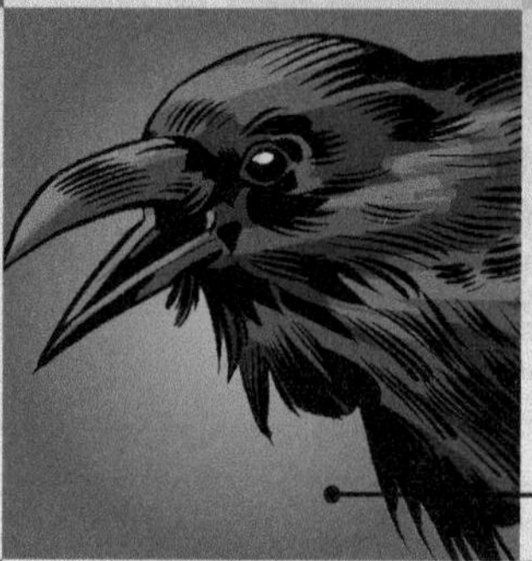

CLARA

A cunningly disguised dragon.

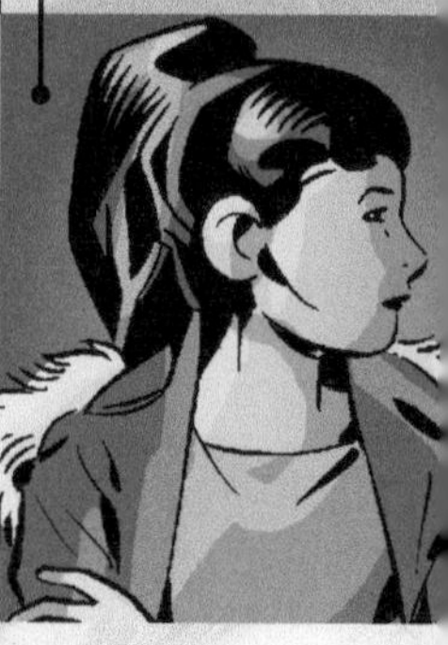

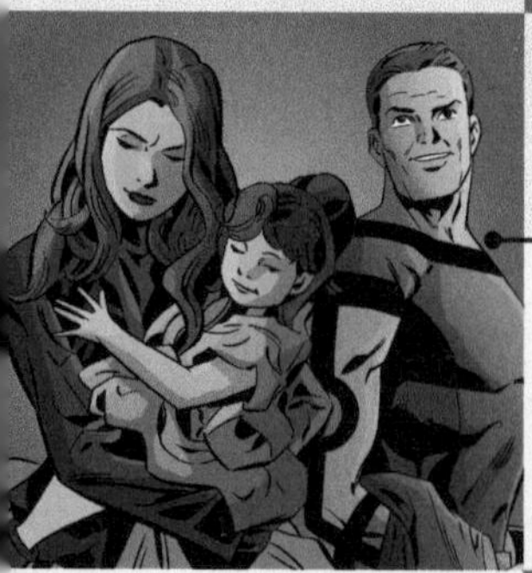

BEAUTY, BEAST AND BLISS

The family unit of Fabletown's former deputy mayor and sheriff.

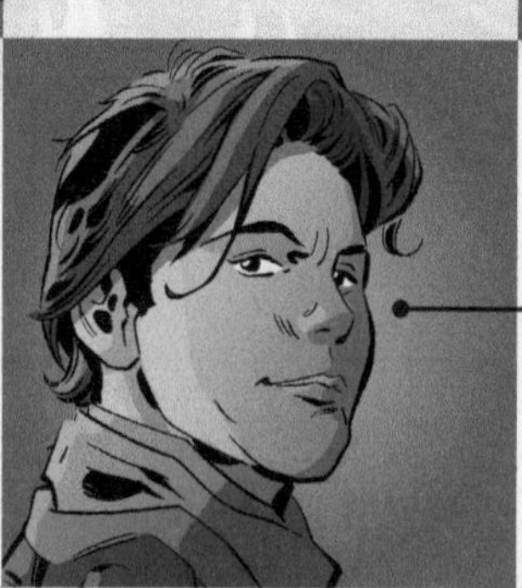

PRINCE BRANDISH

Snow White's first husband, and literally a heartless bastard.

LEIGH DUGLAS

Jack Sprat's slimmed-down widow, groomed for revenge by her deceased patron, Mister Dark.

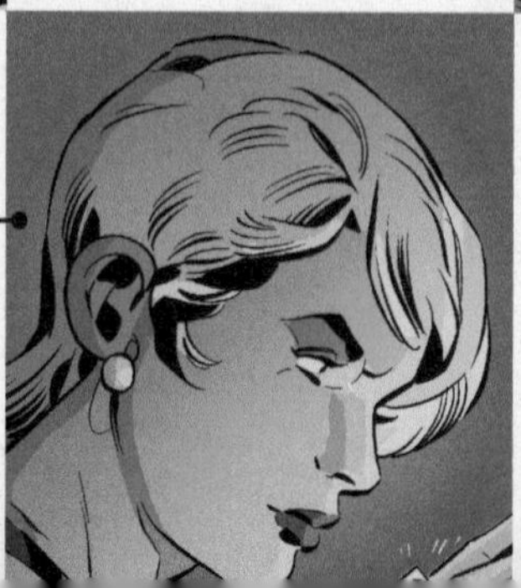

HOPE

Rose Red's patron, the divine embodiment of this most necessary of human attributes.

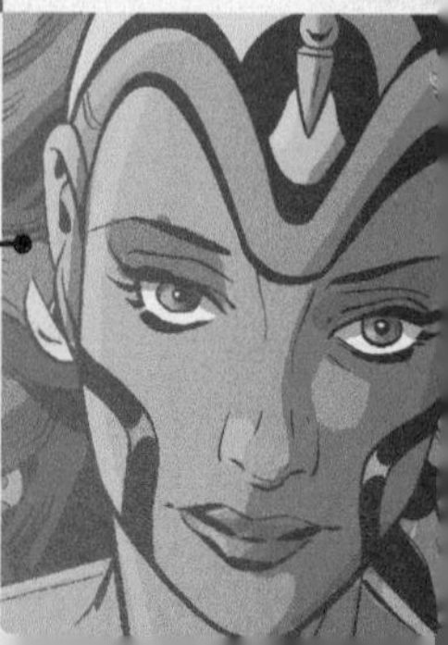

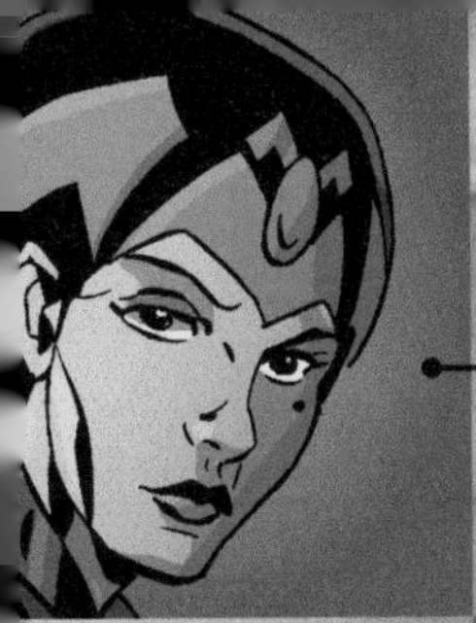

MORGAN LE FEY

The onetime antagonist of King Arthur, now a valued advisor to Rose Red's reconstituted Camelot.

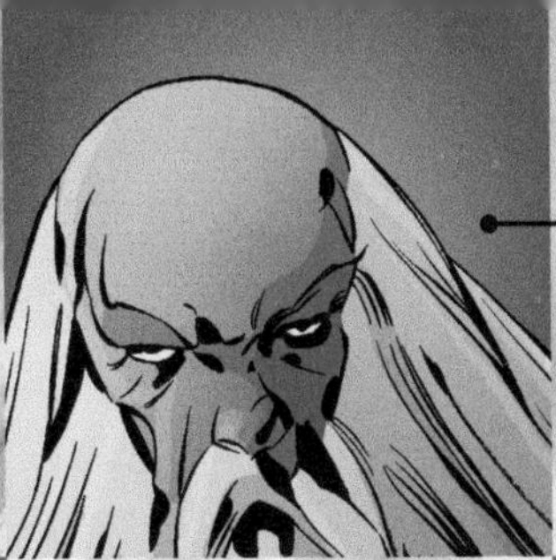

PROSPERO

Another key member of Fabletown's magical community.

BIGBY

The late, lamented Big Bad Wolf, reduced to lifeless broken glass by dire magic.

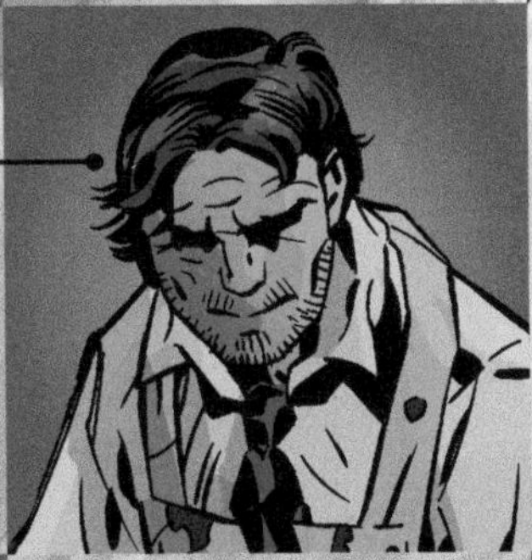

SNOW WHITE

Fabletown's former deputy mayor, widow of Bigby, and mother to their seven cubs.

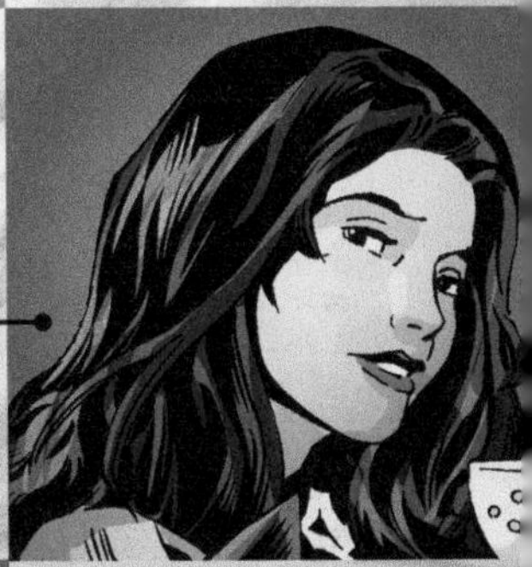

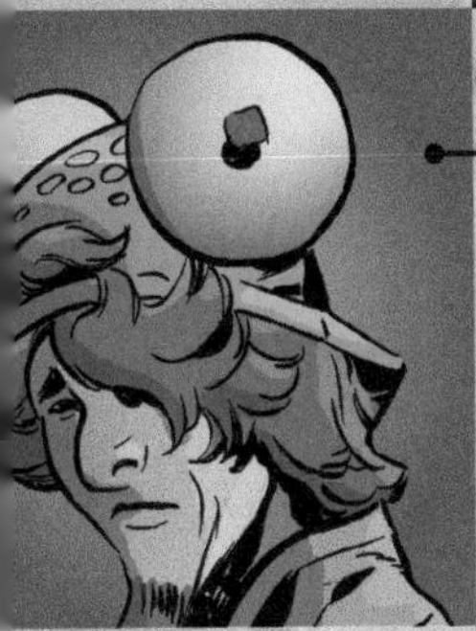

FLYCATCHER

The former Frog Prince and Fabletown janitor, now the ruler of the Kingdom of Haven in the liberated Homelands.

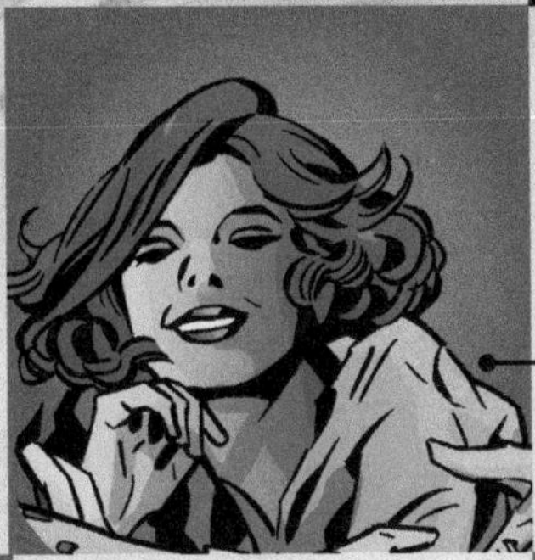

RED RIDING HOOD

Flycatcher's best gal.

KING COLE

The once and future mayor of Fabletown.

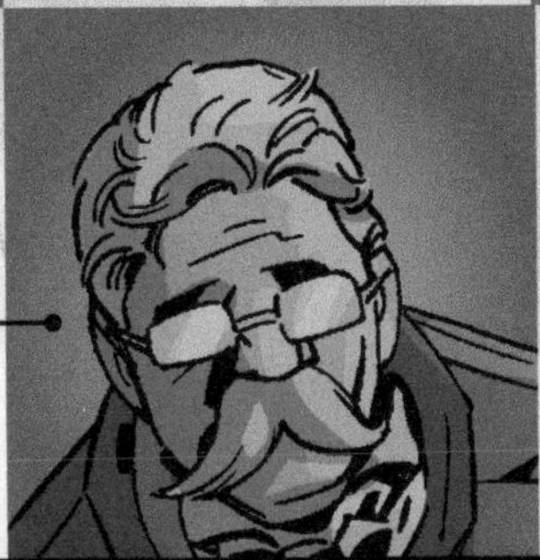

WEYLAND SMITH

A blacksmith and craftsman of great renown, and one of Haven's founding citizens.

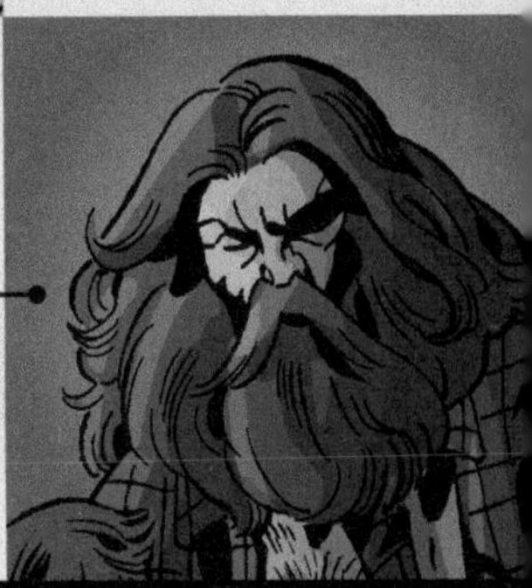

THE STORY SO FAR

After the sorrowful return of her missing daughter and the terrible news of her son's fatal sacrifice, Snow White had more than enough heartache to deal with *before* her age-old betrothed, Prince Brandish, showed up and turned her husband into a pile of shattered glass. Even so, she managed to hold it together while Fabletown's witches and wizards worked tirelessly to bring Bigby Wolf back from the dead. But for all their efforts, a vital piece of Bigby was missing — and the shapely hands that now hold it are neither idle nor well-intentioned.

Meanwhile, Rose Red has gathered a round table's worth of aspiring knights to serve in her New Camelot, complete with a gender-appropriate Guinevere figure to complement her own Arthurian standing. But in this incarnation, the tragic flaw in the court is less of a classic love

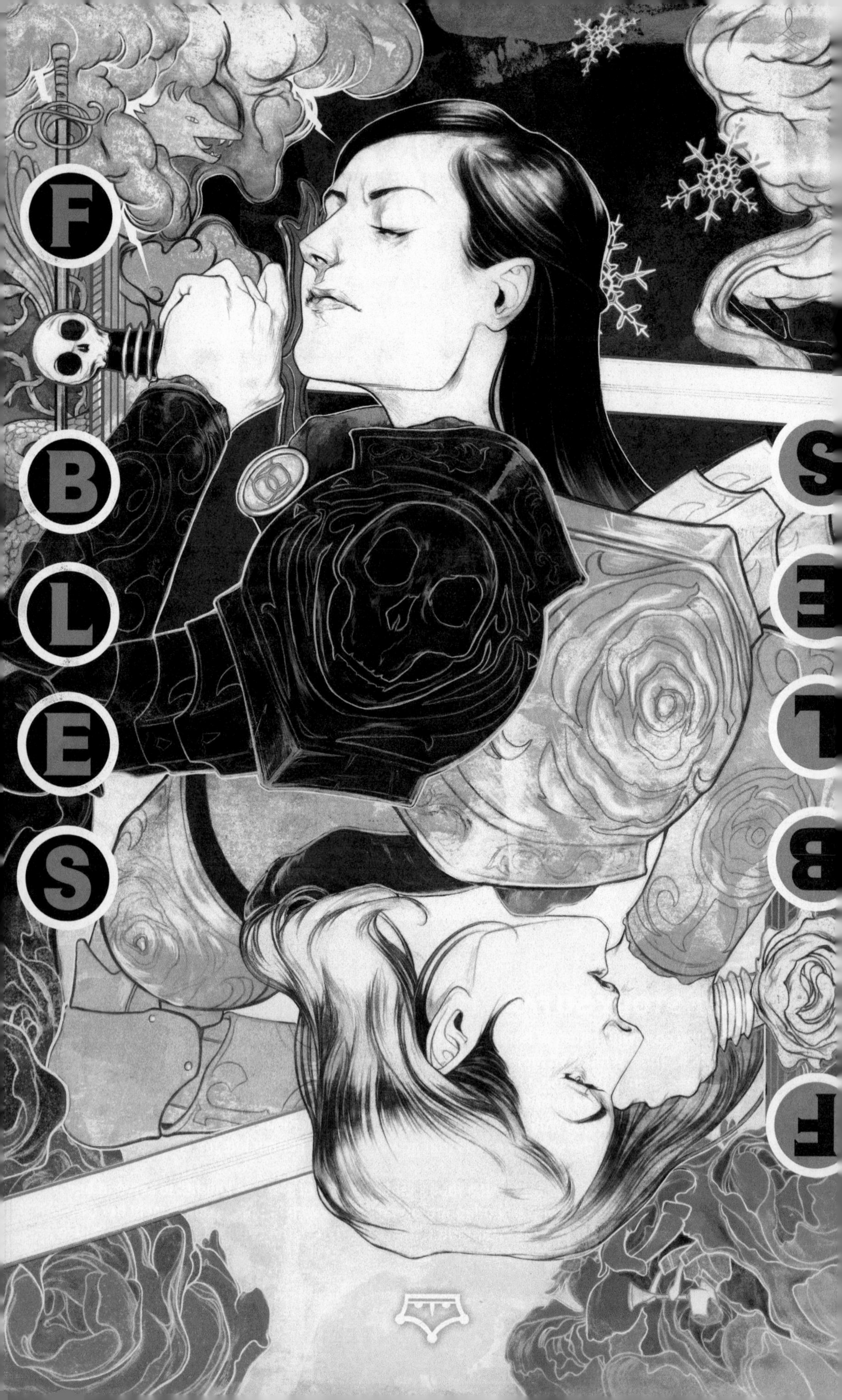
FABLES

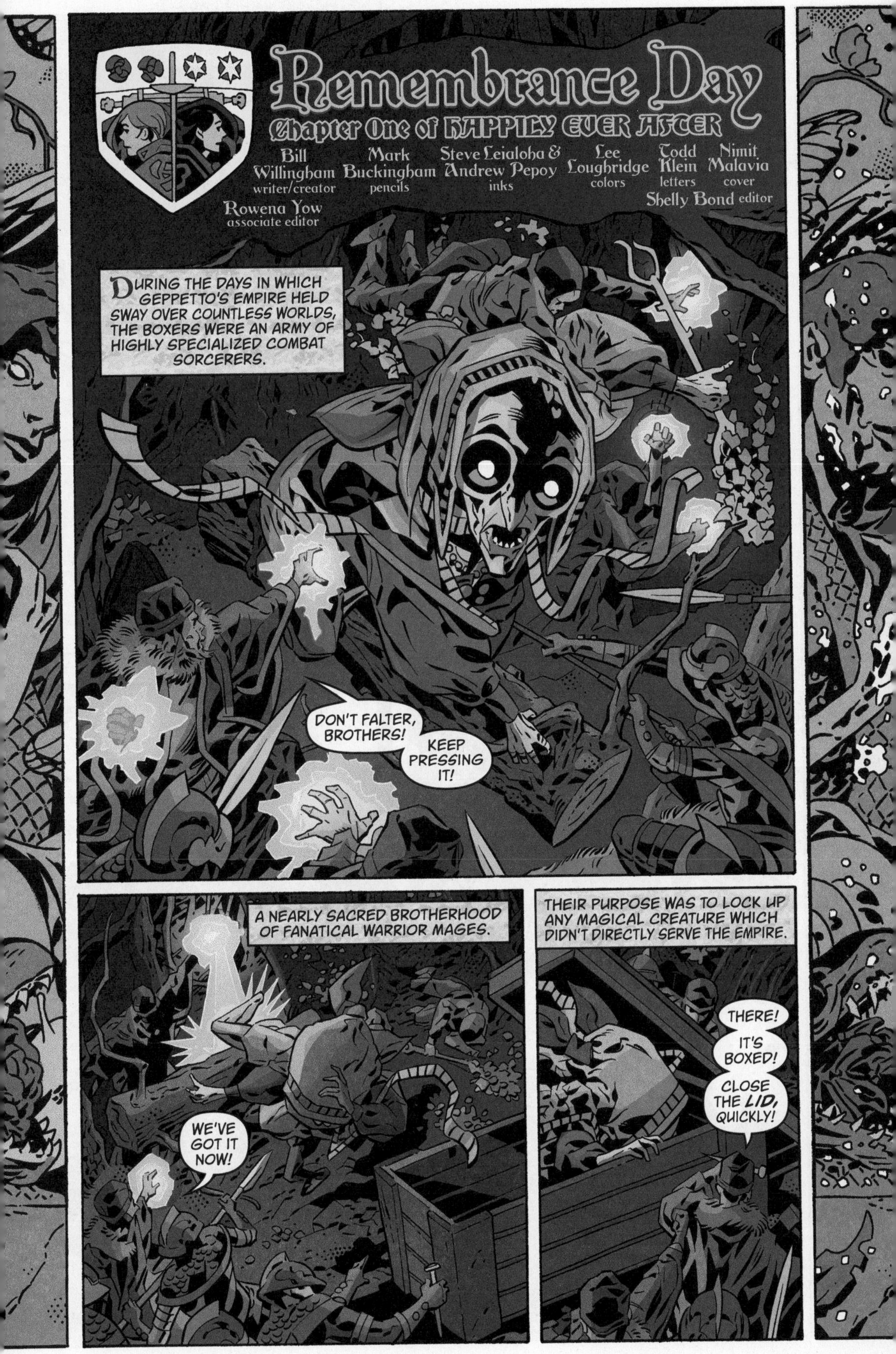
Remembrance Day
Chapter One of HAPPILY EVER AFTER
Bill Willingham writer/creator
Mark Buckingham pencils
Steve Leialoha & Andrew Pepoy inks
Lee Loughridge colors
Todd Klein letters
Nimit Malavia cover
Shelly Bond editor
Rowena Yow associate editor
DURING THE DAYS IN WHICH GEPPETTO'S EMPIRE HELD SWAY OVER COUNTLESS WORLDS, THE BOXERS WERE AN ARMY OF HIGHLY SPECIALIZED COMBAT SORCERERS.
DON'T FALTER, BROTHERS!
KEEP PRESSING IT!
A NEARLY SACRED BROTHERHOOD OF FANATICAL WARRIOR MAGES.
WE'VE GOT IT NOW!
THEIR PURPOSE WAS TO LOCK UP ANY MAGICAL CREATURE WHICH DIDN'T DIRECTLY SERVE THE EMPIRE.
THERE!
IT'S BOXED!
CLOSE THE LID, QUICKLY!

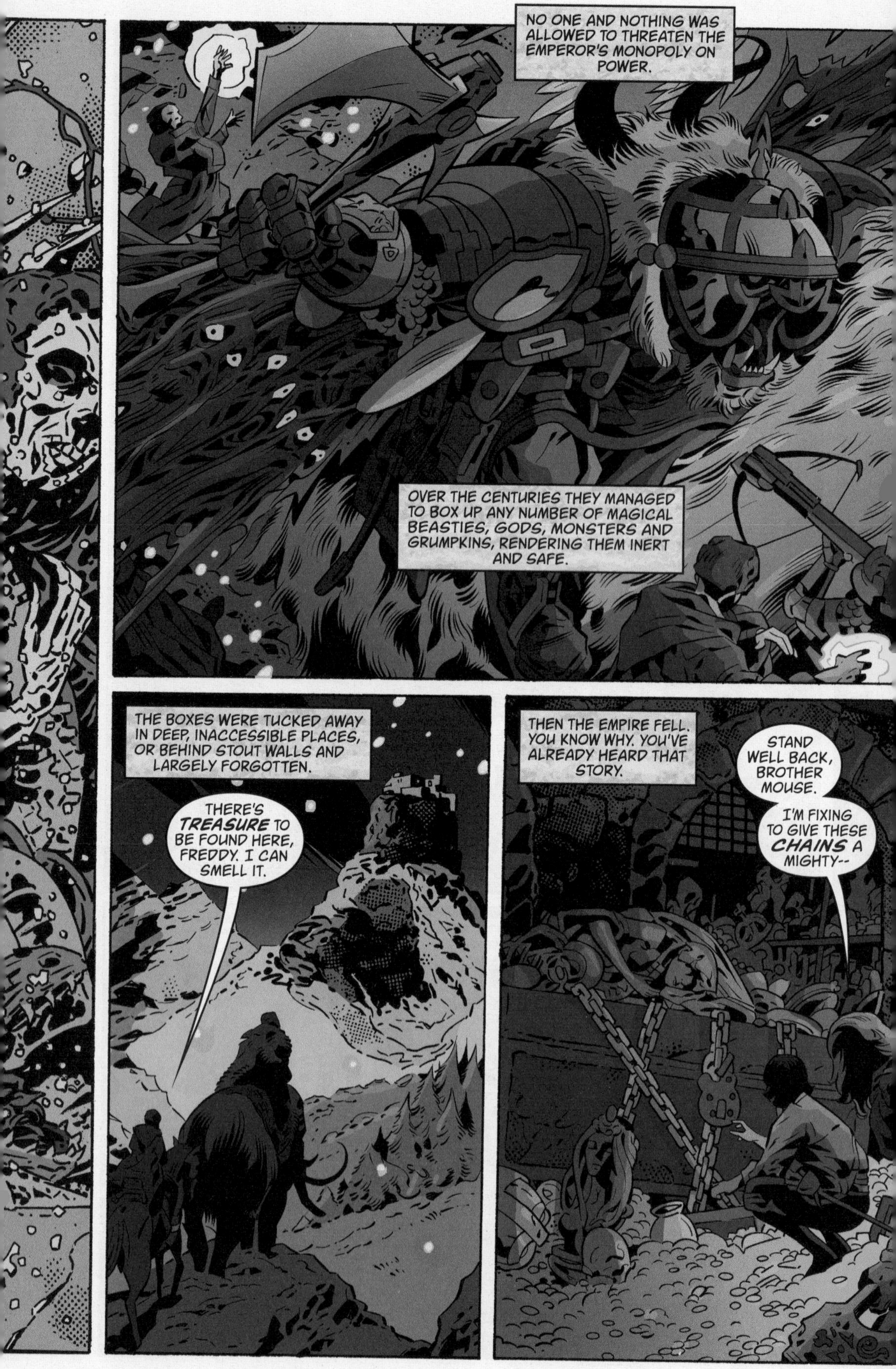
NO ONE AND NOTHING WAS ALLOWED TO THREATEN THE EMPEROR'S MONOPOLY ON POWER.
OVER THE CENTURIES THEY MANAGED TO BOX UP ANY NUMBER OF MAGICAL BEASTIES, GODS, MONSTERS AND GRUMPKINS, RENDERING THEM INERT AND SAFE.
THE BOXES WERE TUCKED AWAY IN DEEP, INACCESSIBLE PLACES, OR BEHIND STOUT WALLS AND LARGELY FORGOTTEN.
THERE'S TREASURE TO BE FOUND HERE, FREDDY. I CAN SMELL IT.
THEN THE EMPIRE FELL. YOU KNOW WHY. YOU'VE ALREADY HEARD THAT STORY.
STAND WELL BACK, BROTHER MOUSE.
I'M FIXING TO GIVE THESE CHAINS A MIGHTY--

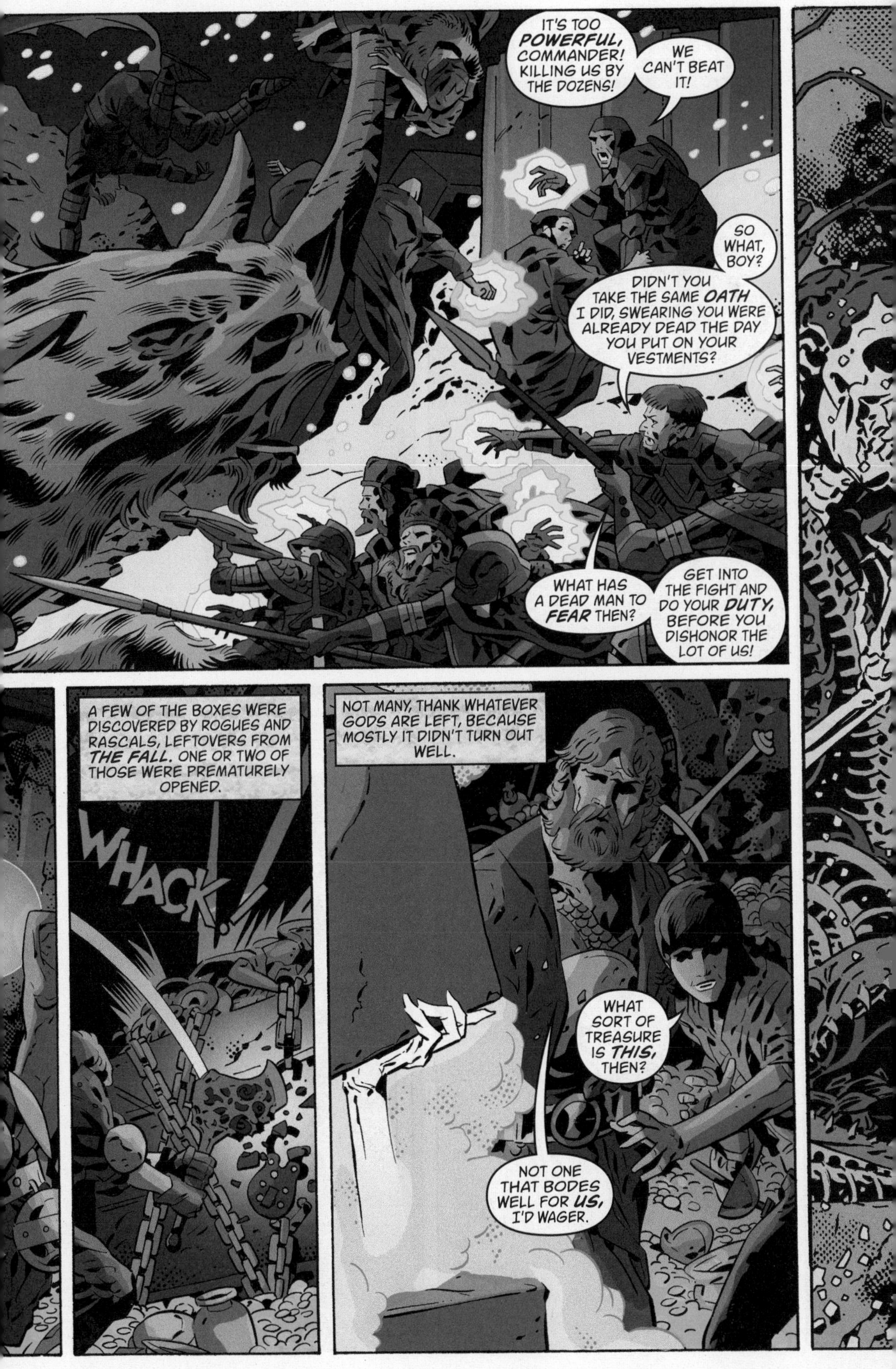
IT'S TOO POWERFUL, COMMANDER! KILLING US BY THE DOZENS!
WE CAN'T BEAT IT!
SO WHAT, BOY?
DIDN'T YOU TAKE THE SAME OATH I DID, SWEARING YOU WERE ALREADY DEAD THE DAY YOU PUT ON YOUR VESTMENTS?
WHAT HAS A DEAD MAN TO FEAR THEN?
GET INTO THE FIGHT AND DO YOUR DUTY, BEFORE YOU DISHONOR THE LOT OF US!
A FEW OF THE BOXES WERE DISCOVERED BY ROGUES AND RASCALS, LEFTOVERS FROM THE FALL. ONE OR TWO OF THOSE WERE PREMATURELY OPENED.
WHACK
NOT MANY, THANK WHATEVER GODS ARE LEFT, BECAUSE MOSTLY IT DIDN'T TURN OUT WELL.
WHAT SORT OF TREASURE IS THIS, THEN?
NOT ONE THAT BODES WELL FOR US, I'D WAGER.

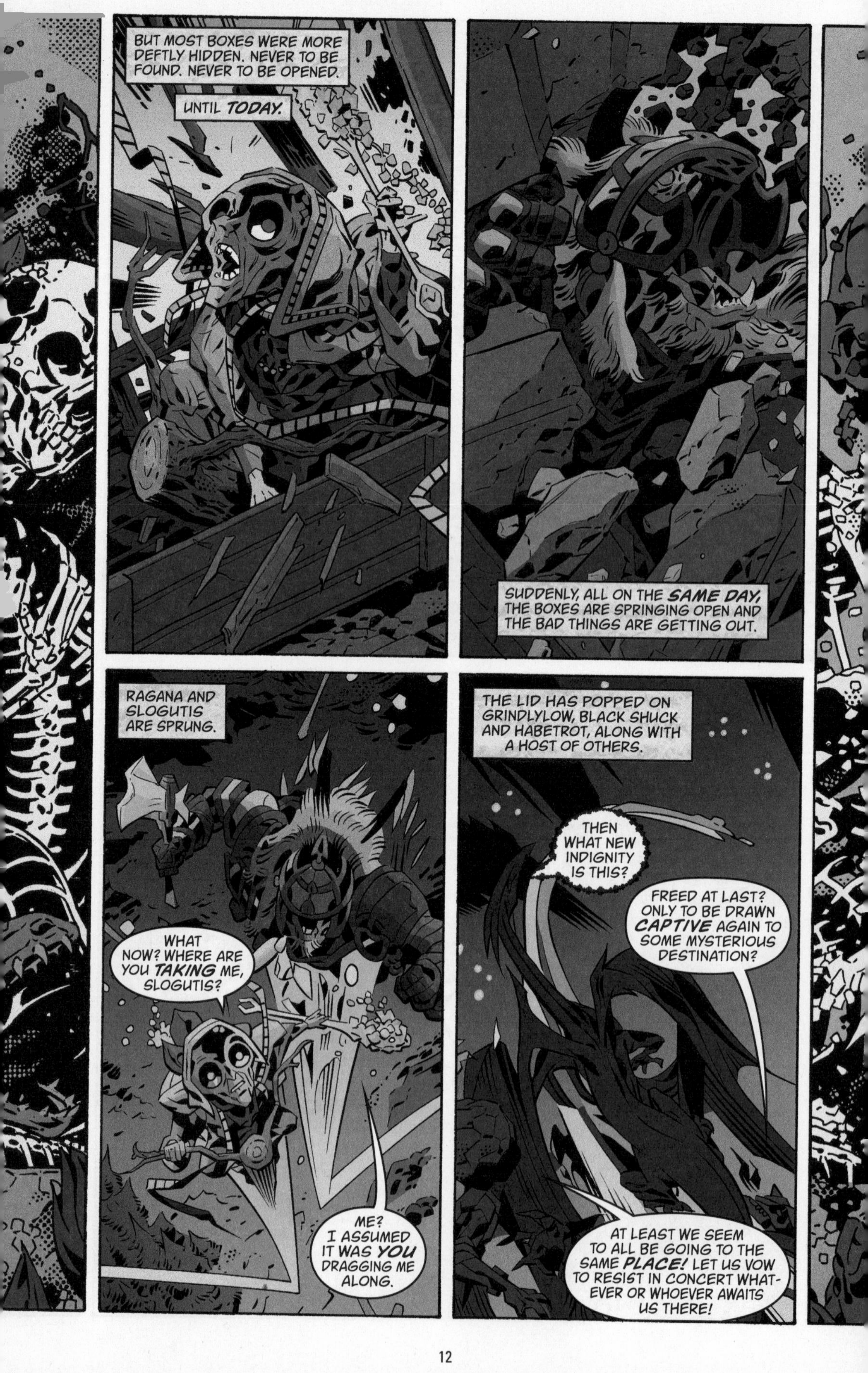
BUT MOST BOXES WERE MORE DEFTLY HIDDEN. NEVER TO BE FOUND. NEVER TO BE OPENED.
UNTIL TODAY.
SUDDENLY, ALL ON THE SAME DAY, THE BOXES ARE SPRINGING OPEN AND THE BAD THINGS ARE GETTING OUT.
RAGANA AND SLOGUTIS ARE SPRUNG.
WHAT NOW? WHERE ARE YOU TAKING ME, SLOGUTIS?
ME? I ASSUMED IT WAS YOU DRAGGING ME ALONG.
THE LID HAS POPPED ON GRINDLYLOW, BLACK SHUCK AND HABETROT, ALONG WITH A HOST OF OTHERS.
THEN WHAT NEW INDIGNITY IS THIS?
FREED AT LAST? ONLY TO BE DRAWN CAPTIVE AGAIN TO SOME MYSTERIOUS DESTINATION?
AT LEAST WE SEEM TO ALL BE GOING TO THE SAME PLACE! LET US VOW TO RESIST IN CONCERT WHAT-EVER OR WHOEVER AWAITS US THERE!

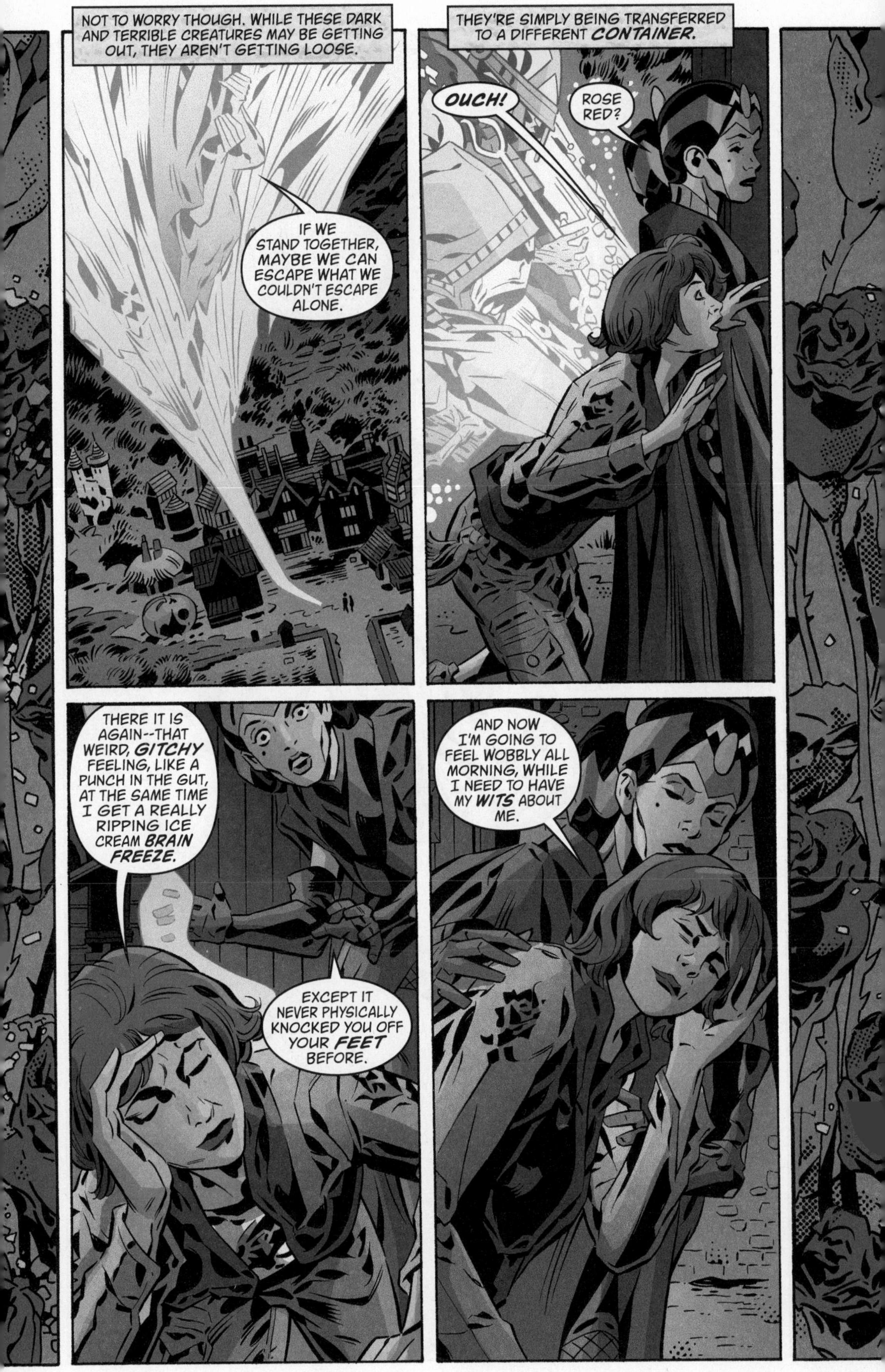
NOT TO WORRY THOUGH. WHILE THESE DARK AND TERRIBLE CREATURES MAY BE GETTING OUT, THEY AREN'T GETTING LOOSE.
IF WE STAND TOGETHER, MAYBE WE CAN ESCAPE WHAT WE COULDN'T ESCAPE ALONE.
THEY'RE SIMPLY BEING TRANSFERRED TO A DIFFERENT CONTAINER.
OUCH!
ROSE RED?
THERE IT IS AGAIN--THAT WEIRD, GITCHY FEELING, LIKE A PUNCH IN THE GUT, AT THE SAME TIME I GET A REALLY RIPPING ICE CREAM BRAIN FREEZE.
EXCEPT IT NEVER PHYSICALLY KNOCKED YOU OFF YOUR FEET BEFORE.
AND NOW I'M GOING TO FEEL WOBBLY ALL MORNING, WHILE I NEED TO HAVE MY WITS ABOUT ME.

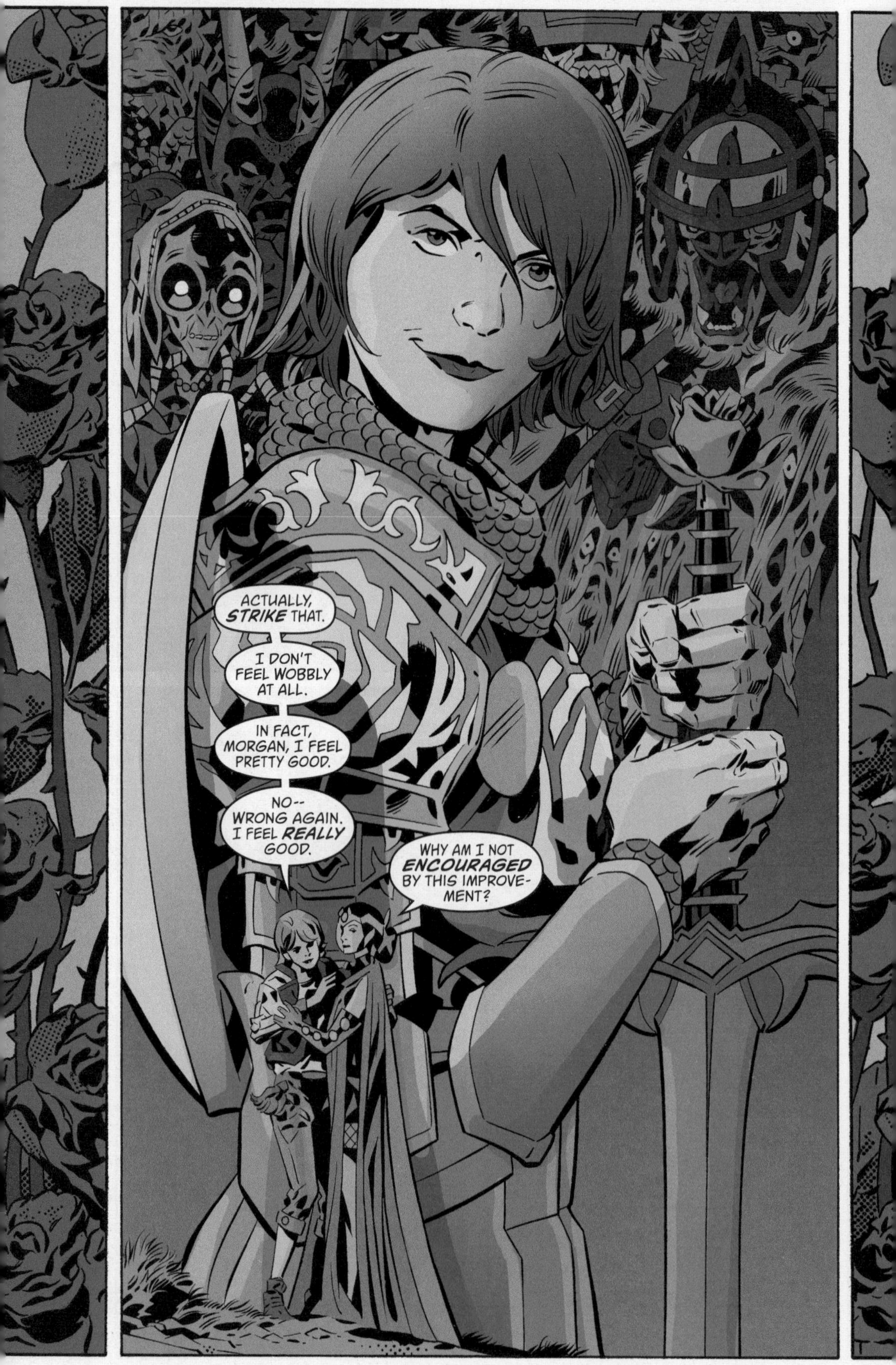
ACTUALLY, STRIKE THAT.
I DON'T FEEL WOBBLY AT ALL.
IN FACT, MORGAN, I FEEL PRETTY GOOD.
NO-- WRONG AGAIN. I FEEL REALLY GOOD.
WHY AM I NOT ENCOURAGED BY THIS IMPROVE-MENT?

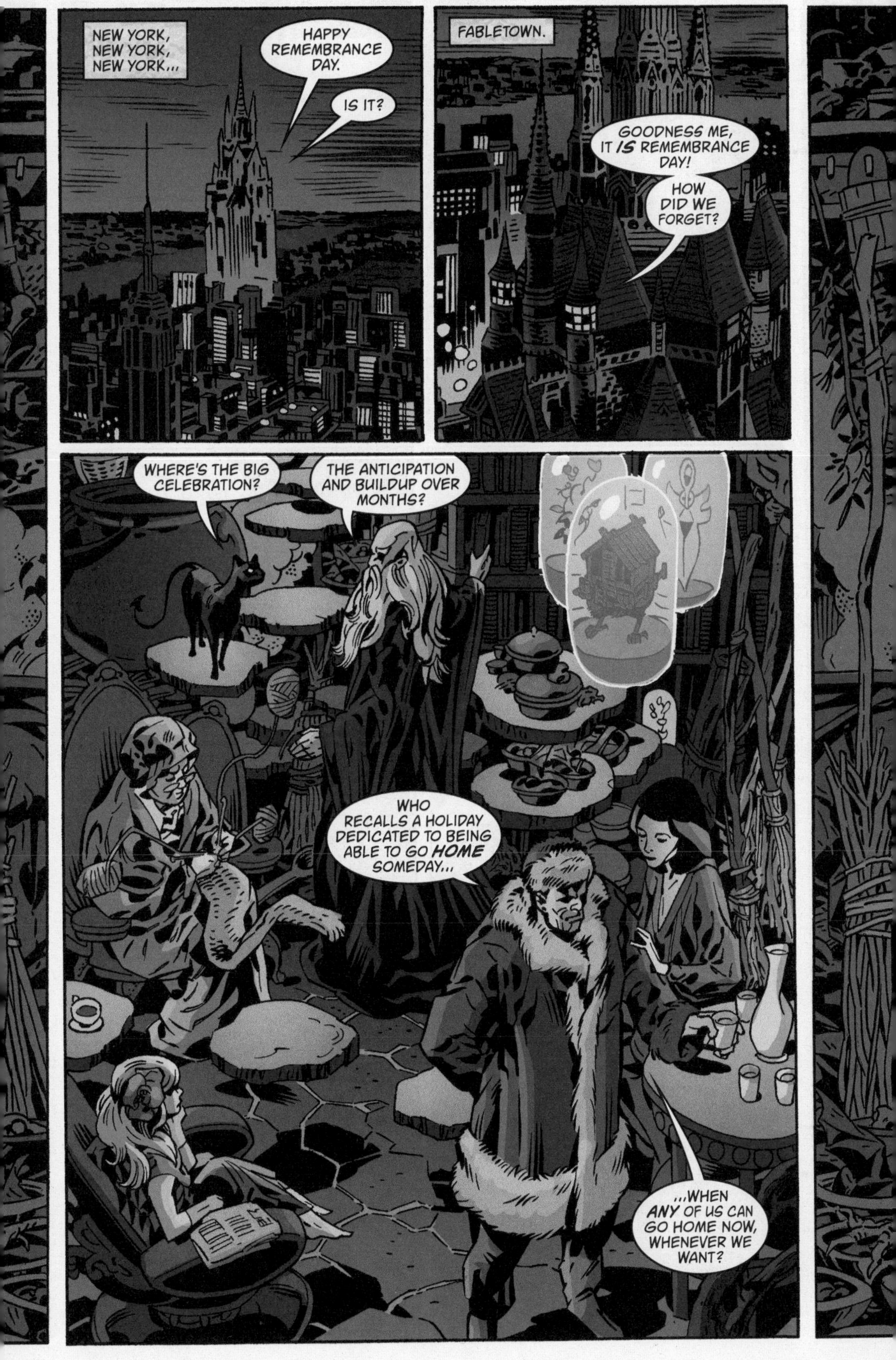
NEW YORK, NEW YORK, NEW YORK...
HAPPY REMEMBRANCE DAY.
IS IT?
FABLETOWN.
GOODNESS ME, IT *IS* REMEMBRANCE DAY!
HOW DID WE FORGET?
WHERE'S THE BIG CELEBRATION?
THE ANTICIPATION AND BUILDUP OVER MONTHS?
WHO RECALLS A HOLIDAY DEDICATED TO BEING ABLE TO GO *HOME* SOMEDAY...
...WHEN *ANY* OF US CAN GO HOME NOW, WHENEVER WE WANT?

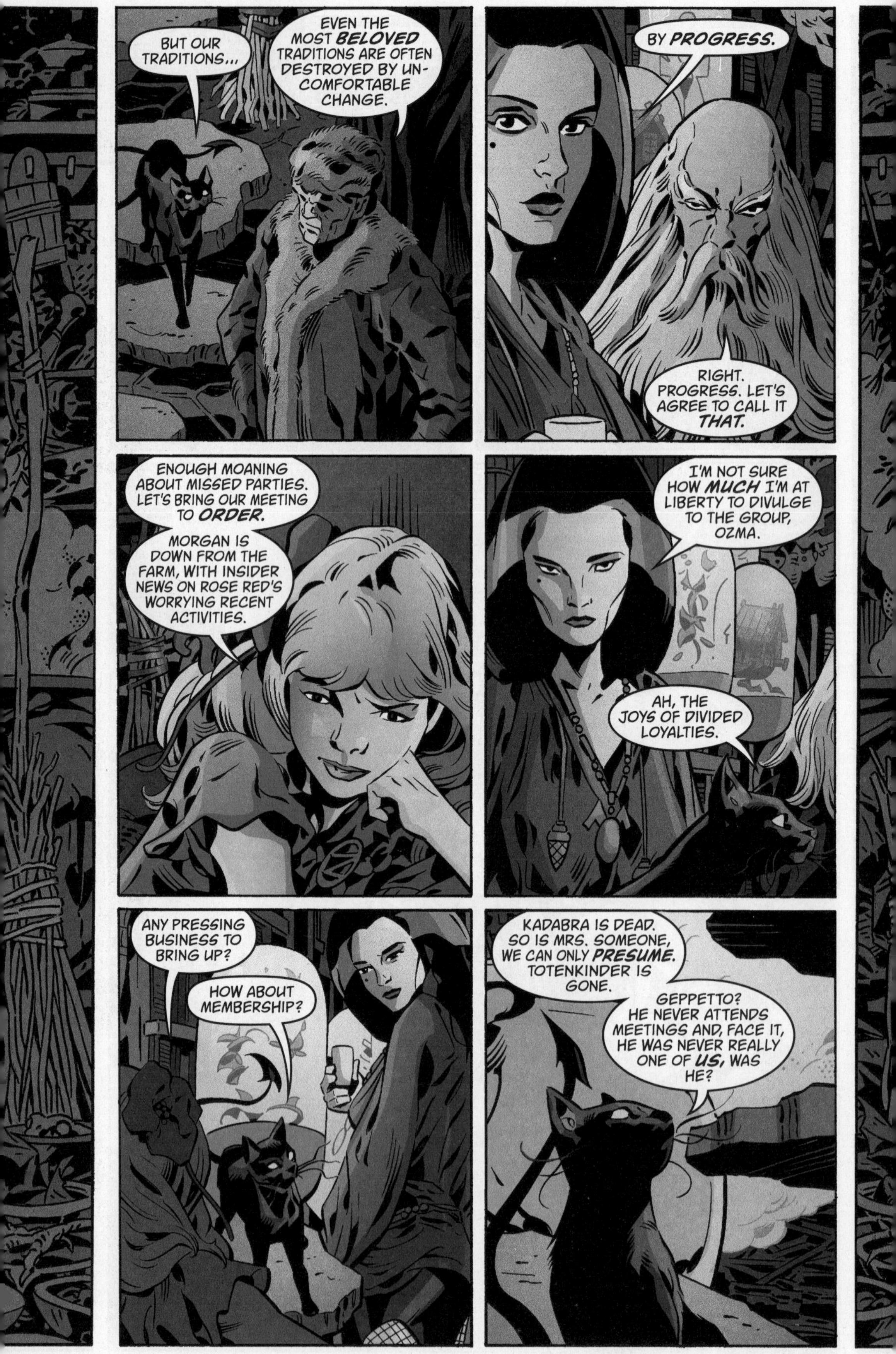
BUT OUR TRADITIONS...
EVEN THE MOST BELOVED TRADITIONS ARE OFTEN DESTROYED BY UN-COMFORTABLE CHANGE.
BY PROGRESS.
RIGHT. PROGRESS. LET'S AGREE TO CALL IT THAT.
ENOUGH MOANING ABOUT MISSED PARTIES. LET'S BRING OUR MEETING TO ORDER.
MORGAN IS DOWN FROM THE FARM, WITH INSIDER NEWS ON ROSE RED'S WORRYING RECENT ACTIVITIES.
I'M NOT SURE HOW MUCH I'M AT LIBERTY TO DIVULGE TO THE GROUP, OZMA.
AH, THE JOYS OF DIVIDED LOYALTIES.
ANY PRESSING BUSINESS TO BRING UP?
HOW ABOUT MEMBERSHIP?
KADABRA IS DEAD. SO IS MRS. SOMEONE, WE CAN ONLY PRESUME. TOTENKINDER IS GONE.
GEPPETTO? HE NEVER ATTENDS MEETINGS AND, FACE IT, HE WAS NEVER REALLY ONE OF US, WAS HE?

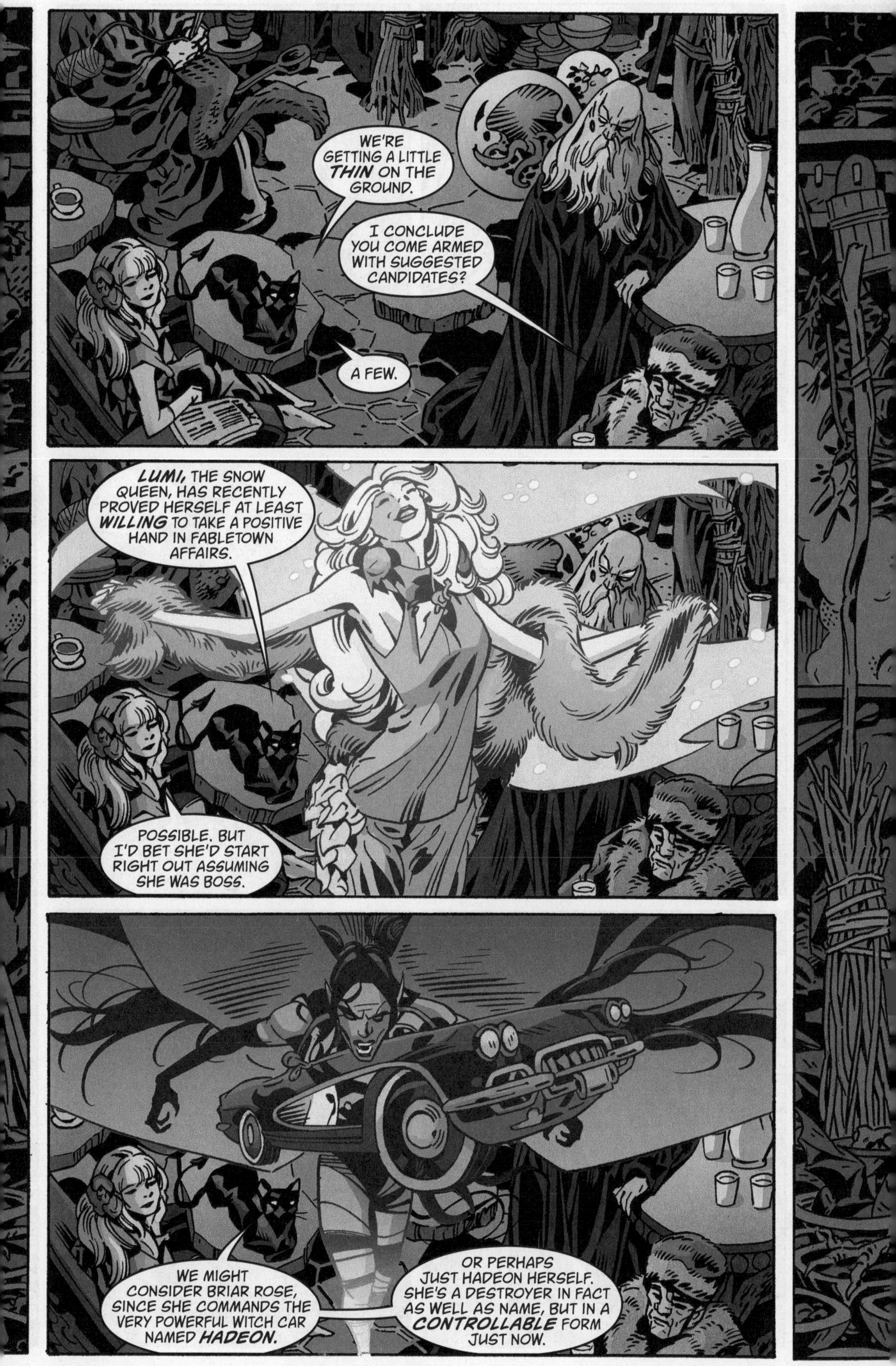
WE'RE GETTING A LITTLE **THIN** ON THE GROUND.
I CONCLUDE YOU COME ARMED WITH SUGGESTED CANDIDATES?
A FEW.
LUMI, THE SNOW QUEEN, HAS RECENTLY PROVED HERSELF AT LEAST **WILLING** TO TAKE A POSITIVE HAND IN FABLETOWN AFFAIRS.
POSSIBLE. BUT I'D BET SHE'D START RIGHT OUT ASSUMING SHE WAS BOSS.
WE MIGHT CONSIDER BRIAR ROSE, SINCE SHE COMMANDS THE VERY POWERFUL WITCH CAR NAMED **HADEON.**
OR PERHAPS JUST HADEON HERSELF. SHE'S A DESTROYER IN FACT AS WELL AS NAME, BUT IN A **CONTROLLABLE** FORM JUST NOW.

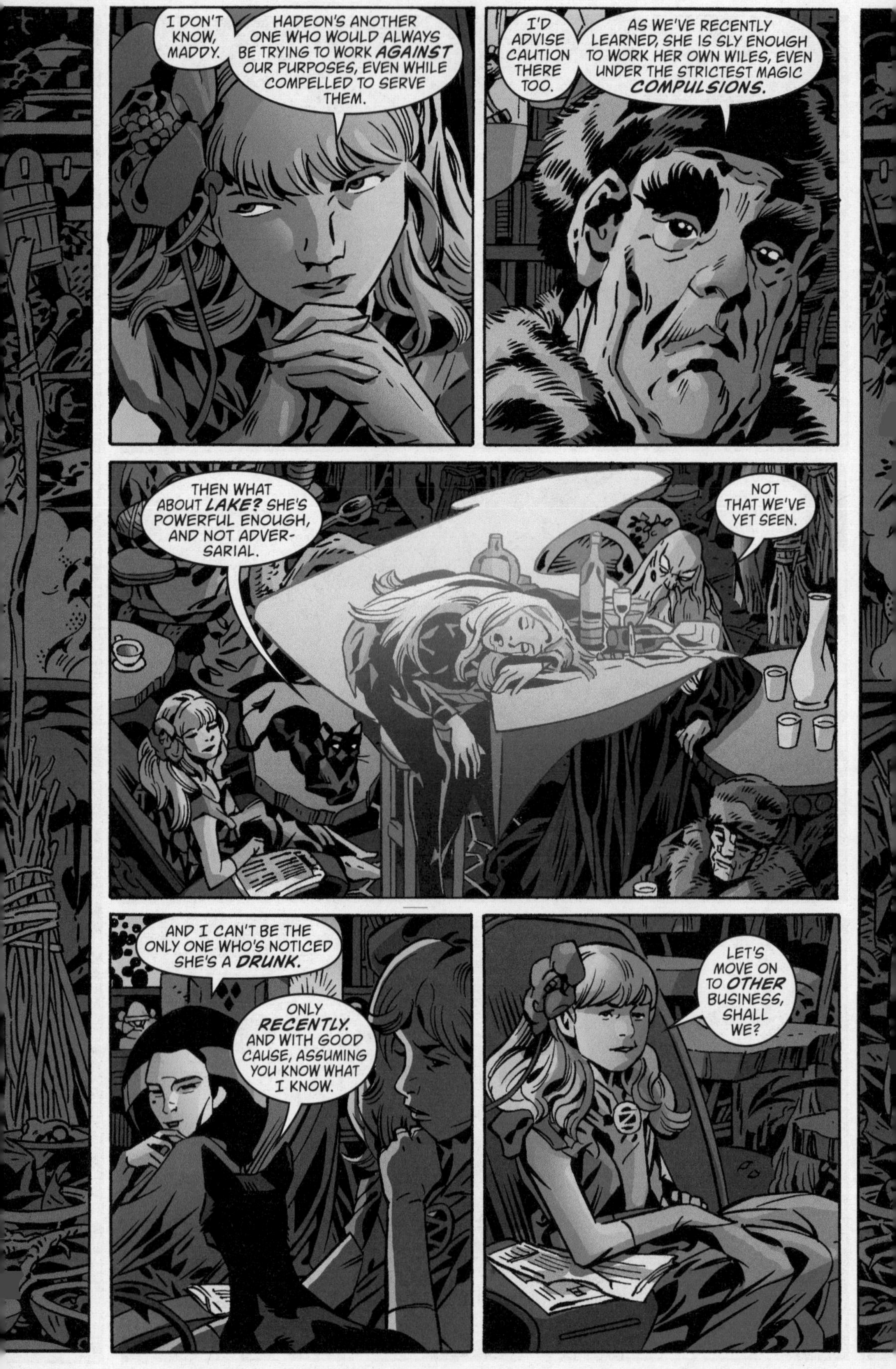
I DON'T KNOW, MADDY.
HADEON'S ANOTHER ONE WHO WOULD ALWAYS BE TRYING TO WORK AGAINST OUR PURPOSES, EVEN WHILE COMPELLED TO SERVE THEM.
I'D ADVISE CAUTION THERE TOO.
AS WE'VE RECENTLY LEARNED, SHE IS SLY ENOUGH TO WORK HER OWN WILES, EVEN UNDER THE STRICTEST MAGIC COMPULSIONS.
THEN WHAT ABOUT LAKE? SHE'S POWERFUL ENOUGH, AND NOT ADVERSARIAL.
NOT THAT WE'VE YET SEEN.
AND I CAN'T BE THE ONLY ONE WHO'S NOTICED SHE'S A DRUNK.
ONLY RECENTLY. AND WITH GOOD CAUSE, ASSUMING YOU KNOW WHAT I KNOW.
LET'S MOVE ON TO OTHER BUSINESS, SHALL WE?

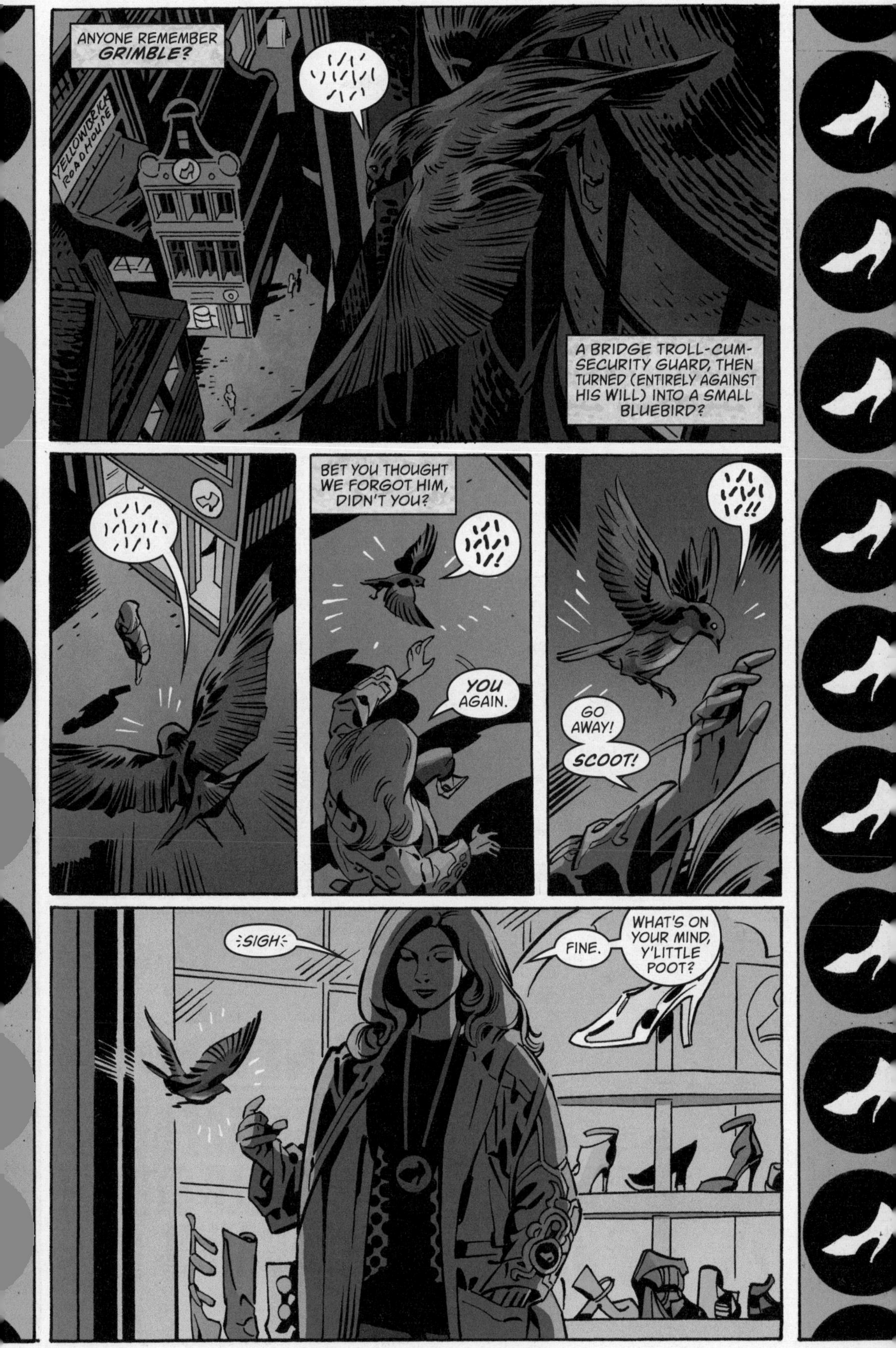
ANYONE REMEMBER GRIMBLE?
YELLOWBRICK ROADHOUSE
A BRIDGE TROLL-CUM-SECURITY GUARD, THEN TURNED (ENTIRELY AGAINST HIS WILL) INTO A SMALL BLUEBIRD?
BET YOU THOUGHT WE FORGOT HIM, DIDN'T YOU?
YOU AGAIN.
GO AWAY!
SCOOT!
SIGH
FINE.
WHAT'S ON YOUR MIND, Y'LITTLE POOT?

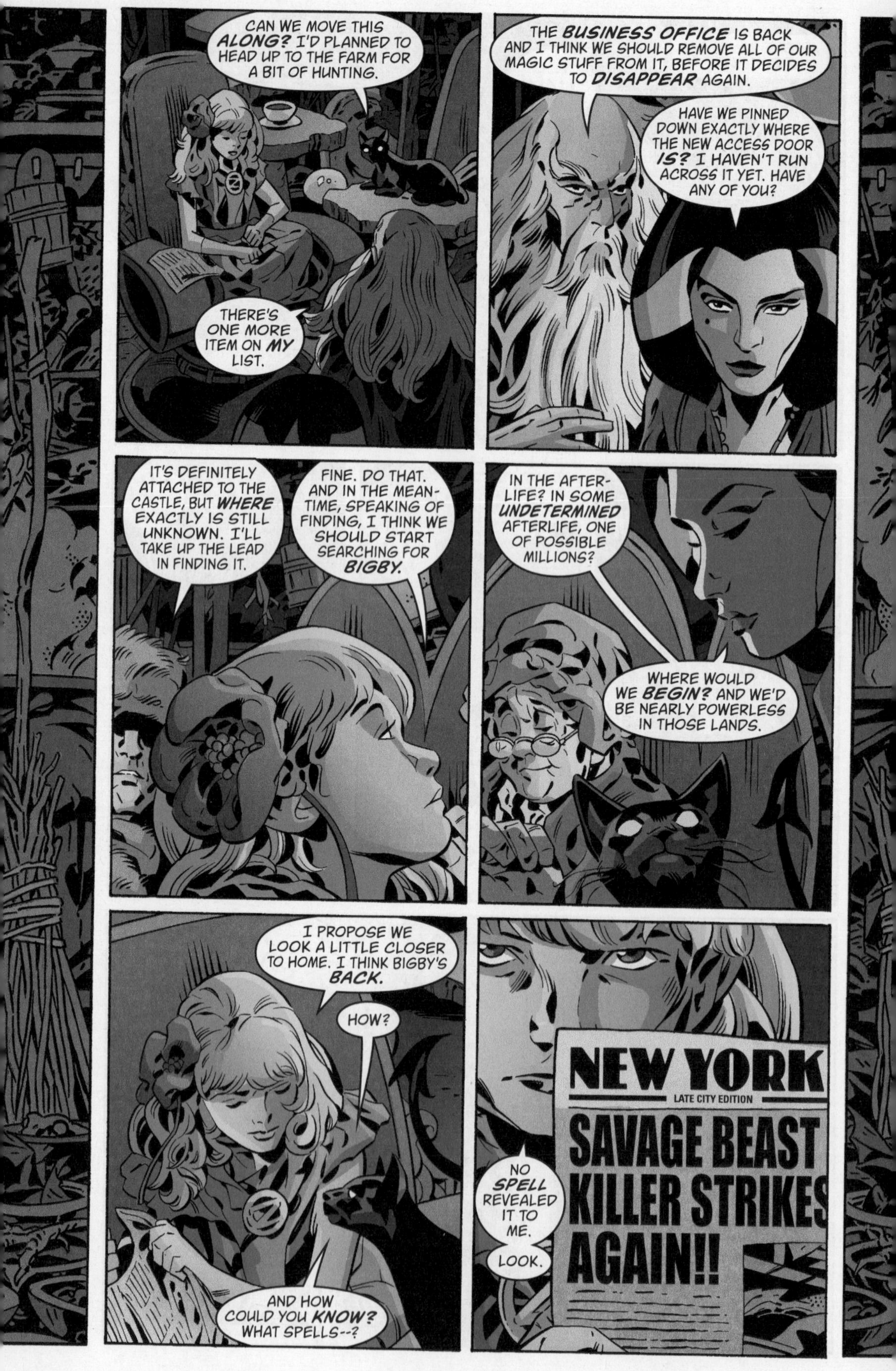
CAN WE MOVE THIS ALONG? I'D PLANNED TO HEAD UP TO THE FARM FOR A BIT OF HUNTING.
THERE'S ONE MORE ITEM ON MY LIST.
THE BUSINESS OFFICE IS BACK AND I THINK WE SHOULD REMOVE ALL OF OUR MAGIC STUFF FROM IT, BEFORE IT DECIDES TO DISAPPEAR AGAIN.
HAVE WE PINNED DOWN EXACTLY WHERE THE NEW ACCESS DOOR IS? I HAVEN'T RUN ACROSS IT YET. HAVE ANY OF YOU?
IT'S DEFINITELY ATTACHED TO THE CASTLE, BUT WHERE EXACTLY IS STILL UNKNOWN. I'LL TAKE UP THE LEAD IN FINDING IT.
FINE. DO THAT. AND IN THE MEAN-TIME, SPEAKING OF FINDING, I THINK WE SHOULD START SEARCHING FOR BIGBY.
IN THE AFTER-LIFE? IN SOME UNDETERMINED AFTERLIFE, ONE OF POSSIBLE MILLIONS?
WHERE WOULD WE BEGIN? AND WE'D BE NEARLY POWERLESS IN THOSE LANDS.
I PROPOSE WE LOOK A LITTLE CLOSER TO HOME. I THINK BIGBY'S BACK.
HOW?
AND HOW COULD YOU KNOW? WHAT SPELLS--?
NO SPELL REVEALED IT TO ME.
LOOK.
NEW YORK
LATE CITY EDITION
SAVAGE BEAST KILLER STRIKES AGAIN!!

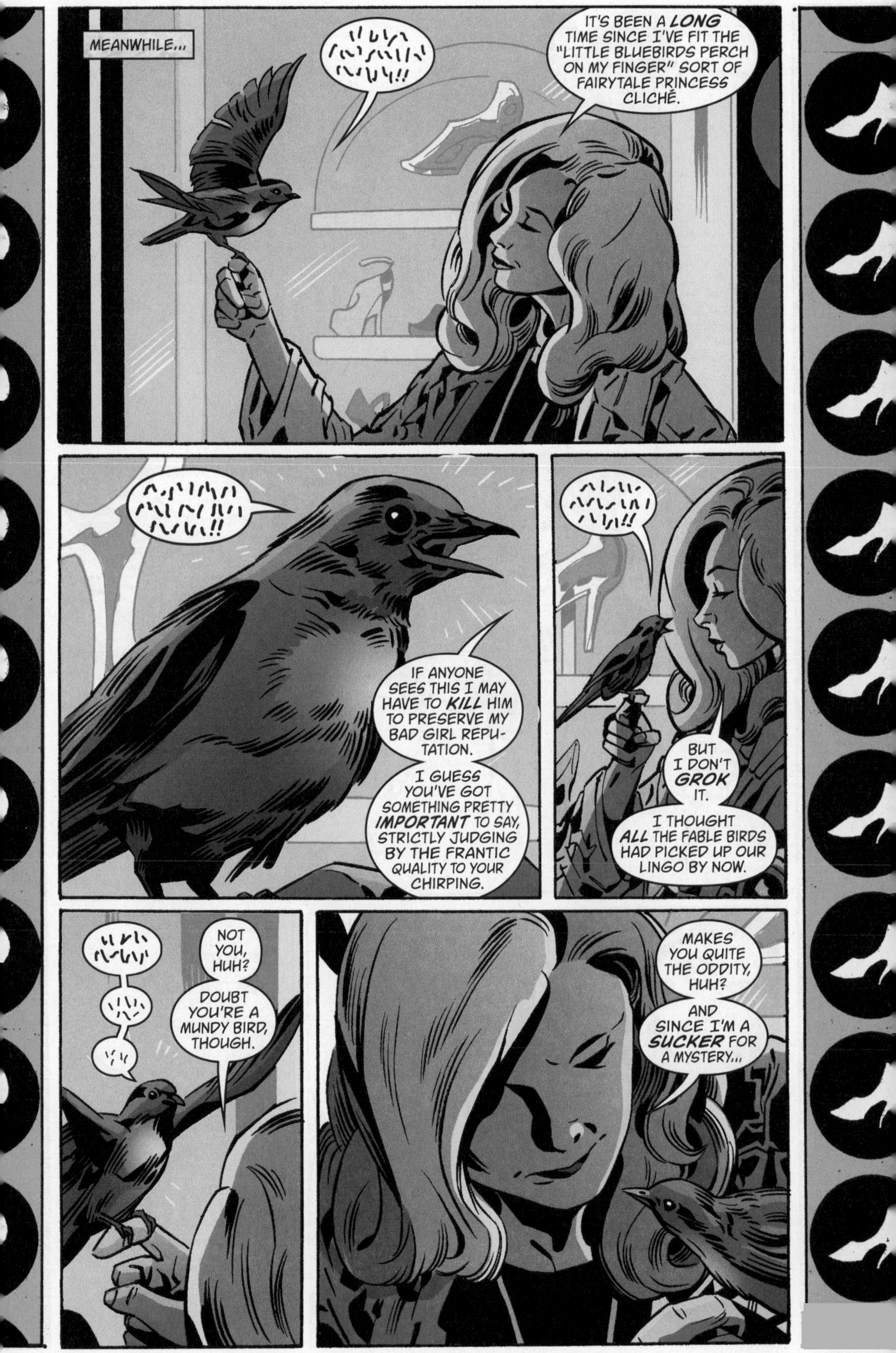
MEANWHILE...
IT'S BEEN A LONG TIME SINCE I'VE FIT THE "LITTLE BLUEBIRDS PERCH ON MY FINGER" SORT OF FAIRYTALE PRINCESS CLICHÉ.
IF ANYONE SEES THIS I MAY HAVE TO KILL HIM TO PRESERVE MY BAD GIRL REPUTATION.
I GUESS YOU'VE GOT SOMETHING PRETTY IMPORTANT TO SAY, STRICTLY JUDGING BY THE FRANTIC QUALITY TO YOUR CHIRPING.
BUT I DON'T GROK IT.
I THOUGHT ALL THE FABLE BIRDS HAD PICKED UP OUR LINGO BY NOW.
NOT YOU, HUH?
DOUBT YOU'RE A MUNDY BIRD, THOUGH.
MAKES YOU QUITE THE ODDITY, HUH?
AND SINCE I'M A SUCKER FOR A MYSTERY...

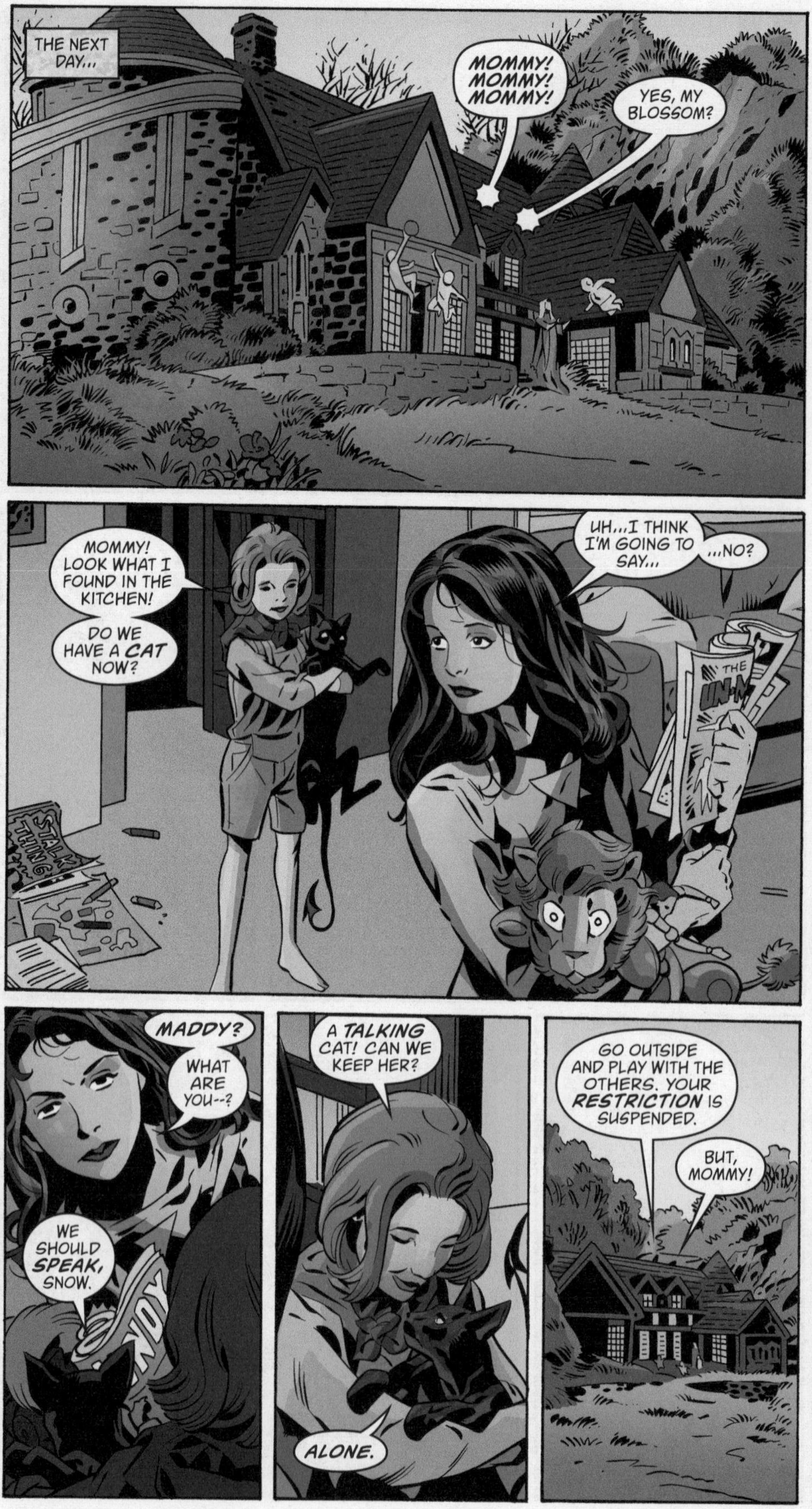
THE NEXT DAY...
MOMMY! MOMMY! MOMMY!
YES, MY BLOSSOM?
MOMMY! LOOK WHAT I FOUND IN THE KITCHEN!
DO WE HAVE A CAT NOW?
UH...I THINK I'M GOING TO SAY...
...NO?
MADDY?
WHAT ARE YOU--?
WE SHOULD SPEAK, SNOW.
A TALKING CAT! CAN WE KEEP HER?
ALONE.
GO OUTSIDE AND PLAY WITH THE OTHERS. YOUR RESTRICTION IS SUSPENDED.
BUT, MOMMY!

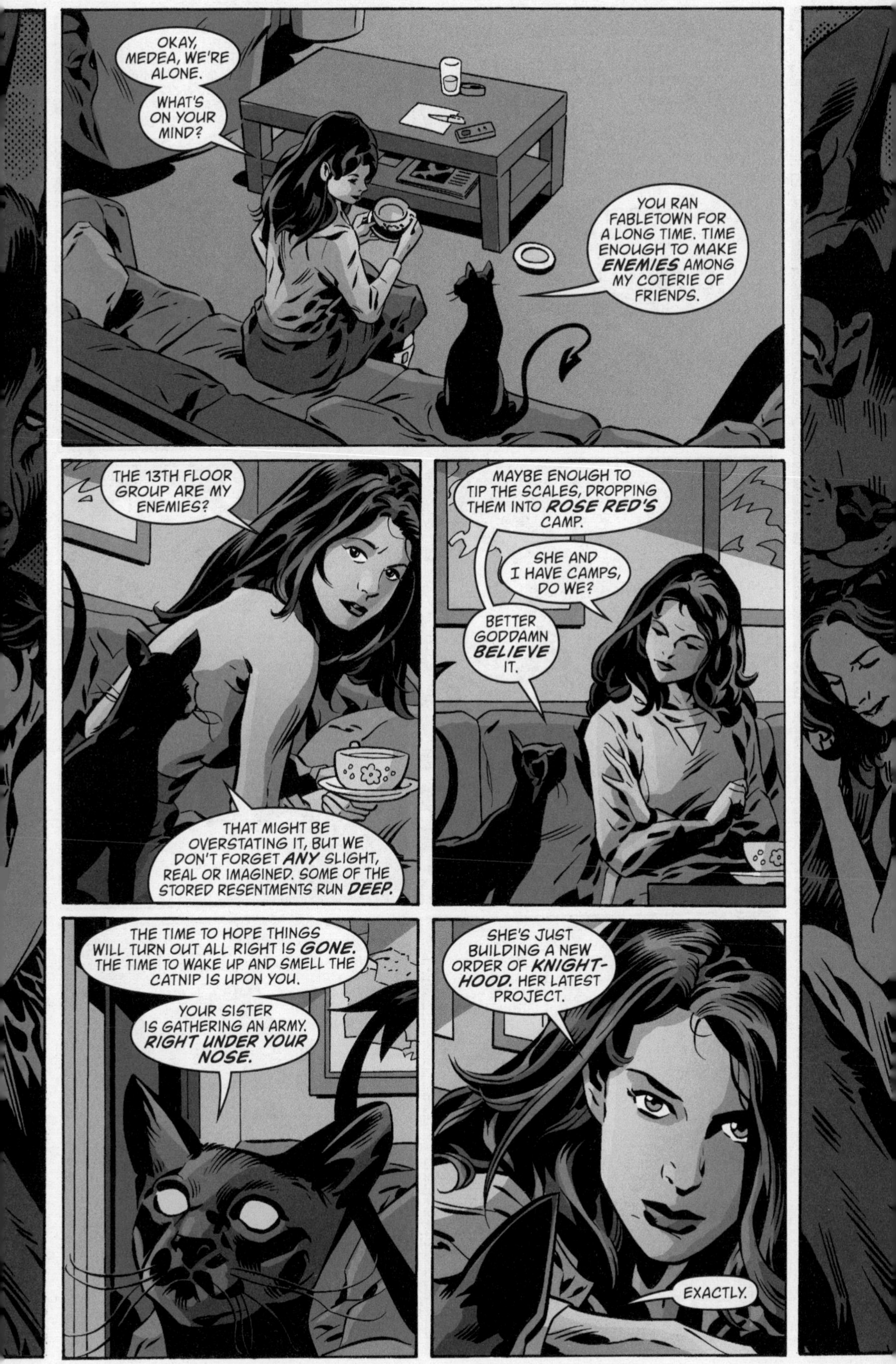
OKAY, MEDEA, WE'RE ALONE.
WHAT'S ON YOUR MIND?
YOU RAN FABLETOWN FOR A LONG TIME. TIME ENOUGH TO MAKE ENEMIES AMONG MY COTERIE OF FRIENDS.
THE 13TH FLOOR GROUP ARE MY ENEMIES?
THAT MIGHT BE OVERSTATING IT, BUT WE DON'T FORGET ANY SLIGHT, REAL OR IMAGINED. SOME OF THE STORED RESENTMENTS RUN DEEP.
MAYBE ENOUGH TO TIP THE SCALES, DROPPING THEM INTO ROSE RED'S CAMP.
SHE AND I HAVE CAMPS, DO WE?
BETTER GODDAMN BELIEVE IT.
THE TIME TO HOPE THINGS WILL TURN OUT ALL RIGHT IS GONE. THE TIME TO WAKE UP AND SMELL THE CATNIP IS UPON YOU.
YOUR SISTER IS GATHERING AN ARMY. RIGHT UNDER YOUR NOSE.
SHE'S JUST BUILDING A NEW ORDER OF KNIGHT-HOOD. HER LATEST PROJECT.
EXACTLY.

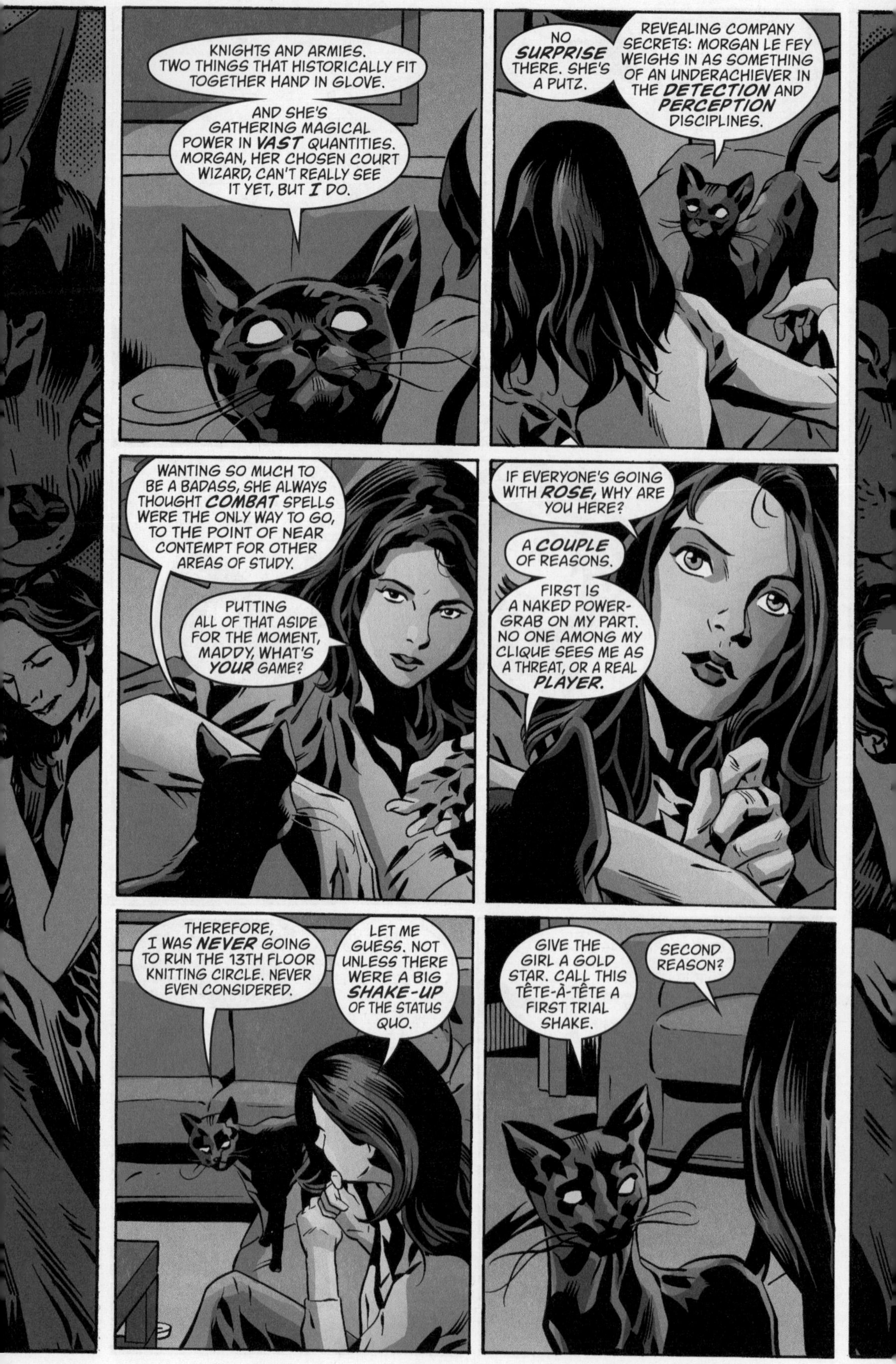
KNIGHTS AND ARMIES. TWO THINGS THAT HISTORICALLY FIT TOGETHER HAND IN GLOVE.
AND SHE'S GATHERING MAGICAL POWER IN VAST QUANTITIES. MORGAN, HER CHOSEN COURT WIZARD, CAN'T REALLY SEE IT YET, BUT I DO.
NO SURPRISE THERE. SHE'S A PUTZ.
REVEALING COMPANY SECRETS: MORGAN LE FEY WEIGHS IN AS SOMETHING OF AN UNDERACHIEVER IN THE DETECTION AND PERCEPTION DISCIPLINES.
WANTING SO MUCH TO BE A BADASS, SHE ALWAYS THOUGHT COMBAT SPELLS WERE THE ONLY WAY TO GO, TO THE POINT OF NEAR CONTEMPT FOR OTHER AREAS OF STUDY.
PUTTING ALL OF THAT ASIDE FOR THE MOMENT, MADDY, WHAT'S YOUR GAME?
IF EVERYONE'S GOING WITH ROSE, WHY ARE YOU HERE?
A COUPLE OF REASONS.
FIRST IS A NAKED POWER-GRAB ON MY PART. NO ONE AMONG MY CLIQUE SEES ME AS A THREAT, OR A REAL PLAYER.
THEREFORE, I WAS NEVER GOING TO RUN THE 13TH FLOOR KNITTING CIRCLE. NEVER EVEN CONSIDERED.
LET ME GUESS. NOT UNLESS THERE WERE A BIG SHAKE-UP OF THE STATUS QUO.
GIVE THE GIRL A GOLD STAR. CALL THIS TÊTE-À-TÊTE A FIRST TRIAL SHAKE.
SECOND REASON?

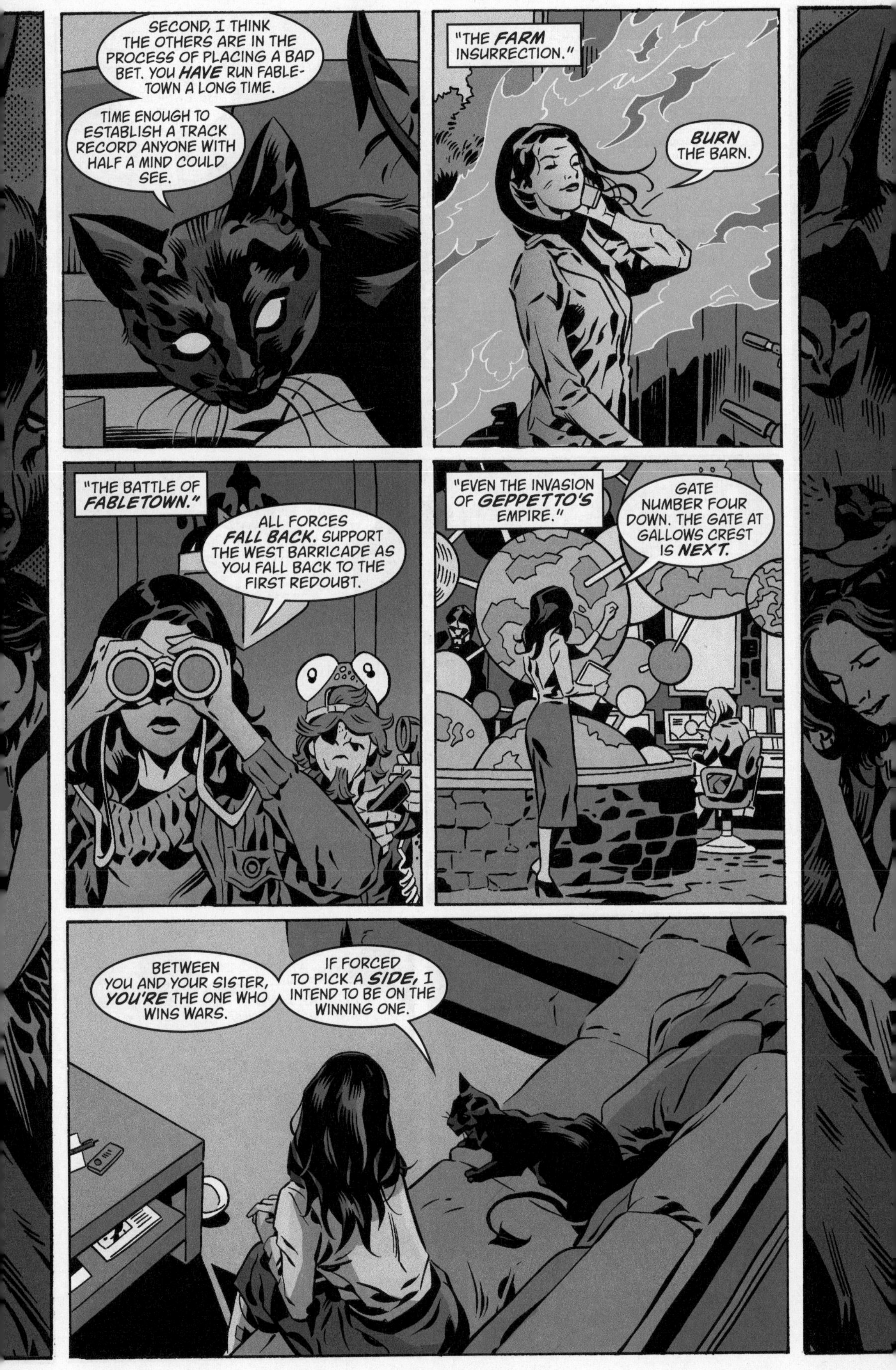
SECOND, I THINK THE OTHERS ARE IN THE PROCESS OF PLACING A BAD BET. YOU HAVE RUN FABLE-TOWN A LONG TIME.
TIME ENOUGH TO ESTABLISH A TRACK RECORD ANYONE WITH HALF A MIND COULD SEE.
"THE FARM INSURRECTION."
BURN THE BARN.
"THE BATTLE OF FABLETOWN."
ALL FORCES FALL BACK. SUPPORT THE WEST BARRICADE AS YOU FALL BACK TO THE FIRST REDOUBT.
"EVEN THE INVASION OF GEPPETTO'S EMPIRE."
GATE NUMBER FOUR DOWN. THE GATE AT GALLOWS CREST IS NEXT.
BETWEEN YOU AND YOUR SISTER, YOU'RE THE ONE WHO WINS WARS.
IF FORCED TO PICK A SIDE, I INTEND TO BE ON THE WINNING ONE.

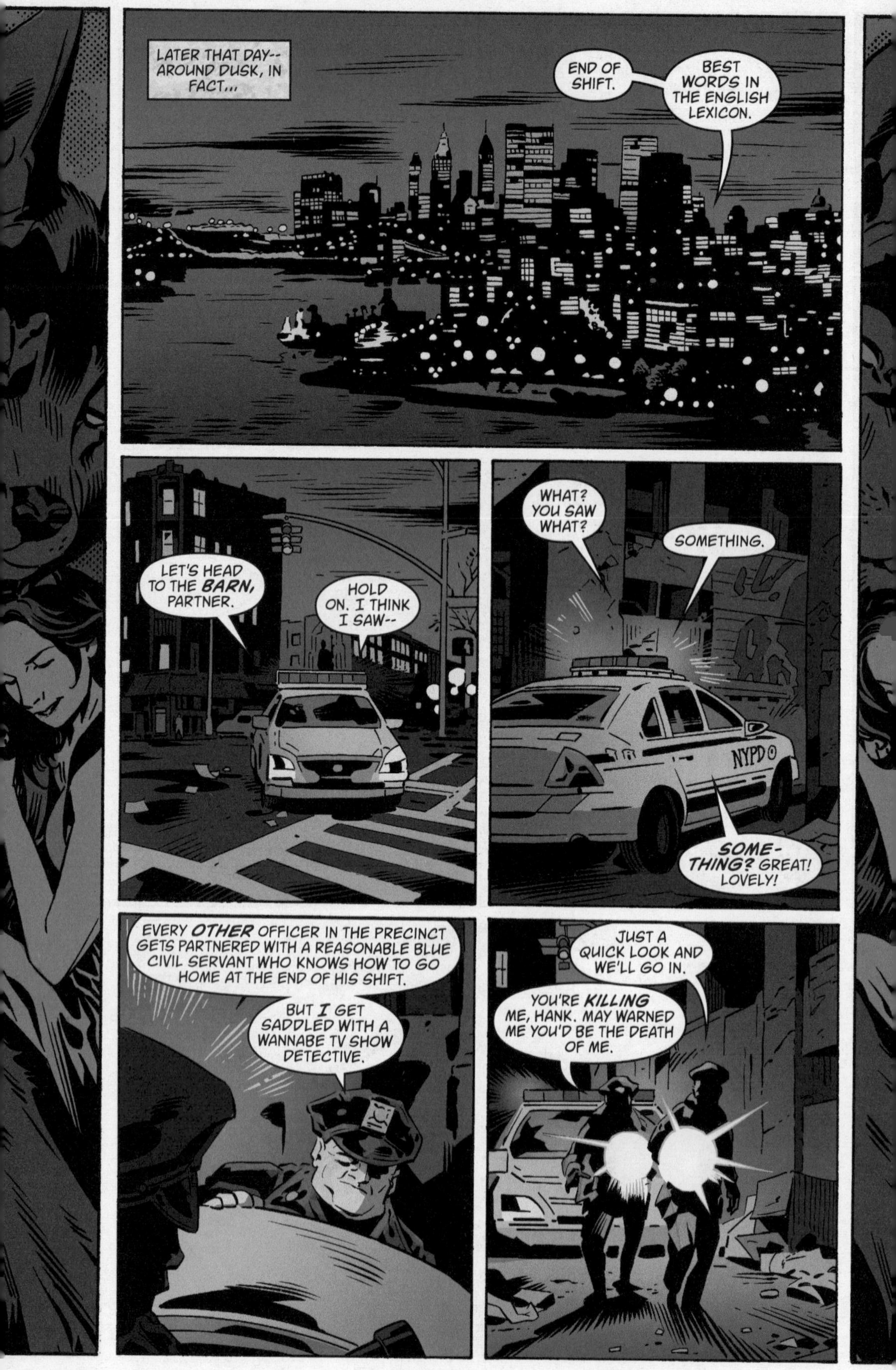
LATER THAT DAY-- AROUND DUSK, IN FACT...
END OF SHIFT.
BEST WORDS IN THE ENGLISH LEXICON.
LET'S HEAD TO THE BARN, PARTNER.
HOLD ON. I THINK I SAW--
WHAT? YOU SAW WHAT?
SOMETHING.
SOME-THING? GREAT! LOVELY!
EVERY OTHER OFFICER IN THE PRECINCT GETS PARTNERED WITH A REASONABLE BLUE CIVIL SERVANT WHO KNOWS HOW TO GO HOME AT THE END OF HIS SHIFT.
BUT I GET SADDLED WITH A WANNABE TV SHOW DETECTIVE.
JUST A QUICK LOOK AND WE'LL GO IN.
YOU'RE KILLING ME, HANK. MAY WARNED ME YOU'D BE THE DEATH OF ME.
NYPD

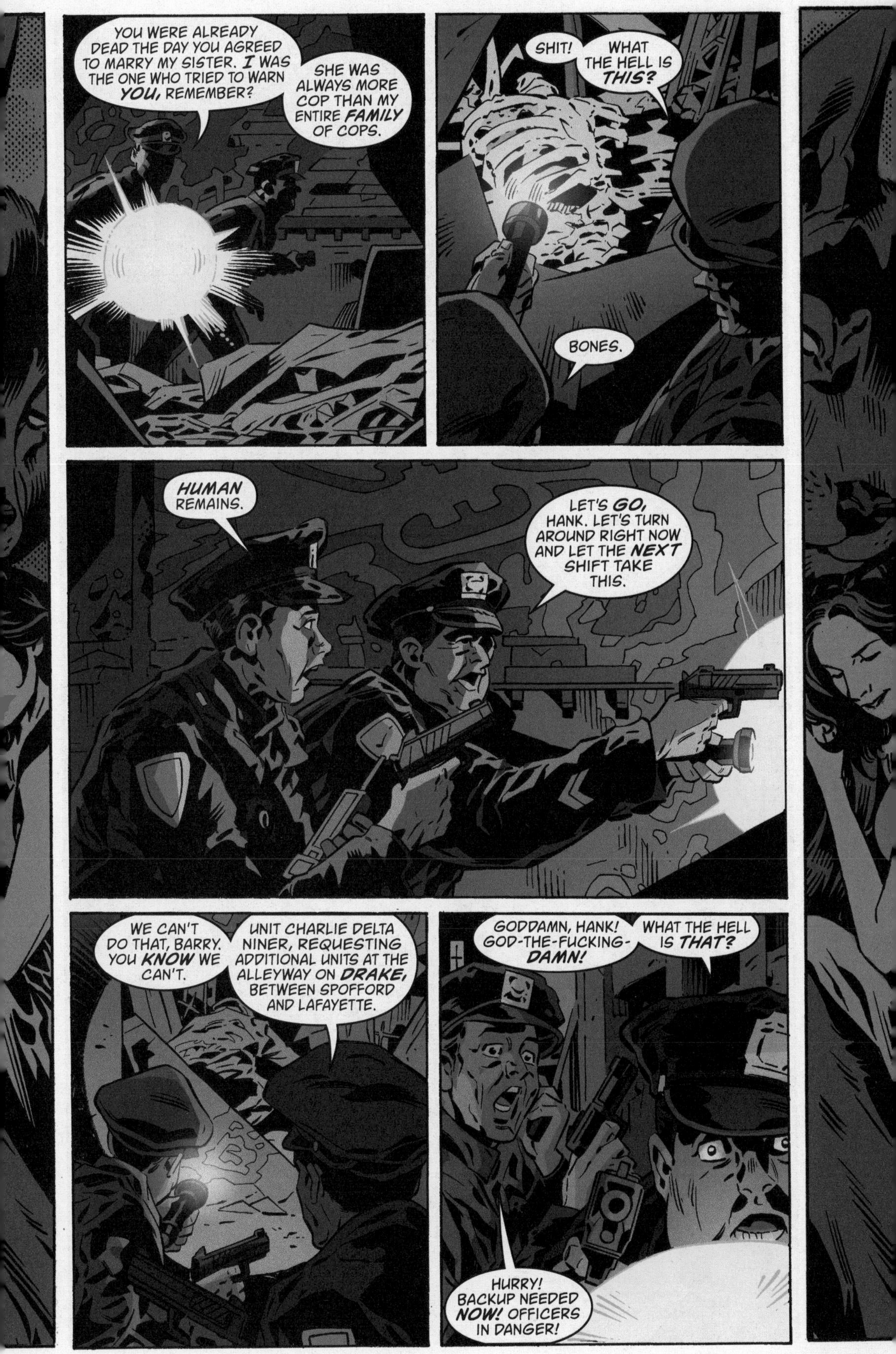

YOU WERE ALREADY DEAD THE DAY YOU AGREED TO MARRY MY SISTER. I WAS THE ONE WHO TRIED TO WARN YOU, REMEMBER?
SHE WAS ALWAYS MORE COP THAN MY ENTIRE FAMILY OF COPS.
SHIT!
WHAT THE HELL IS THIS?
BONES.
HUMAN REMAINS.
LET'S GO, HANK. LET'S TURN AROUND RIGHT NOW AND LET THE NEXT SHIFT TAKE THIS.
WE CAN'T DO THAT, BARRY. YOU KNOW WE CAN'T.
UNIT CHARLIE DELTA NINER, REQUESTING ADDITIONAL UNITS AT THE ALLEYWAY ON DRAKE, BETWEEN SPOFFORD AND LAFAYETTE.
GODDAMN, HANK! GOD-THE-FUCKING-DAMN!
WHAT THE HELL IS THAT?
HURRY! BACKUP NEEDED NOW! OFFICERS IN DANGER!

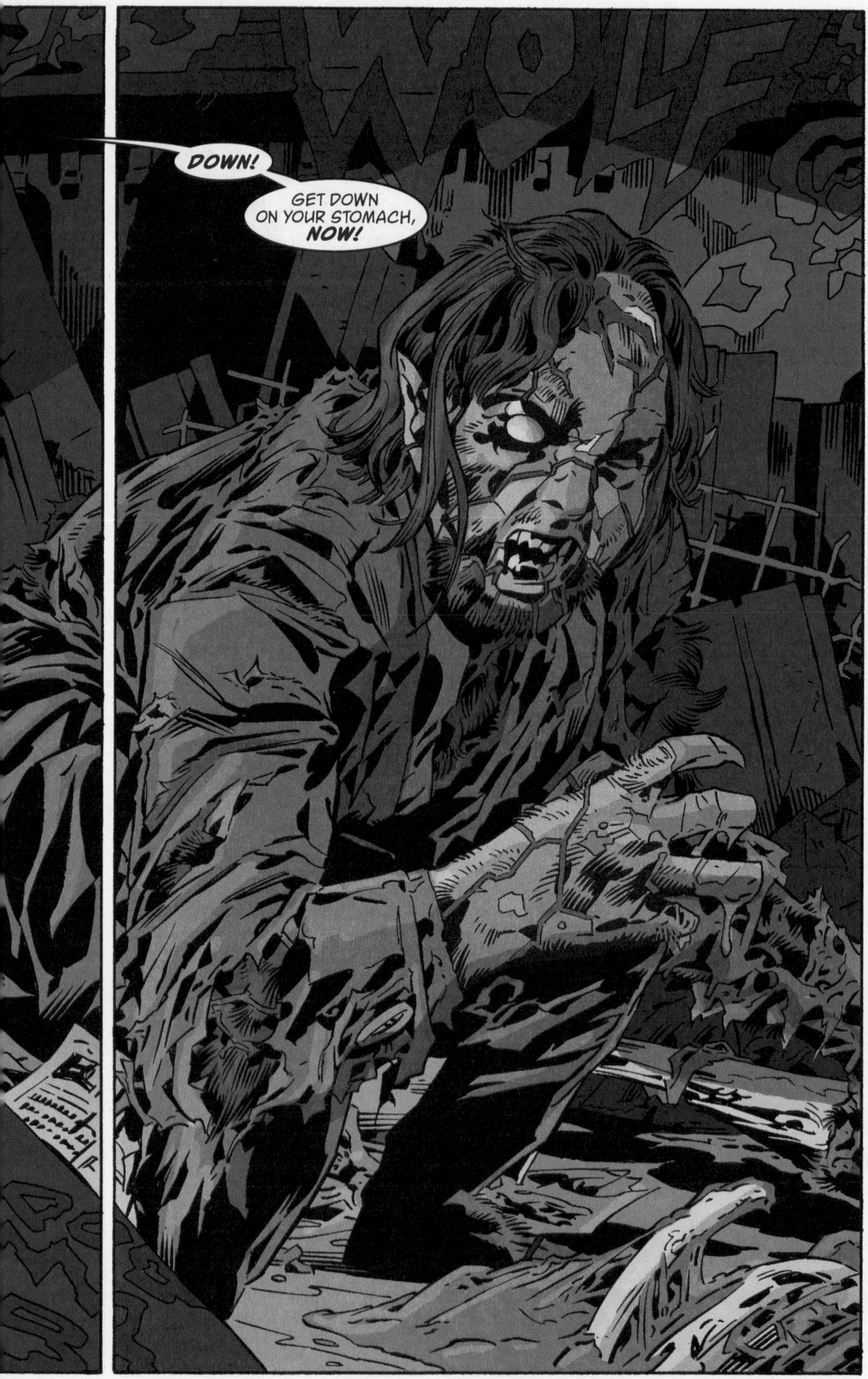
DOWN!
GET DOWN ON YOUR STOMACH, NOW!

NEXT: RETURN OF THE GLASS-SHATTERED WOLF!

The Last Flycatcher Story

Bill Willingham writer/creator
Mark Buckingham artist
Lee Loughridge colors
Todd Klein letters
Rowena Yow assoc. ed.
Shelly Bond editor

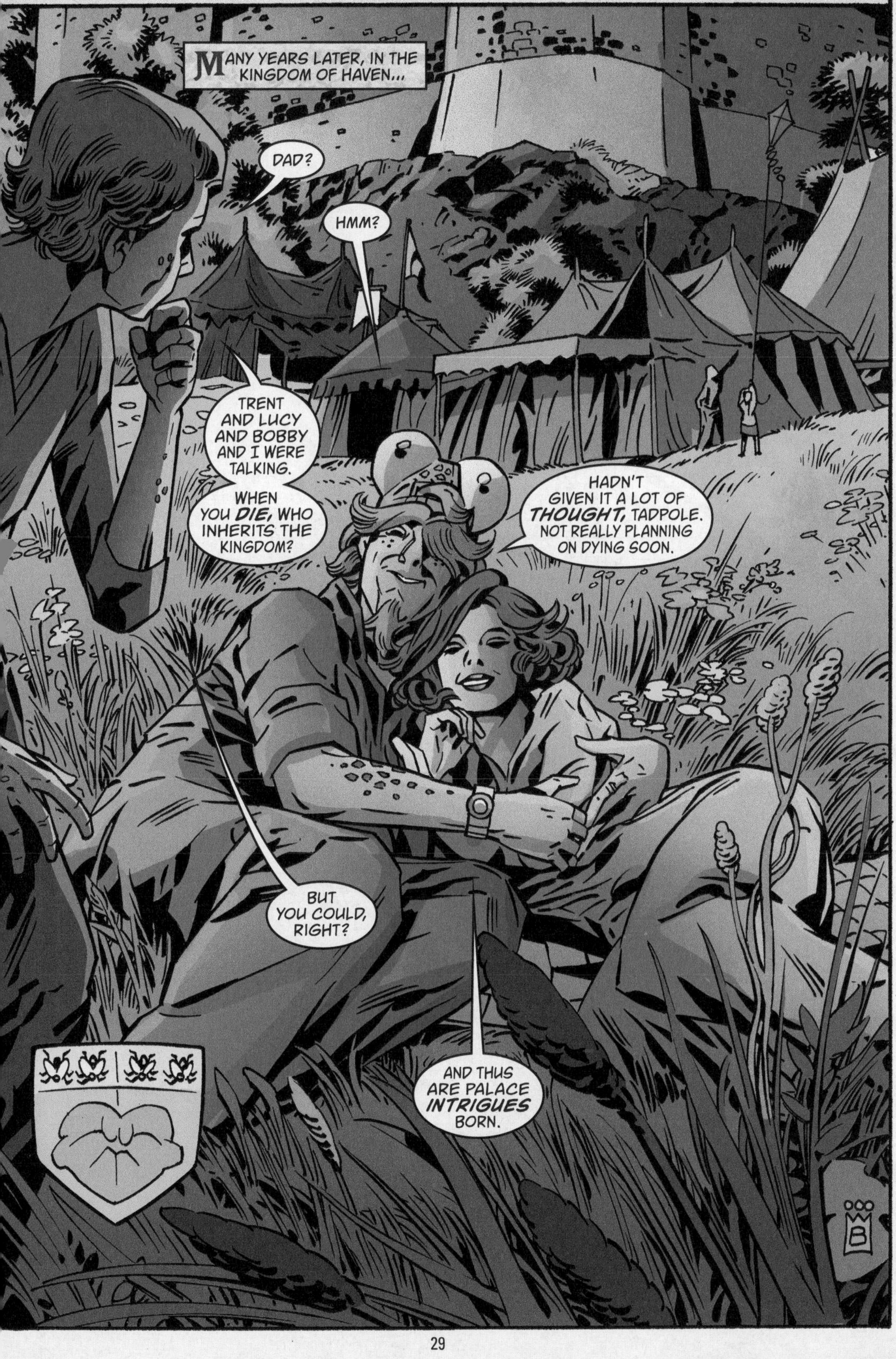
MANY YEARS LATER, IN THE KINGDOM OF HAVEN...
DAD?
HMM?
TRENT AND LUCY AND BOBBY AND I WERE TALKING.
WHEN YOU DIE, WHO INHERITS THE KINGDOM?
HADN'T GIVEN IT A LOT OF THOUGHT, TADPOLE. NOT REALLY PLANNING ON DYING SOON.
BUT YOU COULD, RIGHT?
AND THUS ARE PALACE INTRIGUES BORN.

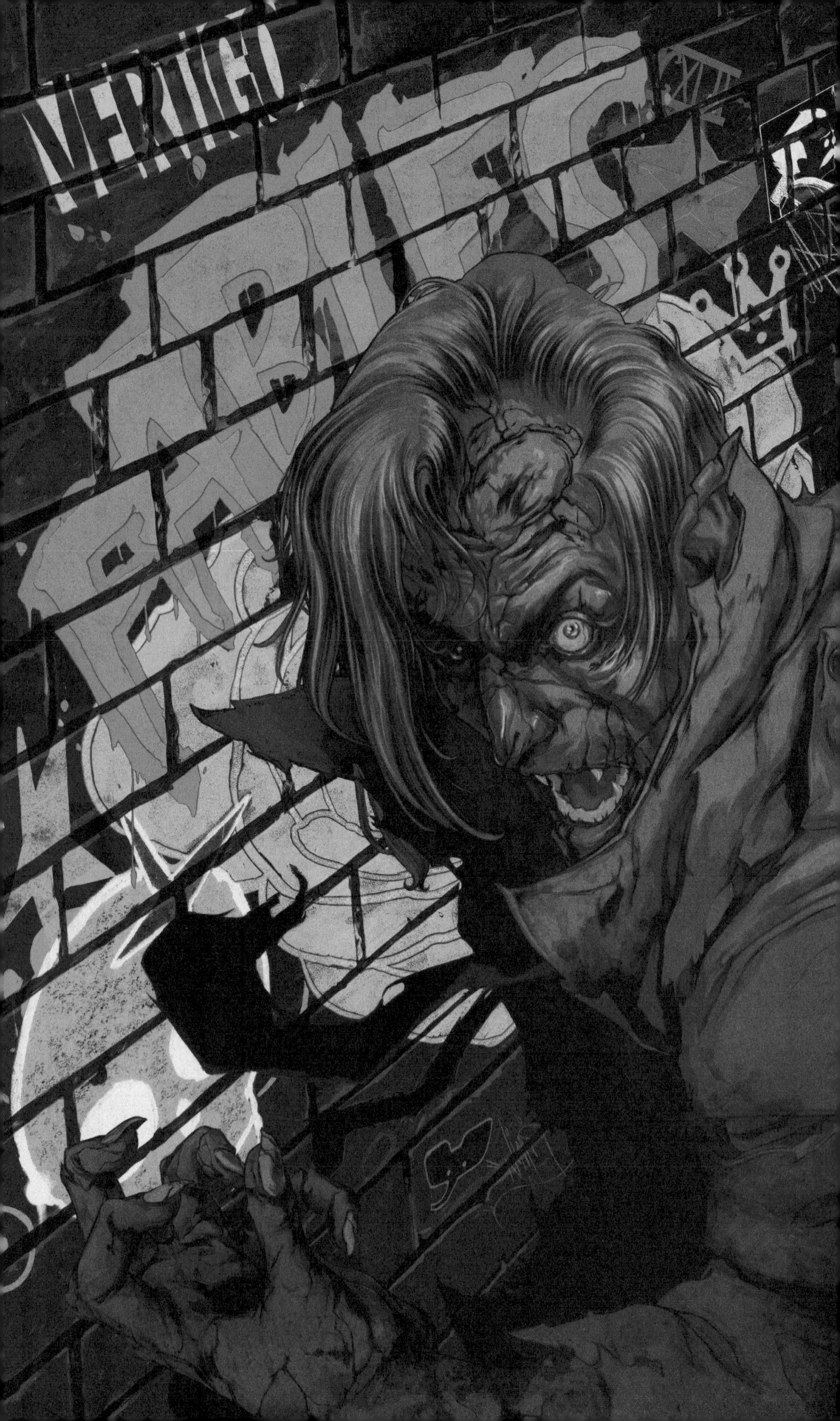
VERTIGO

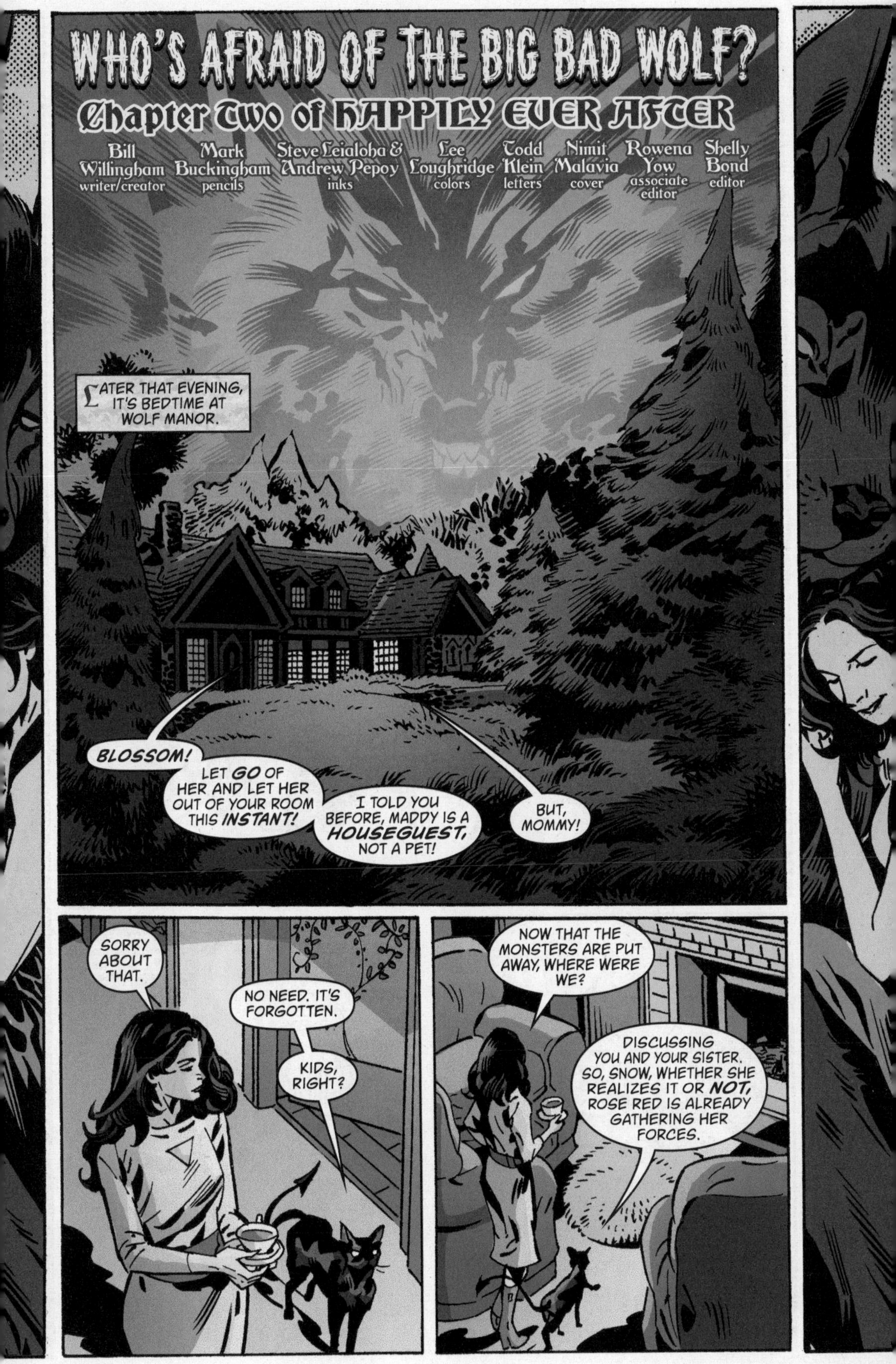
WHO'S AFRAID OF THE BIG BAD WOLF?
Chapter Two of HAPPILY EVER AFTER
Bill Willingham writer/creator
Mark Buckingham pencils
Steve Leialoha & Andrew Pepoy inks
Lee Loughridge colors
Todd Klein letters
Nimit Malavia cover
Rowena Yow associate editor
Shelly Bond editor
LATER THAT EVENING, IT'S BEDTIME AT WOLF MANOR.
BLOSSOM!
LET GO OF HER AND LET HER OUT OF YOUR ROOM THIS INSTANT!
I TOLD YOU BEFORE, MADDY IS A HOUSEGUEST, NOT A PET!
BUT, MOMMY!
SORRY ABOUT THAT.
NO NEED. IT'S FORGOTTEN.
KIDS, RIGHT?
NOW THAT THE MONSTERS ARE PUT AWAY, WHERE WERE WE?
DISCUSSING YOU AND YOUR SISTER. SO, SNOW, WHETHER SHE REALIZES IT OR NOT, ROSE RED IS ALREADY GATHERING HER FORCES.

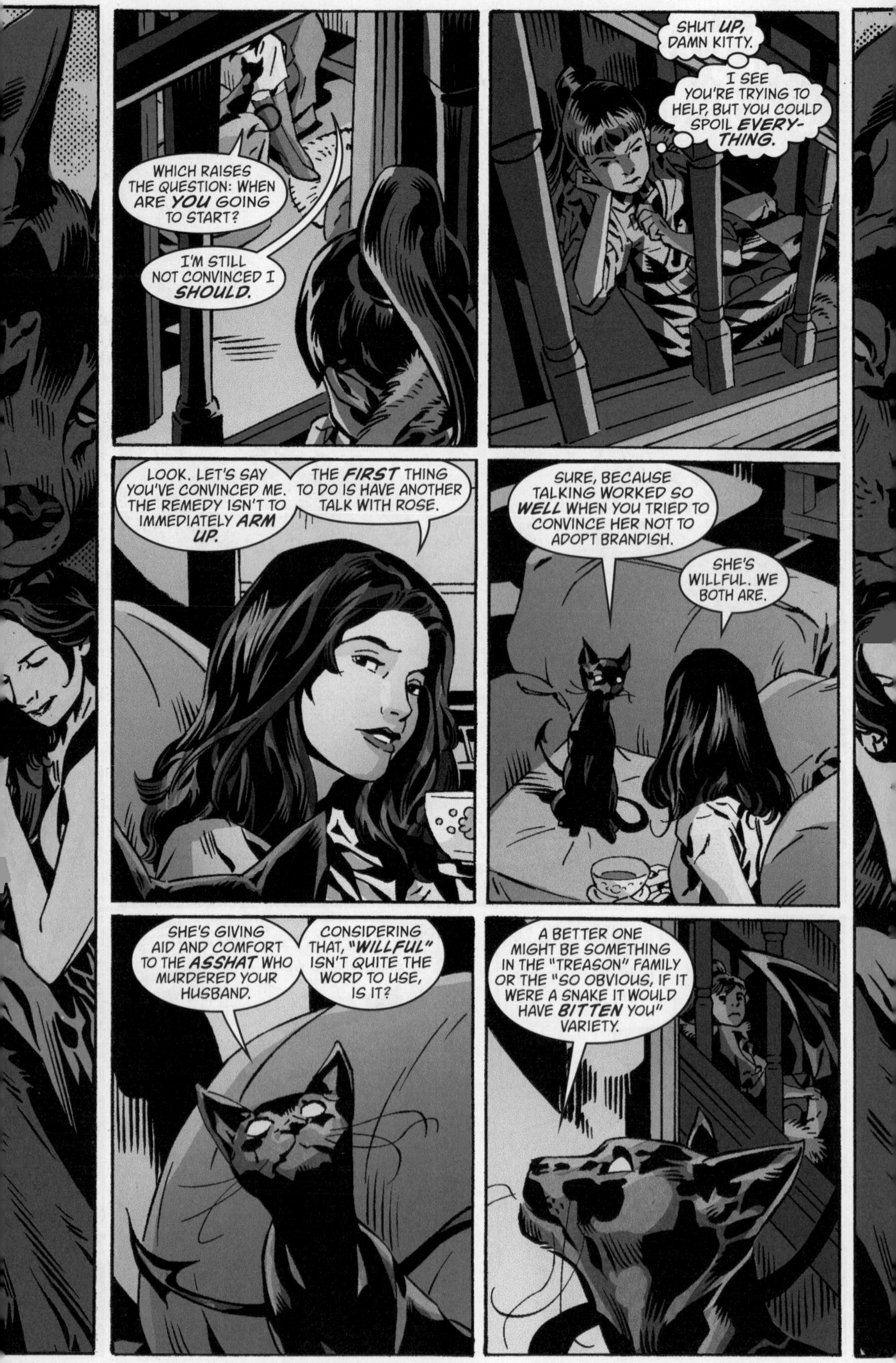
WHICH RAISES THE QUESTION: WHEN ARE YOU GOING TO START?
I'M STILL NOT CONVINCED I SHOULD.
SHUT UP, DAMN KITTY.
I SEE YOU'RE TRYING TO HELP, BUT YOU COULD SPOIL EVERY-THING.
LOOK. LET'S SAY YOU'VE CONVINCED ME. THE REMEDY ISN'T TO IMMEDIATELY ARM UP.
THE FIRST THING TO DO IS HAVE ANOTHER TALK WITH ROSE.
SURE, BECAUSE TALKING WORKED SO WELL WHEN YOU TRIED TO CONVINCE HER NOT TO ADOPT BRANDISH.
SHE'S WILLFUL. WE BOTH ARE.
SHE'S GIVING AID AND COMFORT TO THE ASSHAT WHO MURDERED YOUR HUSBAND.
CONSIDERING THAT, "WILLFUL" ISN'T QUITE THE WORD TO USE, IS IT?
A BETTER ONE MIGHT BE SOMETHING IN THE "TREASON" FAMILY OR THE "SO OBVIOUS, IF IT WERE A SNAKE IT WOULD HAVE BITTEN YOU" VARIETY.

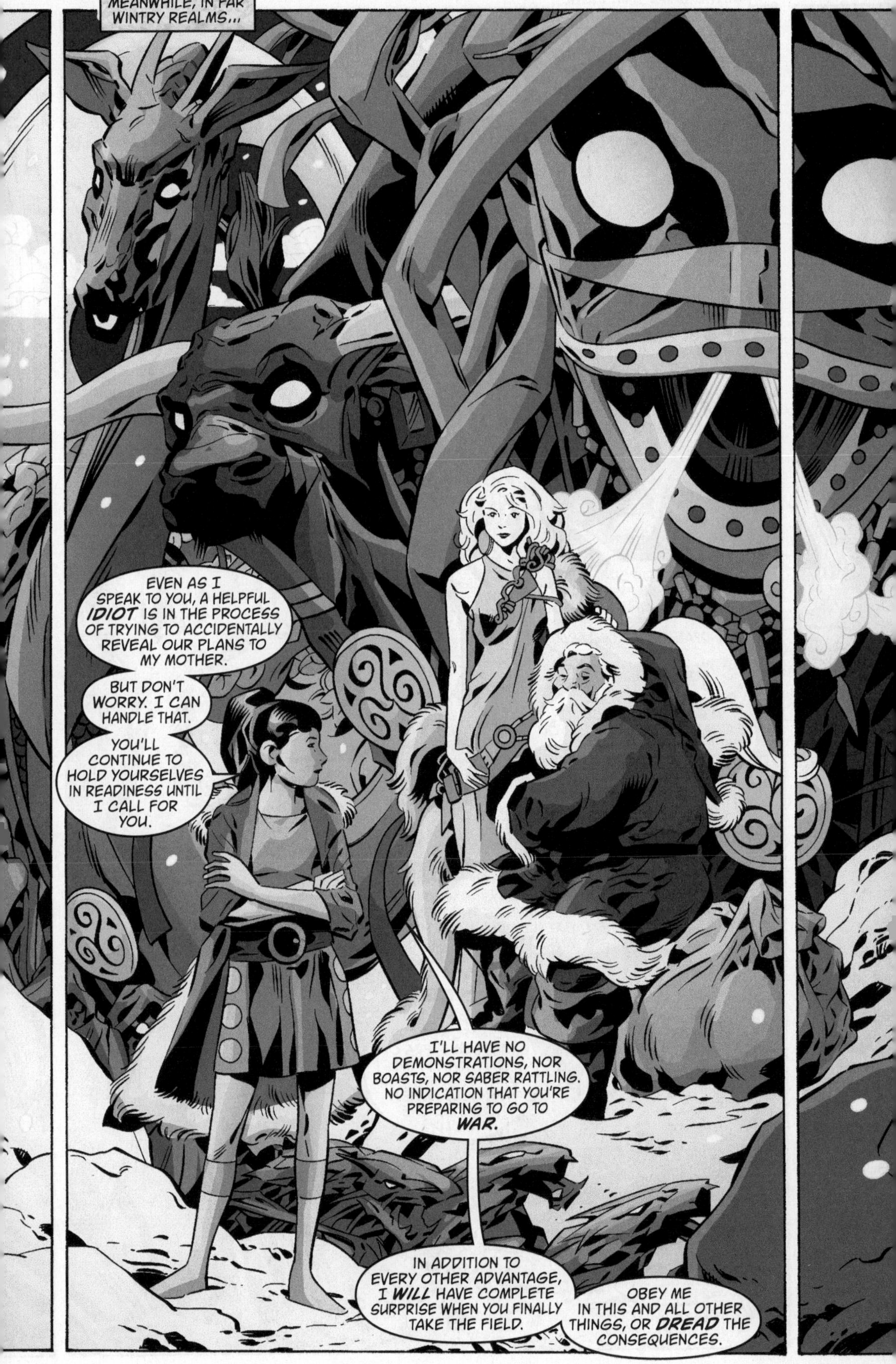
MEANWHILE, IN FAR WINTRY REALMS...
EVEN AS I SPEAK TO YOU, A HELPFUL IDIOT IS IN THE PROCESS OF TRYING TO ACCIDENTALLY REVEAL OUR PLANS TO MY MOTHER.
BUT DON'T WORRY. I CAN HANDLE THAT.
YOU'LL CONTINUE TO HOLD YOURSELVES IN READINESS UNTIL I CALL FOR YOU.
I'LL HAVE NO DEMONSTRATIONS, NOR BOASTS, NOR SABER RATTLING. NO INDICATION THAT YOU'RE PREPARING TO GO TO WAR.
IN ADDITION TO EVERY OTHER ADVANTAGE, I WILL HAVE COMPLETE SURPRISE WHEN YOU FINALLY TAKE THE FIELD.
OBEY ME IN THIS AND ALL OTHER THINGS, OR DREAD THE CONSEQUENCES.

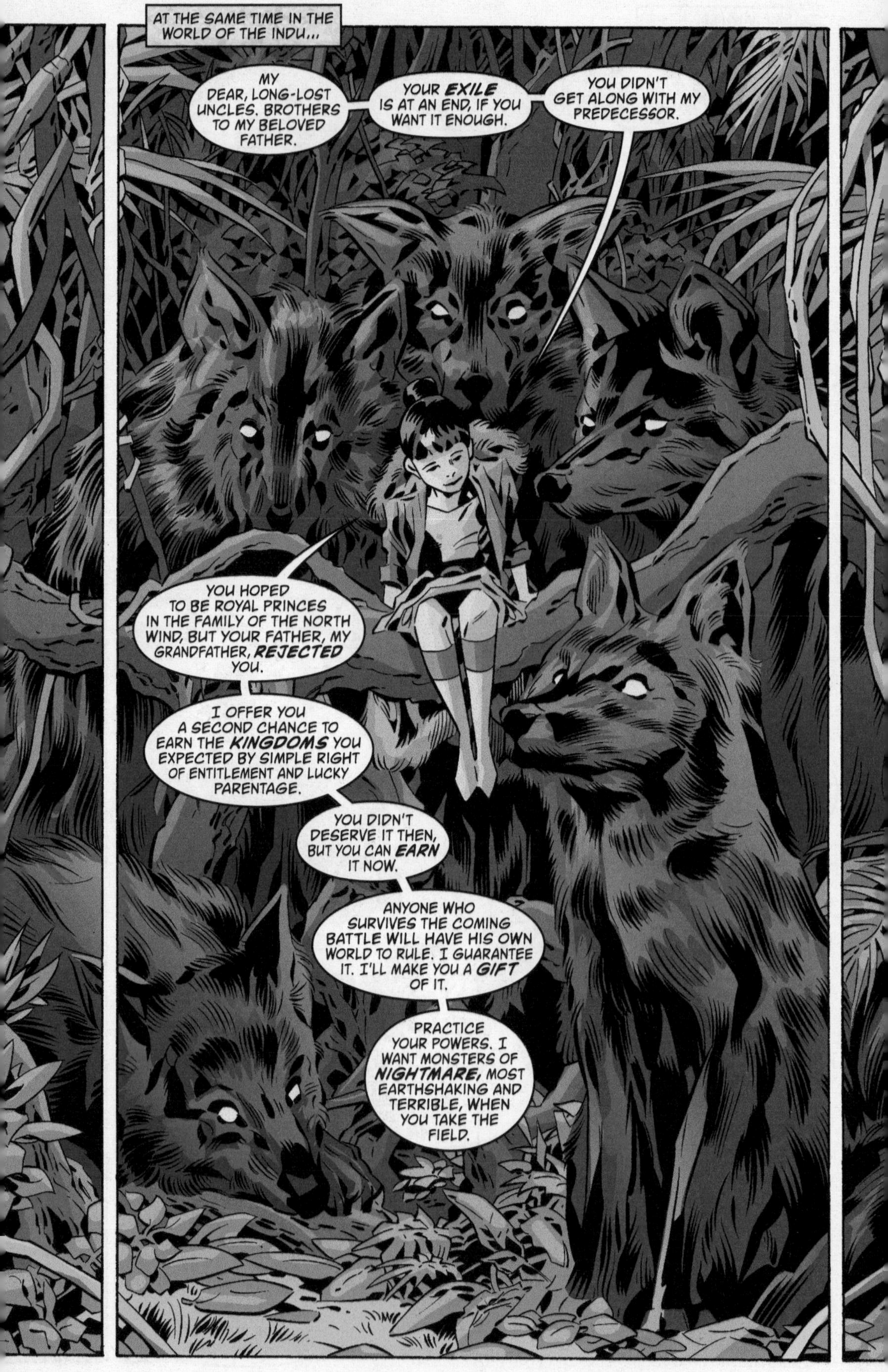
AT THE SAME TIME IN THE WORLD OF THE INDU...
MY DEAR, LONG-LOST UNCLES. BROTHERS TO MY BELOVED FATHER.
YOUR EXILE IS AT AN END, IF YOU WANT IT ENOUGH.
YOU DIDN'T GET ALONG WITH MY PREDECESSOR.
YOU HOPED TO BE ROYAL PRINCES IN THE FAMILY OF THE NORTH WIND, BUT YOUR FATHER, MY GRANDFATHER, REJECTED YOU.
I OFFER YOU A SECOND CHANCE TO EARN THE KINGDOMS YOU EXPECTED BY SIMPLE RIGHT OF ENTITLEMENT AND LUCKY PARENTAGE.
YOU DIDN'T DESERVE IT THEN, BUT YOU CAN EARN IT NOW.
ANYONE WHO SURVIVES THE COMING BATTLE WILL HAVE HIS OWN WORLD TO RULE. I GUARANTEE IT. I'LL MAKE YOU A GIFT OF IT.
PRACTICE YOUR POWERS. I WANT MONSTERS OF NIGHTMARE, MOST EARTHSHAKING AND TERRIBLE, WHEN YOU TAKE THE FIELD.

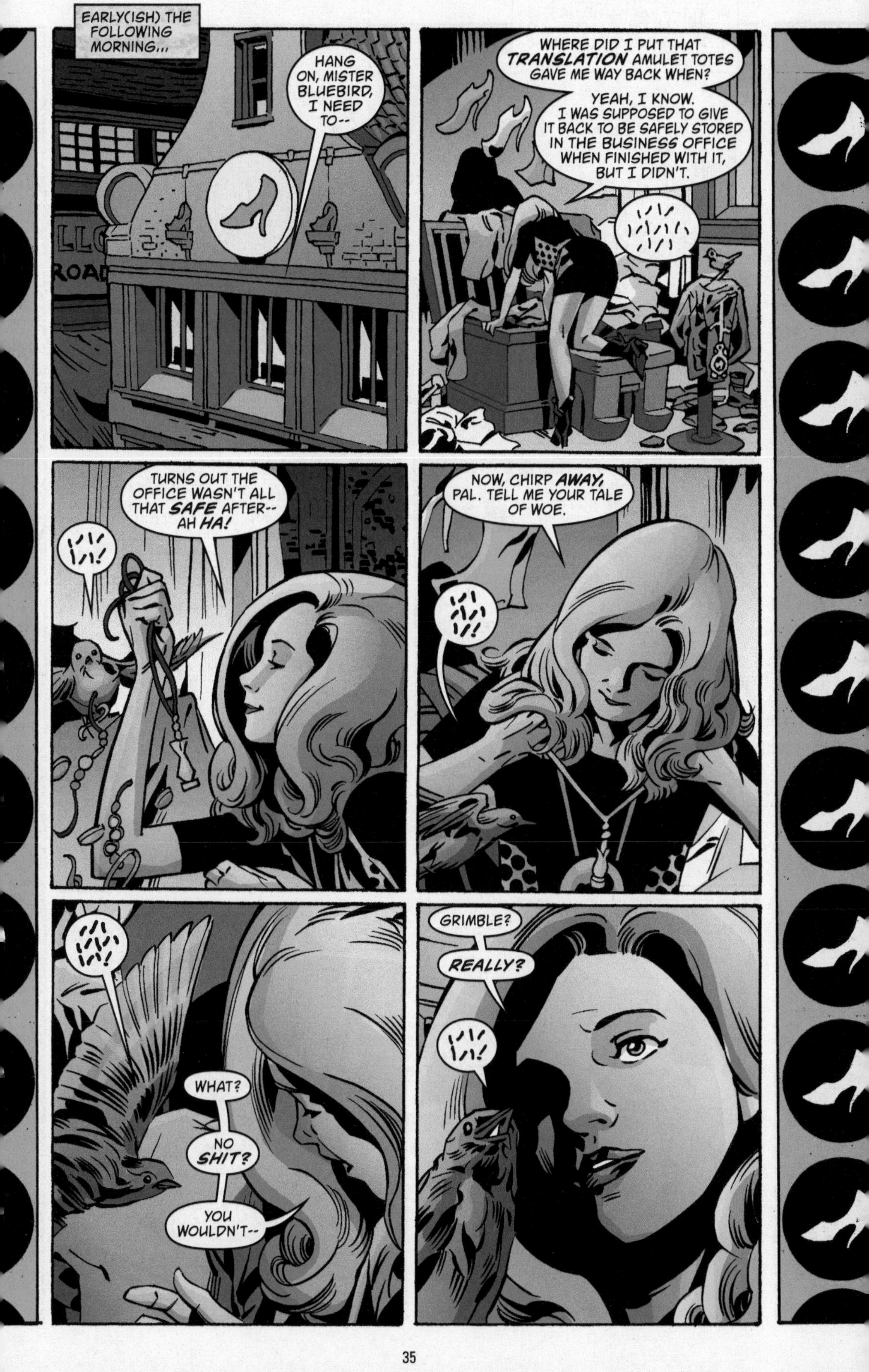

EARLY(ISH) THE FOLLOWING MORNING...
HANG ON, MISTER BLUEBIRD, I NEED TO--
WHERE DID I PUT THAT TRANSLATION AMULET TOTES GAVE ME WAY BACK WHEN?
YEAH, I KNOW. I WAS SUPPOSED TO GIVE IT BACK TO BE SAFELY STORED IN THE BUSINESS OFFICE WHEN FINISHED WITH IT, BUT I DIDN'T.
TURNS OUT THE OFFICE WASN'T ALL THAT SAFE AFTER--AH HA!
NOW, CHIRP AWAY, PAL. TELL ME YOUR TALE OF WOE.
WHAT?
NO SHIT?
YOU WOULDN'T--
GRIMBLE?
REALLY?

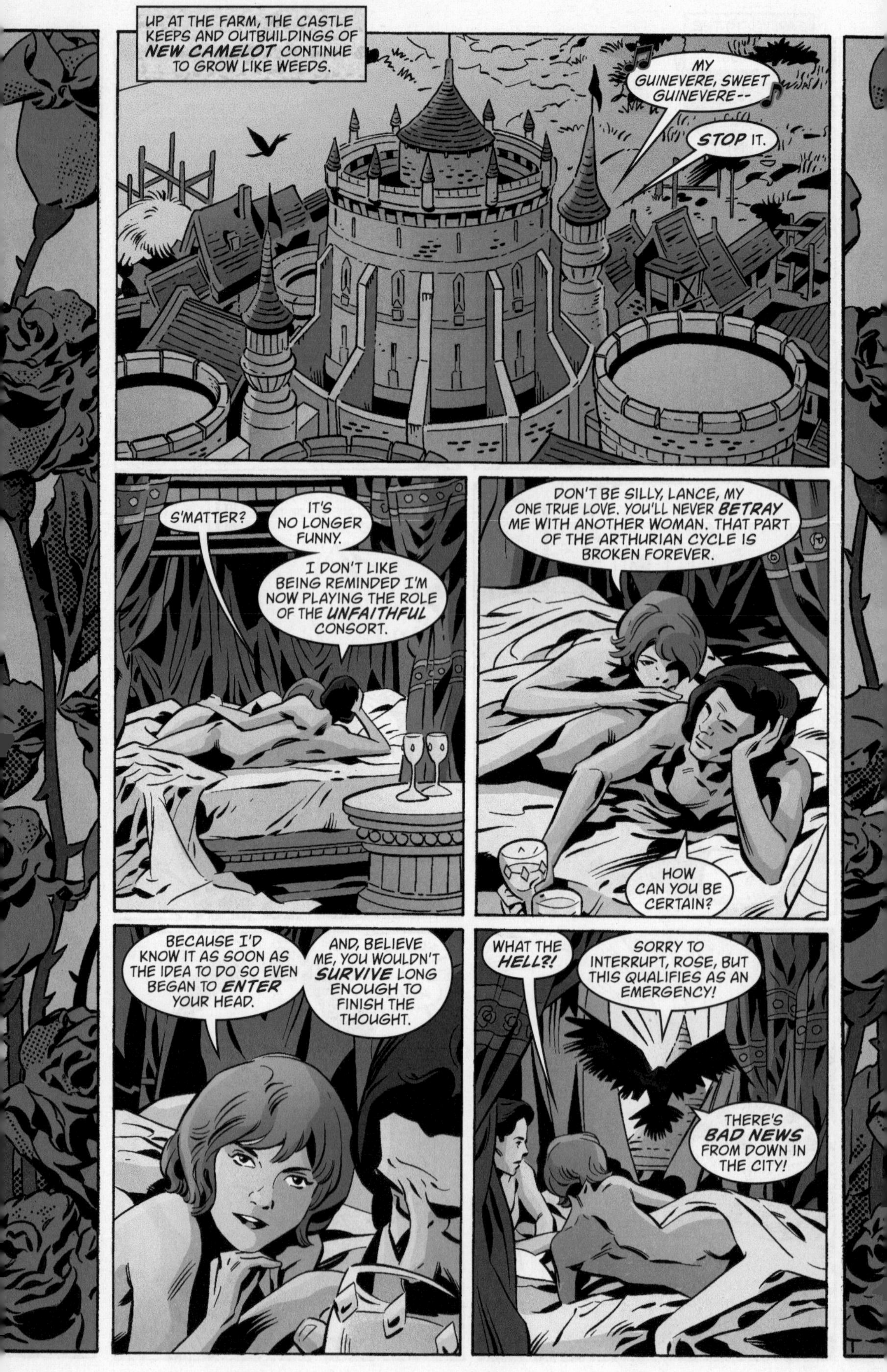
UP AT THE FARM, THE CASTLE KEEPS AND OUTBUILDINGS OF NEW CAMELOT CONTINUE TO GROW LIKE WEEDS.
MY GUINEVERE, SWEET GUINEVERE--
STOP IT.
S'MATTER?
IT'S NO LONGER FUNNY.
I DON'T LIKE BEING REMINDED I'M NOW PLAYING THE ROLE OF THE UNFAITHFUL CONSORT.
DON'T BE SILLY, LANCE, MY ONE TRUE LOVE. YOU'LL NEVER BETRAY ME WITH ANOTHER WOMAN. THAT PART OF THE ARTHURIAN CYCLE IS BROKEN FOREVER.
HOW CAN YOU BE CERTAIN?
BECAUSE I'D KNOW IT AS SOON AS THE IDEA TO DO SO EVEN BEGAN TO ENTER YOUR HEAD.
AND, BELIEVE ME, YOU WOULDN'T SURVIVE LONG ENOUGH TO FINISH THE THOUGHT.
WHAT THE HELL?!
SORRY TO INTERRUPT, ROSE, BUT THIS QUALIFIES AS AN EMERGENCY!
THERE'S BAD NEWS FROM DOWN IN THE CITY!

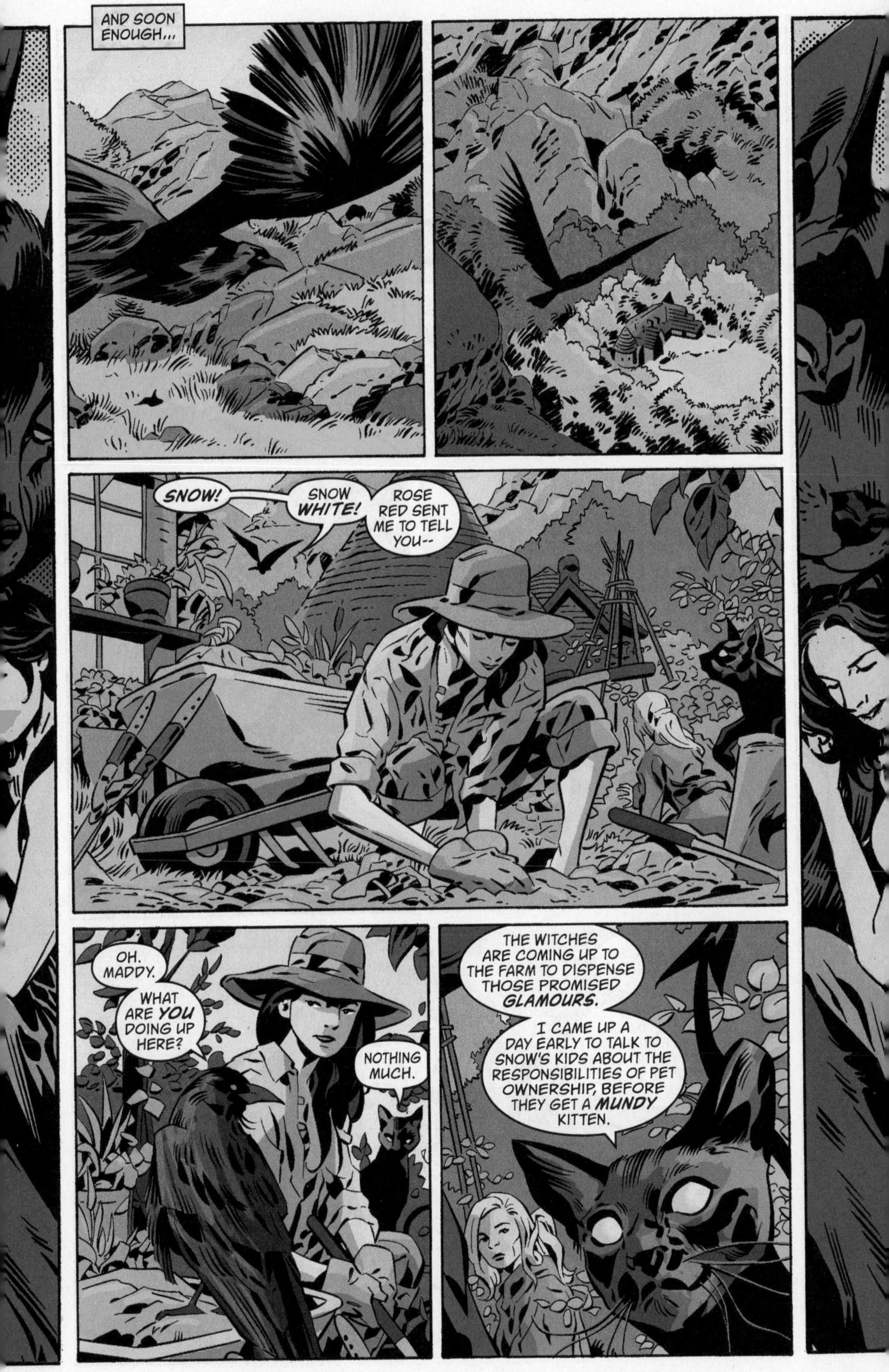
AND SOON ENOUGH...
SNOW!
SNOW WHITE!
ROSE RED SENT ME TO TELL YOU--
OH. MADDY.
WHAT ARE YOU DOING UP HERE?
NOTHING MUCH.
THE WITCHES ARE COMING UP TO THE FARM TO DISPENSE THOSE PROMISED GLAMOURS.
I CAME UP A DAY EARLY TO TALK TO SNOW'S KIDS ABOUT THE RESPONSIBILITIES OF PET OWNERSHIP, BEFORE THEY GET A MUNDY KITTEN.

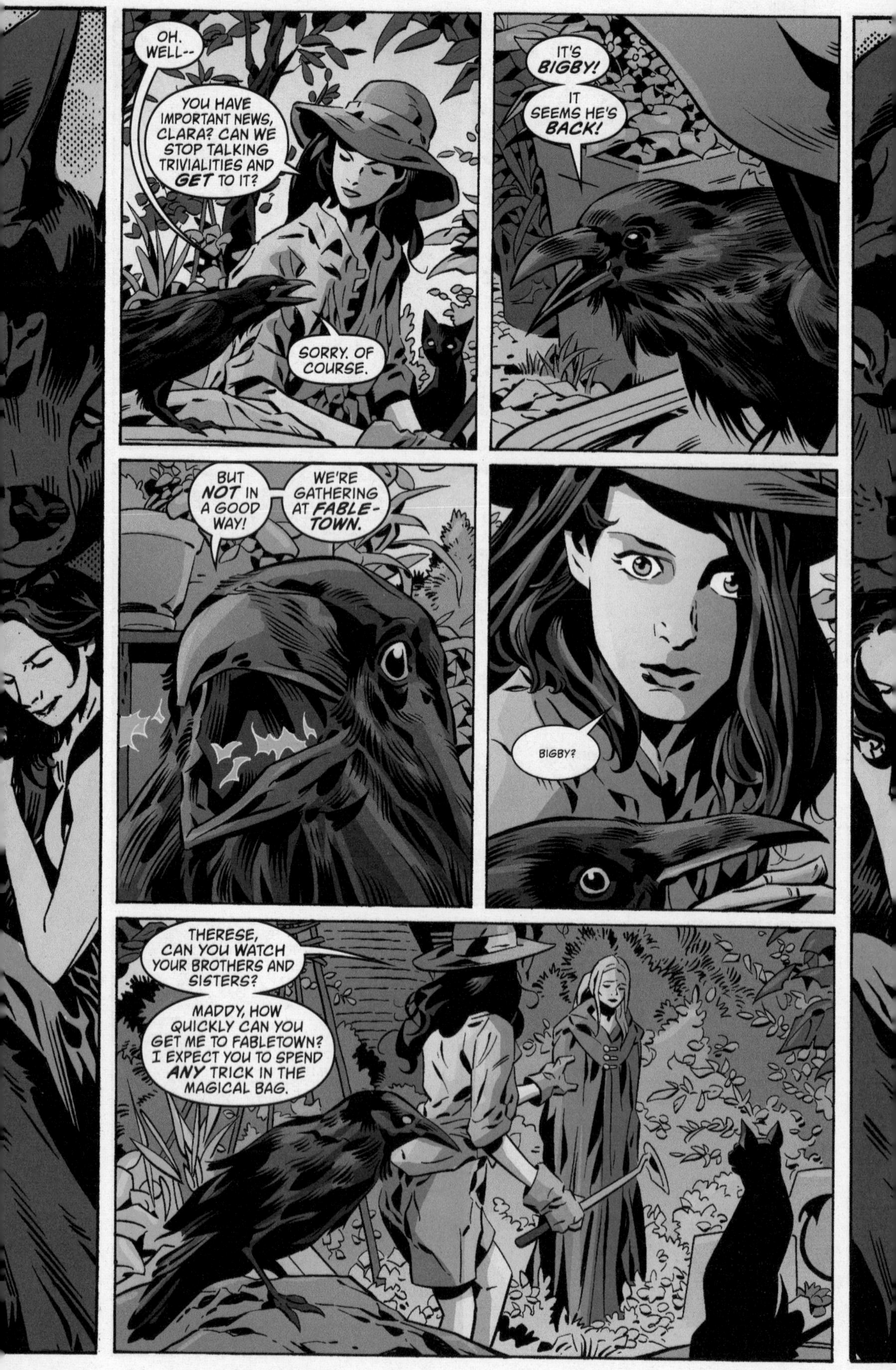
OH. WELL--
YOU HAVE IMPORTANT NEWS, CLARA? CAN WE STOP TALKING TRIVIALITIES AND GET TO IT?
SORRY. OF COURSE.
IT'S BIGBY!
IT SEEMS HE'S BACK!
BUT NOT IN A GOOD WAY!
WE'RE GATHERING AT FABLE-TOWN.
BIGBY?
THERESE, CAN YOU WATCH YOUR BROTHERS AND SISTERS?
MADDY, HOW QUICKLY CAN YOU GET ME TO FABLETOWN? I EXPECT YOU TO SPEND ANY TRICK IN THE MAGICAL BAG.

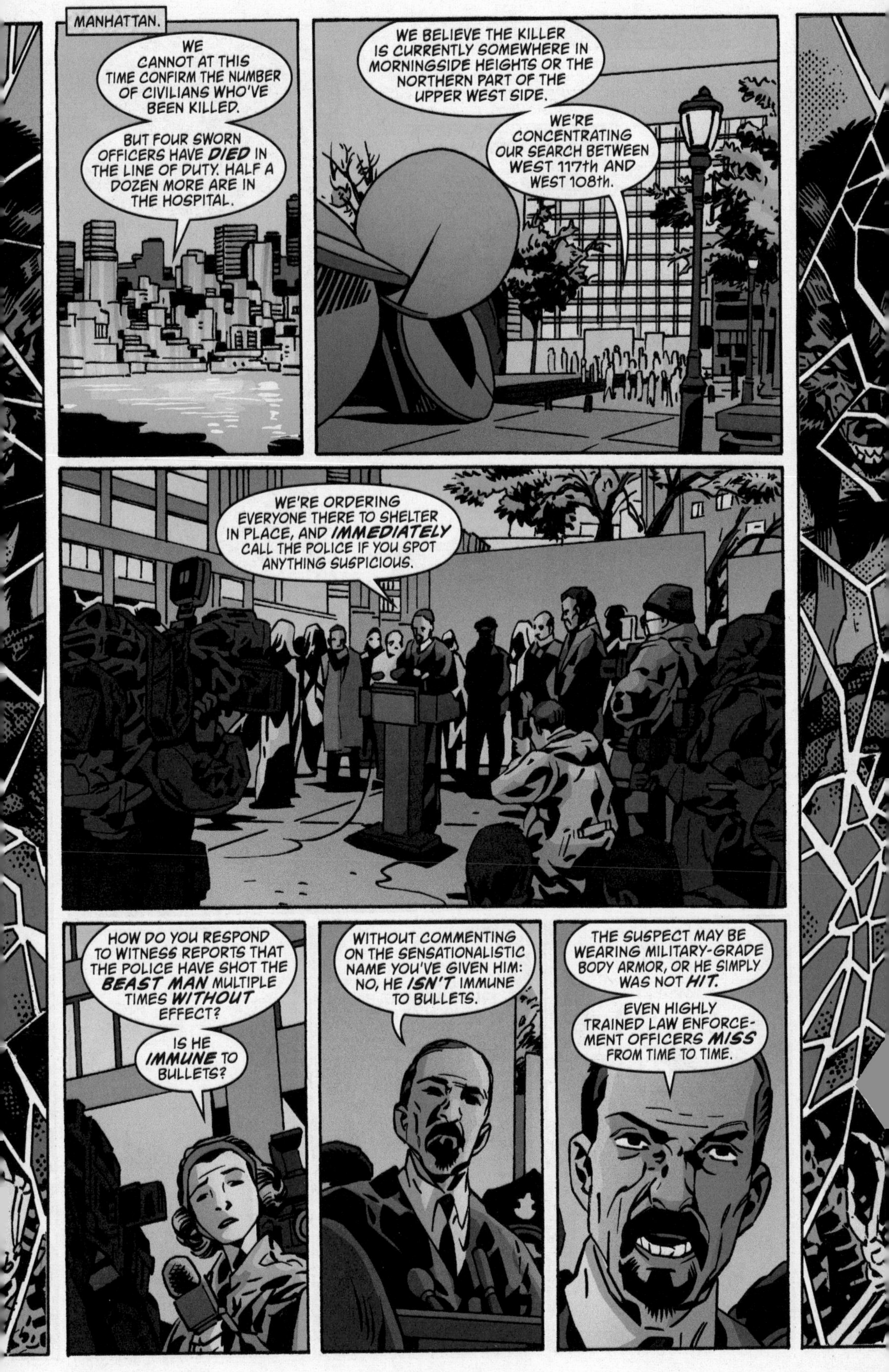
MANHATTAN.
WE CANNOT AT THIS TIME CONFIRM THE NUMBER OF CIVILIANS WHO'VE BEEN KILLED.
BUT FOUR SWORN OFFICERS HAVE DIED IN THE LINE OF DUTY. HALF A DOZEN MORE ARE IN THE HOSPITAL.
WE BELIEVE THE KILLER IS CURRENTLY SOMEWHERE IN MORNINGSIDE HEIGHTS OR THE NORTHERN PART OF THE UPPER WEST SIDE.
WE'RE CONCENTRATING OUR SEARCH BETWEEN WEST 117th AND WEST 108th.
WE'RE ORDERING EVERYONE THERE TO SHELTER IN PLACE, AND IMMEDIATELY CALL THE POLICE IF YOU SPOT ANYTHING SUSPICIOUS.
HOW DO YOU RESPOND TO WITNESS REPORTS THAT THE POLICE HAVE SHOT THE BEAST MAN MULTIPLE TIMES WITHOUT EFFECT?
IS HE IMMUNE TO BULLETS?
WITHOUT COMMENTING ON THE SENSATIONALISTIC NAME YOU'VE GIVEN HIM: NO, HE ISN'T IMMUNE TO BULLETS.
THE SUSPECT MAY BE WEARING MILITARY-GRADE BODY ARMOR, OR HE SIMPLY WAS NOT HIT.
EVEN HIGHLY TRAINED LAW ENFORCEMENT OFFICERS MISS FROM TIME TO TIME.

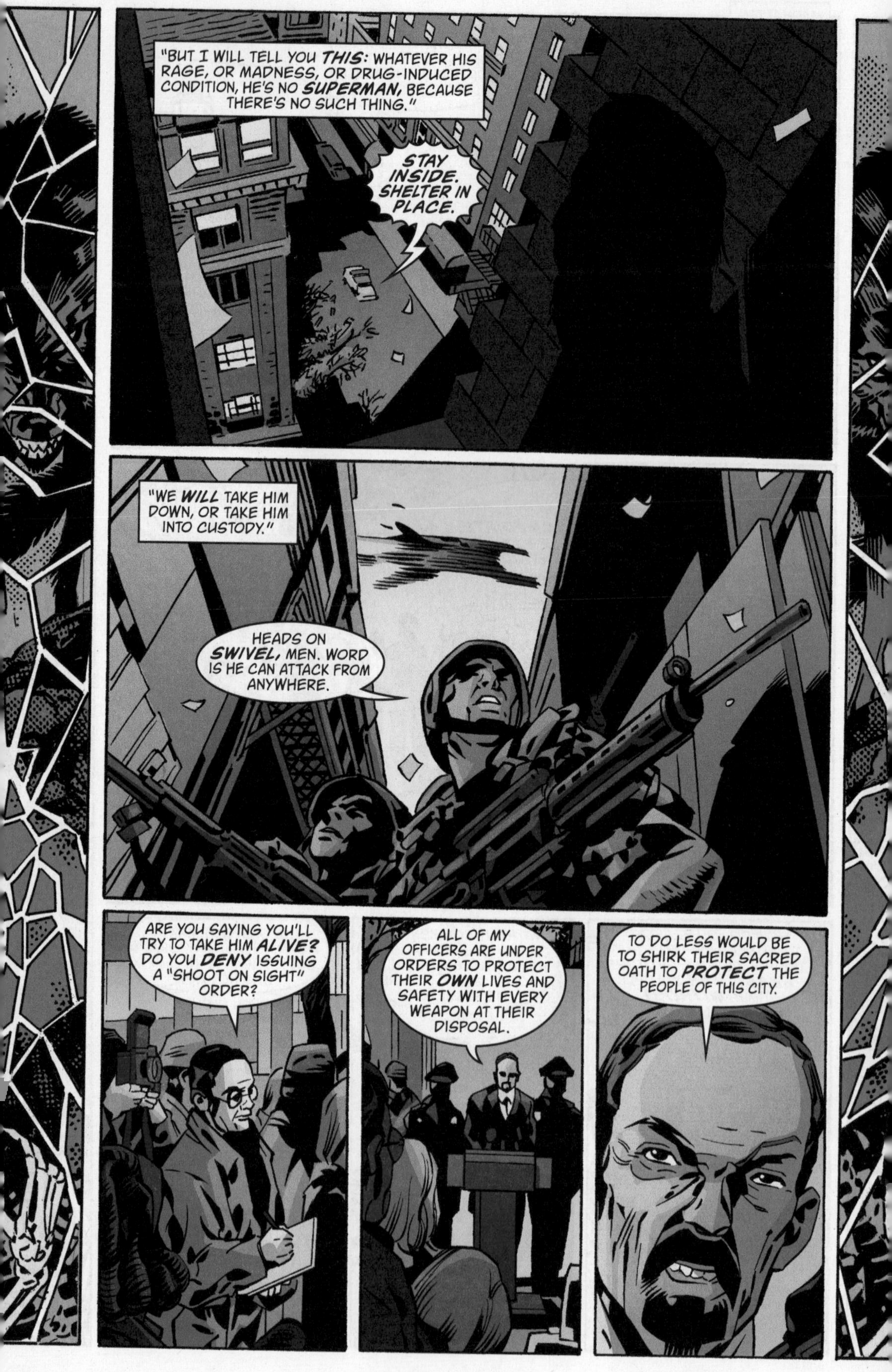
"BUT I WILL TELL YOU THIS: WHATEVER HIS RAGE, OR MADNESS, OR DRUG-INDUCED CONDITION, HE'S NO SUPERMAN, BECAUSE THERE'S NO SUCH THING."
STAY INSIDE. SHELTER IN PLACE.
"WE WILL TAKE HIM DOWN, OR TAKE HIM INTO CUSTODY."
HEADS ON SWIVEL, MEN. WORD IS HE CAN ATTACK FROM ANYWHERE.
ARE YOU SAYING YOU'LL TRY TO TAKE HIM ALIVE? DO YOU DENY ISSUING A "SHOOT ON SIGHT" ORDER?
ALL OF MY OFFICERS ARE UNDER ORDERS TO PROTECT THEIR OWN LIVES AND SAFETY WITH EVERY WEAPON AT THEIR DISPOSAL.
TO DO LESS WOULD BE TO SHIRK THEIR SACRED OATH TO PROTECT THE PEOPLE OF THIS CITY.

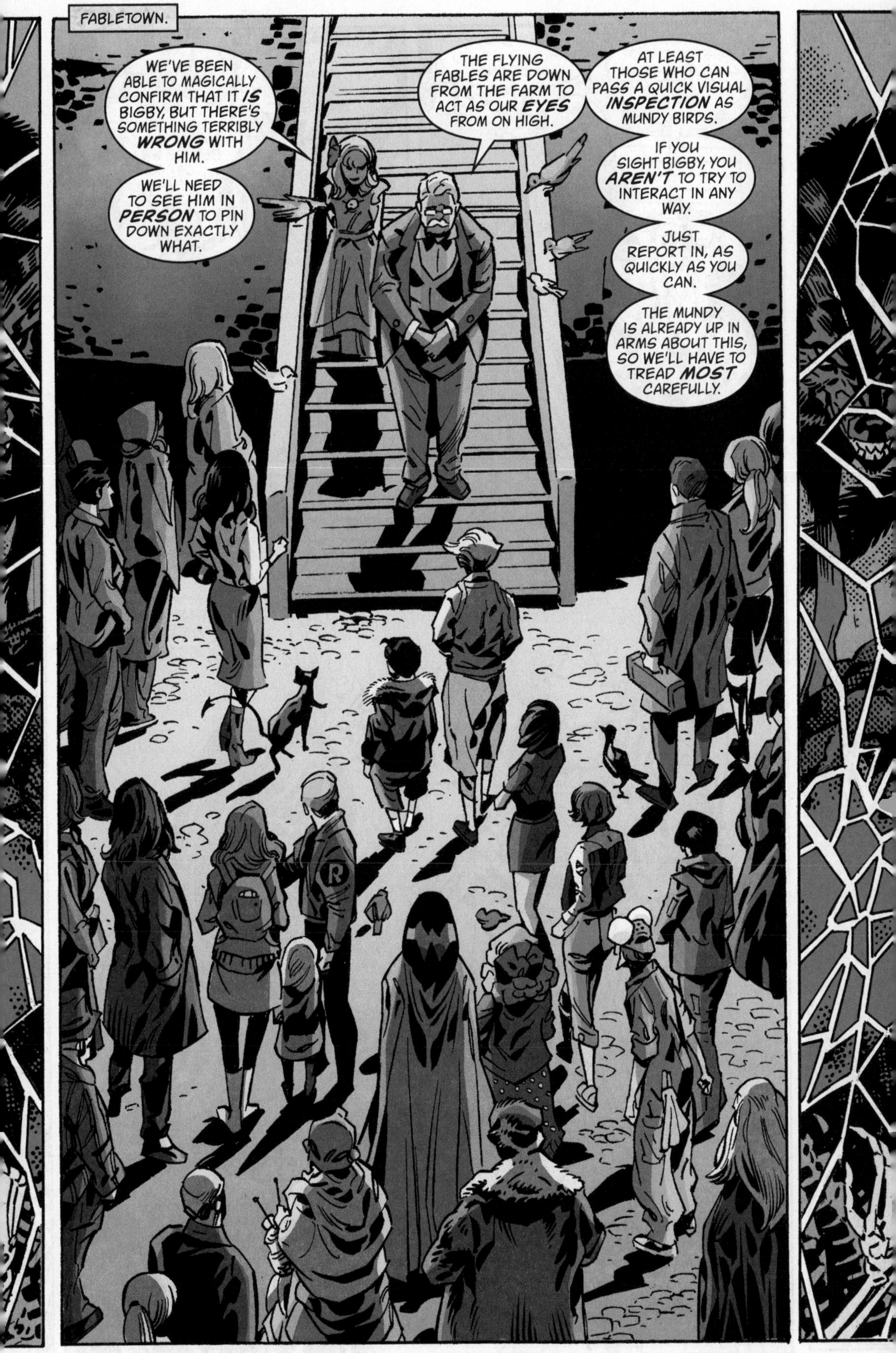

FABLETOWN.
WE'VE BEEN ABLE TO MAGICALLY CONFIRM THAT IT IS BIGBY, BUT THERE'S SOMETHING TERRIBLY WRONG WITH HIM.
WE'LL NEED TO SEE HIM IN PERSON TO PIN DOWN EXACTLY WHAT.
THE FLYING FABLES ARE DOWN FROM THE FARM TO ACT AS OUR EYES FROM ON HIGH.
AT LEAST THOSE WHO CAN PASS A QUICK VISUAL INSPECTION AS MUNDY BIRDS.
IF YOU SIGHT BIGBY, YOU AREN'T TO TRY TO INTERACT IN ANY WAY.
JUST REPORT IN, AS QUICKLY AS YOU CAN.
THE MUNDY IS ALREADY UP IN ARMS ABOUT THIS, SO WE'LL HAVE TO TREAD MOST CAREFULLY.

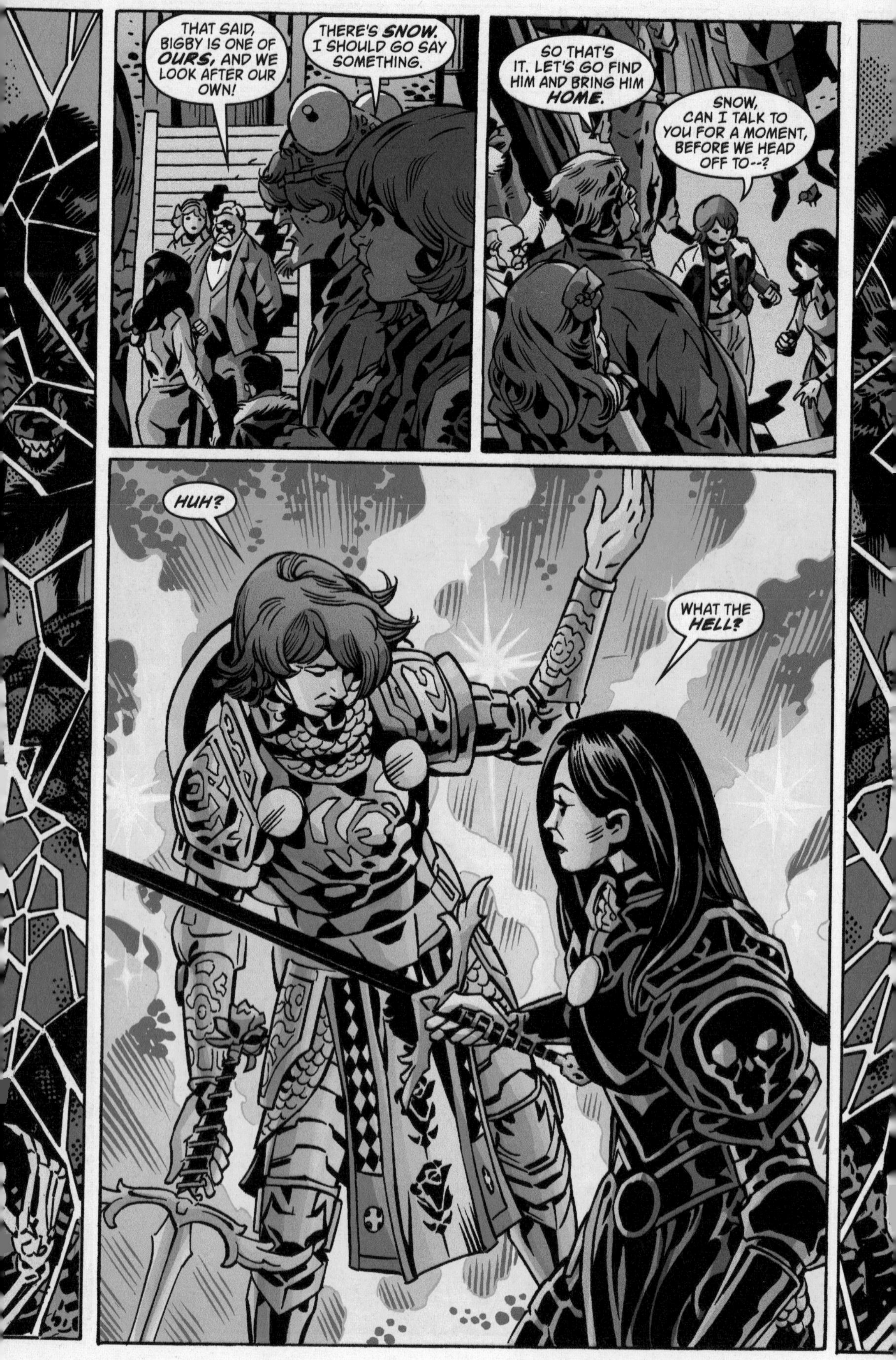
THAT SAID, BIGBY IS ONE OF OURS, AND WE LOOK AFTER OUR OWN!
THERE'S SNOW. I SHOULD GO SAY SOMETHING.
SO THAT'S IT. LET'S GO FIND HIM AND BRING HIM HOME.
SNOW, CAN I TALK TO YOU FOR A MOMENT, BEFORE WE HEAD OFF TO--?
HUH?
WHAT THE HELL?

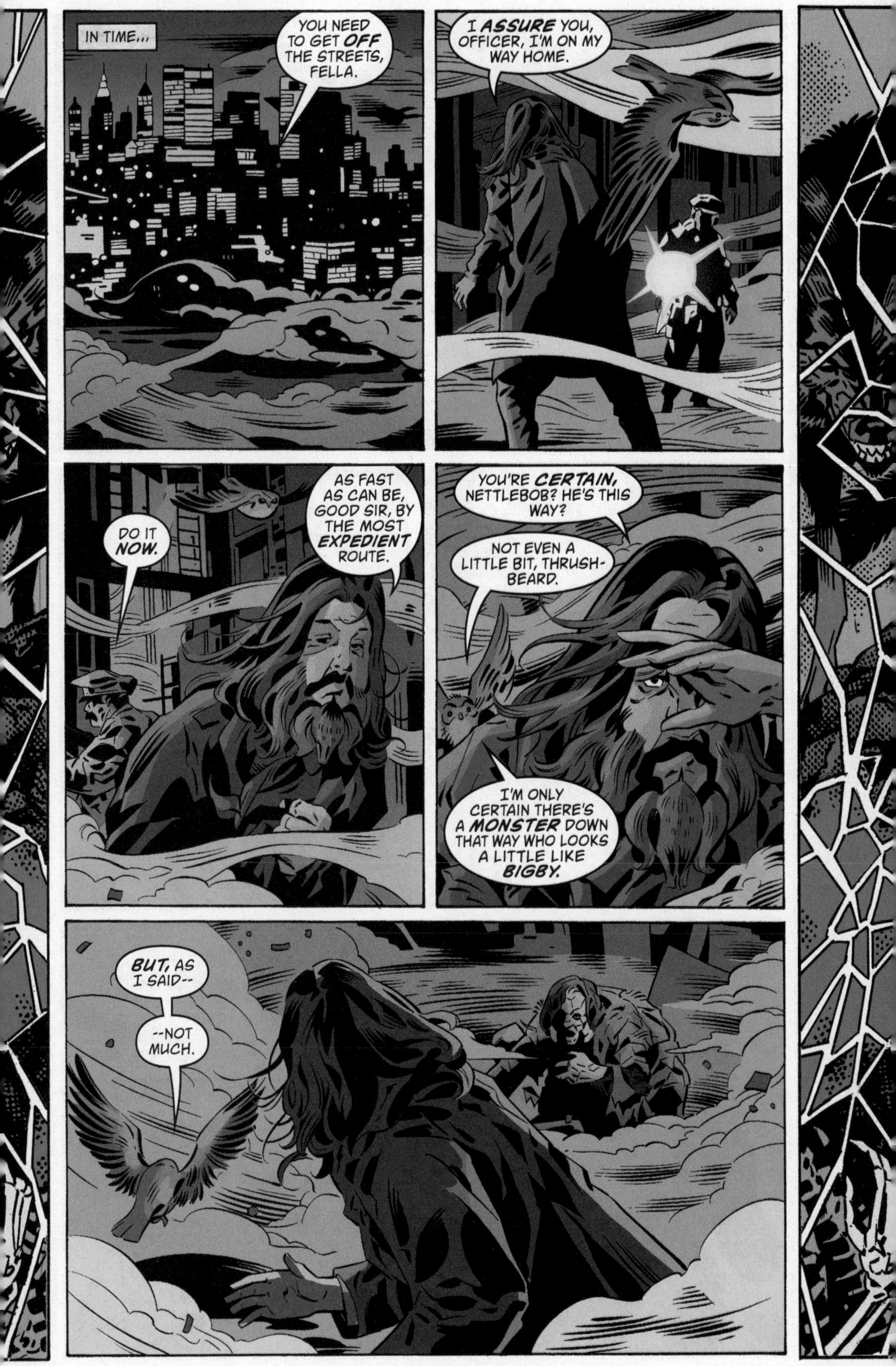
IN TIME...
YOU NEED TO GET OFF THE STREETS, FELLA.
I ASSURE YOU, OFFICER, I'M ON MY WAY HOME.
DO IT NOW.
AS FAST AS CAN BE, GOOD SIR, BY THE MOST EXPEDIENT ROUTE.
YOU'RE CERTAIN, NETTLEBOB? HE'S THIS WAY?
NOT EVEN A LITTLE BIT, THRUSH-BEARD.
I'M ONLY CERTAIN THERE'S A MONSTER DOWN THAT WAY WHO LOOKS A LITTLE LIKE BIGBY.
BUT, AS I SAID--
--NOT MUCH.

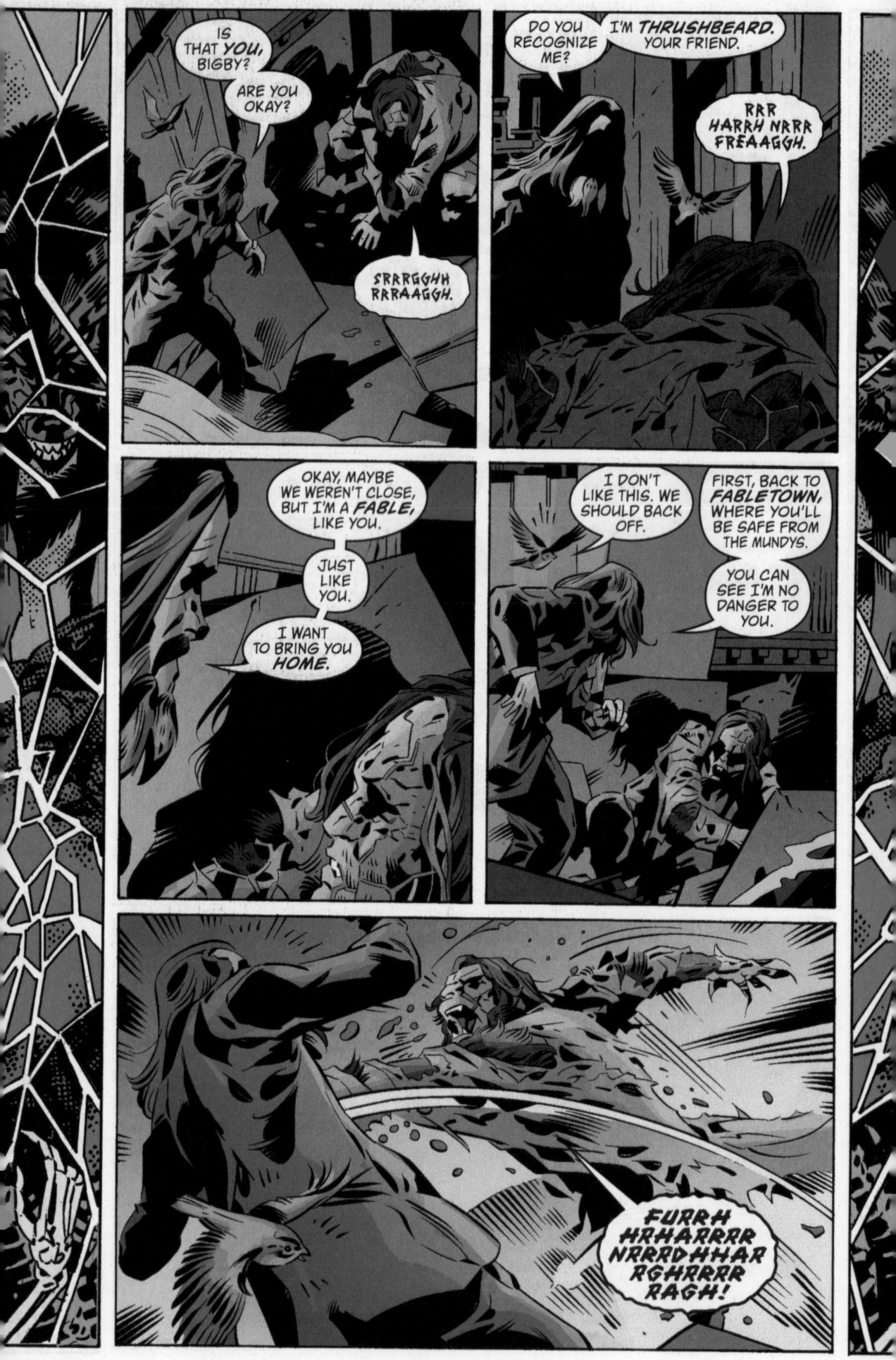
IS THAT YOU, BIGBY?
ARE YOU OKAY?
SRRRGGHH RRRAAGGH.
DO YOU RECOGNIZE ME?
I'M THRUSHBEARD. YOUR FRIEND.
RRR HARRH NRRR FREAAGGH.
OKAY, MAYBE WE WEREN'T CLOSE, BUT I'M A FABLE, LIKE YOU.
JUST LIKE YOU.
I WANT TO BRING YOU HOME.
I DON'T LIKE THIS. WE SHOULD BACK OFF.
FIRST, BACK TO FABLETOWN, WHERE YOU'LL BE SAFE FROM THE MUNDYS.
YOU CAN SEE I'M NO DANGER TO YOU.
FURRH HRHARRRR NRRRDHHAR RGHRRRR RAGH!

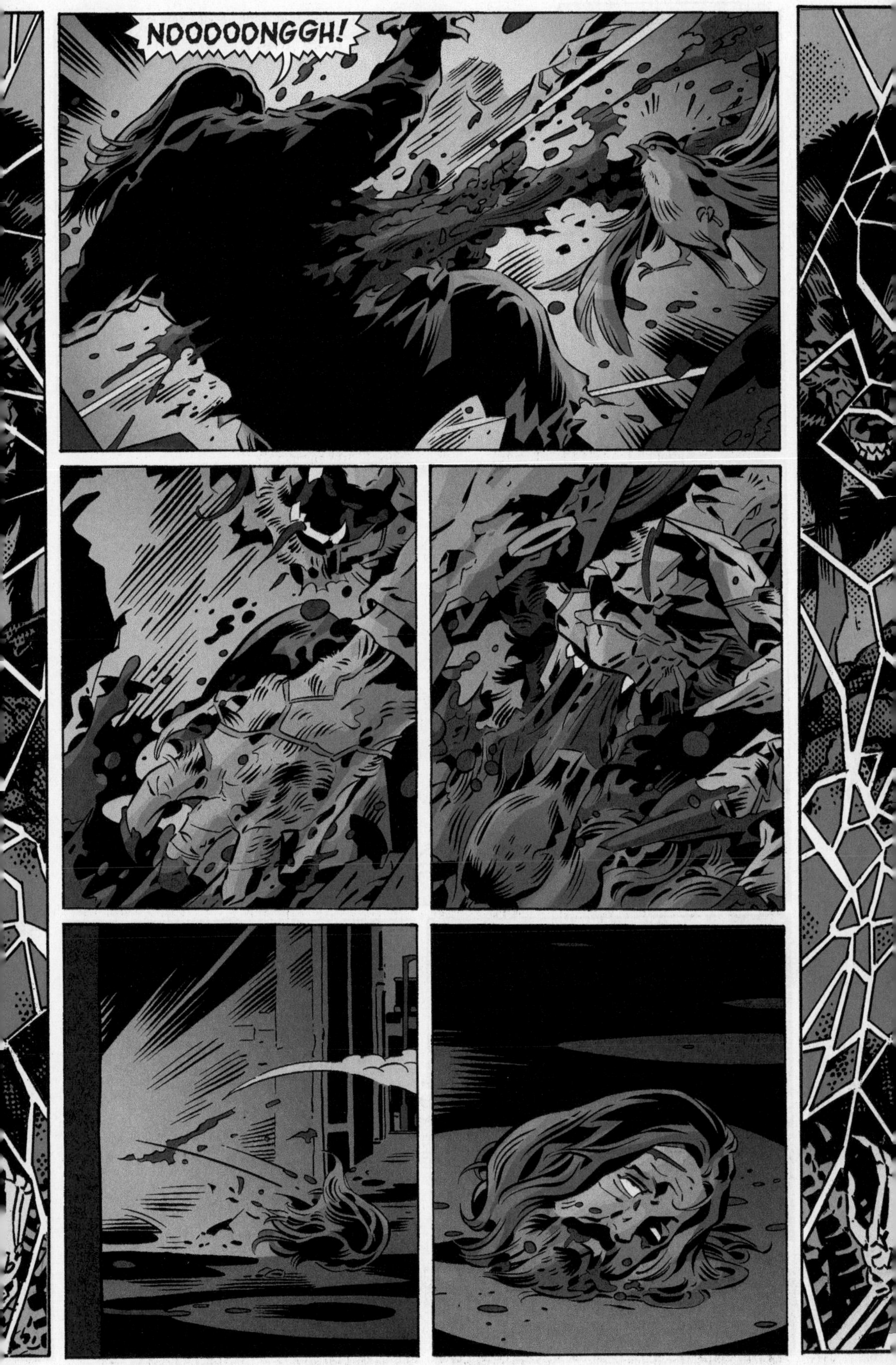
NOOOOONGGH!

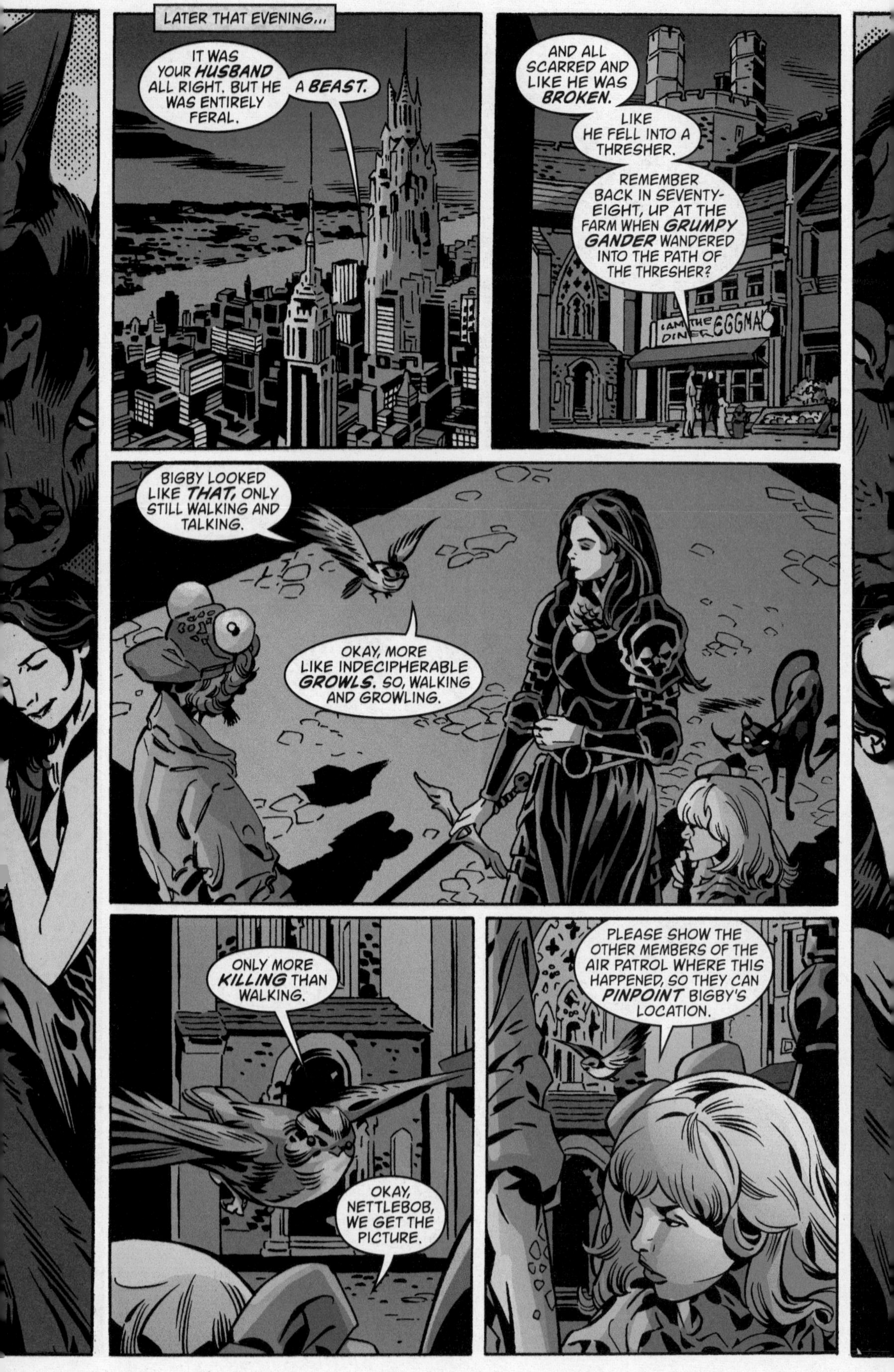
LATER THAT EVENING...
IT WAS YOUR HUSBAND ALL RIGHT. BUT HE WAS ENTIRELY FERAL.
A BEAST.
AND ALL SCARRED AND LIKE HE WAS BROKEN.
LIKE HE FELL INTO A THRESHER.
REMEMBER BACK IN SEVENTY-EIGHT, UP AT THE FARM WHEN GRUMPY GANDER WANDERED INTO THE PATH OF THE THRESHER?
BIGBY LOOKED LIKE THAT, ONLY STILL WALKING AND TALKING.
OKAY, MORE LIKE INDECIPHERABLE GROWLS. SO, WALKING AND GROWLING.
ONLY MORE KILLING THAN WALKING.
OKAY, NETTLEBOB, WE GET THE PICTURE.
PLEASE SHOW THE OTHER MEMBERS OF THE AIR PATROL WHERE THIS HAPPENED, SO THEY CAN PINPOINT BIGBY'S LOCATION.

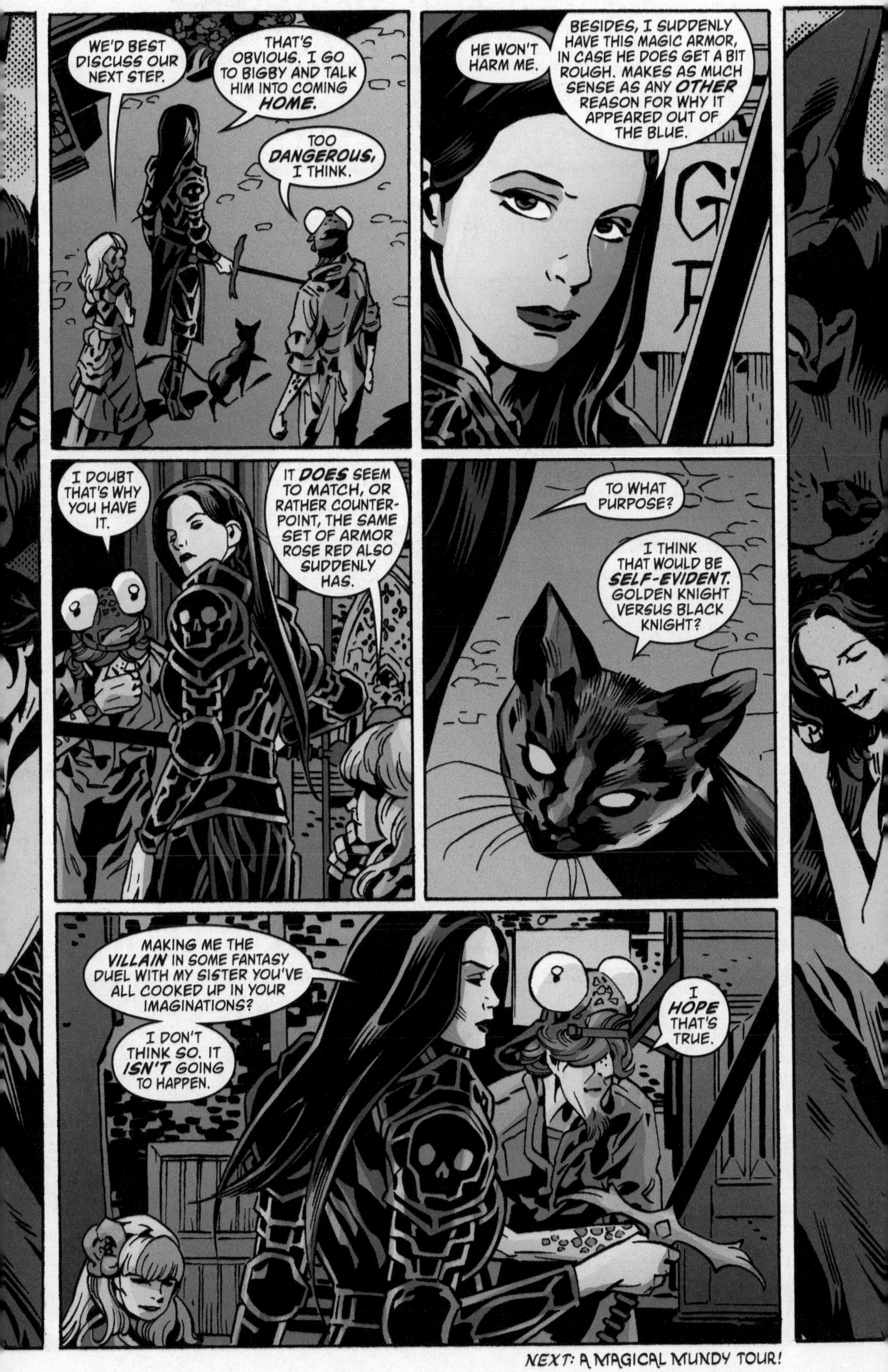
WE'D BEST DISCUSS OUR NEXT STEP.
THAT'S OBVIOUS. I GO TO BIGBY AND TALK HIM INTO COMING HOME.
TOO DANGEROUS, I THINK.
HE WON'T HARM ME.
BESIDES, I SUDDENLY HAVE THIS MAGIC ARMOR, IN CASE HE DOES GET A BIT ROUGH. MAKES AS MUCH SENSE AS ANY OTHER REASON FOR WHY IT APPEARED OUT OF THE BLUE.
I DOUBT THAT'S WHY YOU HAVE IT.
IT DOES SEEM TO MATCH, OR RATHER COUNTER-POINT, THE SAME SET OF ARMOR ROSE RED ALSO SUDDENLY HAS.
TO WHAT PURPOSE?
I THINK THAT WOULD BE SELF-EVIDENT. GOLDEN KNIGHT VERSUS BLACK KNIGHT?
MAKING ME THE VILLAIN IN SOME FANTASY DUEL WITH MY SISTER YOU'VE ALL COOKED UP IN YOUR IMAGINATIONS?
I DON'T THINK SO. IT ISN'T GOING TO HAPPEN.
I HOPE THAT'S TRUE.

NEXT: A MAGICAL MUNDY TOUR!

THE LAST SINBAD STORY

Bill Willingham writer/creator | Eric Shanower artist | Lee Loughridge colors | Todd Klein letters | Rowena Yow assoc. ed. | Shelly Bond editor

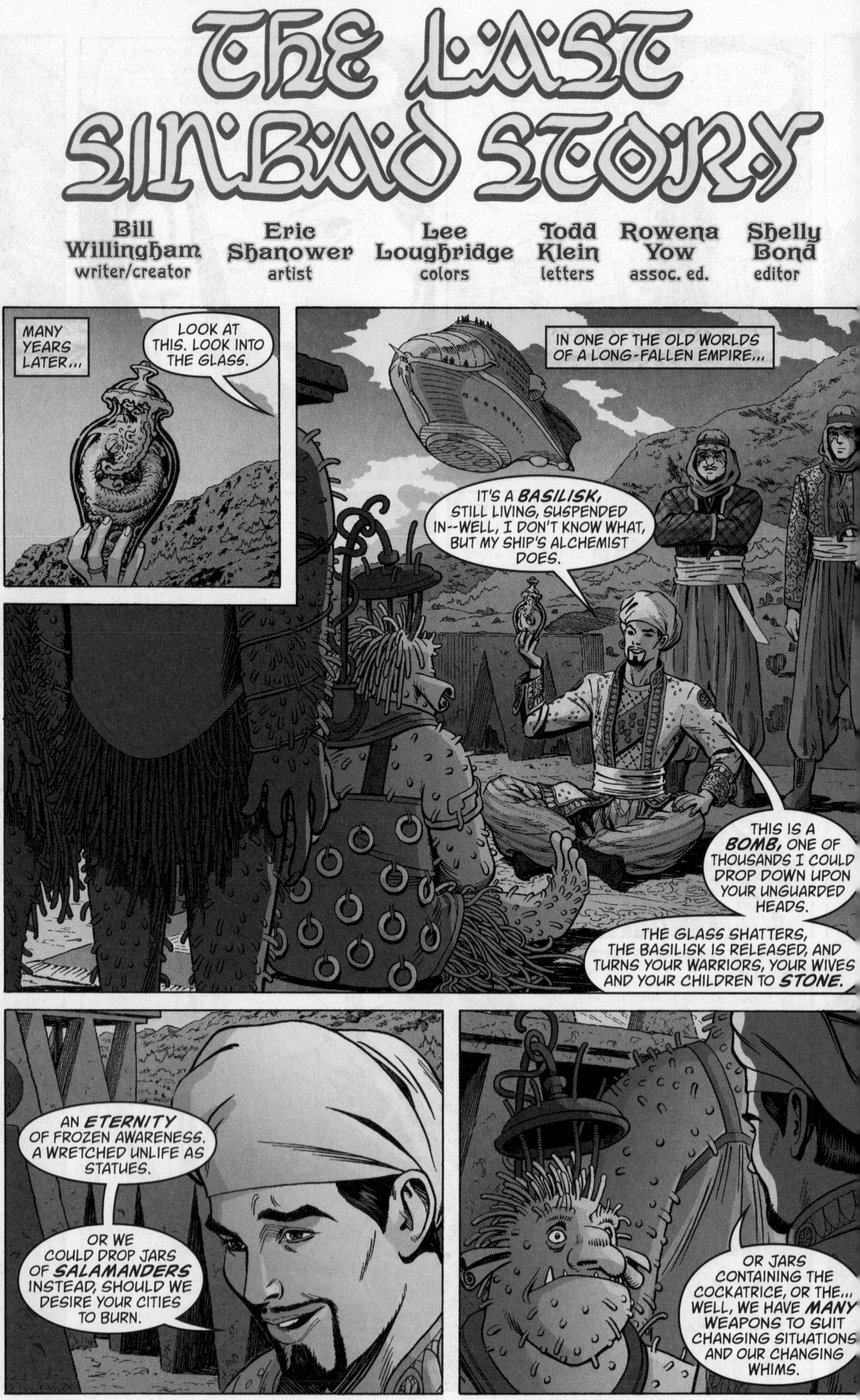

MANY YEARS LATER...
LOOK AT THIS. LOOK INTO THE GLASS.
IN ONE OF THE OLD WORLDS OF A LONG-FALLEN EMPIRE...
IT'S A BASILISK, STILL LIVING, SUSPENDED IN--WELL, I DON'T KNOW WHAT, BUT MY SHIP'S ALCHEMIST DOES.
THIS IS A BOMB, ONE OF THOUSANDS I COULD DROP DOWN UPON YOUR UNGUARDED HEADS.
THE GLASS SHATTERS, THE BASILISK IS RELEASED, AND TURNS YOUR WARRIORS, YOUR WIVES AND YOUR CHILDREN TO STONE.
AN ETERNITY OF FROZEN AWARENESS. A WRETCHED UNLIFE AS STATUES.
OR WE COULD DROP JARS OF SALAMANDERS INSTEAD, SHOULD WE DESIRE YOUR CITIES TO BURN.
OR JARS CONTAINING THE COCKATRICE, OR THE... WELL, WE HAVE MANY WEAPONS TO SUIT CHANGING SITUATIONS AND OUR CHANGING WHIMS.

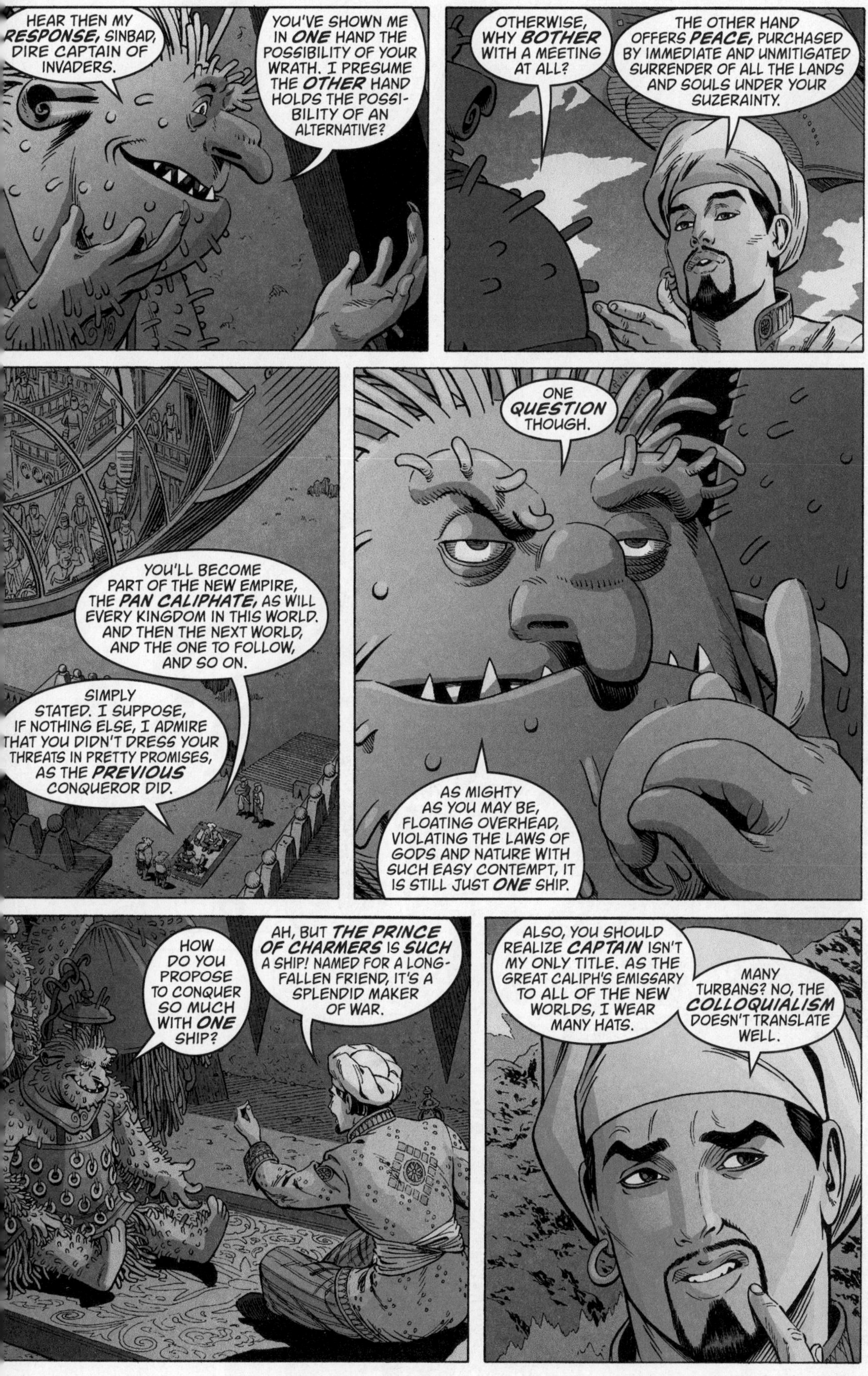
HEAR THEN MY RESPONSE, SINBAD, DIRE CAPTAIN OF INVADERS.
YOU'VE SHOWN ME IN ONE HAND THE POSSIBILITY OF YOUR WRATH. I PRESUME THE OTHER HAND HOLDS THE POSSI-BILITY OF AN ALTERNATIVE?
OTHERWISE, WHY BOTHER WITH A MEETING AT ALL?
THE OTHER HAND OFFERS PEACE, PURCHASED BY IMMEDIATE AND UNMITIGATED SURRENDER OF ALL THE LANDS AND SOULS UNDER YOUR SUZERAINTY.
YOU'LL BECOME PART OF THE NEW EMPIRE, THE PAN CALIPHATE, AS WILL EVERY KINGDOM IN THIS WORLD. AND THEN THE NEXT WORLD, AND THE ONE TO FOLLOW, AND SO ON.
SIMPLY STATED. I SUPPOSE, IF NOTHING ELSE, I ADMIRE THAT YOU DIDN'T DRESS YOUR THREATS IN PRETTY PROMISES, AS THE PREVIOUS CONQUEROR DID.
ONE QUESTION THOUGH.
AS MIGHTY AS YOU MAY BE, FLOATING OVERHEAD, VIOLATING THE LAWS OF GODS AND NATURE WITH SUCH EASY CONTEMPT, IT IS STILL JUST ONE SHIP.
HOW DO YOU PROPOSE TO CONQUER SO MUCH WITH ONE SHIP?
AH, BUT THE PRINCE OF CHARMERS IS SUCH A SHIP! NAMED FOR A LONG-FALLEN FRIEND, IT'S A SPLENDID MAKER OF WAR.
ALSO, YOU SHOULD REALIZE CAPTAIN ISN'T MY ONLY TITLE. AS THE GREAT CALIPH'S EMISSARY TO ALL OF THE NEW WORLDS, I WEAR MANY HATS.
MANY TURBANS? NO, THE COLLOQUIALISM DOESN'T TRANSLATE WELL.

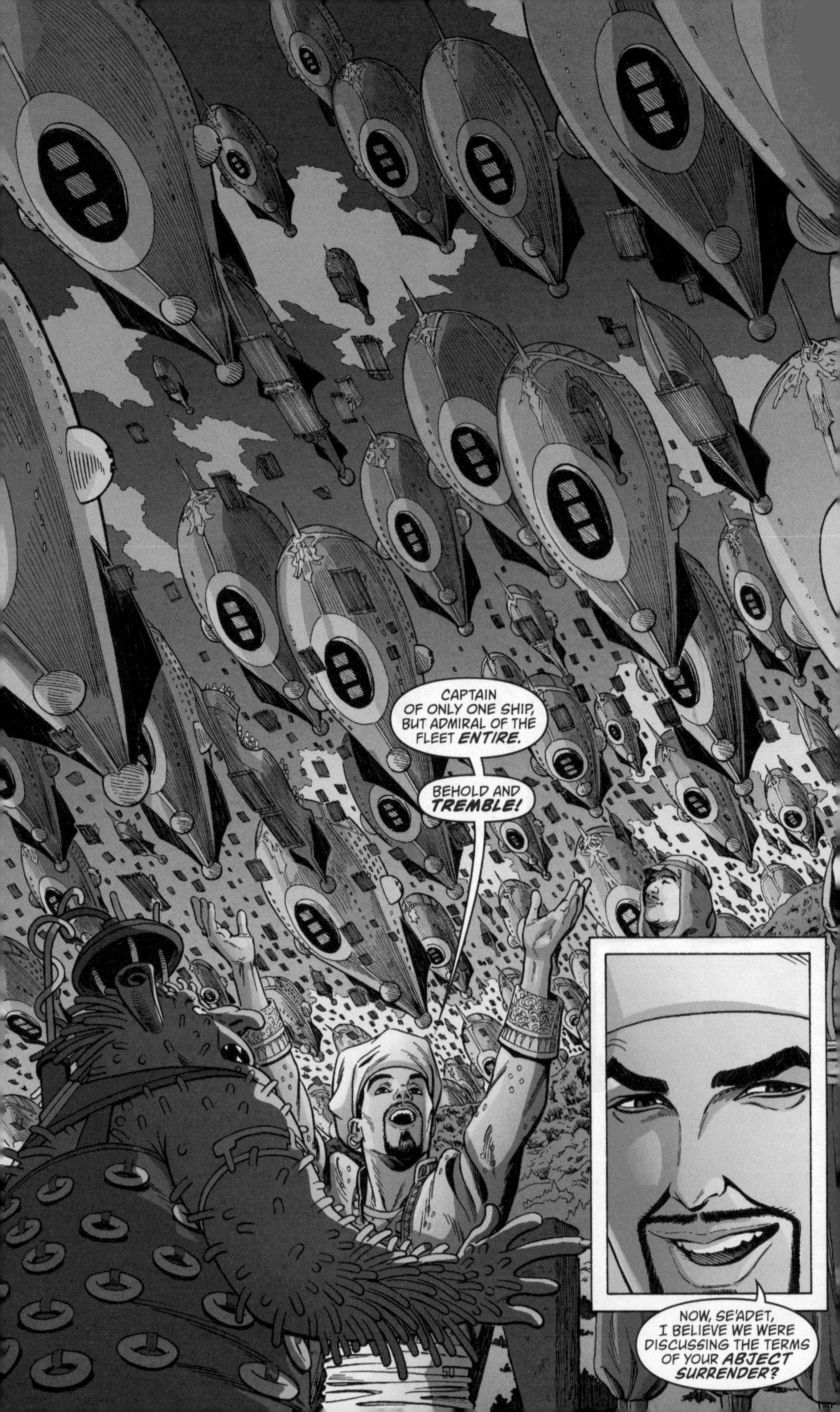
CAPTAIN OF ONLY ONE SHIP, BUT ADMIRAL OF THE FLEET *ENTIRE*.
BEHOLD AND ***TREMBLE!***
NOW, SE'ADET, I BELIEVE WE WERE DISCUSSING THE TERMS OF YOUR ***ABJECT SURRENDER?***

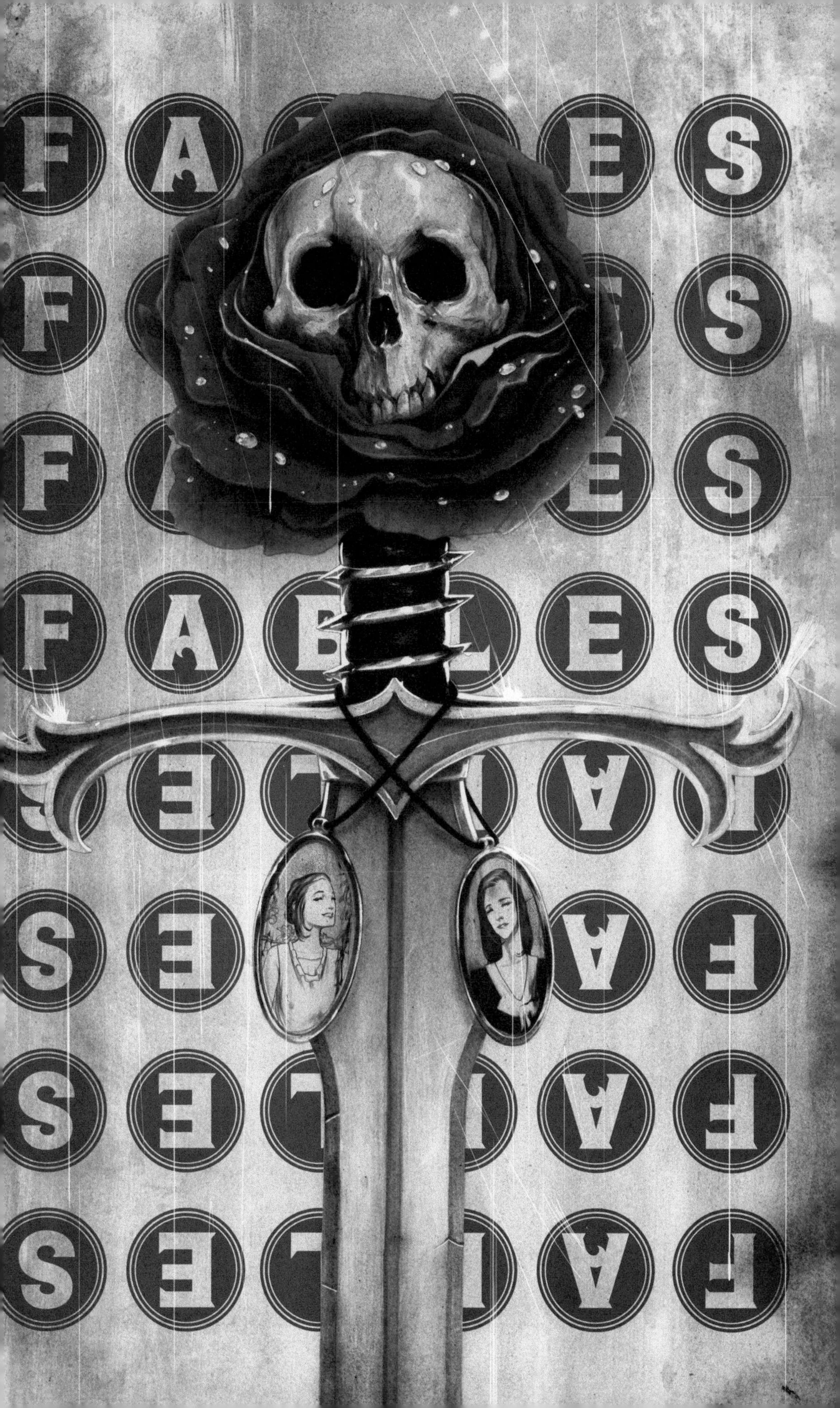
FABLES

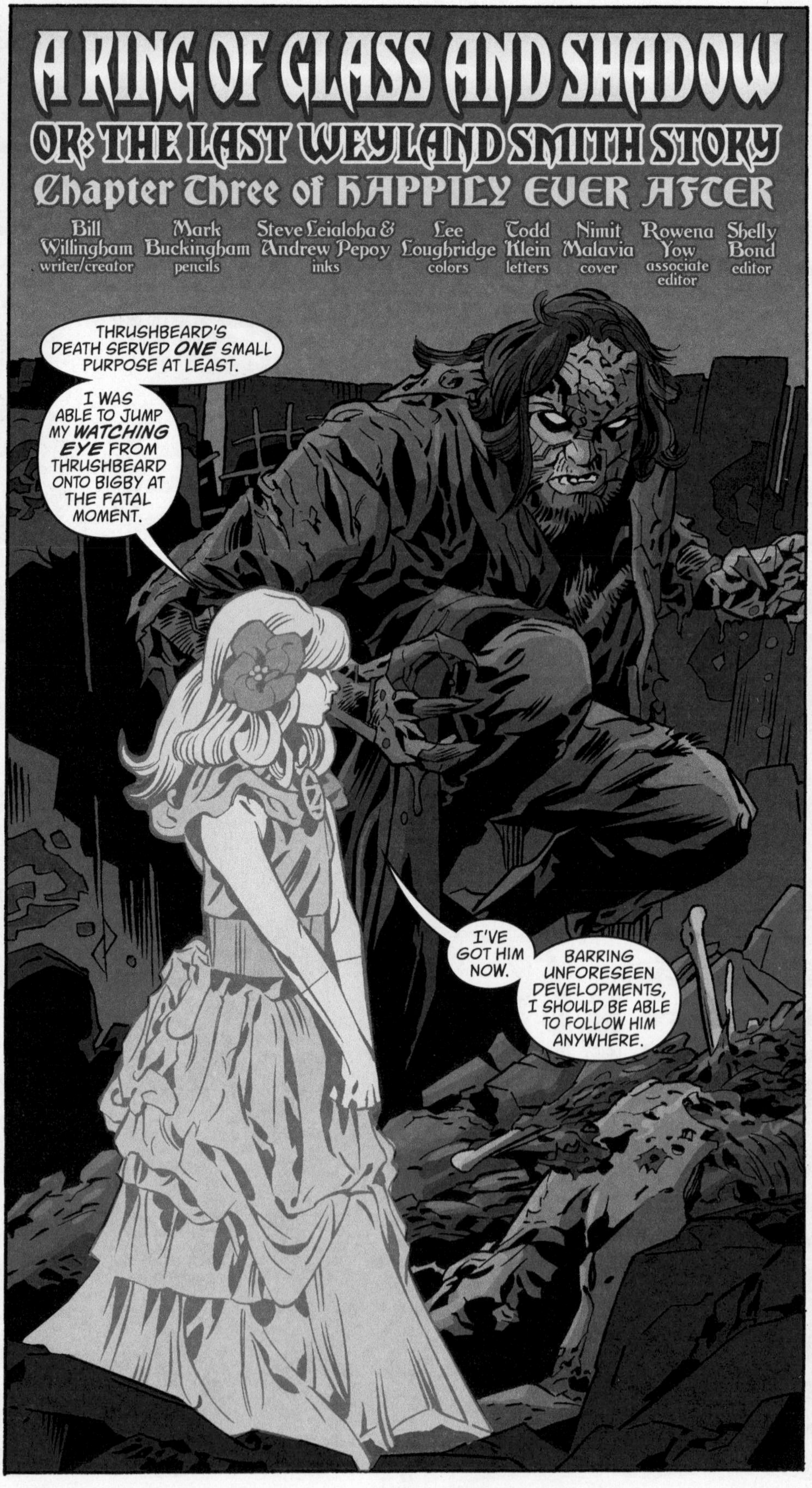
A RING OF GLASS AND SHADOW
OR: THE LAST WEYLAND SMITH STORY
Chapter Three of HAPPILY EVER AFTER
Bill Willingham writer/creator
Mark Buckingham pencils
Steve Leialoha & Andrew Pepoy inks
Lee Loughridge colors
Todd Klein letters
Nimit Malavia cover
Rowena Yow associate editor
Shelly Bond editor
THRUSHBEARD'S DEATH SERVED ONE SMALL PURPOSE AT LEAST.
I WAS ABLE TO JUMP MY WATCHING EYE FROM THRUSHBEARD ONTO BIGBY AT THE FATAL MOMENT.
I'VE GOT HIM NOW.
BARRING UNFORESEEN DEVELOPMENTS, I SHOULD BE ABLE TO FOLLOW HIM ANYWHERE.

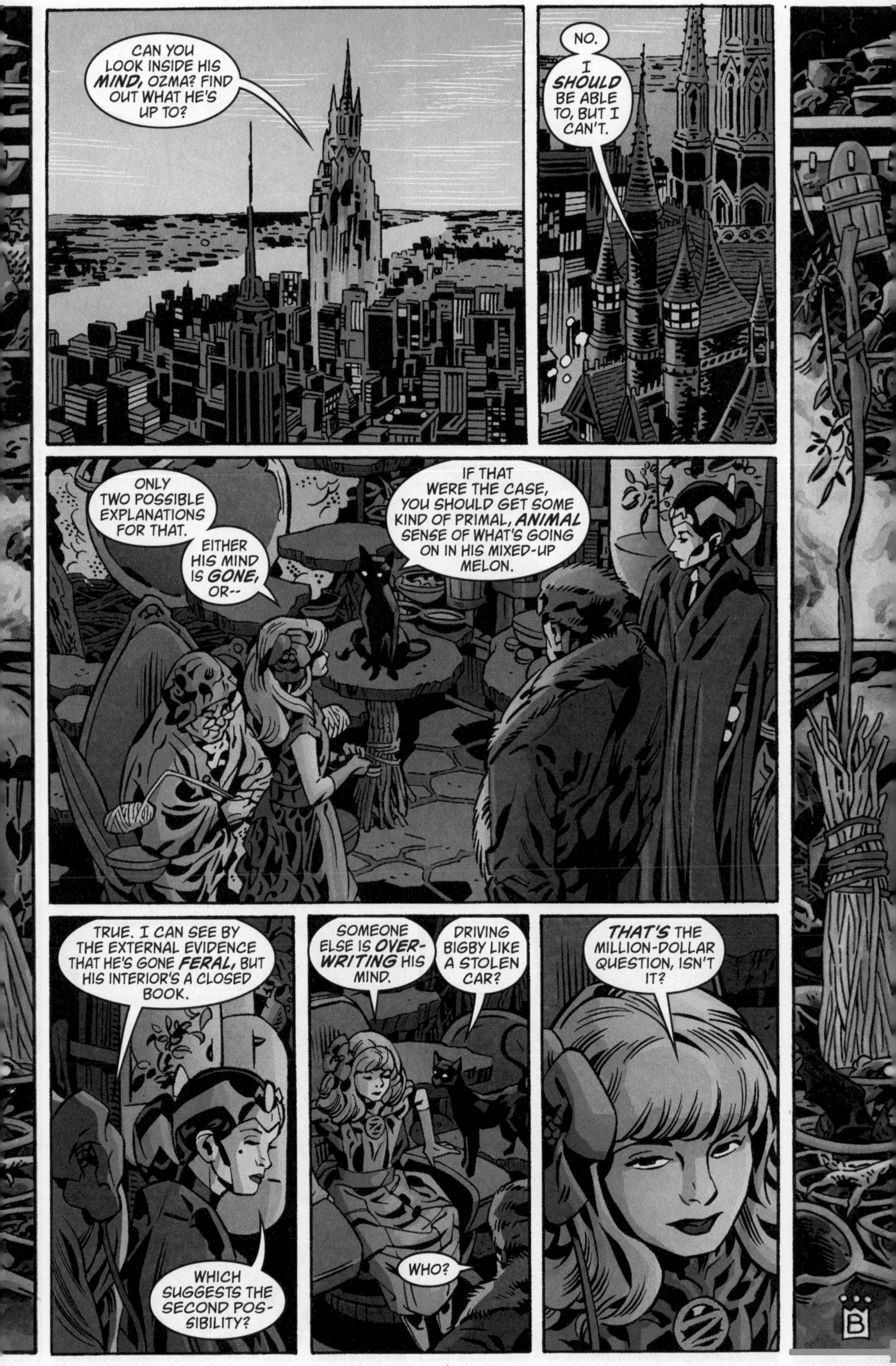
CAN YOU LOOK INSIDE HIS MIND, OZMA? FIND OUT WHAT HE'S UP TO?
NO.
I SHOULD BE ABLE TO, BUT I CAN'T.
ONLY TWO POSSIBLE EXPLANATIONS FOR THAT.
EITHER HIS MIND IS GONE, OR--
IF THAT WERE THE CASE, YOU SHOULD GET SOME KIND OF PRIMAL, ANIMAL SENSE OF WHAT'S GOING ON IN HIS MIXED-UP MELON.
TRUE. I CAN SEE BY THE EXTERNAL EVIDENCE THAT HE'S GONE FERAL, BUT HIS INTERIOR'S A CLOSED BOOK.
WHICH SUGGESTS THE SECOND POS-SIBILITY?
SOMEONE ELSE IS OVER-WRITING HIS MIND.
DRIVING BIGBY LIKE A STOLEN CAR?
WHO?
THAT'S THE MILLION-DOLLAR QUESTION, ISN'T IT?

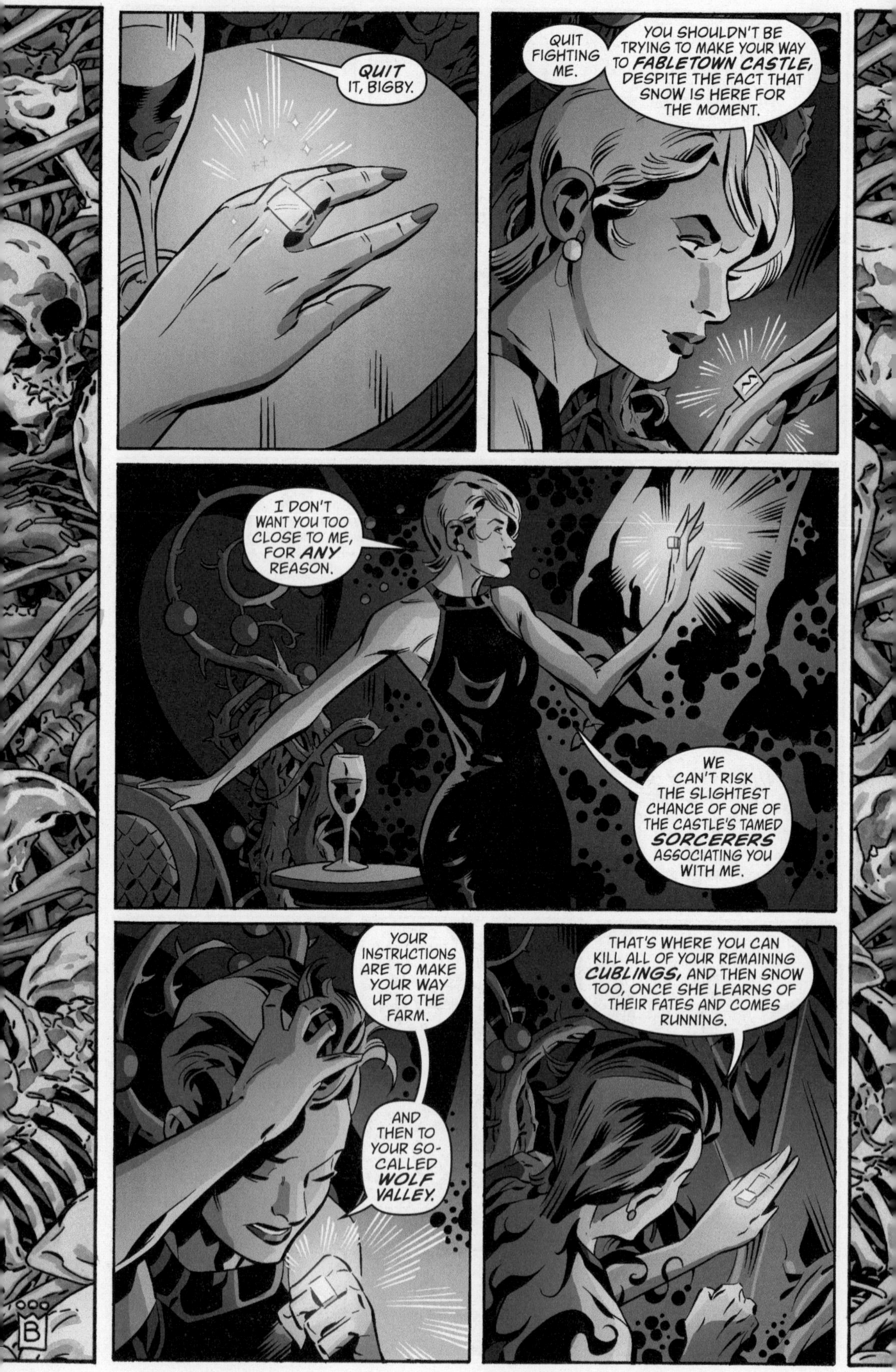
QUIT IT, BIGBY.
QUIT FIGHTING ME.
YOU SHOULDN'T BE TRYING TO MAKE YOUR WAY TO FABLETOWN CASTLE, DESPITE THE FACT THAT SNOW IS HERE FOR THE MOMENT.
I DON'T WANT YOU TOO CLOSE TO ME, FOR ANY REASON.
WE CAN'T RISK THE SLIGHTEST CHANCE OF ONE OF THE CASTLE'S TAMED SORCERERS ASSOCIATING YOU WITH ME.
YOUR INSTRUCTIONS ARE TO MAKE YOUR WAY UP TO THE FARM.
AND THEN TO YOUR SO-CALLED WOLF VALLEY.
THAT'S WHERE YOU CAN KILL ALL OF YOUR REMAINING CUBLINGS, AND THEN SNOW TOO, ONCE SHE LEARNS OF THEIR FATES AND COMES RUNNING.

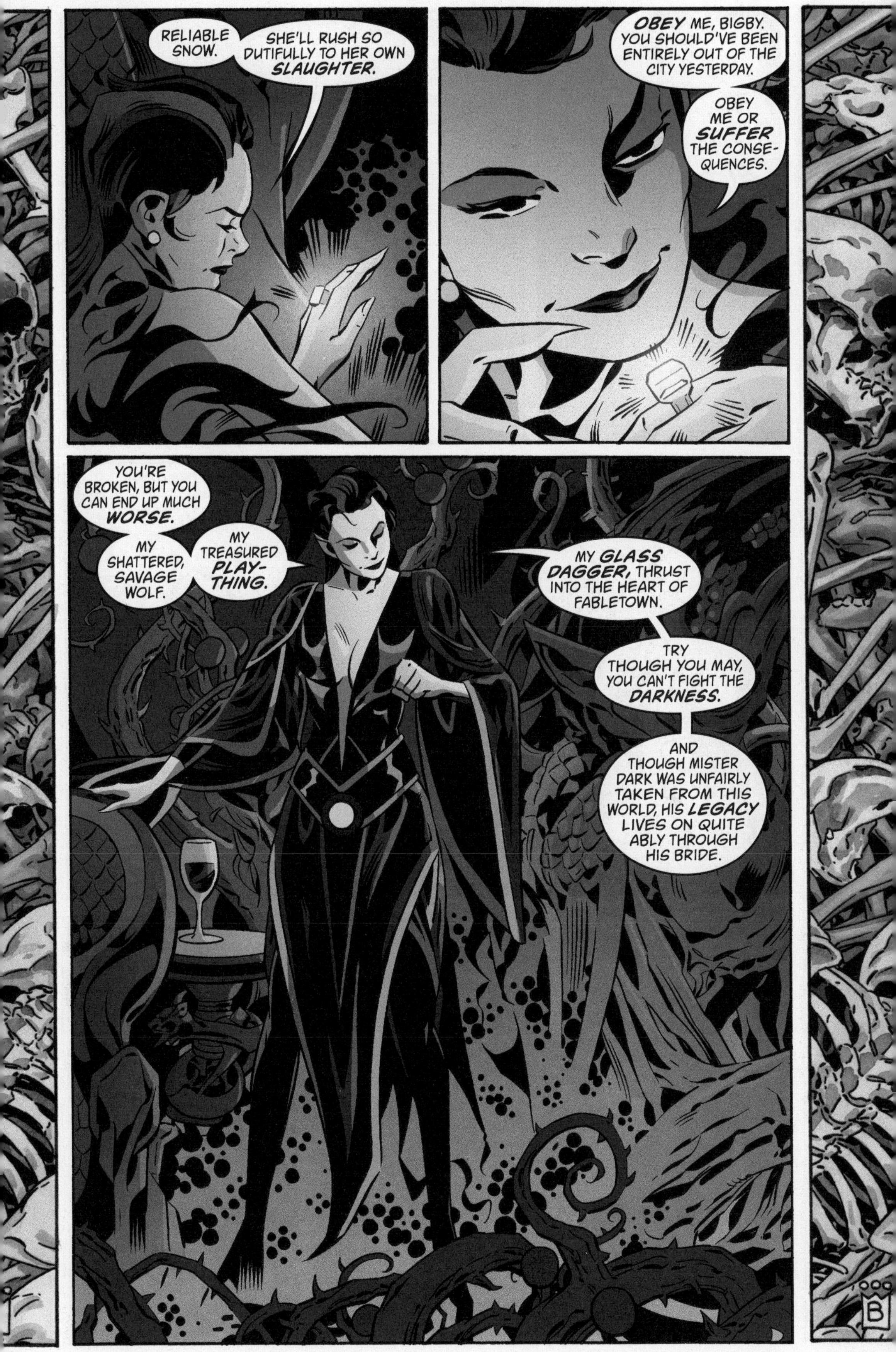
RELIABLE SNOW.
SHE'LL RUSH SO DUTIFULLY TO HER OWN SLAUGHTER.
OBEY ME, BIGBY. YOU SHOULD'VE BEEN ENTIRELY OUT OF THE CITY YESTERDAY.
OBEY ME OR SUFFER THE CONSE- QUENCES.
YOU'RE BROKEN, BUT YOU CAN END UP MUCH WORSE.
MY SHATTERED, SAVAGE WOLF.
MY TREASURED PLAY- THING.
MY GLASS DAGGER, THRUST INTO THE HEART OF FABLETOWN.
TRY THOUGH YOU MAY, YOU CAN'T FIGHT THE DARKNESS.
AND THOUGH MISTER DARK WAS UNFAIRLY TAKEN FROM THIS WORLD, HIS LEGACY LIVES ON QUITE ABLY THROUGH HIS BRIDE.

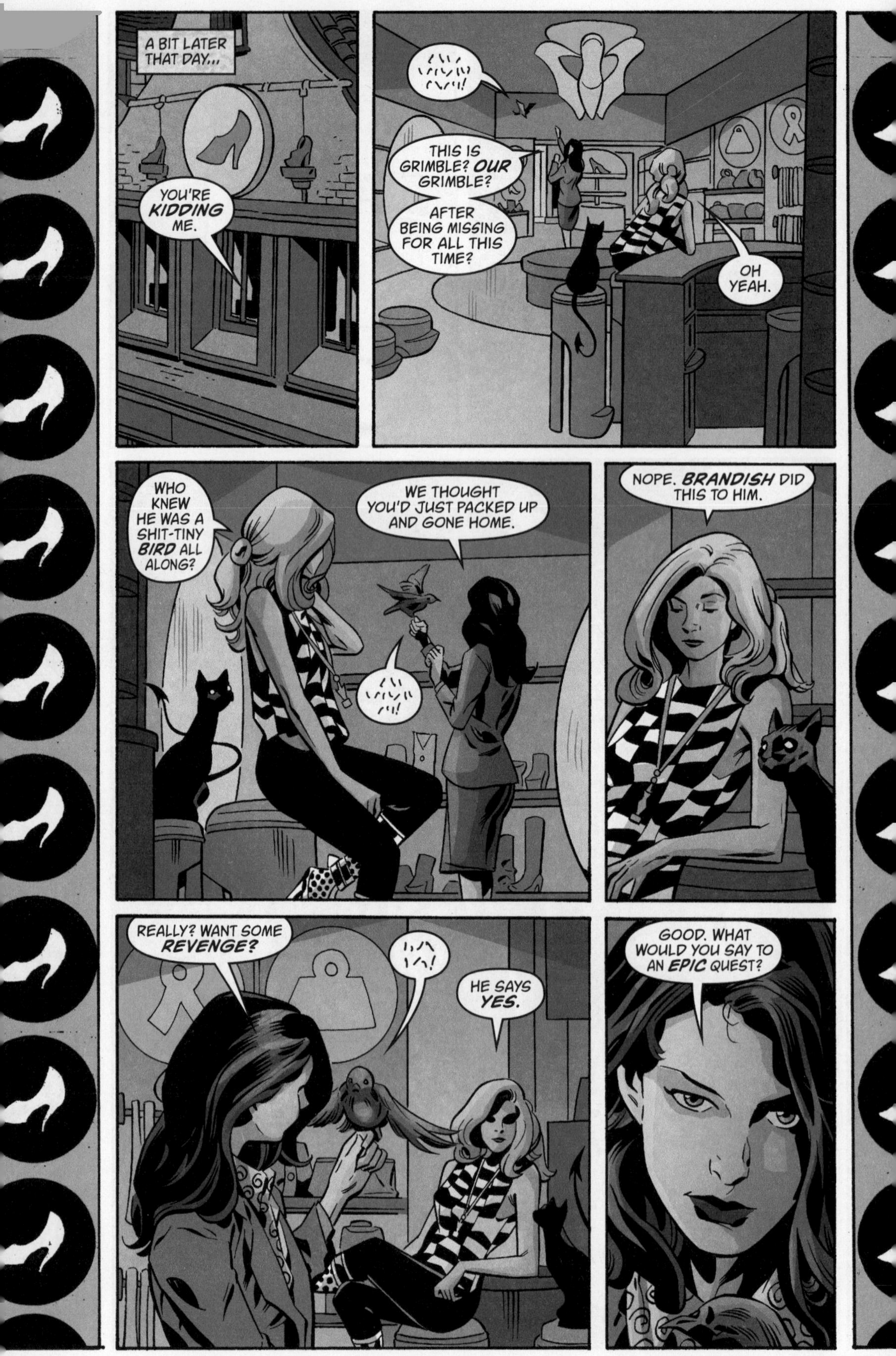
A BIT LATER THAT DAY...
YOU'RE KIDDING ME.
THIS IS GRIMBLE? OUR GRIMBLE?
AFTER BEING MISSING FOR ALL THIS TIME?
OH YEAH.
WHO KNEW HE WAS A SHIT-TINY BIRD ALL ALONG?
WE THOUGHT YOU'D JUST PACKED UP AND GONE HOME.
NOPE. BRANDISH DID THIS TO HIM.
REALLY? WANT SOME REVENGE?
HE SAYS YES.
GOOD. WHAT WOULD YOU SAY TO AN EPIC QUEST?

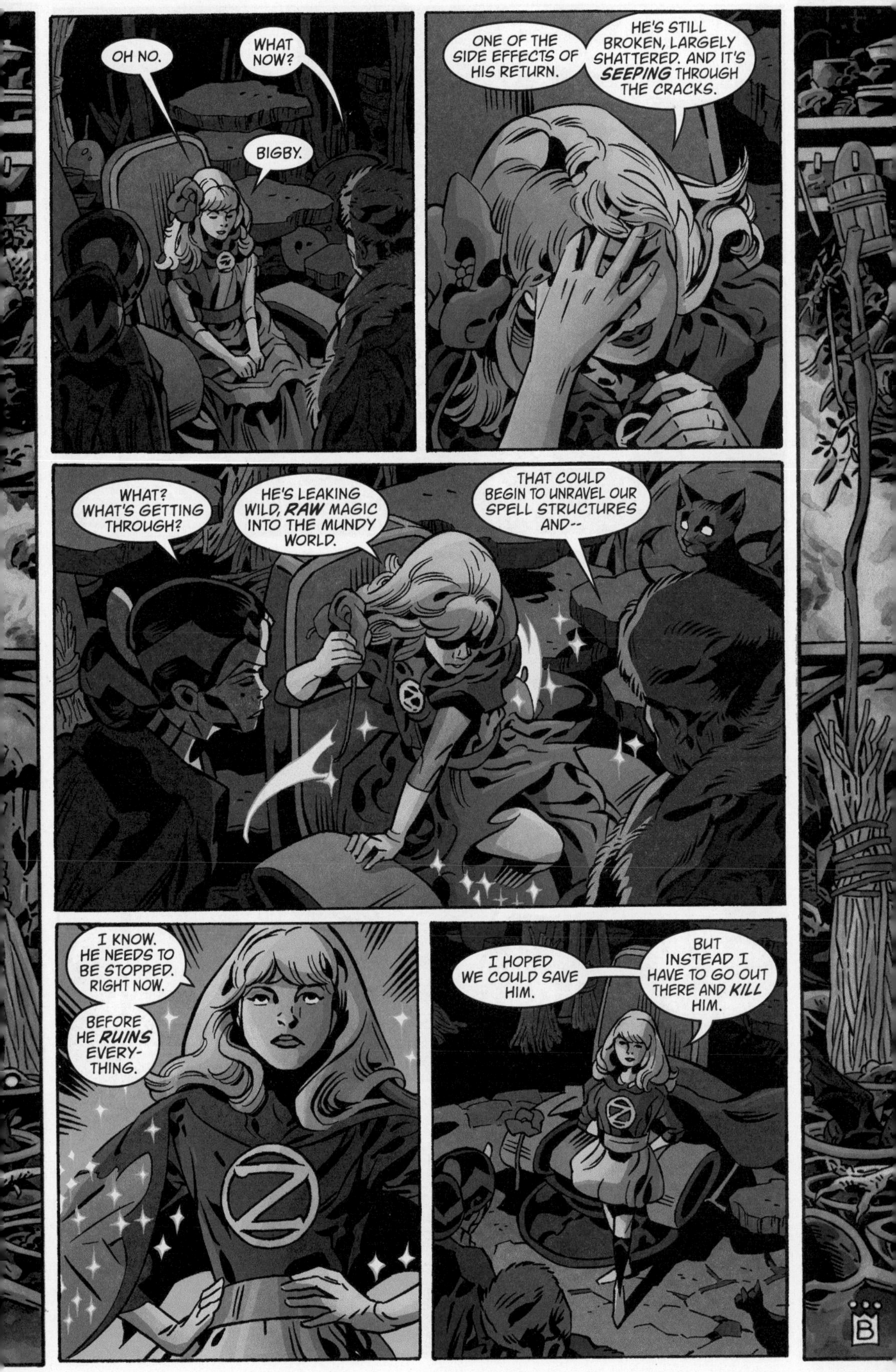
OH NO.
WHAT NOW?
BIGBY.
ONE OF THE SIDE EFFECTS OF HIS RETURN.
HE'S STILL BROKEN, LARGELY SHATTERED. AND IT'S SEEPING THROUGH THE CRACKS.
WHAT? WHAT'S GETTING THROUGH?
HE'S LEAKING WILD, RAW MAGIC INTO THE MUNDY WORLD.
THAT COULD BEGIN TO UNRAVEL OUR SPELL STRUCTURES AND--
I KNOW. HE NEEDS TO BE STOPPED. RIGHT NOW.
BEFORE HE RUINS EVERY-THING.
I HOPED WE COULD SAVE HIM.
BUT INSTEAD I HAVE TO GO OUT THERE AND KILL HIM.

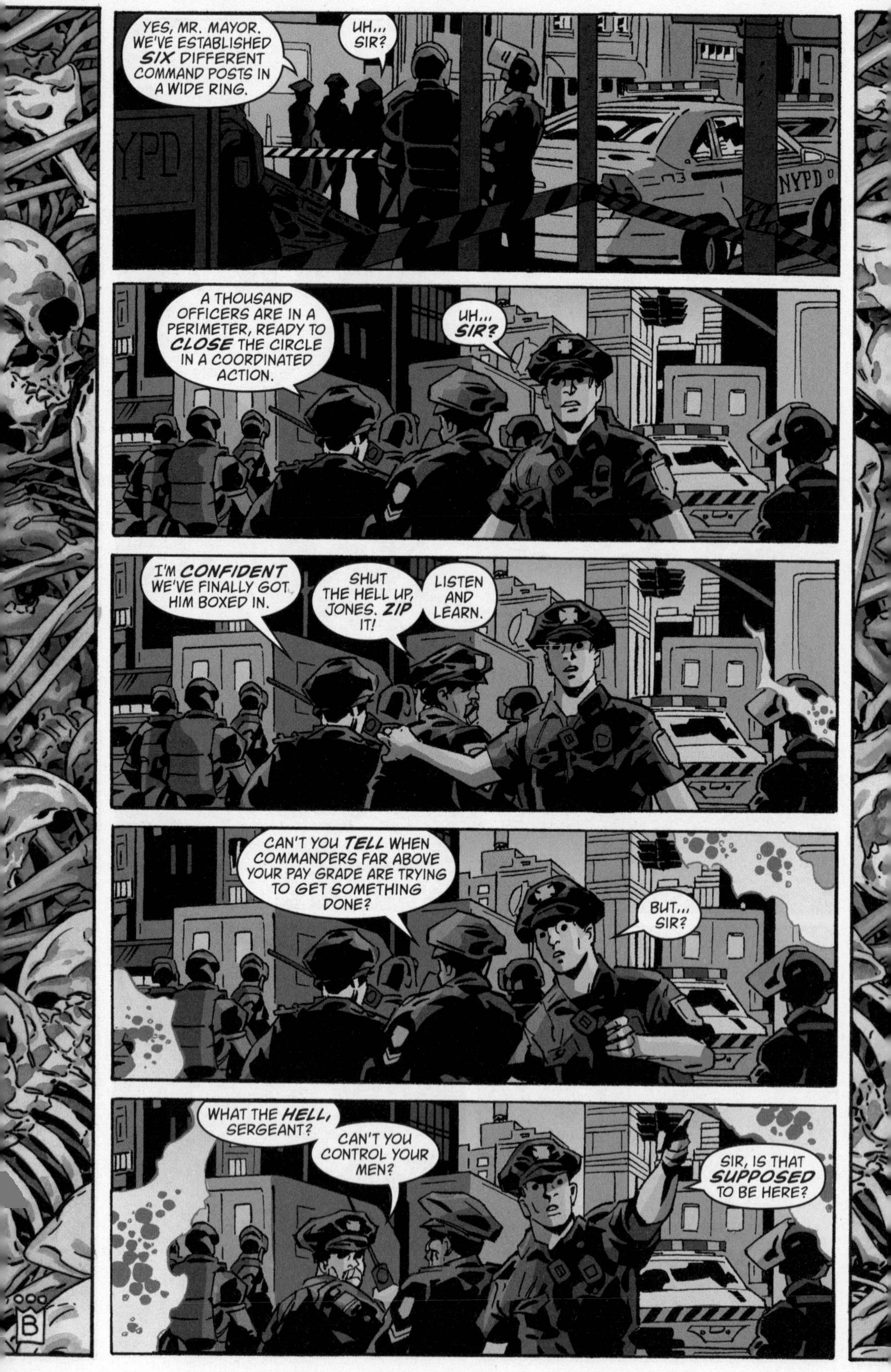
YES, MR. MAYOR. WE'VE ESTABLISHED SIX DIFFERENT COMMAND POSTS IN A WIDE RING.
UH... SIR?
NYPD
NYPD
A THOUSAND OFFICERS ARE IN A PERIMETER, READY TO CLOSE THE CIRCLE IN A COORDINATED ACTION.
UH... SIR?
I'M CONFIDENT WE'VE FINALLY GOT HIM BOXED IN.
SHUT THE HELL UP, JONES. ZIP IT!
LISTEN AND LEARN.
CAN'T YOU TELL WHEN COMMANDERS FAR ABOVE YOUR PAY GRADE ARE TRYING TO GET SOMETHING DONE?
BUT... SIR?
WHAT THE HELL, SERGEANT?
CAN'T YOU CONTROL YOUR MEN?
SIR, IS THAT SUPPOSED TO BE HERE?

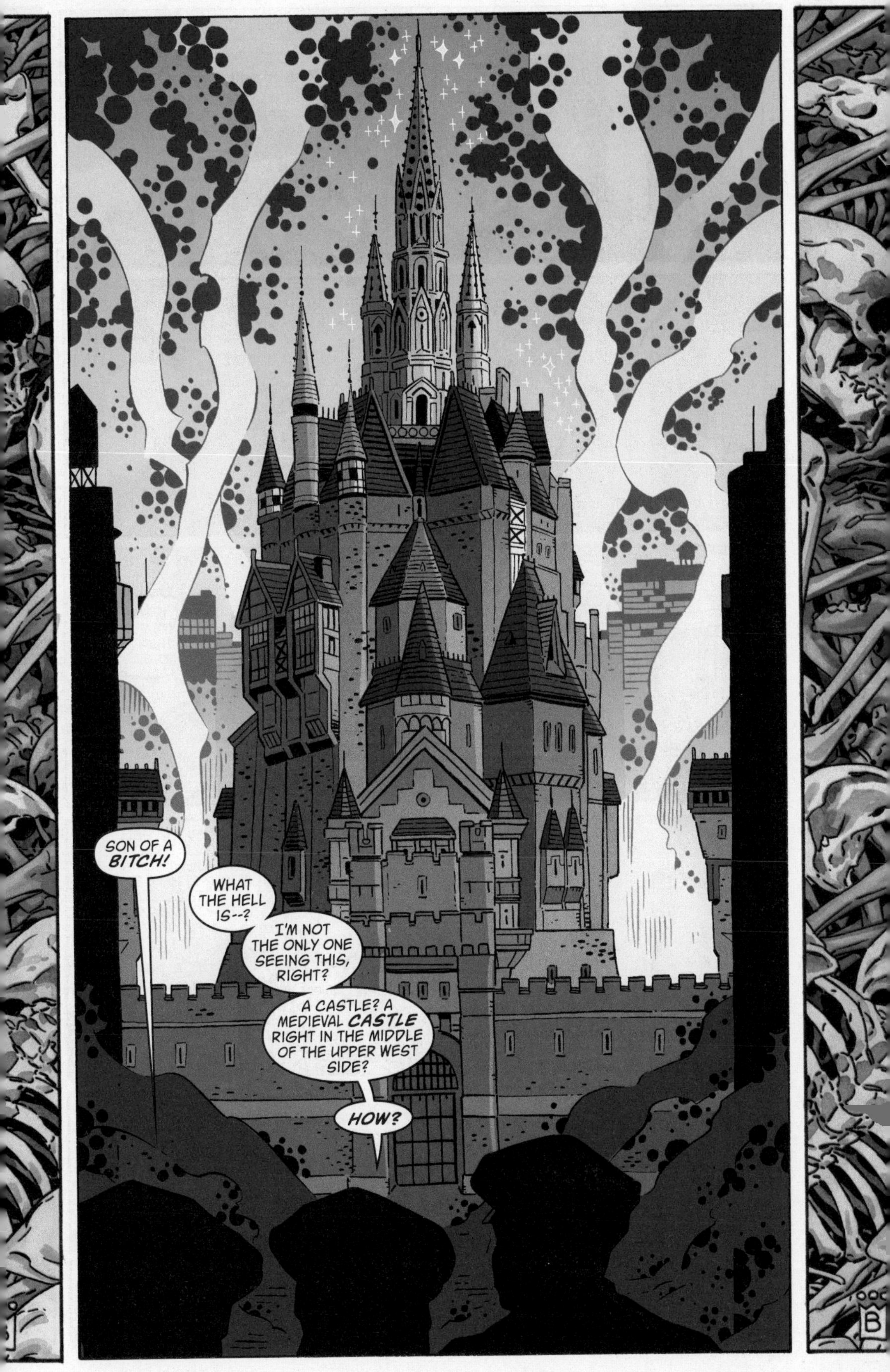
SON OF A BITCH!
WHAT THE HELL IS--?
I'M NOT THE ONLY ONE SEEING THIS, RIGHT?
A CASTLE? A MEDIEVAL CASTLE RIGHT IN THE MIDDLE OF THE UPPER WEST SIDE?
HOW?

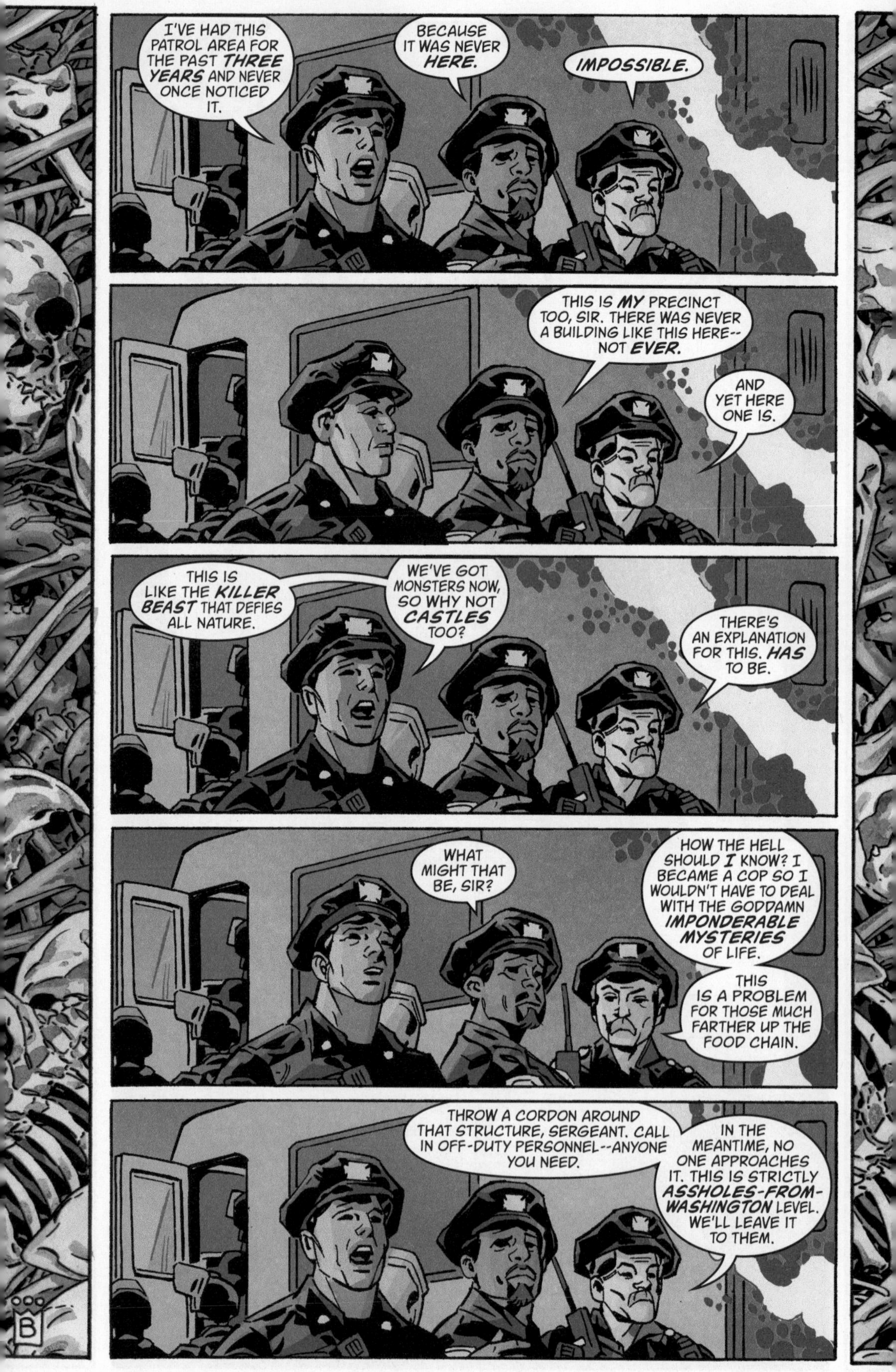
I'VE HAD THIS PATROL AREA FOR THE PAST THREE YEARS AND NEVER ONCE NOTICED IT.
BECAUSE IT WAS NEVER HERE.
IMPOSSIBLE.
THIS IS MY PRECINCT TOO, SIR. THERE WAS NEVER A BUILDING LIKE THIS HERE-- NOT EVER.
AND YET HERE ONE IS.
THIS IS LIKE THE KILLER BEAST THAT DEFIES ALL NATURE.
WE'VE GOT MONSTERS NOW, SO WHY NOT CASTLES TOO?
THERE'S AN EXPLANATION FOR THIS. HAS TO BE.
WHAT MIGHT THAT BE, SIR?
HOW THE HELL SHOULD I KNOW? I BECAME A COP SO I WOULDN'T HAVE TO DEAL WITH THE GODDAMN IMPONDERABLE MYSTERIES OF LIFE.
THIS IS A PROBLEM FOR THOSE MUCH FARTHER UP THE FOOD CHAIN.
THROW A CORDON AROUND THAT STRUCTURE, SERGEANT. CALL IN OFF-DUTY PERSONNEL--ANYONE YOU NEED.
IN THE MEANTIME, NO ONE APPROACHES IT. THIS IS STRICTLY ASSHOLES-FROM-WASHINGTON LEVEL. WE'LL LEAVE IT TO THEM.

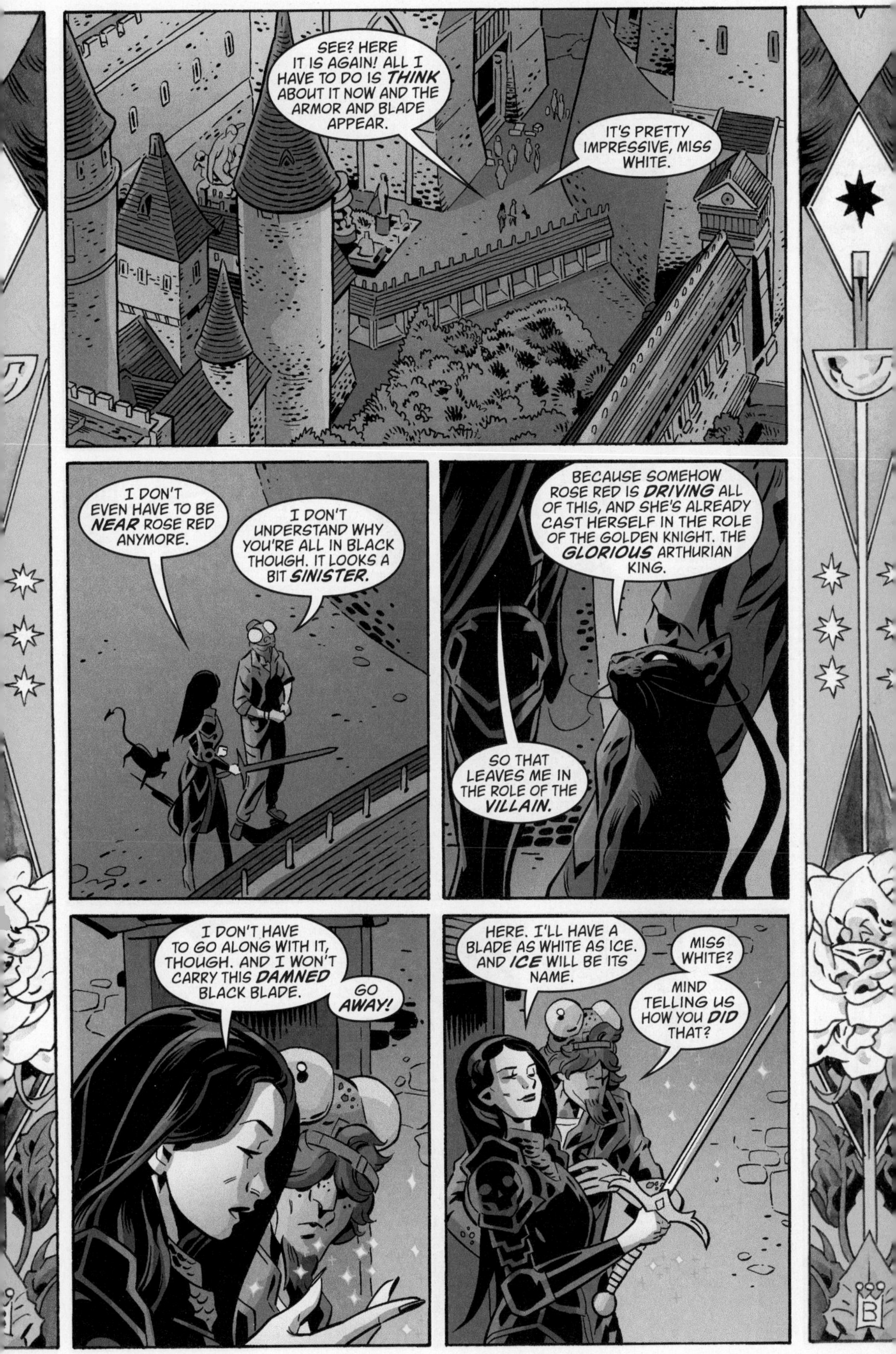
SEE? HERE IT IS AGAIN! ALL I HAVE TO DO IS THINK ABOUT IT NOW AND THE ARMOR AND BLADE APPEAR.
IT'S PRETTY IMPRESSIVE, MISS WHITE.
I DON'T EVEN HAVE TO BE NEAR ROSE RED ANYMORE.
I DON'T UNDERSTAND WHY YOU'RE ALL IN BLACK THOUGH. IT LOOKS A BIT SINISTER.
BECAUSE SOMEHOW ROSE RED IS DRIVING ALL OF THIS, AND SHE'S ALREADY CAST HERSELF IN THE ROLE OF THE GOLDEN KNIGHT. THE GLORIOUS ARTHURIAN KING.
SO THAT LEAVES ME IN THE ROLE OF THE VILLAIN.
I DON'T HAVE TO GO ALONG WITH IT, THOUGH. AND I WON'T CARRY THIS DAMNED BLACK BLADE.
GO AWAY!
HERE. I'LL HAVE A BLADE AS WHITE AS ICE. AND ICE WILL BE ITS NAME.
MISS WHITE?
MIND TELLING US HOW YOU DID THAT?

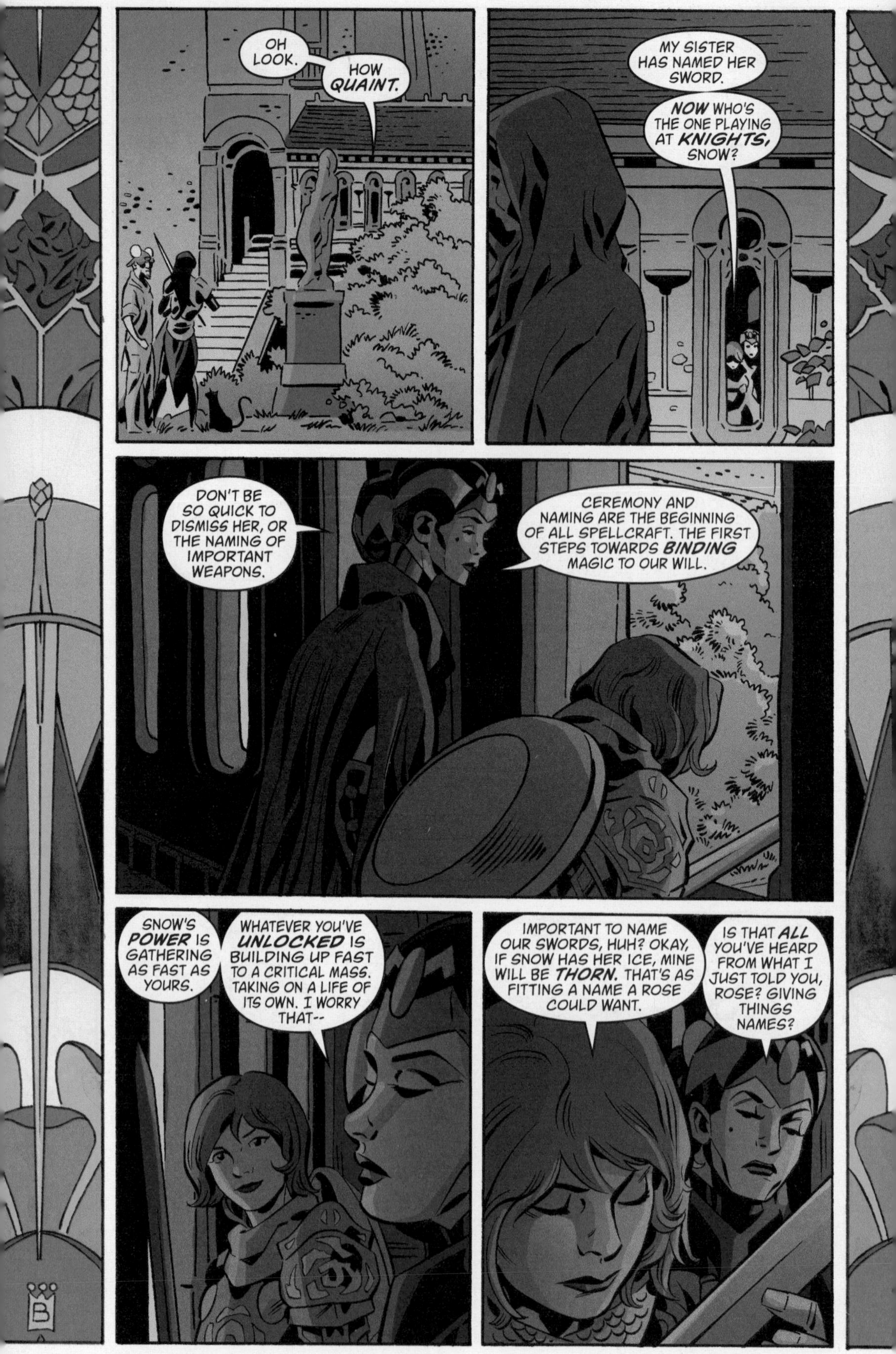
OH LOOK.
HOW QUAINT.
MY SISTER HAS NAMED HER SWORD.
NOW WHO'S THE ONE PLAYING AT KNIGHTS, SNOW?
DON'T BE SO QUICK TO DISMISS HER, OR THE NAMING OF IMPORTANT WEAPONS.
CEREMONY AND NAMING ARE THE BEGINNING OF ALL SPELLCRAFT. THE FIRST STEPS TOWARDS BINDING MAGIC TO OUR WILL.
SNOW'S POWER IS GATHERING AS FAST AS YOURS.
WHATEVER YOU'VE UNLOCKED IS BUILDING UP FAST TO A CRITICAL MASS. TAKING ON A LIFE OF ITS OWN. I WORRY THAT--
IMPORTANT TO NAME OUR SWORDS, HUH? OKAY, IF SNOW HAS HER ICE, MINE WILL BE THORN. THAT'S AS FITTING A NAME A ROSE COULD WANT.
IS THAT ALL YOU'VE HEARD FROM WHAT I JUST TOLD YOU, ROSE? GIVING THINGS NAMES?

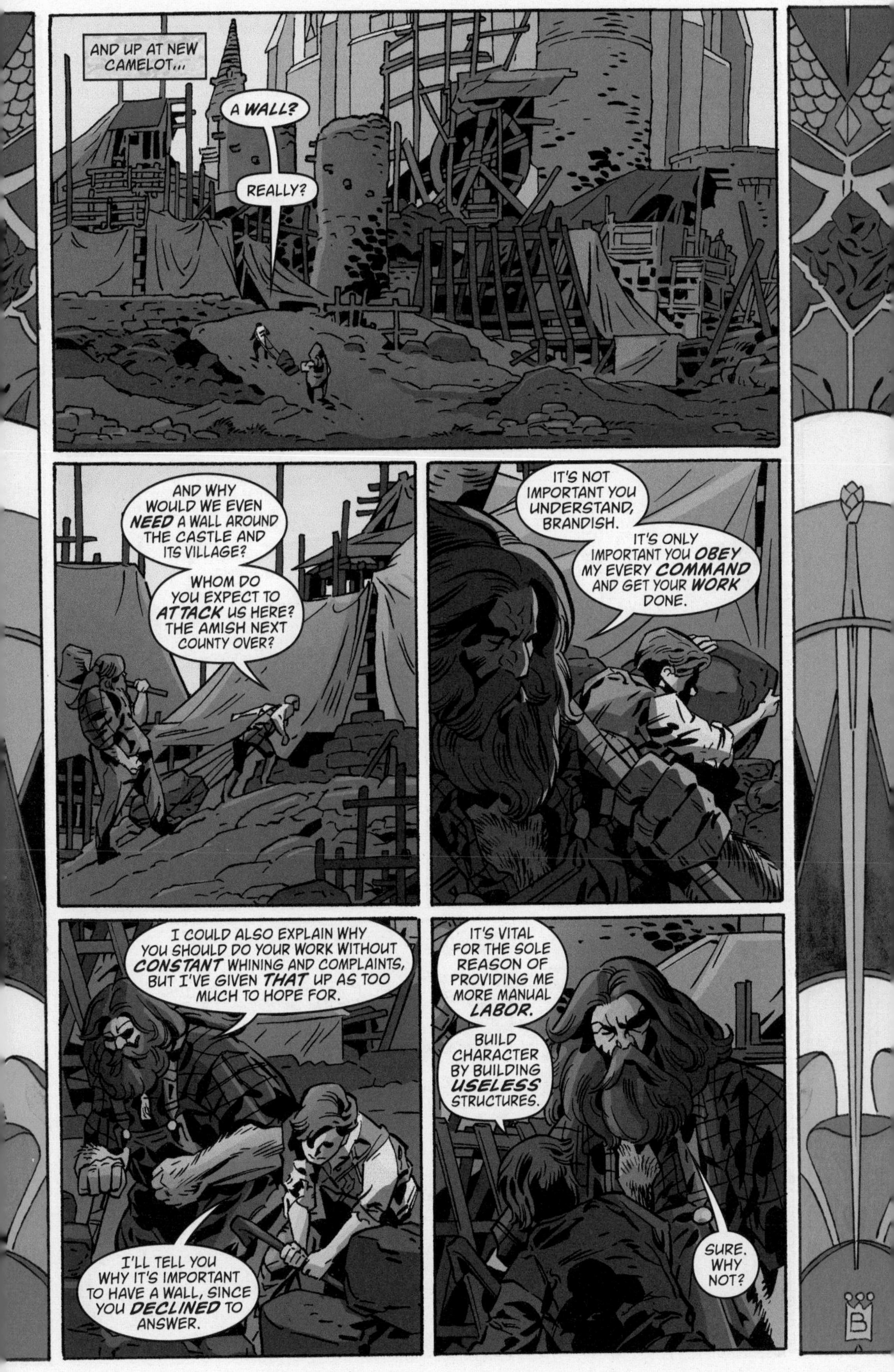
AND UP AT NEW CAMELOT...
A WALL?
REALLY?
AND WHY WOULD WE EVEN NEED A WALL AROUND THE CASTLE AND ITS VILLAGE?
WHOM DO YOU EXPECT TO ATTACK US HERE? THE AMISH NEXT COUNTY OVER?
IT'S NOT IMPORTANT YOU UNDERSTAND, BRANDISH.
IT'S ONLY IMPORTANT YOU OBEY MY EVERY COMMAND AND GET YOUR WORK DONE.
I COULD ALSO EXPLAIN WHY YOU SHOULD DO YOUR WORK WITHOUT CONSTANT WHINING AND COMPLAINTS, BUT I'VE GIVEN THAT UP AS TOO MUCH TO HOPE FOR.
I'LL TELL YOU WHY IT'S IMPORTANT TO HAVE A WALL, SINCE YOU DECLINED TO ANSWER.
IT'S VITAL FOR THE SOLE REASON OF PROVIDING ME MORE MANUAL LABOR.
BUILD CHARACTER BY BUILDING USELESS STRUCTURES.
SURE. WHY NOT?

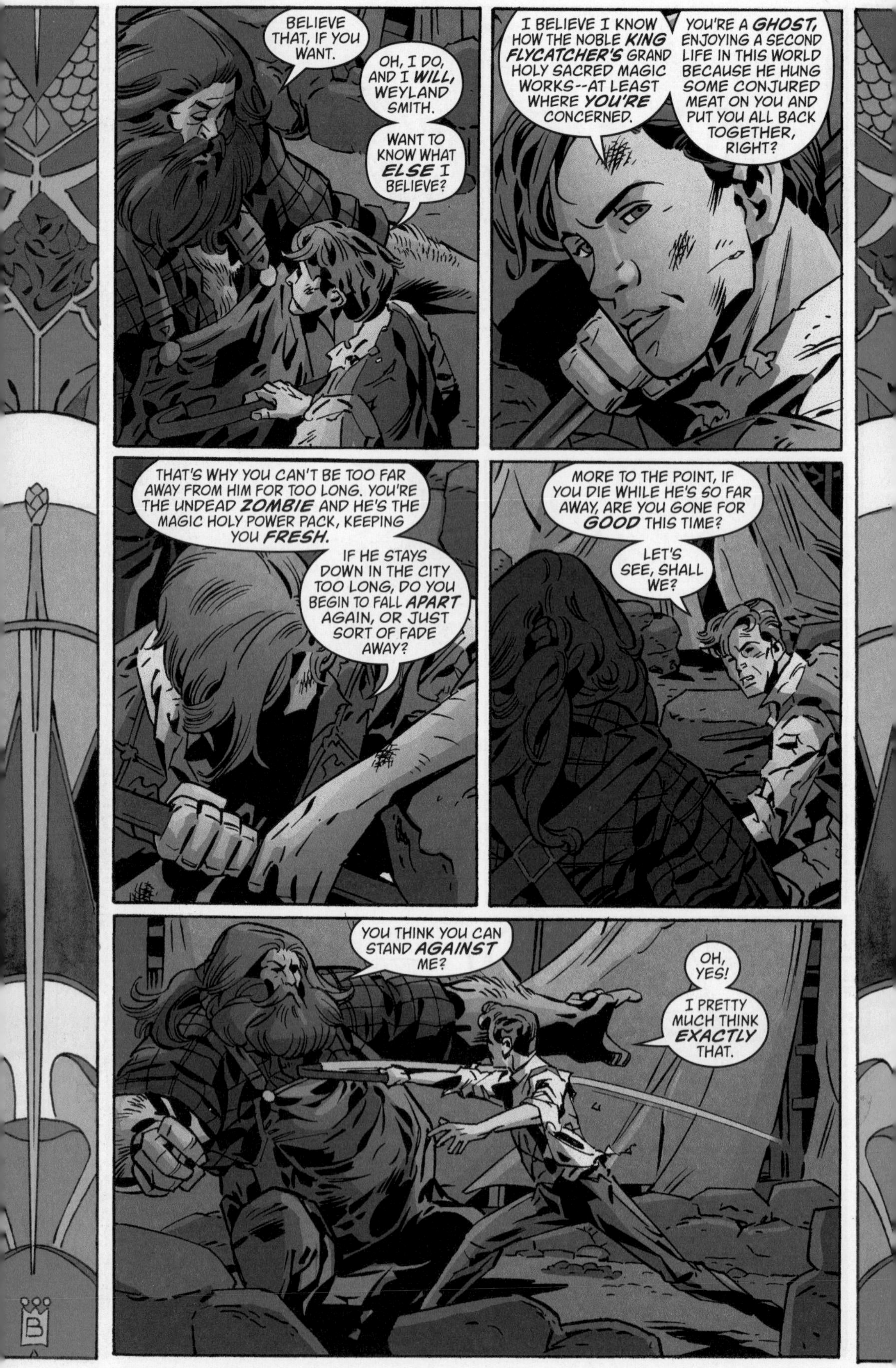
BELIEVE THAT, IF YOU WANT.
OH, I DO, AND I WILL, WEYLAND SMITH.
WANT TO KNOW WHAT ELSE I BELIEVE?
I BELIEVE I KNOW HOW THE NOBLE KING FLYCATCHER'S GRAND HOLY SACRED MAGIC WORKS--AT LEAST WHERE YOU'RE CONCERNED.
YOU'RE A GHOST, ENJOYING A SECOND LIFE IN THIS WORLD BECAUSE HE HUNG SOME CONJURED MEAT ON YOU AND PUT YOU ALL BACK TOGETHER, RIGHT?
THAT'S WHY YOU CAN'T BE TOO FAR AWAY FROM HIM FOR TOO LONG. YOU'RE THE UNDEAD ZOMBIE AND HE'S THE MAGIC HOLY POWER PACK, KEEPING YOU FRESH.
IF HE STAYS DOWN IN THE CITY TOO LONG, DO YOU BEGIN TO FALL APART AGAIN, OR JUST SORT OF FADE AWAY?
MORE TO THE POINT, IF YOU DIE WHILE HE'S SO FAR AWAY, ARE YOU GONE FOR GOOD THIS TIME?
LET'S SEE, SHALL WE?
YOU THINK YOU CAN STAND AGAINST ME?
OH, YES!
I PRETTY MUCH THINK EXACTLY THAT.

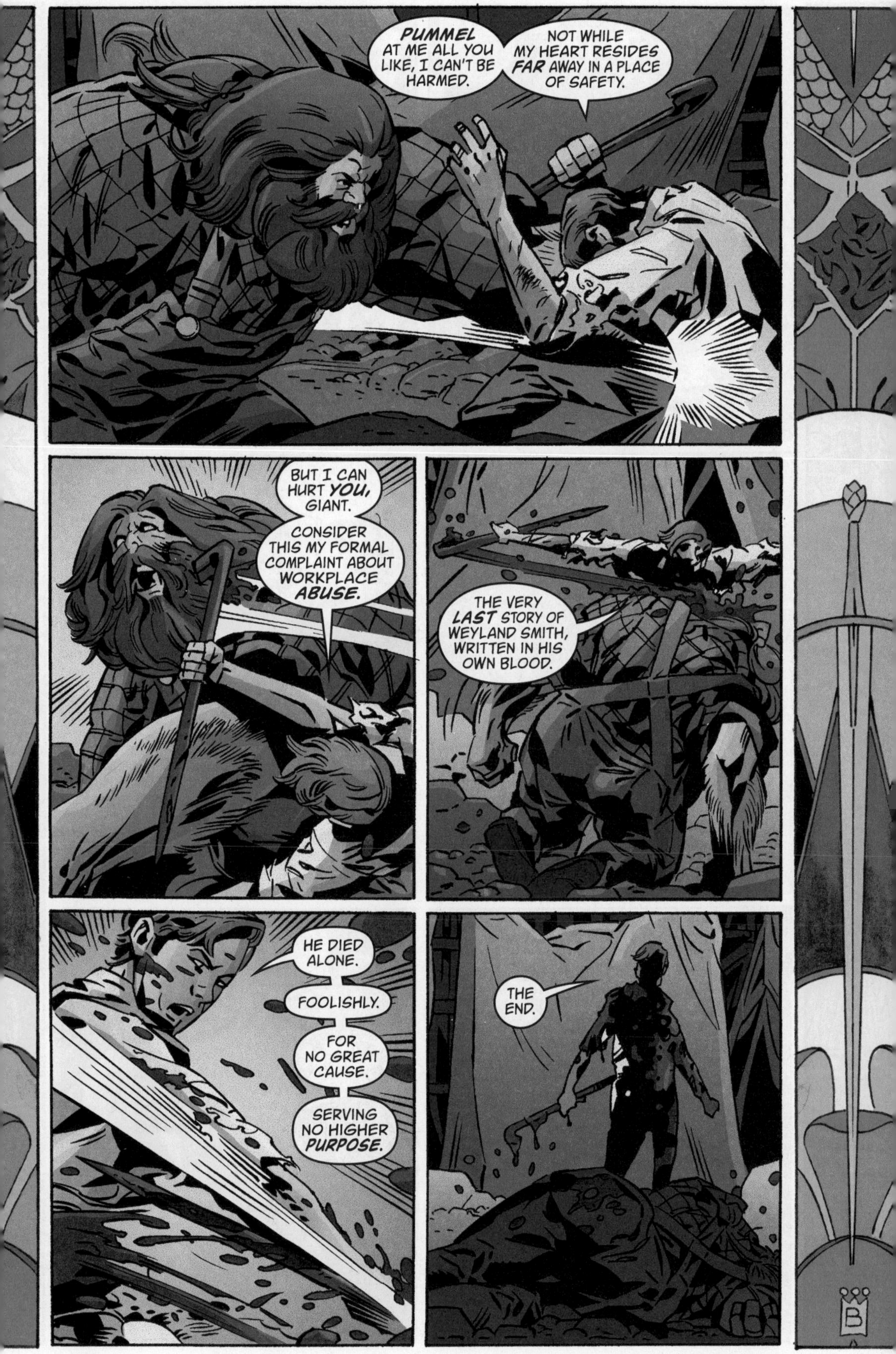
PUMMEL AT ME ALL YOU LIKE, I CAN'T BE HARMED.
NOT WHILE MY HEART RESIDES FAR AWAY IN A PLACE OF SAFETY.
BUT I CAN HURT YOU, GIANT.
CONSIDER THIS MY FORMAL COMPLAINT ABOUT WORKPLACE ABUSE.
THE VERY LAST STORY OF WEYLAND SMITH, WRITTEN IN HIS OWN BLOOD.
HE DIED ALONE.
FOOLISHLY.
FOR NO GREAT CAUSE.
SERVING NO HIGHER PURPOSE.
THE END.

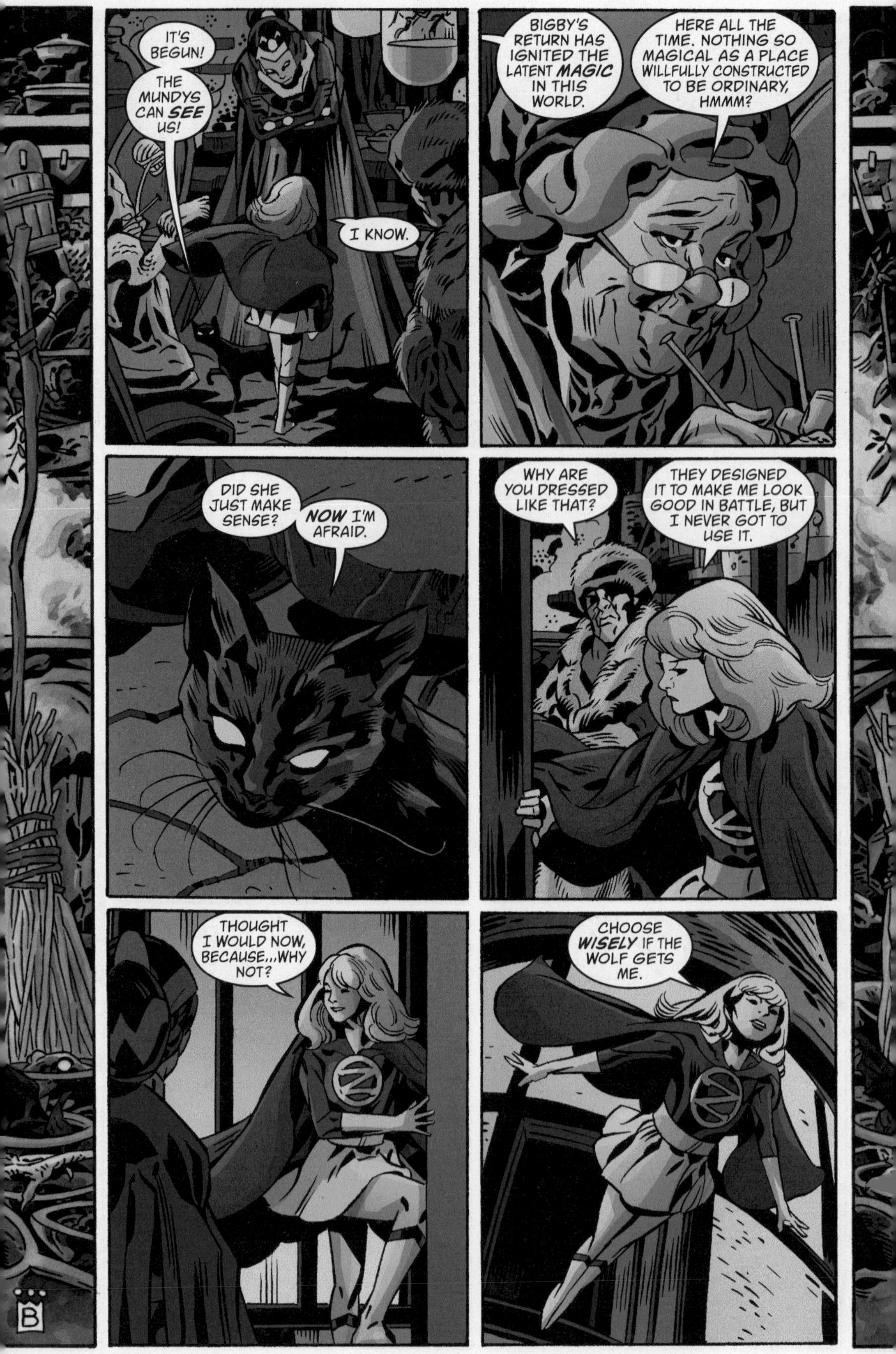
IT'S BEGUN!
THE MUNDYS CAN SEE US!
I KNOW.
BIGBY'S RETURN HAS IGNITED THE LATENT MAGIC IN THIS WORLD.
HERE ALL THE TIME. NOTHING SO MAGICAL AS A PLACE WILLFULLY CONSTRUCTED TO BE ORDINARY, HMMM?
DID SHE JUST MAKE SENSE?
NOW I'M AFRAID.
WHY ARE YOU DRESSED LIKE THAT?
THEY DESIGNED IT TO MAKE ME LOOK GOOD IN BATTLE, BUT I NEVER GOT TO USE IT.
THOUGHT I WOULD NOW, BECAUSE...WHY NOT?
CHOOSE WISELY IF THE WOLF GETS ME.

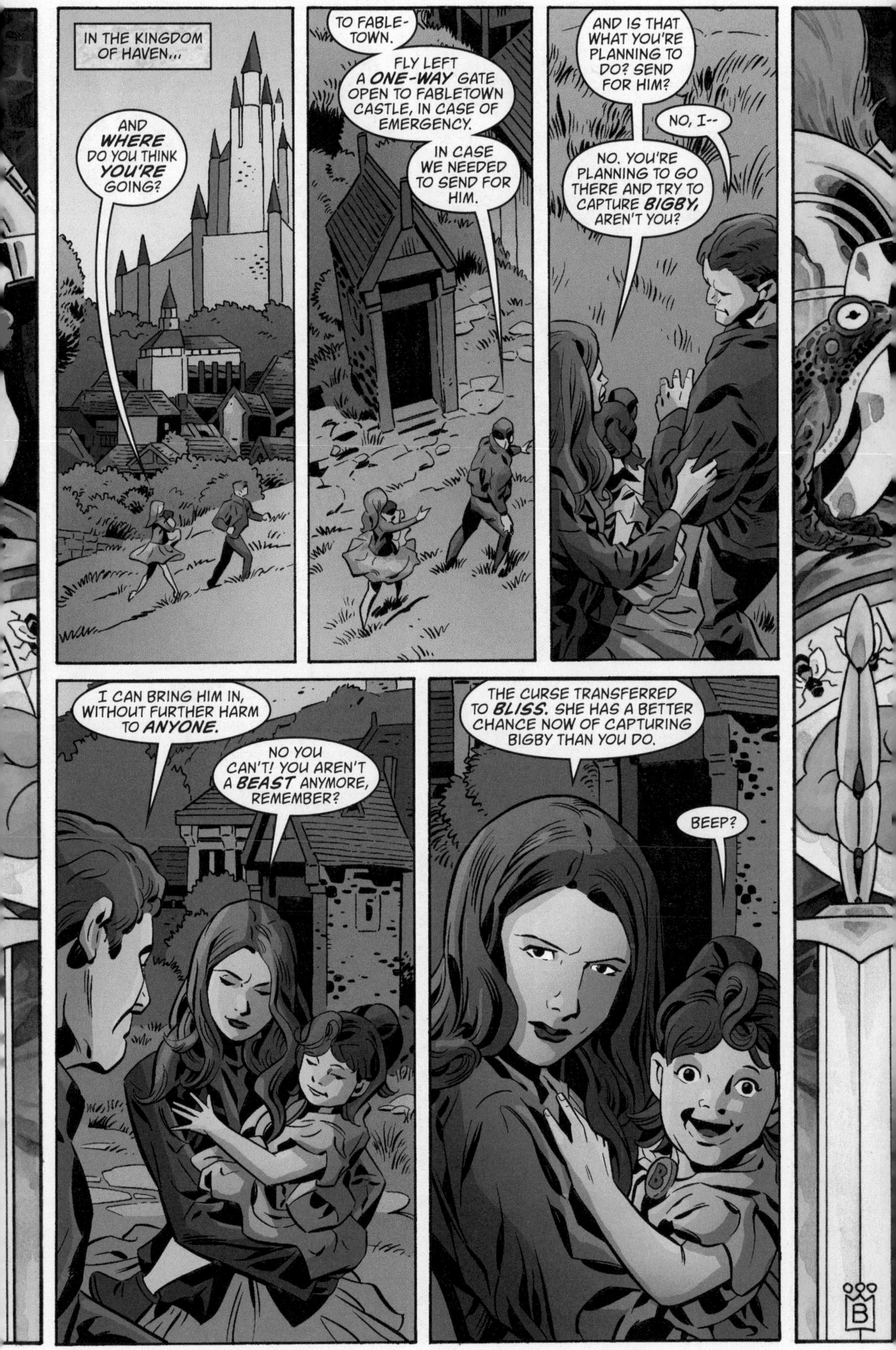
IN THE KINGDOM OF HAVEN...
AND WHERE DO YOU THINK YOU'RE GOING?
TO FABLE-TOWN.
FLY LEFT A ONE-WAY GATE OPEN TO FABLETOWN CASTLE, IN CASE OF EMERGENCY.
IN CASE WE NEEDED TO SEND FOR HIM.
AND IS THAT WHAT YOU'RE PLANNING TO DO? SEND FOR HIM?
NO, I--
NO. YOU'RE PLANNING TO GO THERE AND TRY TO CAPTURE BIGBY, AREN'T YOU?
I CAN BRING HIM IN, WITHOUT FURTHER HARM TO ANYONE.
NO YOU CAN'T! YOU AREN'T A BEAST ANYMORE, REMEMBER?
THE CURSE TRANSFERRED TO BLISS. SHE HAS A BETTER CHANCE NOW OF CAPTURING BIGBY THAN YOU DO.
BEEP?

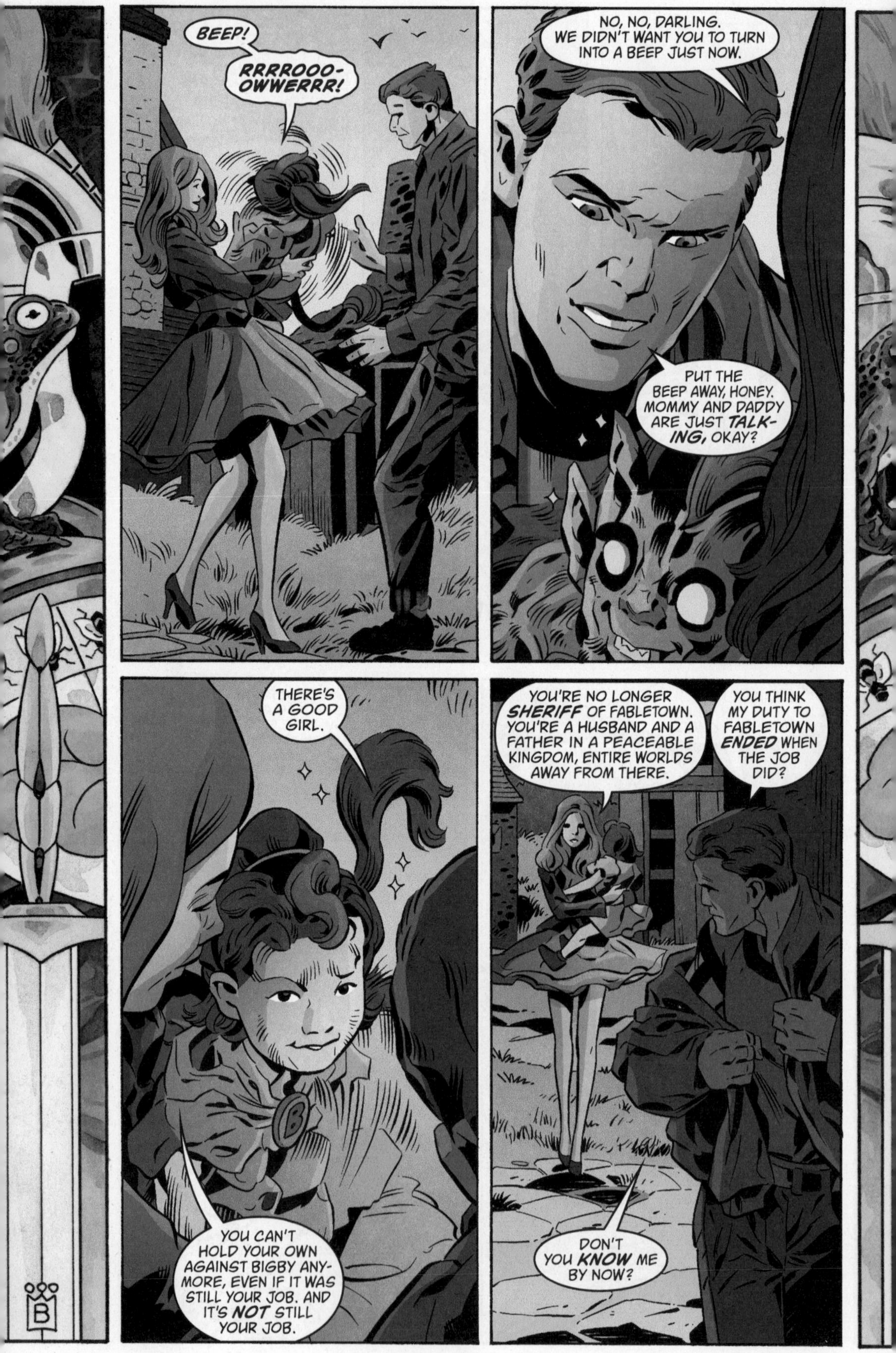
BEEP!
RRRROOO-OWWERRR!
NO, NO, DARLING. WE DIDN'T WANT YOU TO TURN INTO A BEEP JUST NOW.
PUT THE BEEP AWAY, HONEY. MOMMY AND DADDY ARE JUST TALKING, OKAY?
THERE'S A GOOD GIRL.
YOU CAN'T HOLD YOUR OWN AGAINST BIGBY ANYMORE, EVEN IF IT WAS STILL YOUR JOB. AND IT'S NOT STILL YOUR JOB.
YOU'RE NO LONGER SHERIFF OF FABLETOWN. YOU'RE A HUSBAND AND A FATHER IN A PEACEABLE KINGDOM, ENTIRE WORLDS AWAY FROM THERE.
YOU THINK MY DUTY TO FABLETOWN ENDED WHEN THE JOB DID?
DON'T YOU KNOW ME BY NOW?

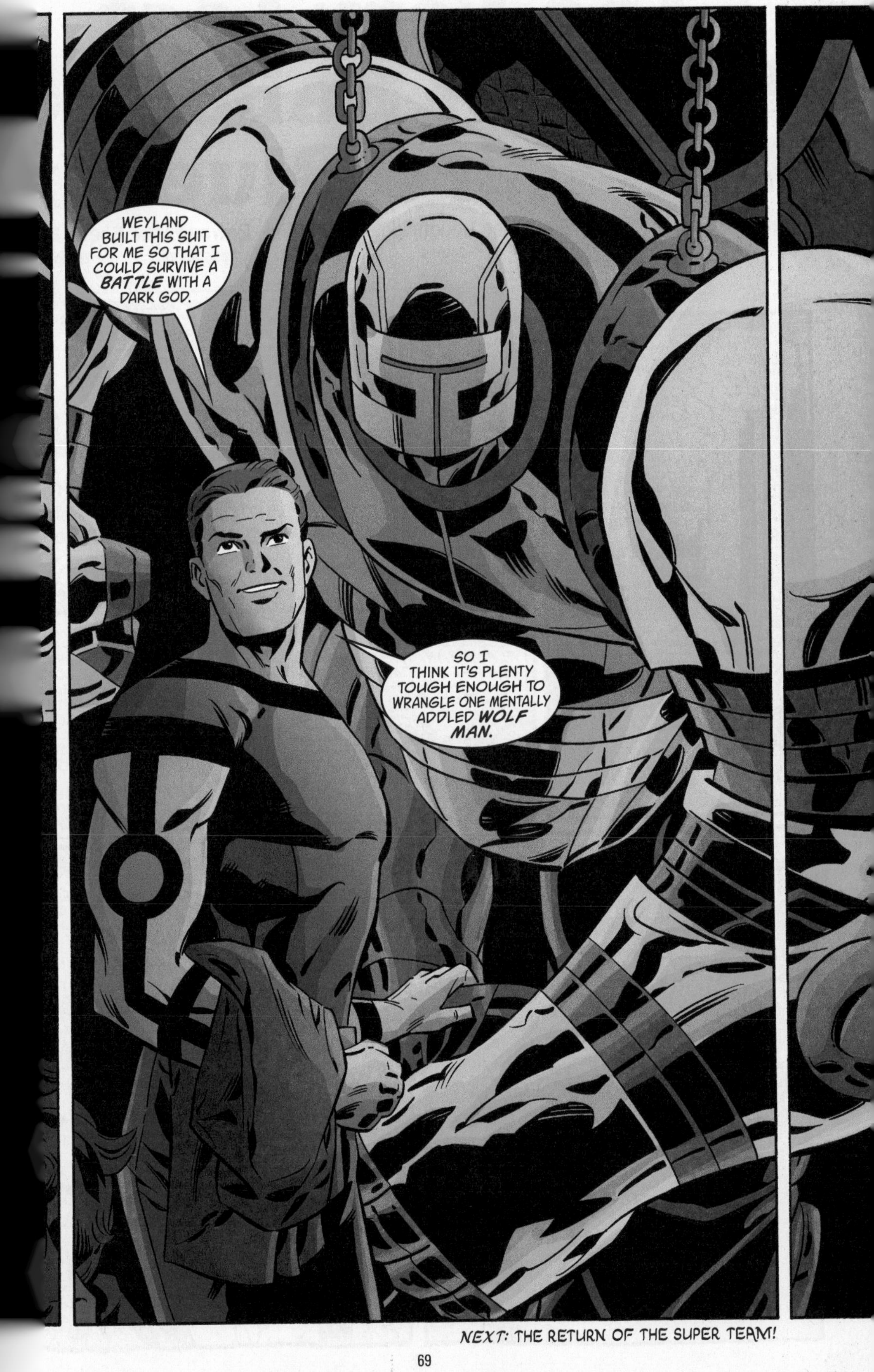
WEYLAND BUILT THIS SUIT FOR ME SO THAT I COULD SURVIVE A BATTLE WITH A DARK GOD.
SO I THINK IT'S PLENTY TOUGH ENOUGH TO WRANGLE ONE MENTALLY ADDLED WOLF MAN.

NEXT: THE RETURN OF THE SUPER TEAM!

The Very Last Story of Babe the Miniature Blue Ox

Matthew Sturges writer · Tony Akins artist · Lee Loughridge colors · Todd Klein letters · Rowena Yow assoc. ed. · Shelly Bond editor

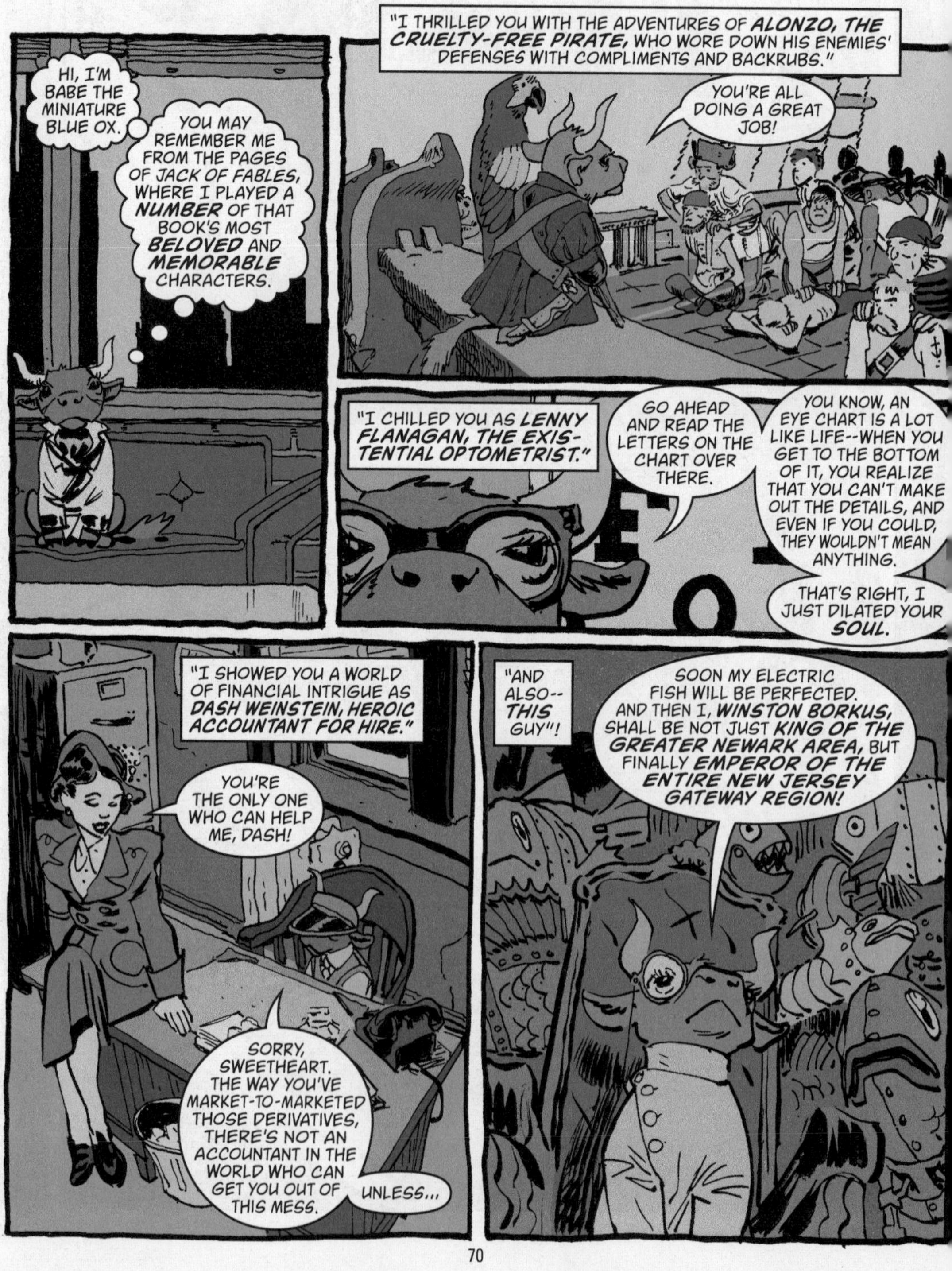

HI, I'M BABE THE MINIATURE BLUE OX.
YOU MAY REMEMBER ME FROM THE PAGES OF JACK OF FABLES, WHERE I PLAYED A NUMBER OF THAT BOOK'S MOST BELOVED AND MEMORABLE CHARACTERS.
"I THRILLED YOU WITH THE ADVENTURES OF ALONZO, THE CRUELTY-FREE PIRATE, WHO WORE DOWN HIS ENEMIES' DEFENSES WITH COMPLIMENTS AND BACKRUBS."
YOU'RE ALL DOING A GREAT JOB!
"I CHILLED YOU AS LENNY FLANAGAN, THE EXIS-TENTIAL OPTOMETRIST."
GO AHEAD AND READ THE LETTERS ON THE CHART OVER THERE.
YOU KNOW, AN EYE CHART IS A LOT LIKE LIFE--WHEN YOU GET TO THE BOTTOM OF IT, YOU REALIZE THAT YOU CAN'T MAKE OUT THE DETAILS, AND EVEN IF YOU COULD, THEY WOULDN'T MEAN ANYTHING.
THAT'S RIGHT, I JUST DILATED YOUR SOUL.
"I SHOWED YOU A WORLD OF FINANCIAL INTRIGUE AS DASH WEINSTEIN, HEROIC ACCOUNTANT FOR HIRE."
YOU'RE THE ONLY ONE WHO CAN HELP ME, DASH!
SORRY, SWEETHEART. THE WAY YOU'VE MARKET-TO-MARKETED THOSE DERIVATIVES, THERE'S NOT AN ACCOUNTANT IN THE WORLD WHO CAN GET YOU OUT OF THIS MESS.
UNLESS...
"AND ALSO-- THIS GUY"!
SOON MY ELECTRIC FISH WILL BE PERFECTED. AND THEN I, WINSTON BORKUS, SHALL BE NOT JUST KING OF THE GREATER NEWARK AREA, BUT FINALLY EMPEROR OF THE ENTIRE NEW JERSEY GATEWAY REGION!

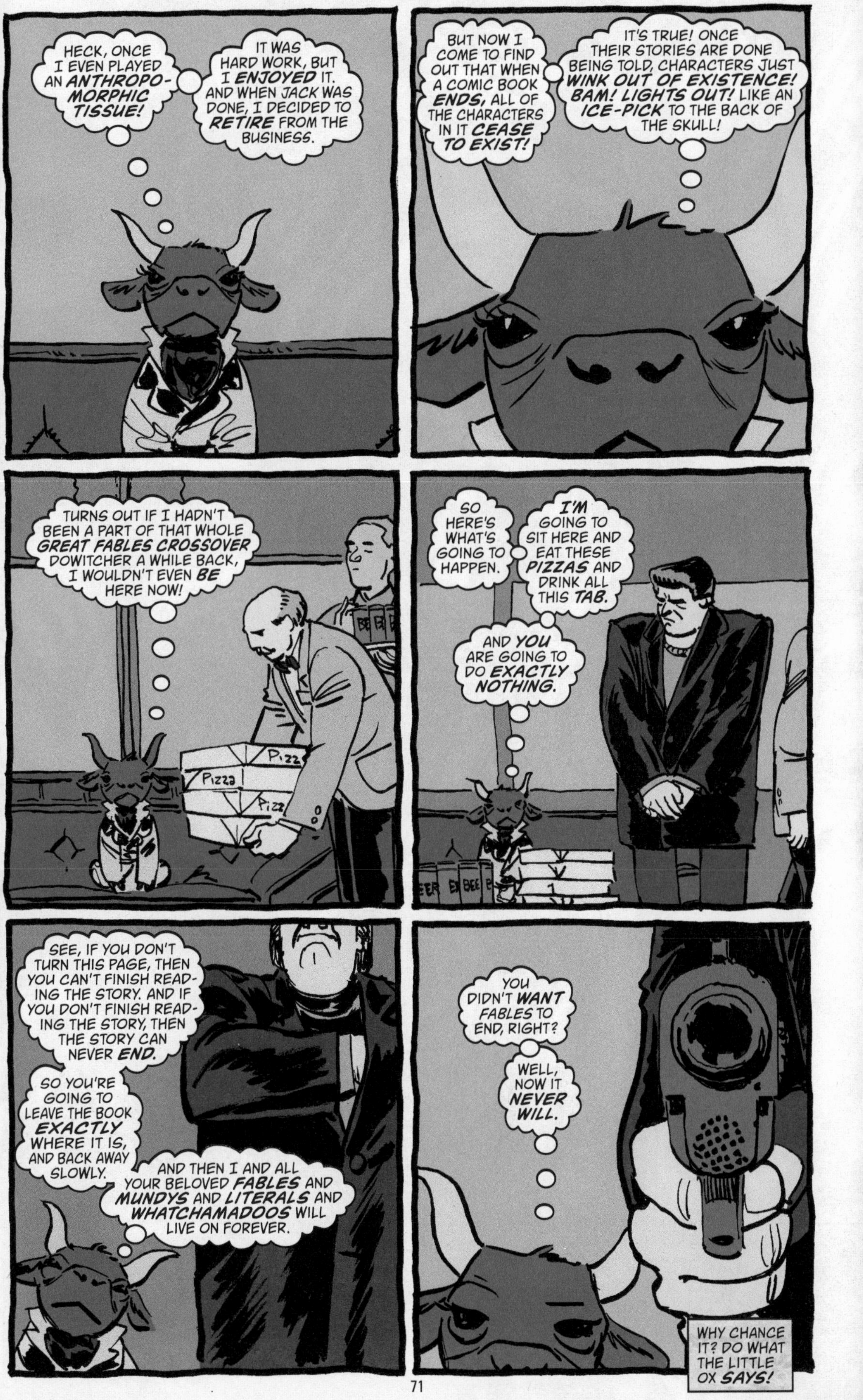
HECK, ONCE I EVEN PLAYED AN ANTHROPO-MORPHIC TISSUE!
IT WAS HARD WORK, BUT I ENJOYED IT. AND WHEN JACK WAS DONE, I DECIDED TO RETIRE FROM THE BUSINESS.
BUT NOW I COME TO FIND OUT THAT WHEN A COMIC BOOK ENDS, ALL OF THE CHARACTERS IN IT CEASE TO EXIST!
IT'S TRUE! ONCE THEIR STORIES ARE DONE BEING TOLD, CHARACTERS JUST WINK OUT OF EXISTENCE! BAM! LIGHTS OUT! LIKE AN ICE-PICK TO THE BACK OF THE SKULL!
TURNS OUT IF I HADN'T BEEN A PART OF THAT WHOLE GREAT FABLES CROSSOVER DOWITCHER A WHILE BACK, I WOULDN'T EVEN BE HERE NOW!
PIZZA
PIZZA
PIZZA
SO HERE'S WHAT'S GOING TO HAPPEN.
I'M GOING TO SIT HERE AND EAT THESE PIZZAS AND DRINK ALL THIS TAB.
AND YOU ARE GOING TO DO EXACTLY NOTHING.
SEE, IF YOU DON'T TURN THIS PAGE, THEN YOU CAN'T FINISH READ-ING THE STORY. AND IF YOU DON'T FINISH READ-ING THE STORY, THEN THE STORY CAN NEVER END.
SO YOU'RE GOING TO LEAVE THE BOOK EXACTLY WHERE IT IS, AND BACK AWAY SLOWLY.
AND THEN I AND ALL YOUR BELOVED FABLES AND MUNDYS AND LITERALS AND WHATCHAMADOOS WILL LIVE ON FOREVER.
YOU DIDN'T WANT FABLES TO END, RIGHT?
WELL, NOW IT NEVER WILL.
WHY CHANCE IT? DO WHAT THE LITTLE OX SAYS!

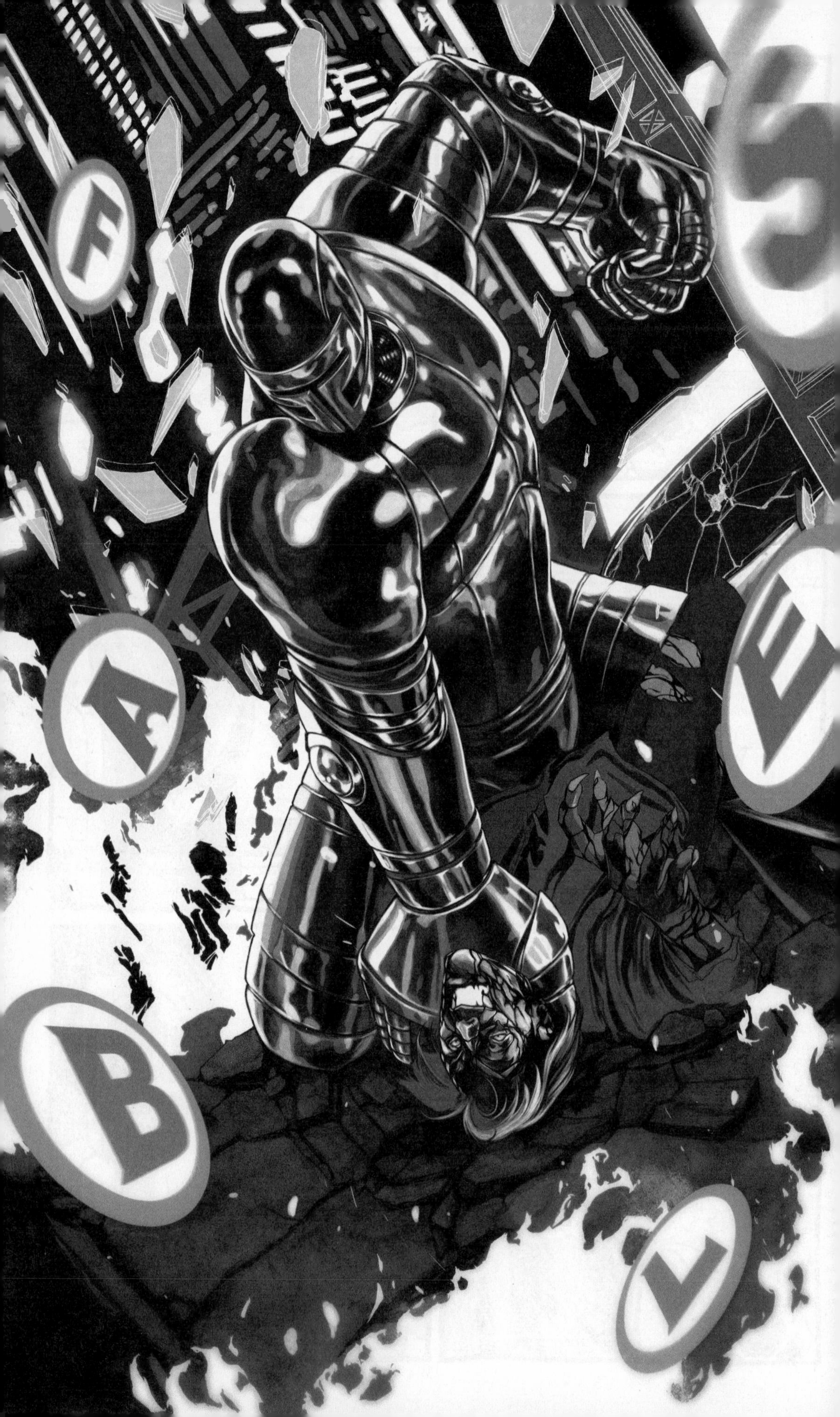

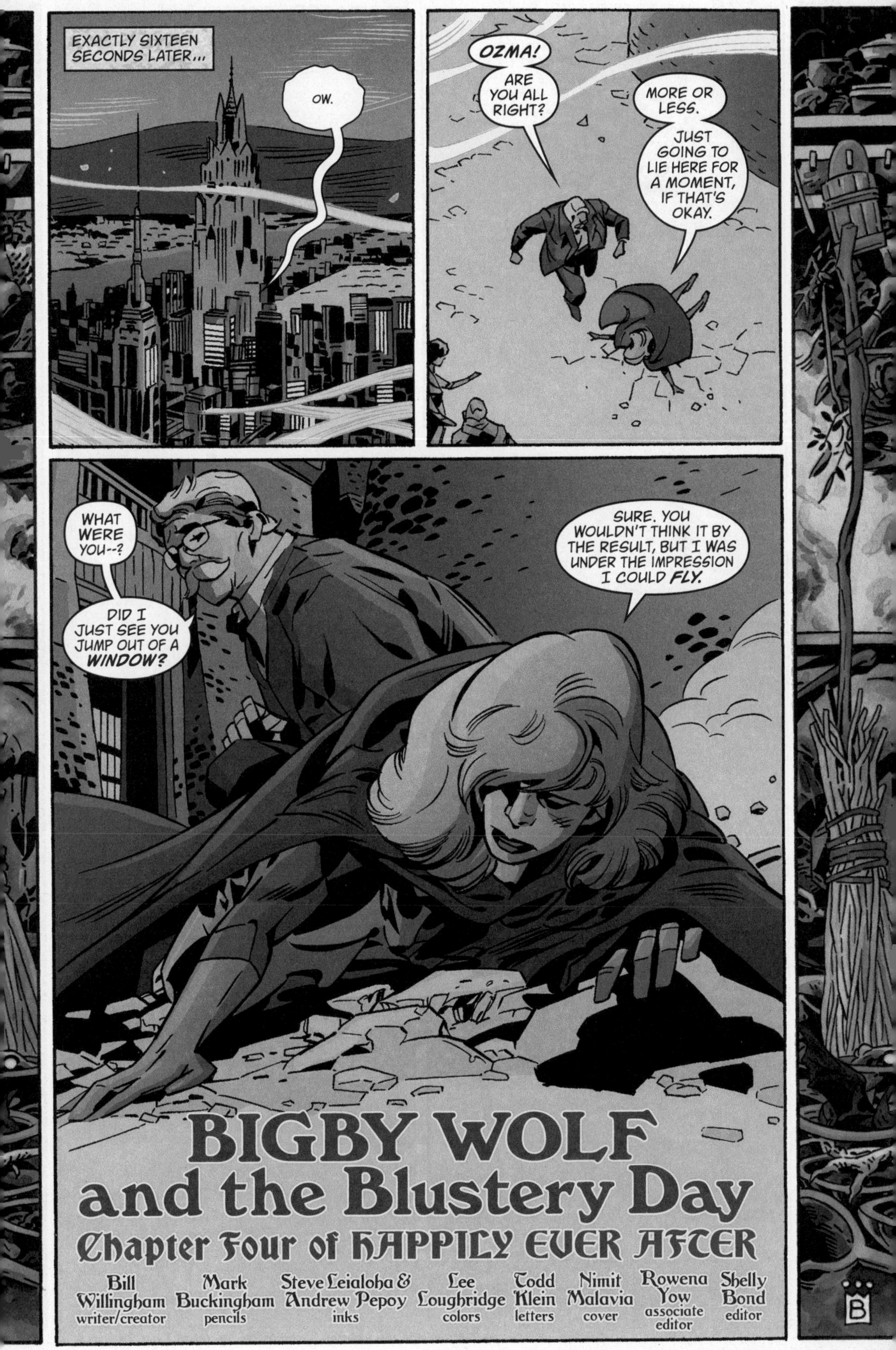
EXACTLY SIXTEEN SECONDS LATER...
OW.
OZMA!
ARE YOU ALL RIGHT?
MORE OR LESS.
JUST GOING TO LIE HERE FOR A MOMENT, IF THAT'S OKAY.
WHAT WERE YOU--?
DID I JUST SEE YOU JUMP OUT OF A WINDOW?
SURE. YOU WOULDN'T THINK IT BY THE RESULT, BUT I WAS UNDER THE IMPRESSION I COULD FLY.
BIGBY WOLF and the Blustery Day
Chapter Four of HAPPILY EVER AFTER
Bill Willingham writer/creator
Mark Buckingham pencils
Steve Leialoha & Andrew Pepoy inks
Lee Loughridge colors
Todd Klein letters
Nimit Malavia cover
Rowena Yow associate editor
Shelly Bond editor

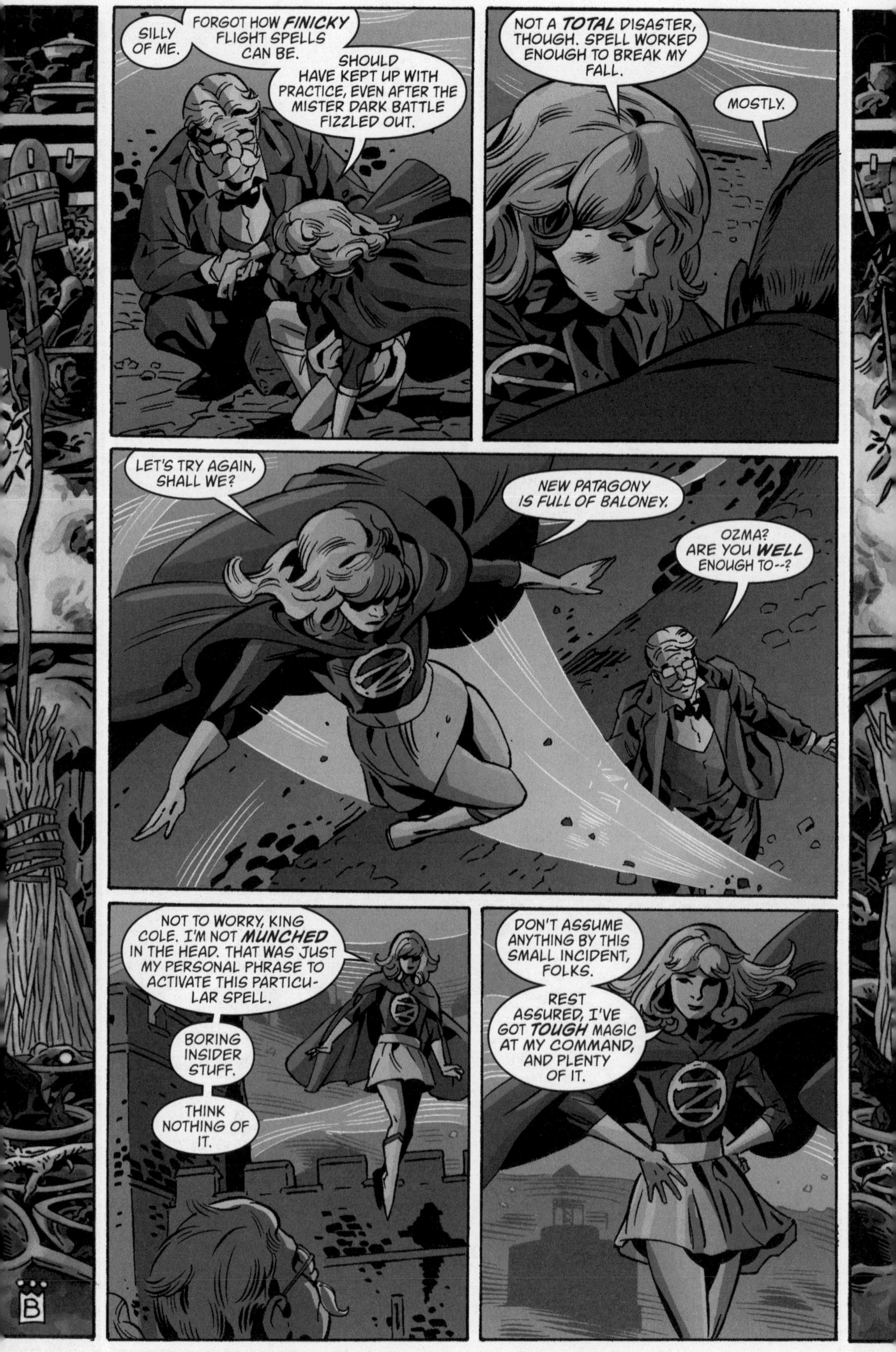
SILLY OF ME.
FORGOT HOW FINICKY FLIGHT SPELLS CAN BE.
SHOULD HAVE KEPT UP WITH PRACTICE, EVEN AFTER THE MISTER DARK BATTLE FIZZLED OUT.
NOT A TOTAL DISASTER, THOUGH. SPELL WORKED ENOUGH TO BREAK MY FALL.
MOSTLY.
LET'S TRY AGAIN, SHALL WE?
NEW PATAGONY IS FULL OF BALONEY.
OZMA? ARE YOU WELL ENOUGH TO--?
NOT TO WORRY, KING COLE. I'M NOT MUNCHED IN THE HEAD. THAT WAS JUST MY PERSONAL PHRASE TO ACTIVATE THIS PARTICU-LAR SPELL.
BORING INSIDER STUFF.
THINK NOTHING OF IT.
DON'T ASSUME ANYTHING BY THIS SMALL INCIDENT, FOLKS.
REST ASSURED, I'VE GOT TOUGH MAGIC AT MY COMMAND, AND PLENTY OF IT.

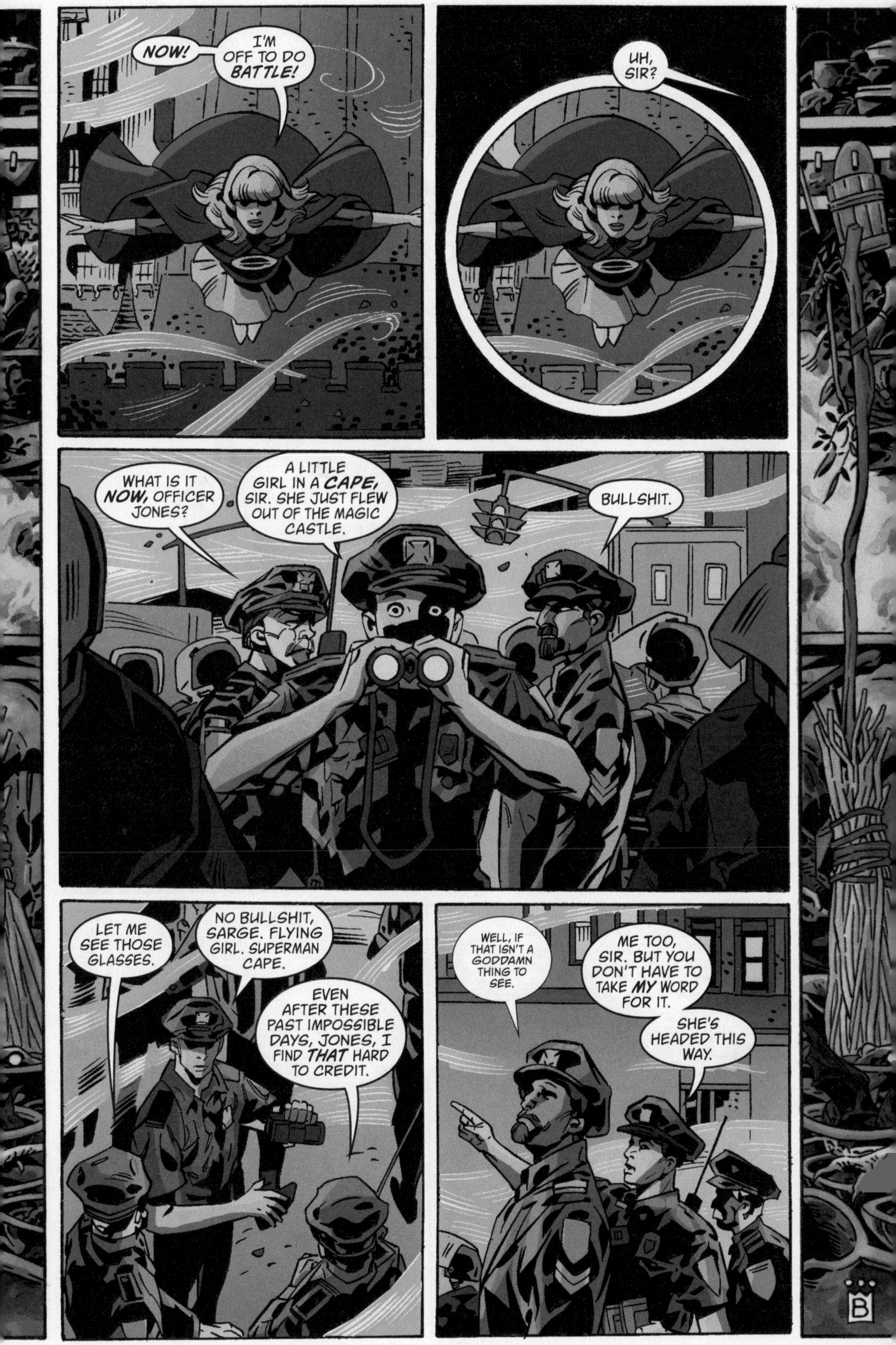
NOW!
I'M OFF TO DO BATTLE!
UH, SIR?
WHAT IS IT NOW, OFFICER JONES?
A LITTLE GIRL IN A CAPE, SIR. SHE JUST FLEW OUT OF THE MAGIC CASTLE.
BULLSHIT.
LET ME SEE THOSE GLASSES.
NO BULLSHIT, SARGE. FLYING GIRL. SUPERMAN CAPE.
EVEN AFTER THESE PAST IMPOSSIBLE DAYS, JONES, I FIND THAT HARD TO CREDIT.
WELL, IF THAT ISN'T A GODDAMN THING TO SEE.
ME TOO, SIR. BUT YOU DON'T HAVE TO TAKE MY WORD FOR IT.
SHE'S HEADED THIS WAY.

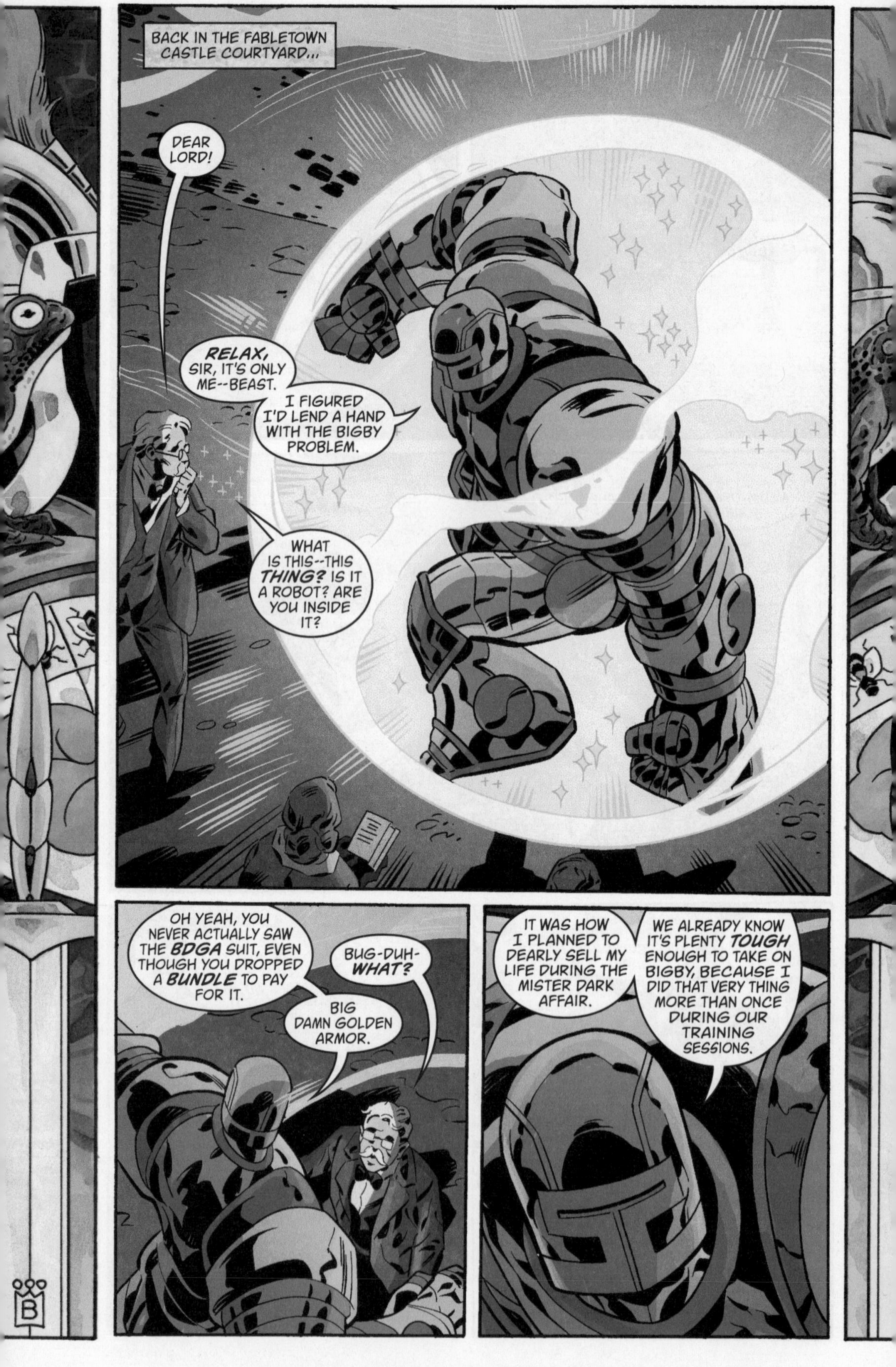

BACK IN THE FABLETOWN CASTLE COURTYARD...
DEAR LORD!
RELAX, SIR, IT'S ONLY ME--BEAST.
I FIGURED I'D LEND A HAND WITH THE BIGBY PROBLEM.
WHAT IS THIS--THIS THING? IS IT A ROBOT? ARE YOU INSIDE IT?
OH YEAH, YOU NEVER ACTUALLY SAW THE BDGA SUIT, EVEN THOUGH YOU DROPPED A BUNDLE TO PAY FOR IT.
BUG-DUH-WHAT?
BIG DAMN GOLDEN ARMOR.
IT WAS HOW I PLANNED TO DEARLY SELL MY LIFE DURING THE MISTER DARK AFFAIR.
WE ALREADY KNOW IT'S PLENTY TOUGH ENOUGH TO TAKE ON BIGBY, BECAUSE I DID THAT VERY THING MORE THAN ONCE DURING OUR TRAINING SESSIONS.

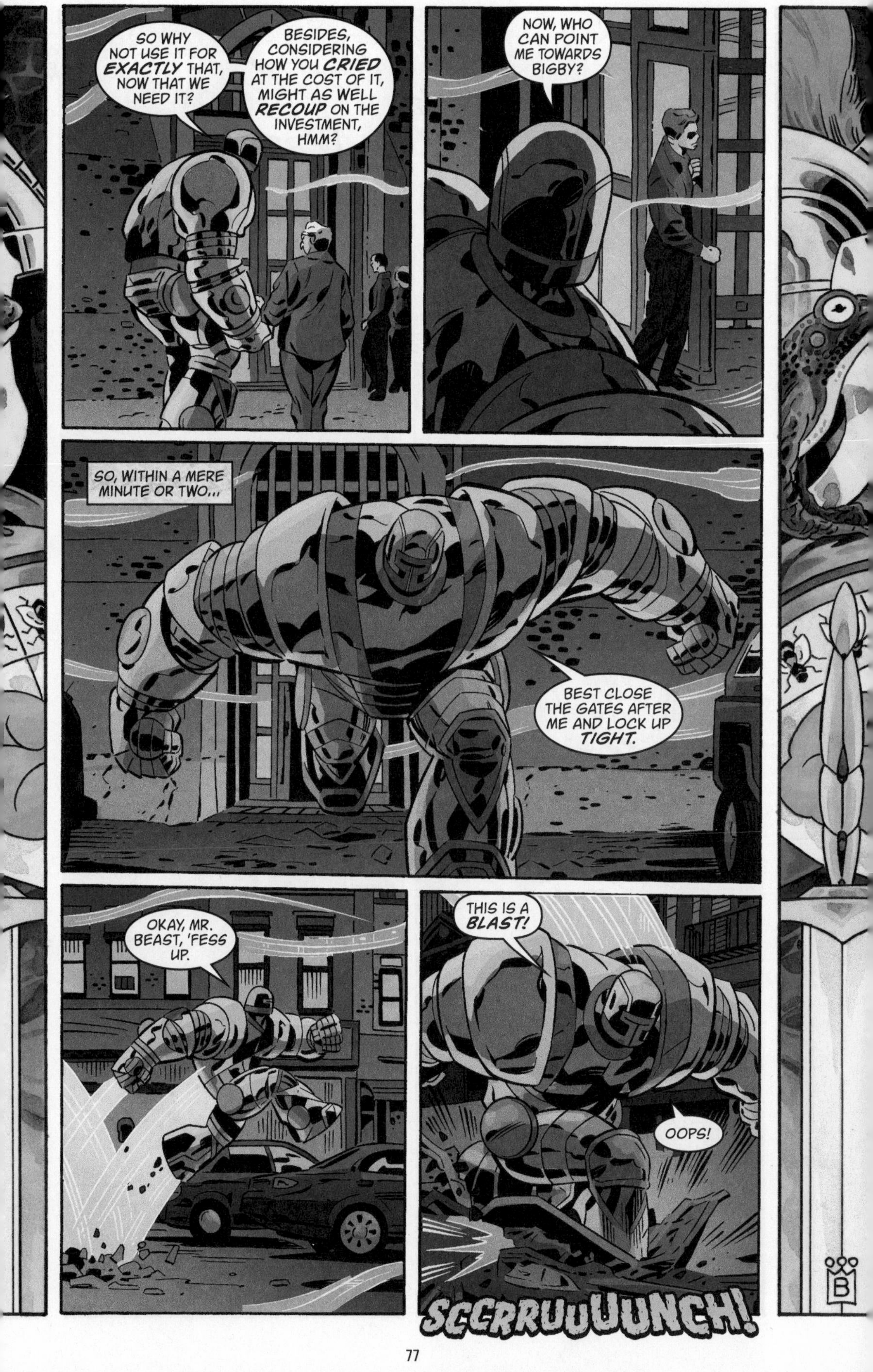
SO WHY NOT USE IT FOR EXACTLY THAT, NOW THAT WE NEED IT?
BESIDES, CONSIDERING HOW YOU CRIED AT THE COST OF IT, MIGHT AS WELL RECOUP ON THE INVESTMENT, HMM?
NOW, WHO CAN POINT ME TOWARDS BIGBY?
SO, WITHIN A MERE MINUTE OR TWO...
BEST CLOSE THE GATES AFTER ME AND LOCK UP TIGHT.
OKAY, MR. BEAST, 'FESS UP.
THIS IS A BLAST!
OOPS!
SCCRRUUUUUNCH!

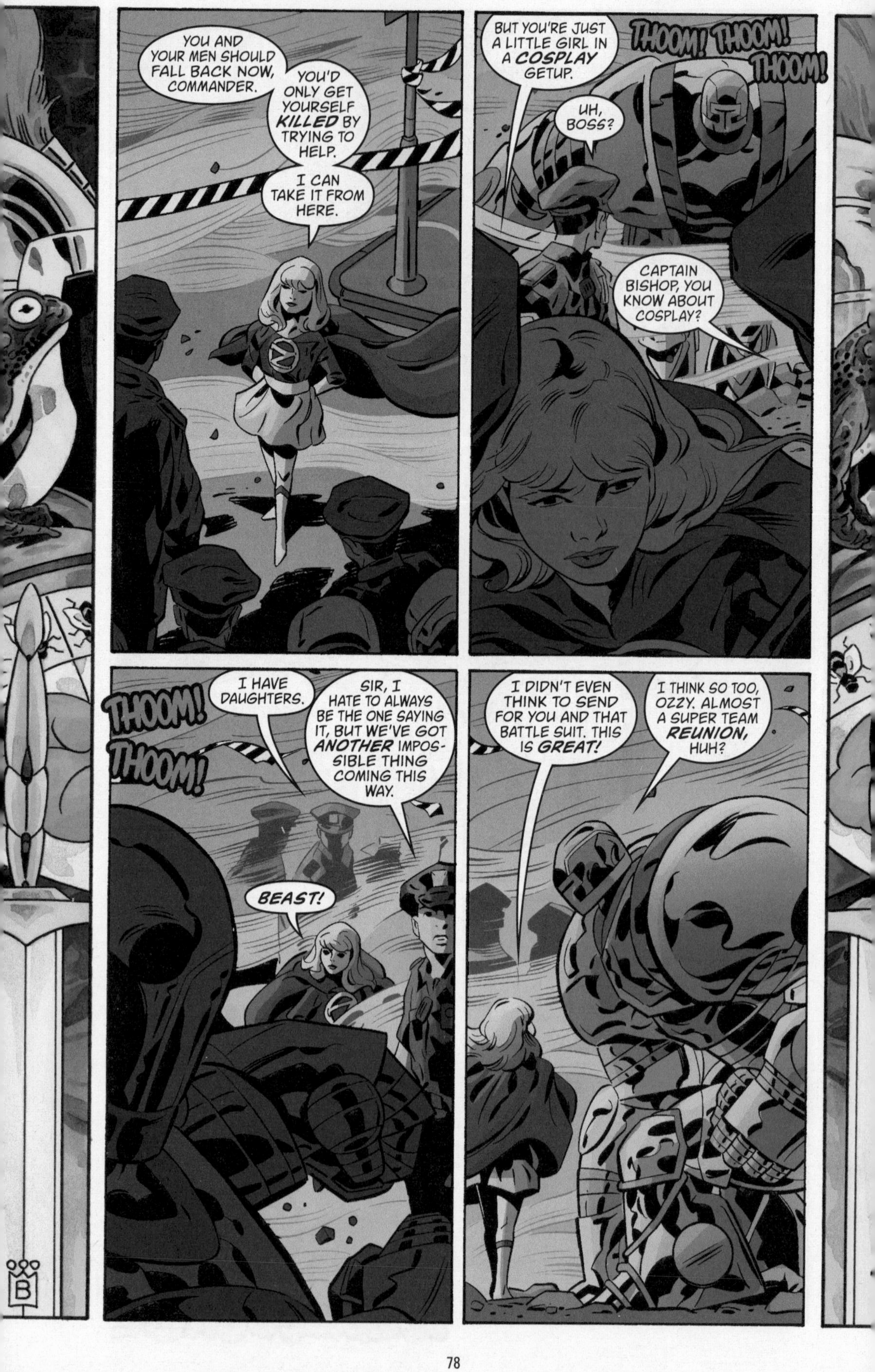
YOU AND YOUR MEN SHOULD FALL BACK NOW, COMMANDER.
YOU'D ONLY GET YOURSELF KILLED BY TRYING TO HELP.
I CAN TAKE IT FROM HERE.
BUT YOU'RE JUST A LITTLE GIRL IN A COSPLAY GETUP.
THOOM! THOOM! THOOM!
UH, BOSS?
CAPTAIN BISHOP, YOU KNOW ABOUT COSPLAY?
THOOM! THOOM!
I HAVE DAUGHTERS.
SIR, I HATE TO ALWAYS BE THE ONE SAYING IT, BUT WE'VE GOT ANOTHER IMPOSSIBLE THING COMING THIS WAY.
BEAST!
I DIDN'T EVEN THINK TO SEND FOR YOU AND THAT BATTLE SUIT. THIS IS GREAT!
I THINK SO TOO, OZZY. ALMOST A SUPER TEAM REUNION, HUH?

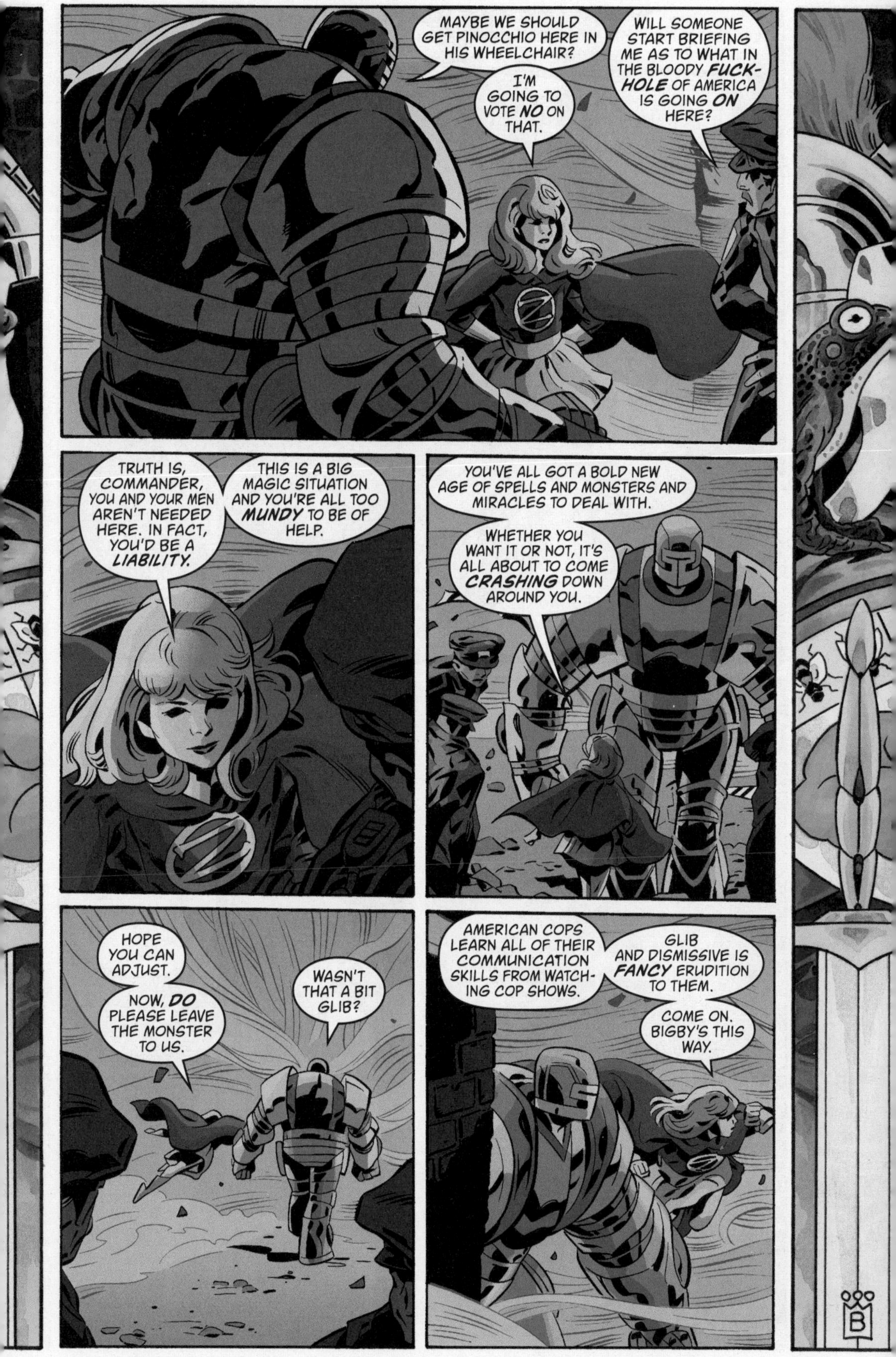
MAYBE WE SHOULD GET PINOCCHIO HERE IN HIS WHEELCHAIR?
I'M GOING TO VOTE NO ON THAT.
WILL SOMEONE START BRIEFING ME AS TO WHAT IN THE BLOODY FUCK-HOLE OF AMERICA IS GOING ON HERE?
TRUTH IS, COMMANDER, YOU AND YOUR MEN AREN'T NEEDED HERE. IN FACT, YOU'D BE A LIABILITY.
THIS IS A BIG MAGIC SITUATION AND YOU'RE ALL TOO MUNDY TO BE OF HELP.
YOU'VE ALL GOT A BOLD NEW AGE OF SPELLS AND MONSTERS AND MIRACLES TO DEAL WITH.
WHETHER YOU WANT IT OR NOT, IT'S ALL ABOUT TO COME CRASHING DOWN AROUND YOU.
HOPE YOU CAN ADJUST.
NOW, DO PLEASE LEAVE THE MONSTER TO US.
WASN'T THAT A BIT GLIB?
AMERICAN COPS LEARN ALL OF THEIR COMMUNICATION SKILLS FROM WATCHING COP SHOWS.
GLIB AND DISMISSIVE IS FANCY ERUDITION TO THEM.
COME ON. BIGBY'S THIS WAY.

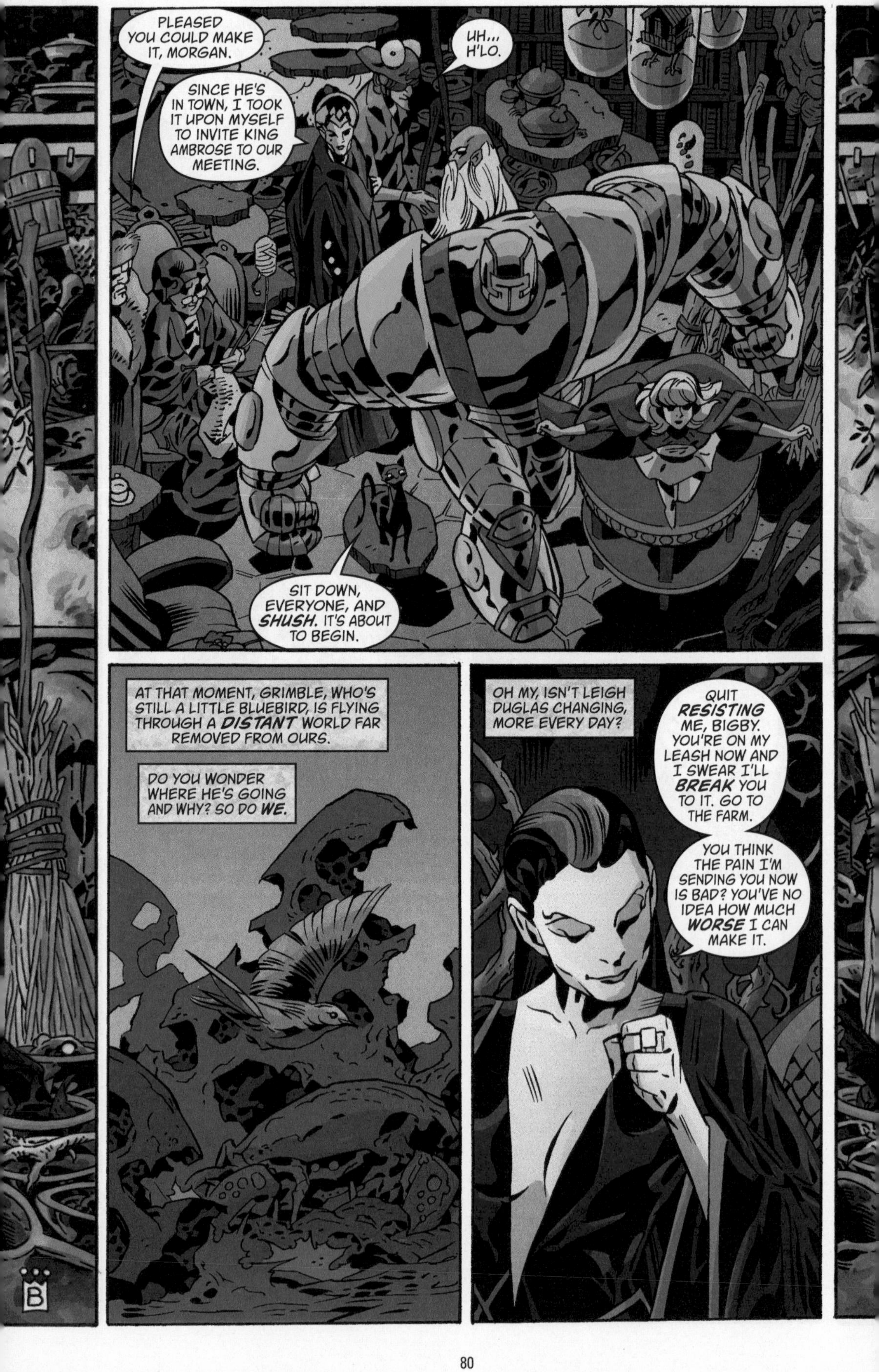
PLEASED YOU COULD MAKE IT, MORGAN.
UH... H'LO.
SINCE HE'S IN TOWN, I TOOK IT UPON MYSELF TO INVITE KING AMBROSE TO OUR MEETING.
SIT DOWN, EVERYONE, AND SHUSH. IT'S ABOUT TO BEGIN.
AT THAT MOMENT, GRIMBLE, WHO'S STILL A LITTLE BLUEBIRD, IS FLYING THROUGH A DISTANT WORLD FAR REMOVED FROM OURS.
DO YOU WONDER WHERE HE'S GOING AND WHY? SO DO WE.
OH MY, ISN'T LEIGH DUGLAS CHANGING, MORE EVERY DAY?
QUIT RESISTING ME, BIGBY. YOU'RE ON MY LEASH NOW AND I SWEAR I'LL BREAK YOU TO IT. GO TO THE FARM.
YOU THINK THE PAIN I'M SENDING YOU NOW IS BAD? YOU'VE NO IDEA HOW MUCH WORSE I CAN MAKE IT.

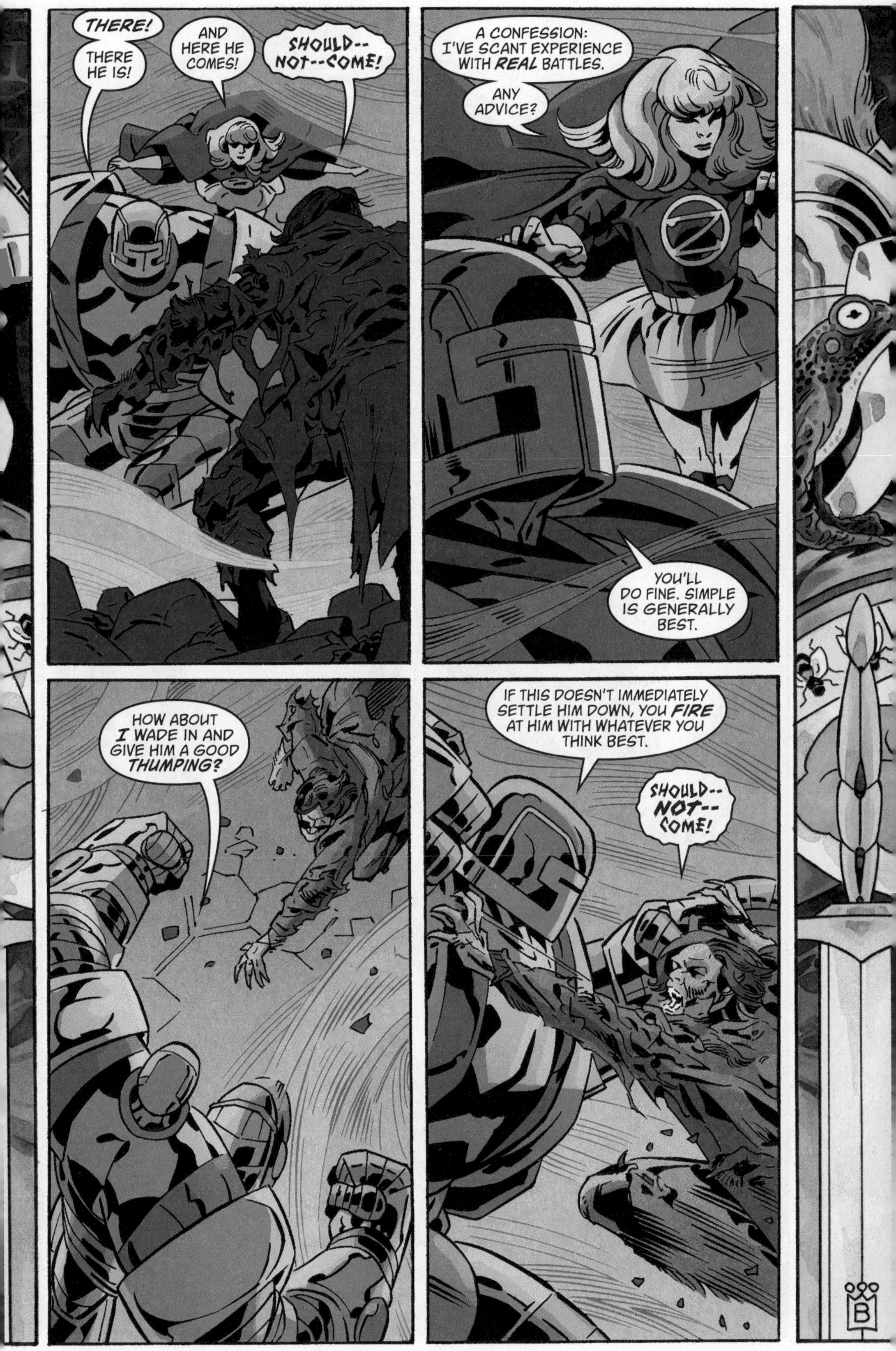
THERE! THERE HE IS!
AND HERE HE COMES!
SHOULD--NOT--COME!
A CONFESSION: I'VE SCANT EXPERIENCE WITH REAL BATTLES.
ANY ADVICE?
YOU'LL DO FINE. SIMPLE IS GENERALLY BEST.
HOW ABOUT I WADE IN AND GIVE HIM A GOOD THUMPING?
IF THIS DOESN'T IMMEDIATELY SETTLE HIM DOWN, YOU FIRE AT HIM WITH WHATEVER YOU THINK BEST.
SHOULD--NOT--COME!

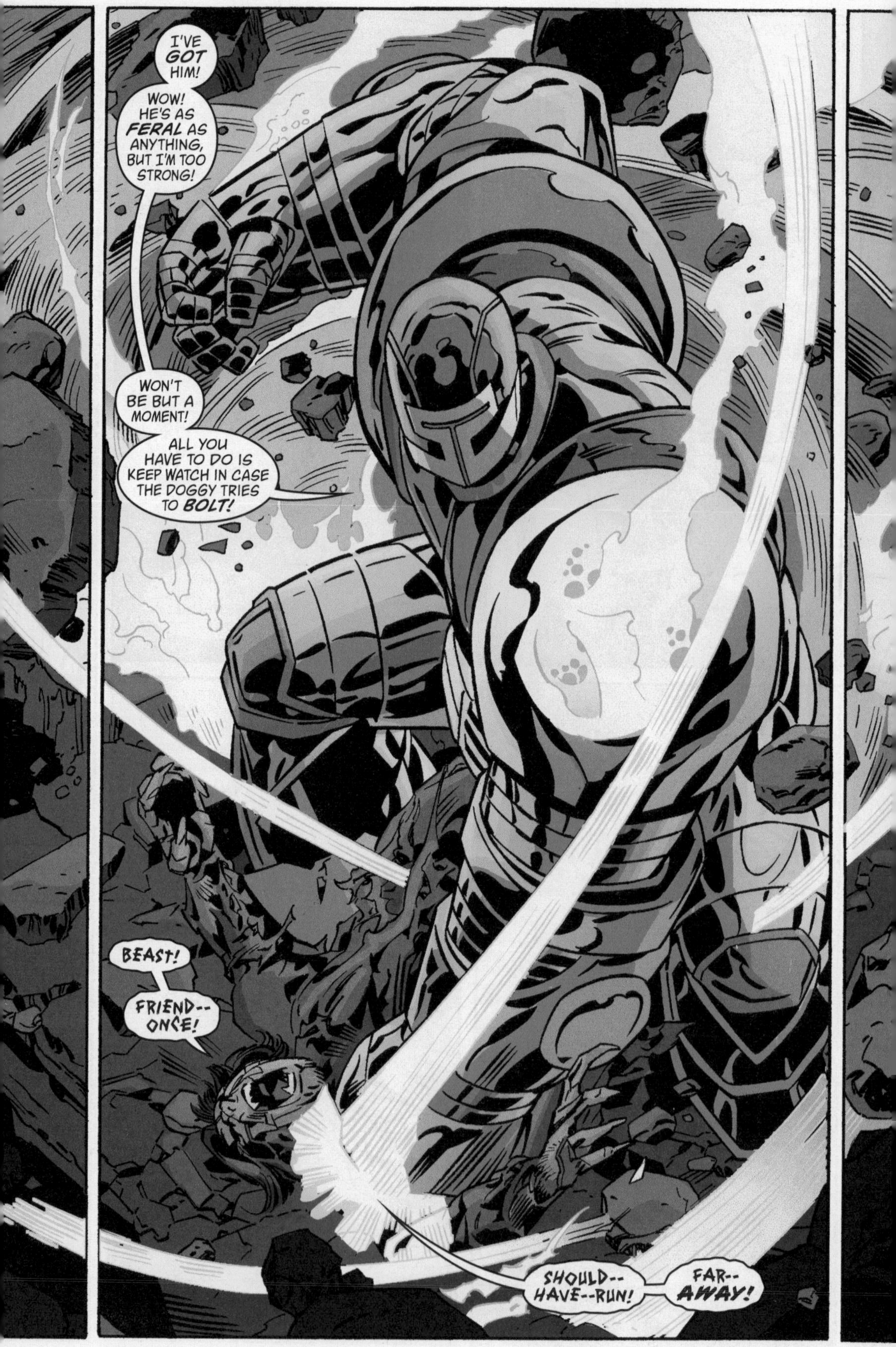
I'VE GOT HIM!
WOW! HE'S AS FERAL AS ANYTHING, BUT I'M TOO STRONG!
WON'T BE BUT A MOMENT!
ALL YOU HAVE TO DO IS KEEP WATCH IN CASE THE DOGGY TRIES TO BOLT!
BEAST!
FRIEND-- ONCE!
SHOULD-- HAVE--RUN!
FAR-- AWAY!

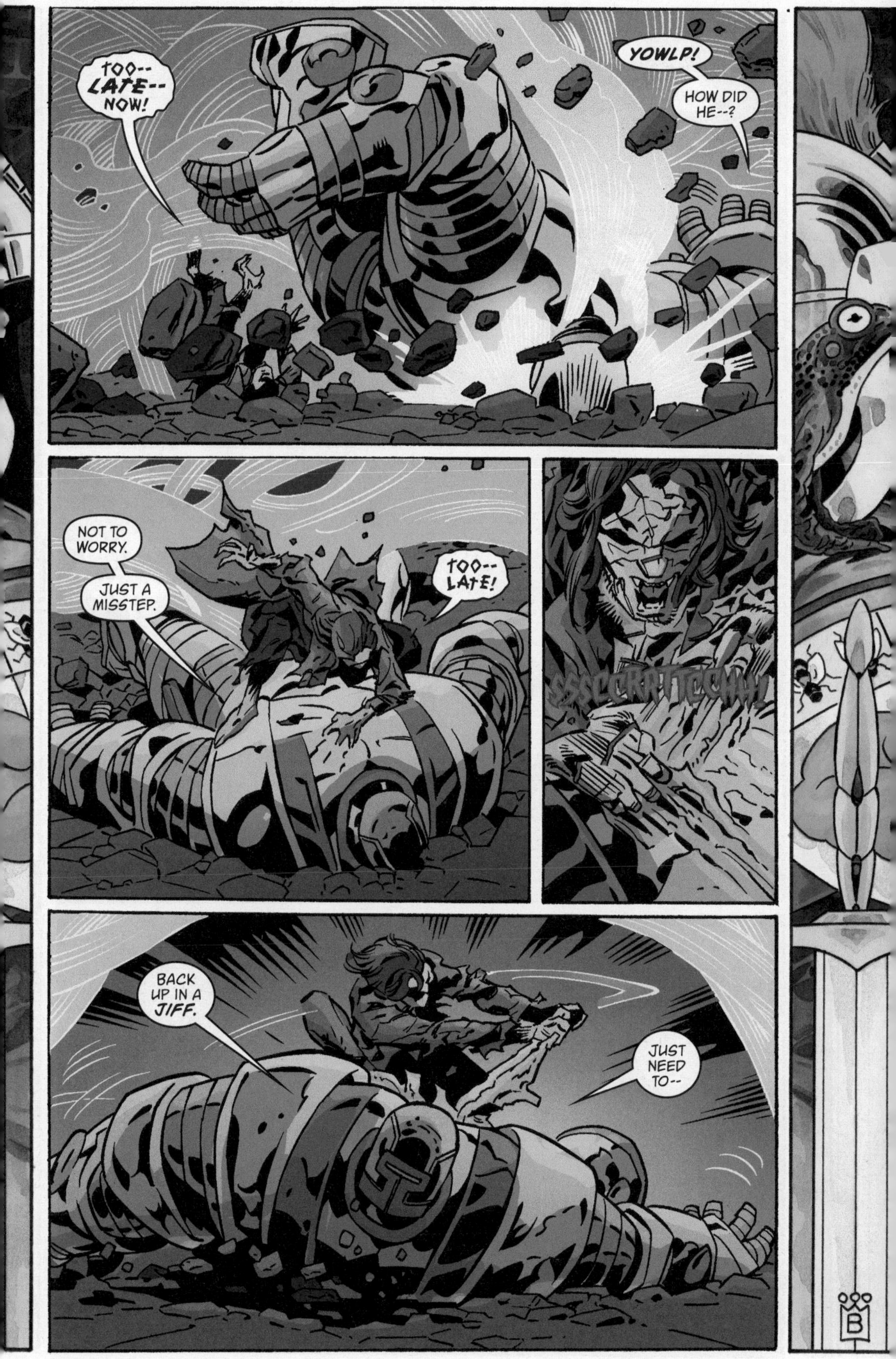
TOO--
LATE--
NOW!
YOWLP!
HOW DID HE--?
NOT TO WORRY.
JUST A MISSTEP.
TOO--
LATE!
BACK UP IN A JIFF.
JUST NEED TO--

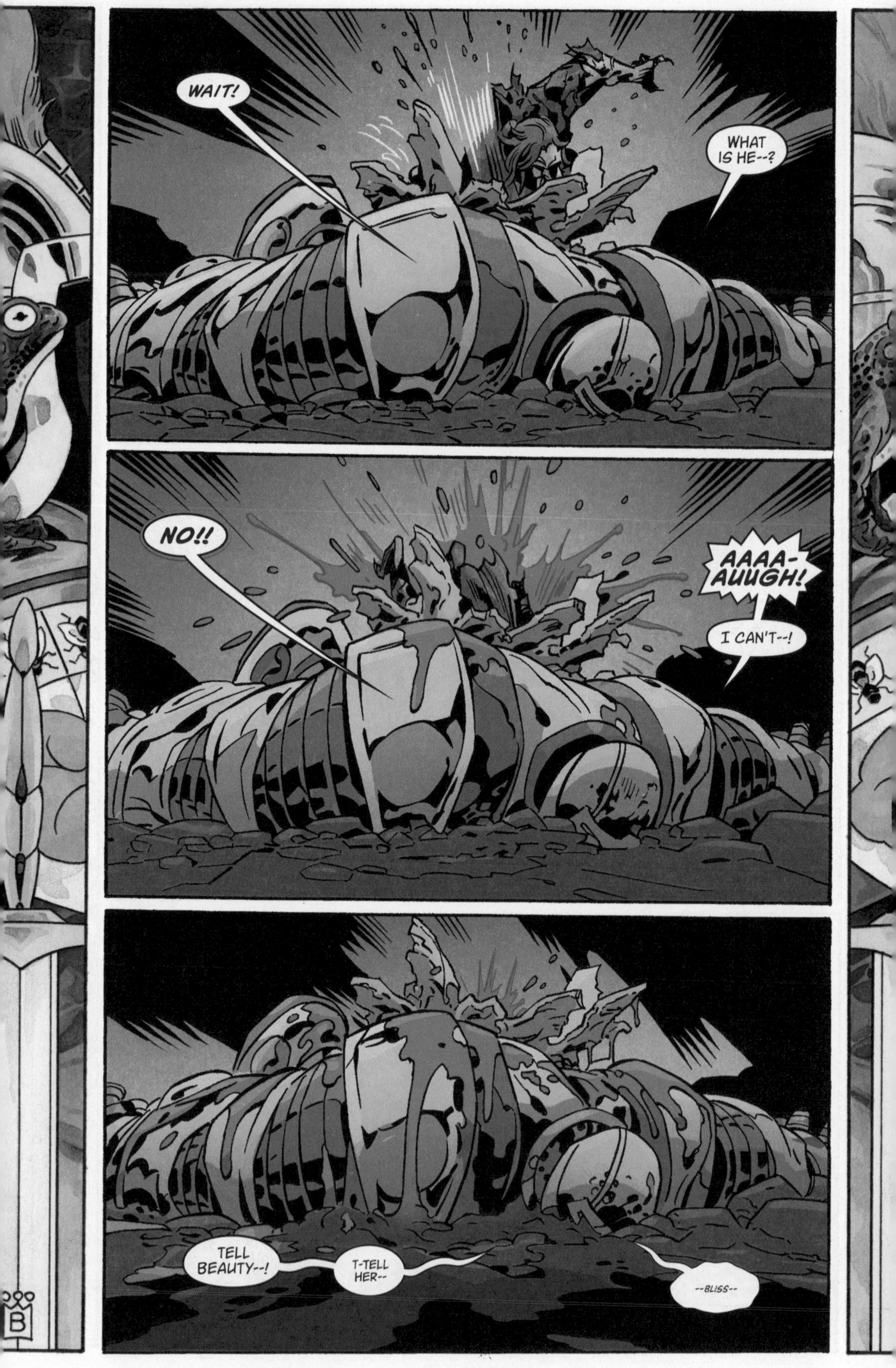
WAIT!
WHAT IS HE--?
NO!!
AAAA-AUUGH!
I CAN'T--!
TELL BEAUTY--!
T-TELL HER--
--BLISS--

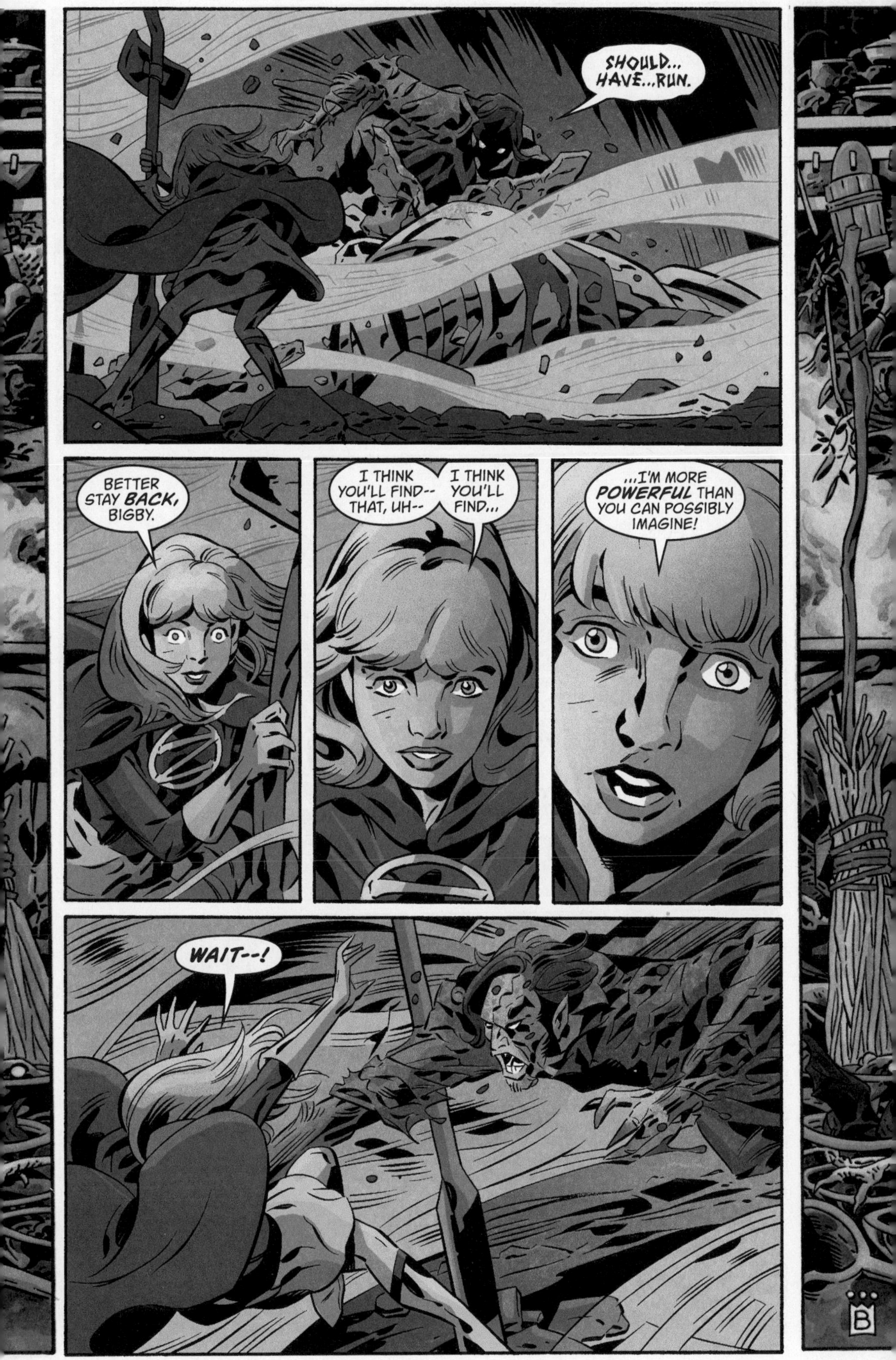
SHOULD... HAVE...RUN.
BETTER STAY BACK, BIGBY.
I THINK YOU'LL FIND-- THAT, UH--
I THINK YOU'LL FIND...
...I'M MORE POWERFUL THAN YOU CAN POSSIBLY IMAGINE!
WAIT--!

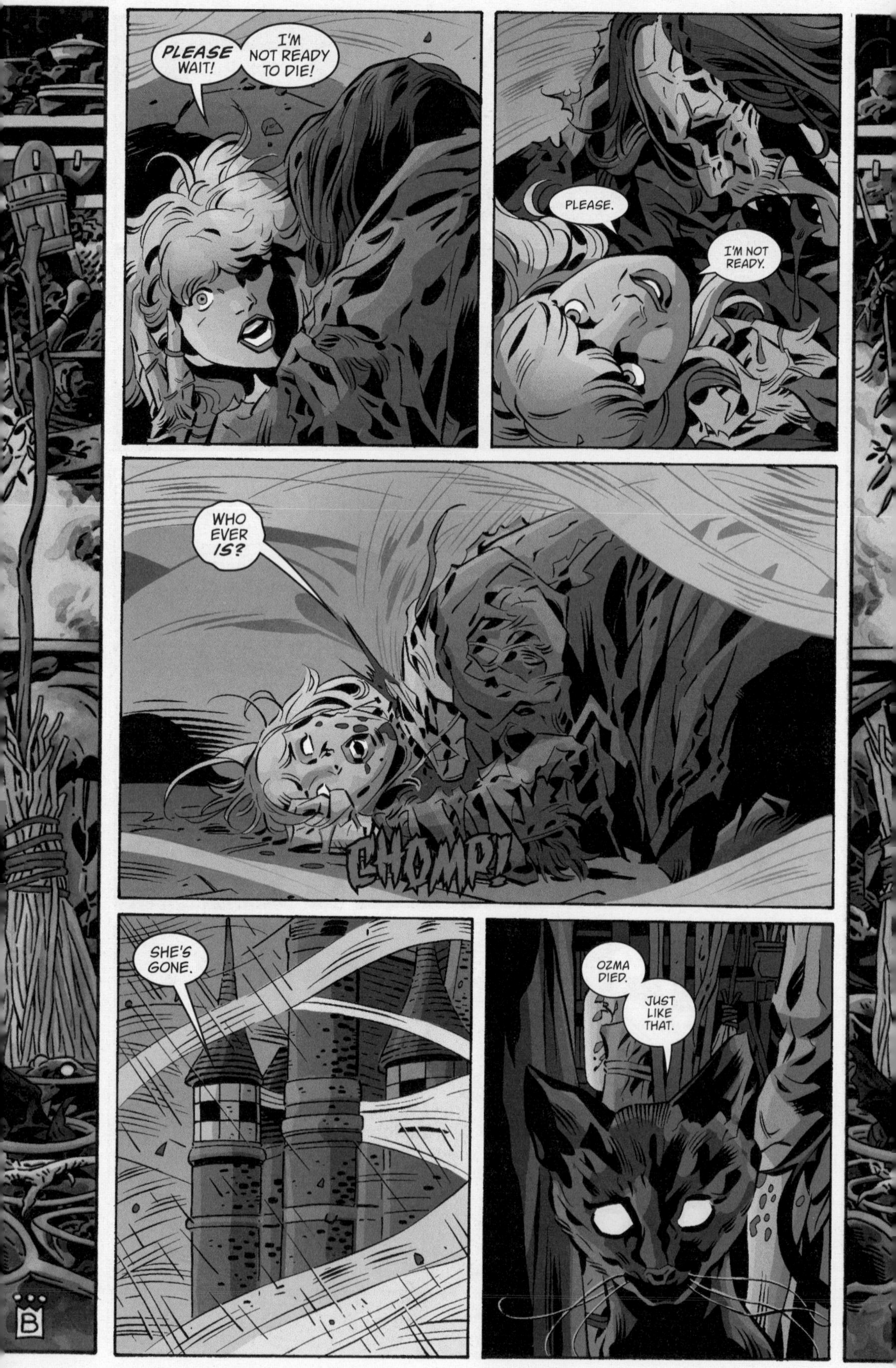
PLEASE WAIT!
I'M NOT READY TO DIE!
PLEASE.
I'M NOT READY.
WHO EVER IS?
CHOMP!
SHE'S GONE.
OZMA DIED.
JUST LIKE THAT.

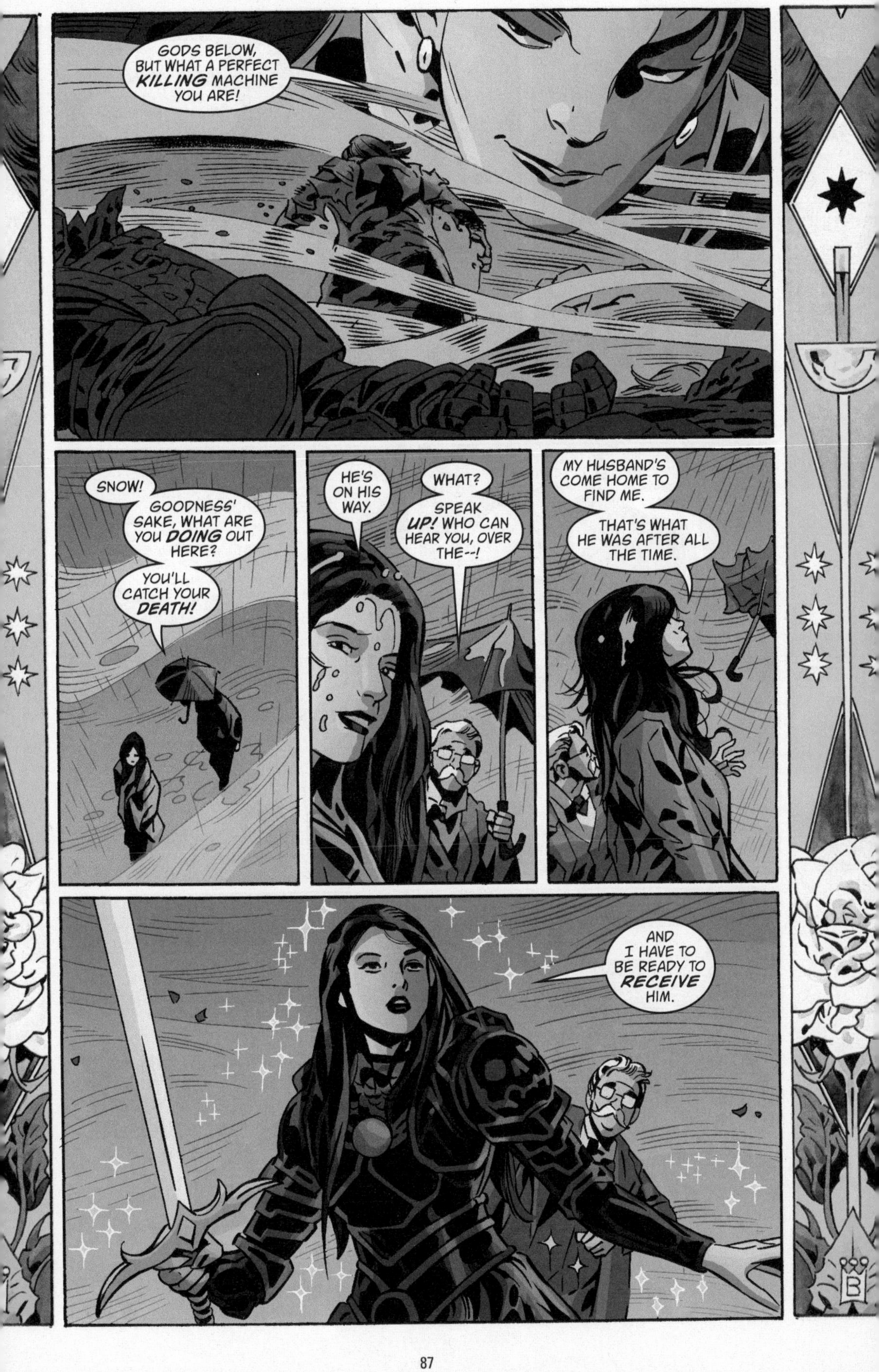
GODS BELOW, BUT WHAT A PERFECT KILLING MACHINE YOU ARE!
SNOW!
GOODNESS' SAKE, WHAT ARE YOU DOING OUT HERE?
YOU'LL CATCH YOUR DEATH!
HE'S ON HIS WAY.
WHAT?
SPEAK UP! WHO CAN HEAR YOU, OVER THE--!
MY HUSBAND'S COME HOME TO FIND ME.
THAT'S WHAT HE WAS AFTER ALL THE TIME.
AND I HAVE TO BE READY TO RECEIVE HIM.

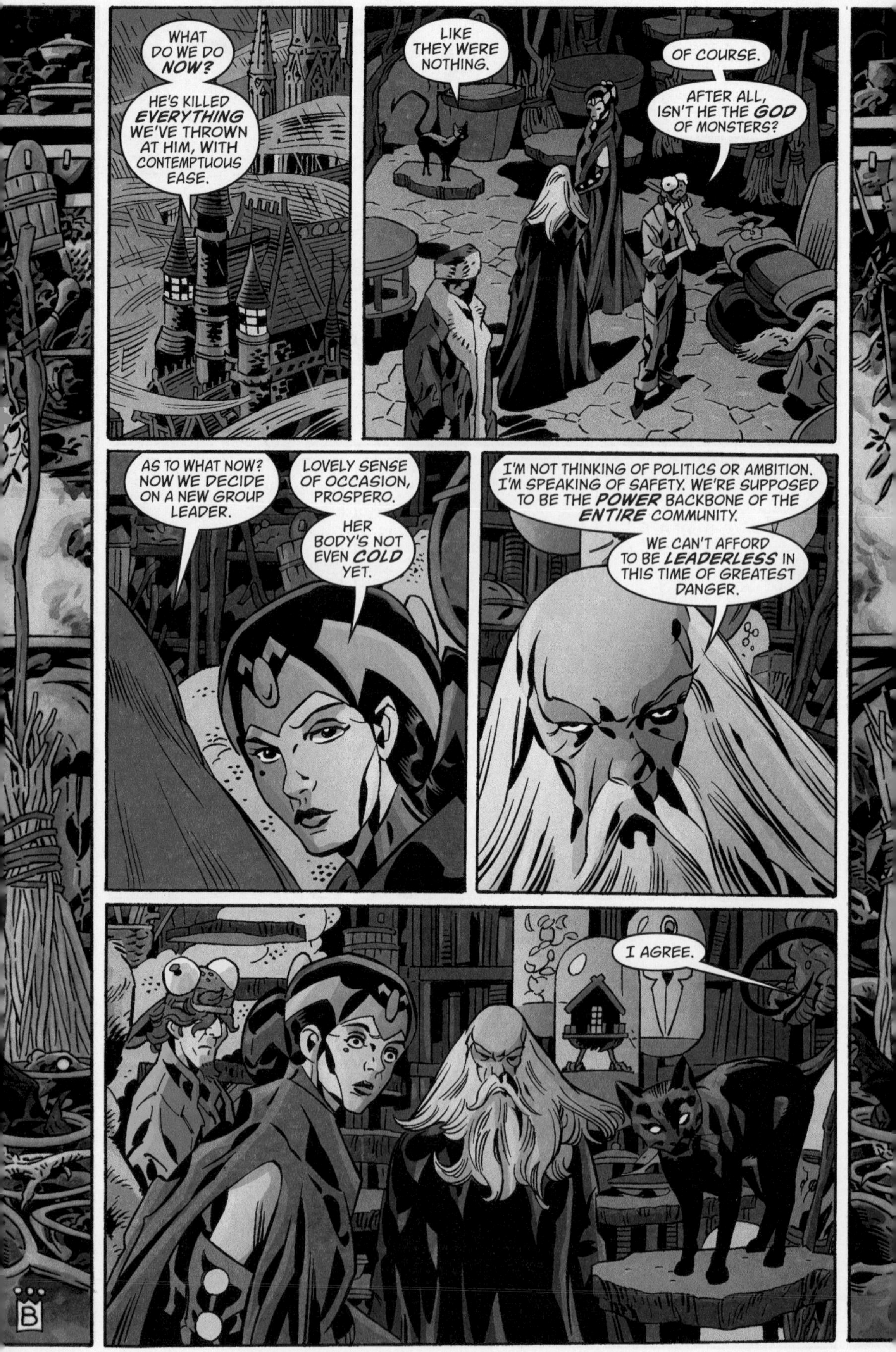
WHAT DO WE DO NOW?
HE'S KILLED EVERYTHING WE'VE THROWN AT HIM, WITH CONTEMPTUOUS EASE.
LIKE THEY WERE NOTHING.
OF COURSE.
AFTER ALL, ISN'T HE THE GOD OF MONSTERS?
AS TO WHAT NOW? NOW WE DECIDE ON A NEW GROUP LEADER.
LOVELY SENSE OF OCCASION, PROSPERO.
HER BODY'S NOT EVEN COLD YET.
I'M NOT THINKING OF POLITICS OR AMBITION. I'M SPEAKING OF SAFETY. WE'RE SUPPOSED TO BE THE POWER BACKBONE OF THE ENTIRE COMMUNITY.
WE CAN'T AFFORD TO BE LEADERLESS IN THIS TIME OF GREATEST DANGER.
I AGREE.

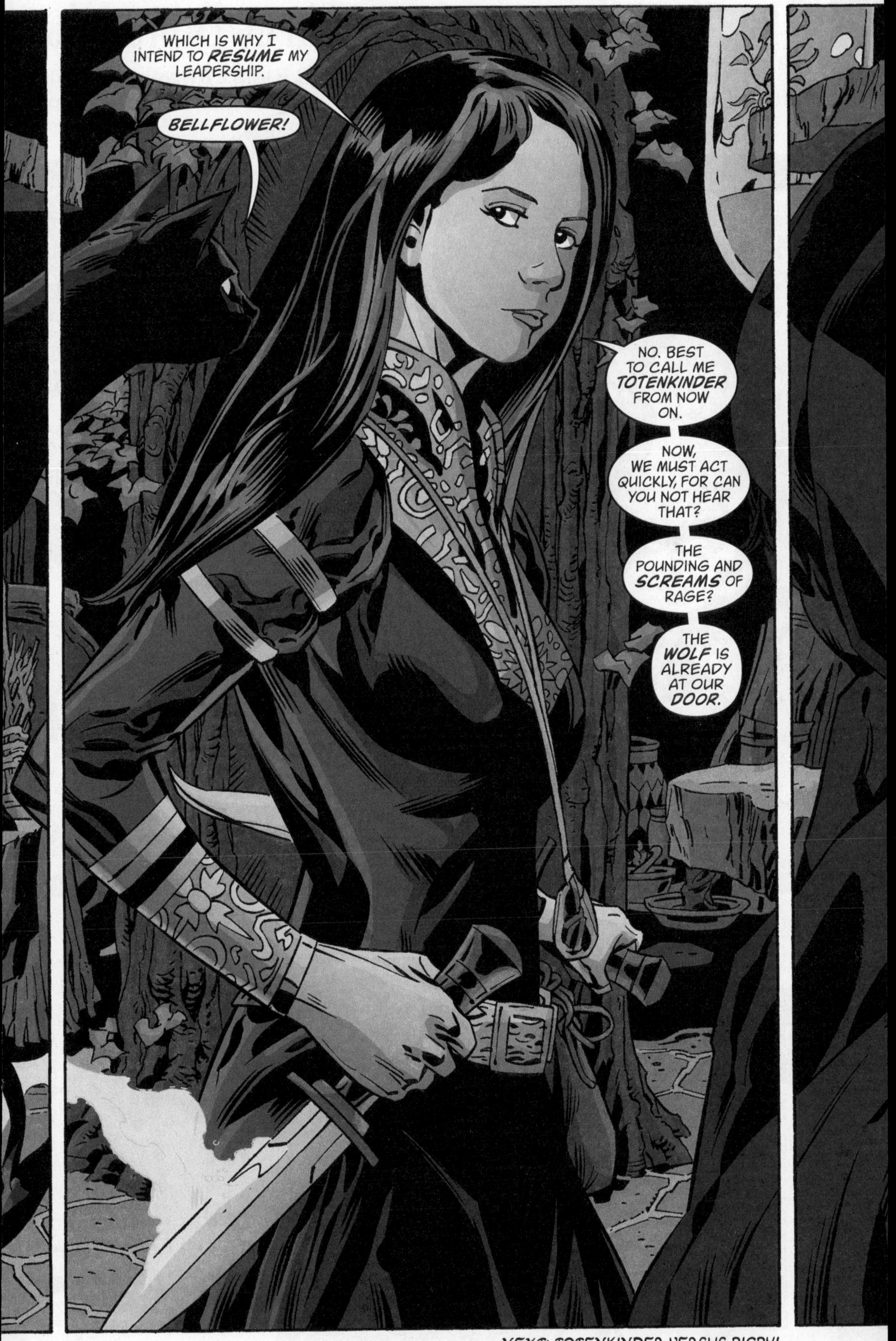
WHICH IS WHY I INTEND TO RESUME MY LEADERSHIP.
BELLFLOWER!
NO. BEST TO CALL ME TOTENKINDER FROM NOW ON.
NOW, WE MUST ACT QUICKLY, FOR CAN YOU NOT HEAR THAT?
THE POUNDING AND SCREAMS OF RAGE?
THE WOLF IS ALREADY AT OUR DOOR.

NEXT: TOTENKINDER VERSUS BIGBY!

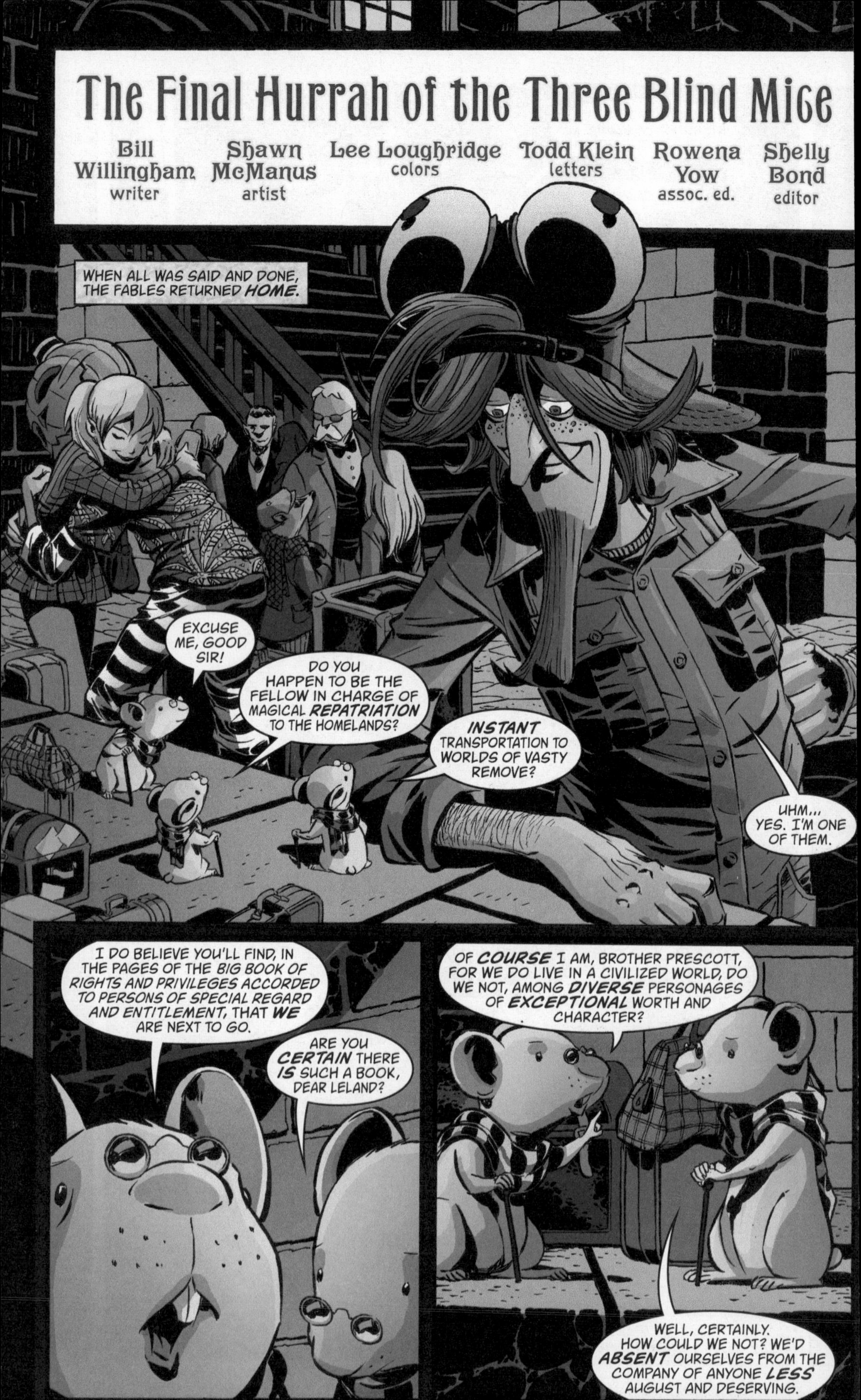

The Final Hurrah of the Three Blind Mice
Bill Willingham writer
Shawn McManus artist
Lee Loughridge colors
Todd Klein letters
Rowena Yow assoc. ed.
Shelly Bond editor
WHEN ALL WAS SAID AND DONE, THE FABLES RETURNED HOME.
EXCUSE ME, GOOD SIR!
DO YOU HAPPEN TO BE THE FELLOW IN CHARGE OF MAGICAL REPATRIATION TO THE HOMELANDS?
INSTANT TRANSPORTATION TO WORLDS OF VASTY REMOVE?
UHM... YES. I'M ONE OF THEM.
I DO BELIEVE YOU'LL FIND, IN THE PAGES OF THE BIG BOOK OF RIGHTS AND PRIVILEGES ACCORDED TO PERSONS OF SPECIAL REGARD AND ENTITLEMENT, THAT WE ARE NEXT TO GO.
ARE YOU CERTAIN THERE IS SUCH A BOOK, DEAR LELAND?
OF COURSE I AM, BROTHER PRESCOTT, FOR WE DO LIVE IN A CIVILIZED WORLD, DO WE NOT, AMONG DIVERSE PERSONAGES OF EXCEPTIONAL WORTH AND CHARACTER?
WELL, CERTAINLY. HOW COULD WE NOT? WE'D ABSENT OURSELVES FROM THE COMPANY OF ANYONE LESS AUGUST AND DESERVING.

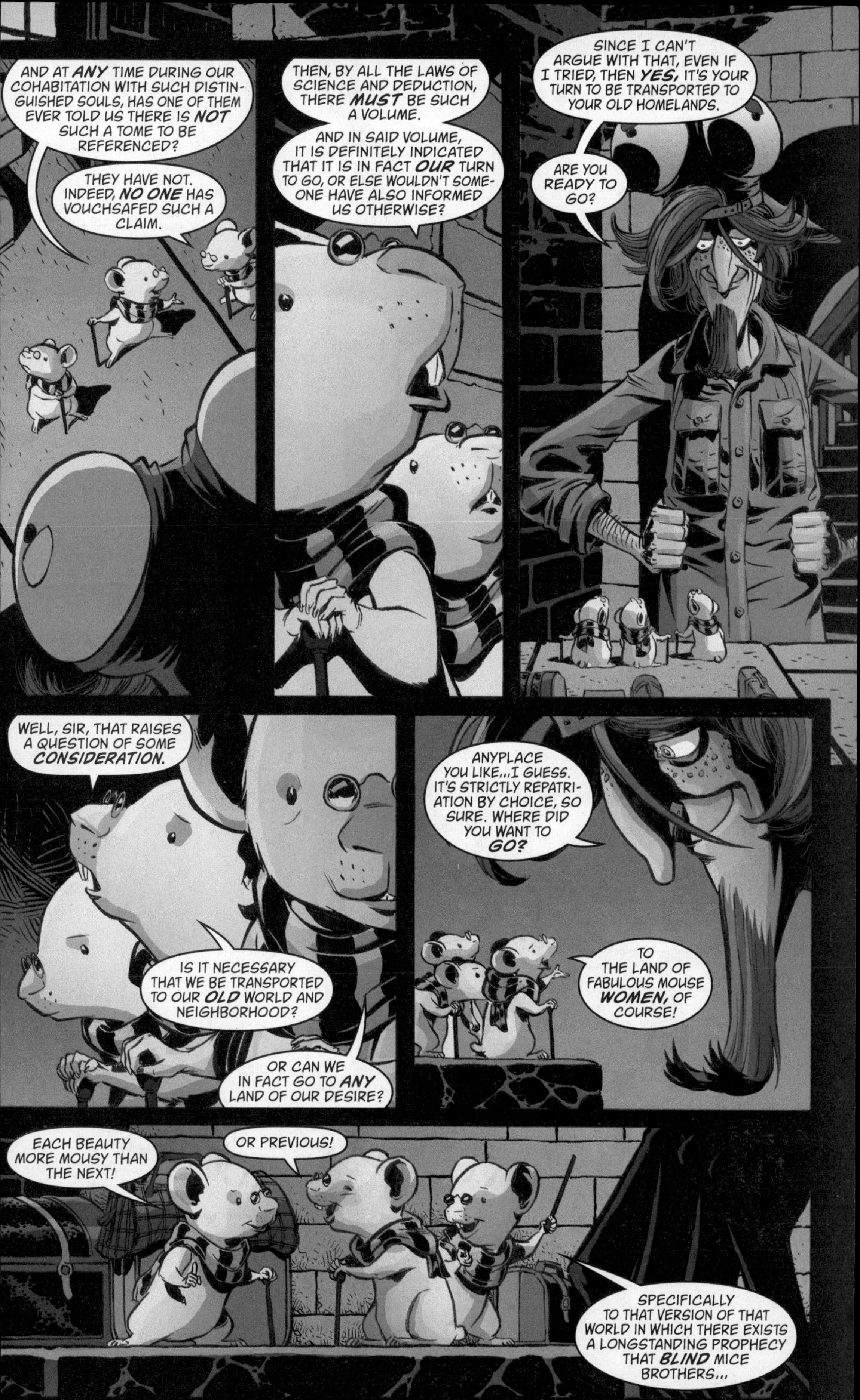
AND AT ANY TIME DURING OUR COHABITATION WITH SUCH DISTINGUISHED SOULS, HAS ONE OF THEM EVER TOLD US THERE IS NOT SUCH A TOME TO BE REFERENCED?
THEY HAVE NOT. INDEED, NO ONE HAS VOUCHSAFED SUCH A CLAIM.
THEN, BY ALL THE LAWS OF SCIENCE AND DEDUCTION, THERE MUST BE SUCH A VOLUME.
AND IN SAID VOLUME, IT IS DEFINITELY INDICATED THAT IT IS IN FACT OUR TURN TO GO, OR ELSE WOULDN'T SOMEONE HAVE ALSO INFORMED US OTHERWISE?
SINCE I CAN'T ARGUE WITH THAT, EVEN IF I TRIED, THEN YES, IT'S YOUR TURN TO BE TRANSPORTED TO YOUR OLD HOMELANDS.
ARE YOU READY TO GO?
WELL, SIR, THAT RAISES A QUESTION OF SOME CONSIDERATION.
IS IT NECESSARY THAT WE BE TRANSPORTED TO OUR OLD WORLD AND NEIGHBORHOOD?
OR CAN WE IN FACT GO TO ANY LAND OF OUR DESIRE?
ANYPLACE YOU LIKE...I GUESS. IT'S STRICTLY REPATRIATION BY CHOICE, SO SURE. WHERE DID YOU WANT TO GO?
TO THE LAND OF FABULOUS MOUSE WOMEN, OF COURSE!
EACH BEAUTY MORE MOUSY THAN THE NEXT!
OR PREVIOUS!
SPECIFICALLY TO THAT VERSION OF THAT WORLD IN WHICH THERE EXISTS A LONGSTANDING PROPHECY THAT BLIND MICE BROTHERS...

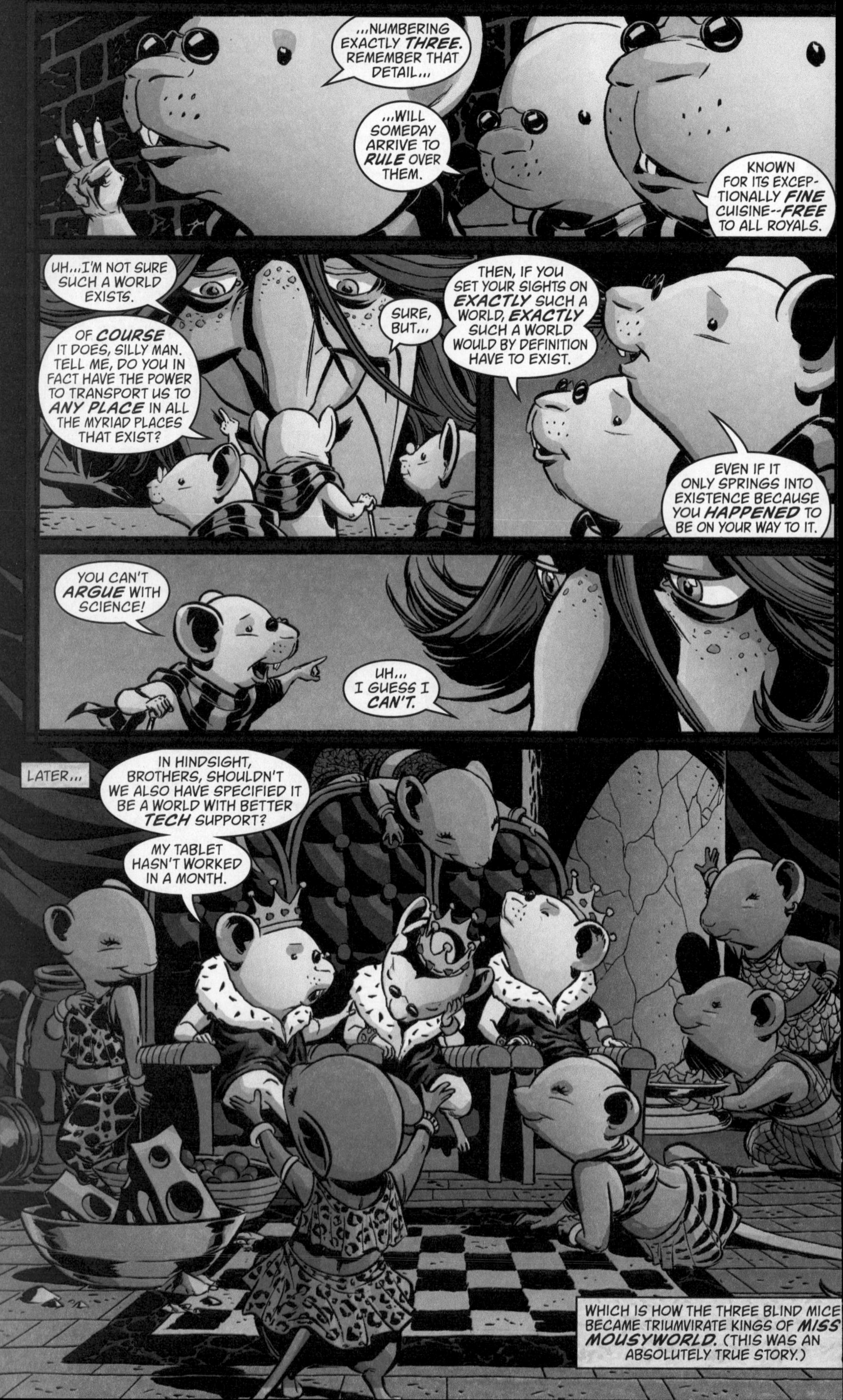

...NUMBERING EXACTLY THREE. REMEMBER THAT DETAIL...
...WILL SOMEDAY ARRIVE TO RULE OVER THEM.
KNOWN FOR ITS EXCEPTIONALLY FINE CUISINE--FREE TO ALL ROYALS.
UH...I'M NOT SURE SUCH A WORLD EXISTS.
OF COURSE IT DOES, SILLY MAN. TELL ME, DO YOU IN FACT HAVE THE POWER TO TRANSPORT US TO ANY PLACE IN ALL THE MYRIAD PLACES THAT EXIST?
SURE, BUT...
THEN, IF YOU SET YOUR SIGHTS ON EXACTLY SUCH A WORLD, EXACTLY SUCH A WORLD WOULD BY DEFINITION HAVE TO EXIST.
EVEN IF IT ONLY SPRINGS INTO EXISTENCE BECAUSE YOU HAPPENED TO BE ON YOUR WAY TO IT.
YOU CAN'T ARGUE WITH SCIENCE!
UH... I GUESS I CAN'T.
LATER...
IN HINDSIGHT, BROTHERS, SHOULDN'T WE ALSO HAVE SPECIFIED IT BE A WORLD WITH BETTER TECH SUPPORT?
MY TABLET HASN'T WORKED IN A MONTH.
WHICH IS HOW THE THREE BLIND MICE BECAME TRIUMVIRATE KINGS OF MISS MOUSYWORLD. (THIS WAS AN ABSOLUTELY TRUE STORY.)

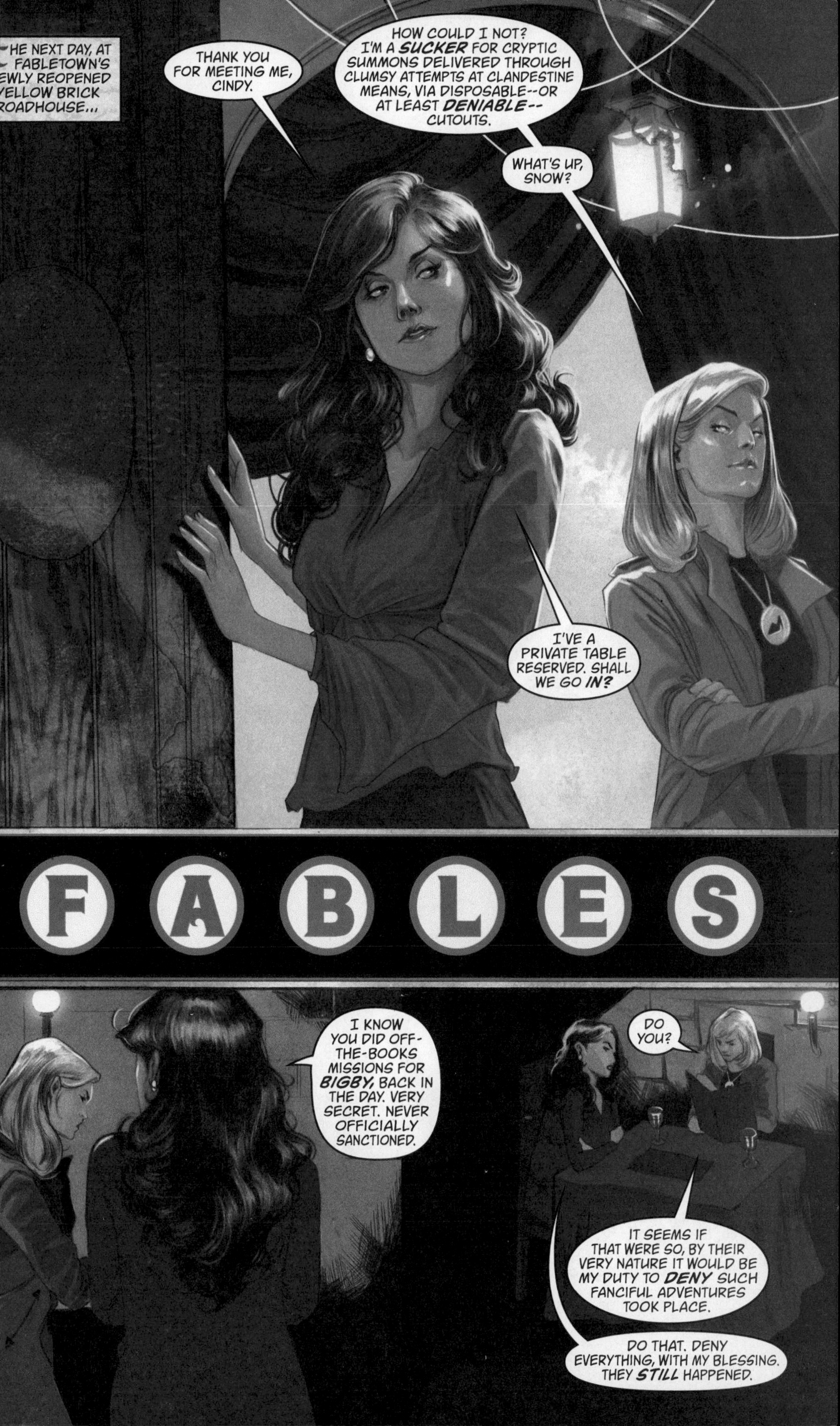
THE NEXT DAY, AT FABLETOWN'S NEWLY REOPENED YELLOW BRICK ROADHOUSE...
THANK YOU FOR MEETING ME, CINDY.
HOW COULD I NOT? I'M A SUCKER FOR CRYPTIC SUMMONS DELIVERED THROUGH CLUMSY ATTEMPTS AT CLANDESTINE MEANS, VIA DISPOSABLE--OR AT LEAST DENIABLE--CUTOUTS.
WHAT'S UP, SNOW?
I'VE A PRIVATE TABLE RESERVED. SHALL WE GO IN?
FABLES
I KNOW YOU DID OFF-THE-BOOKS MISSIONS FOR BIGBY, BACK IN THE DAY. VERY SECRET. NEVER OFFICIALLY SANCTIONED.
DO YOU?
IT SEEMS IF THAT WERE SO, BY THEIR VERY NATURE IT WOULD BE MY DUTY TO DENY SUCH FANCIFUL ADVENTURES TOOK PLACE.
DO THAT. DENY EVERYTHING, WITH MY BLESSING. THEY STILL HAPPENED.

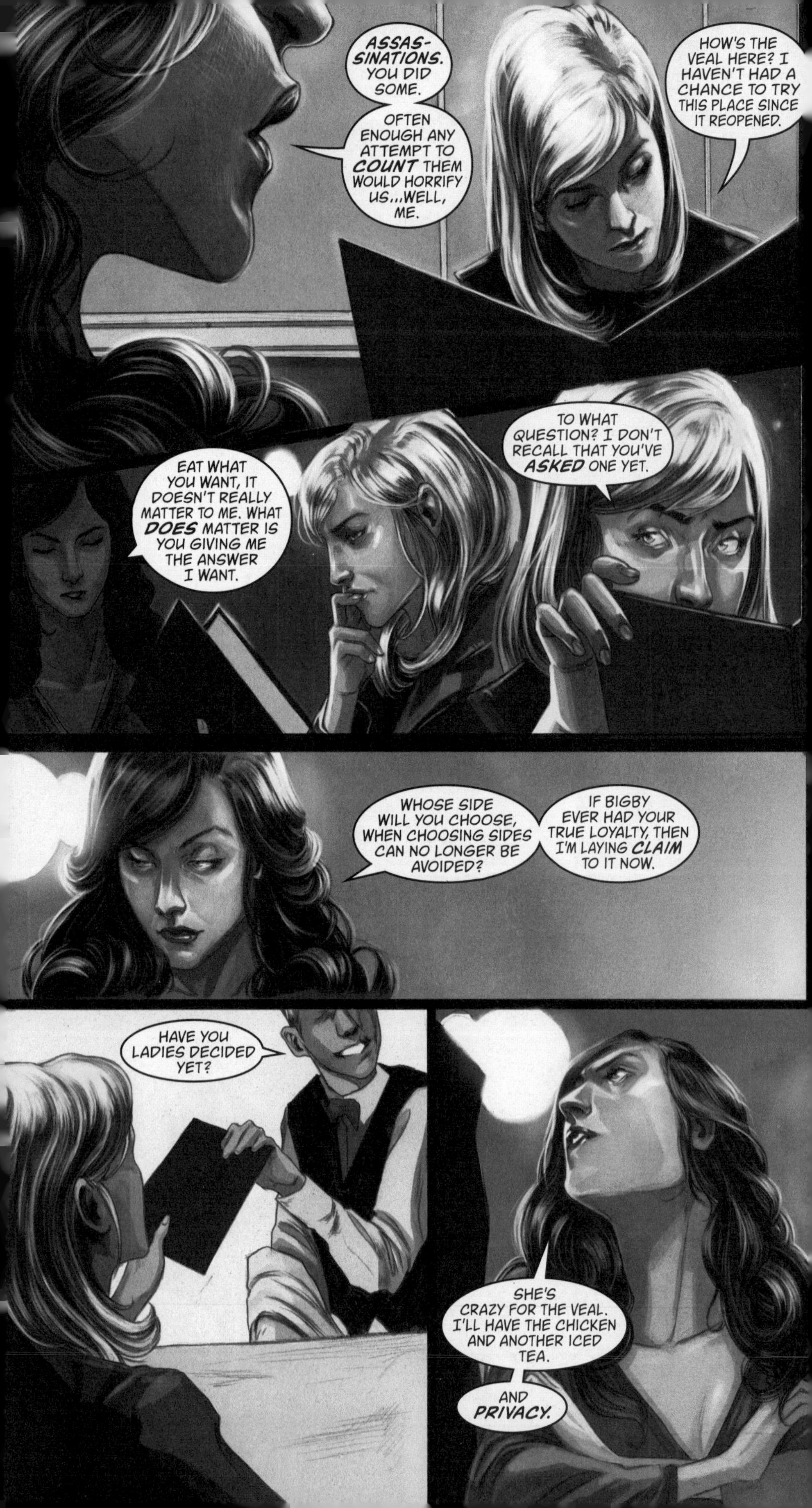
ASSAS-SINATIONS. YOU DID SOME.
OFTEN ENOUGH ANY ATTEMPT TO COUNT THEM WOULD HORRIFY US...WELL, ME.
HOW'S THE VEAL HERE? I HAVEN'T HAD A CHANCE TO TRY THIS PLACE SINCE IT REOPENED.
EAT WHAT YOU WANT, IT DOESN'T REALLY MATTER TO ME. WHAT DOES MATTER IS YOU GIVING ME THE ANSWER I WANT.
TO WHAT QUESTION? I DON'T RECALL THAT YOU'VE ASKED ONE YET.
WHOSE SIDE WILL YOU CHOOSE, WHEN CHOOSING SIDES CAN NO LONGER BE AVOIDED?
IF BIGBY EVER HAD YOUR TRUE LOYALTY, THEN I'M LAYING CLAIM TO IT NOW.
HAVE YOU LADIES DECIDED YET?
SHE'S CRAZY FOR THE VEAL. I'LL HAVE THE CHICKEN AND ANOTHER ICED TEA.
AND PRIVACY.

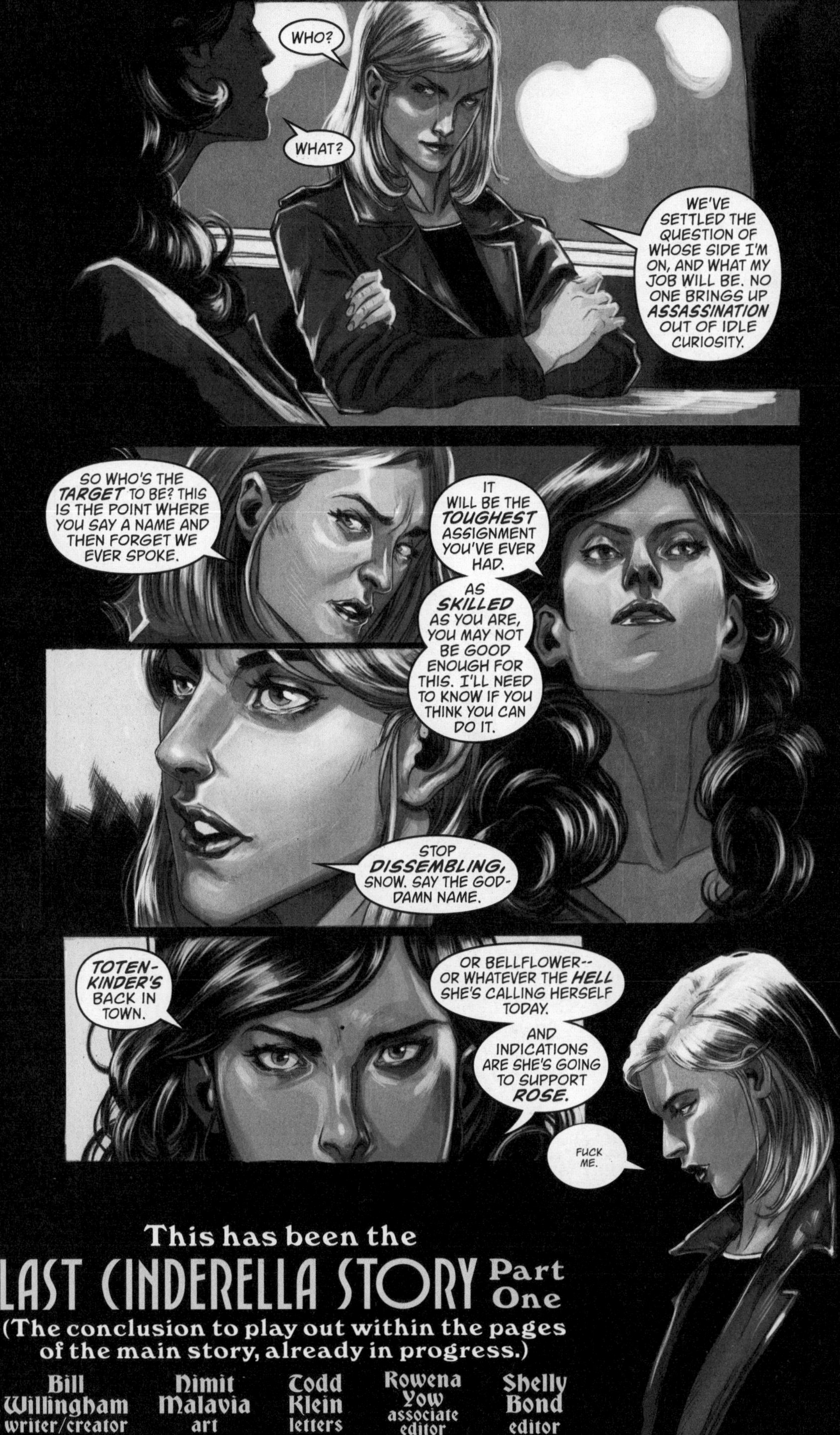
WHO?
WHAT?
WE'VE SETTLED THE QUESTION OF WHOSE SIDE I'M ON, AND WHAT MY JOB WILL BE. NO ONE BRINGS UP ASSASSINATION OUT OF IDLE CURIOSITY.
SO WHO'S THE TARGET TO BE? THIS IS THE POINT WHERE YOU SAY A NAME AND THEN FORGET WE EVER SPOKE.
IT WILL BE THE TOUGHEST ASSIGNMENT YOU'VE EVER HAD.
AS SKILLED AS YOU ARE, YOU MAY NOT BE GOOD ENOUGH FOR THIS. I'LL NEED TO KNOW IF YOU THINK YOU CAN DO IT.
STOP DISSEMBLING, SNOW. SAY THE GOD-DAMN NAME.
TOTEN-KINDER'S BACK IN TOWN.
OR BELLFLOWER-- OR WHATEVER THE HELL SHE'S CALLING HERSELF TODAY.
AND INDICATIONS ARE SHE'S GOING TO SUPPORT ROSE.
FUCK ME.

This has been the

LAST CINDERELLA STORY Part One

(The conclusion to play out within the pages of the main story, already in progress.)

Bill Willingham writer/creator | Nimit Malavia art | Todd Klein letters | Rowena Yow associate editor | Shelly Bond editor

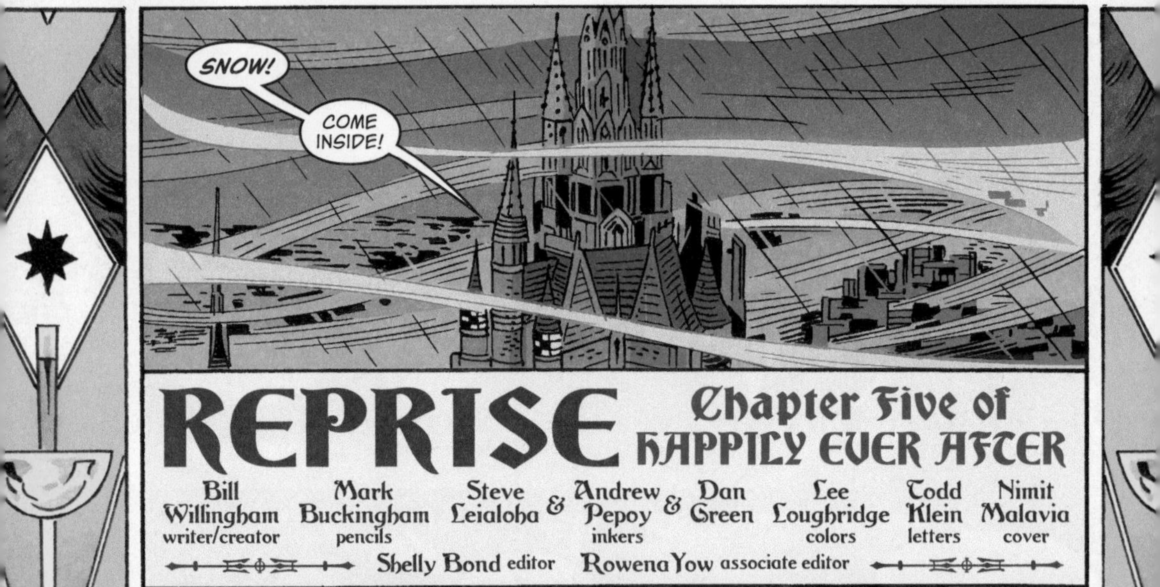
SNOW!
COME INSIDE!

REPRISE
Chapter Five of HAPPILY EVER AFTER

Bill Willingham writer/creator
Mark Buckingham pencils
Steve Leialoha & Andrew Pepoy & Dan Green inkers
Lee Loughridge colors
Todd Klein letters
Nimit Malavia cover
Shelly Bond editor Rowena Yow associate editor

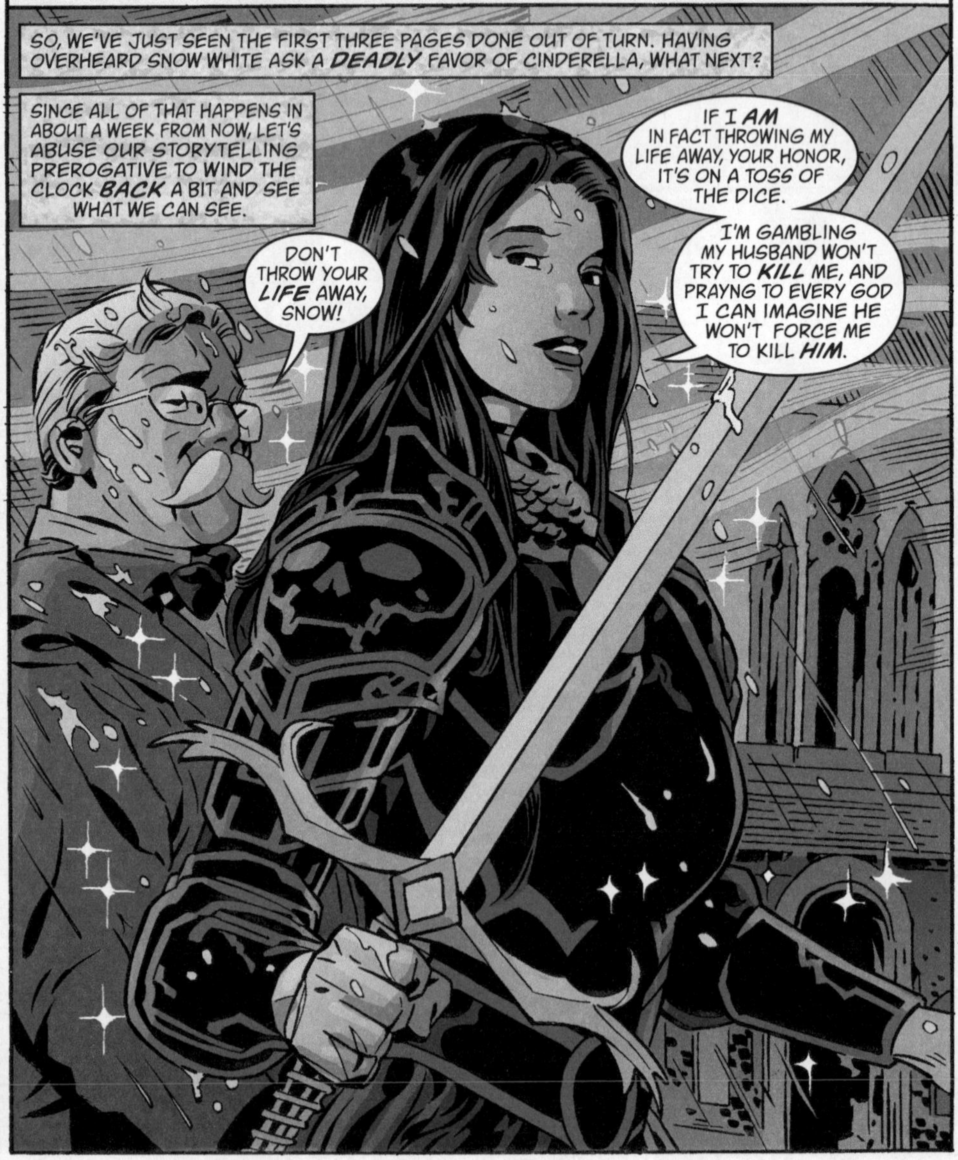
SO, WE'VE JUST SEEN THE FIRST THREE PAGES DONE OUT OF TURN. HAVING OVERHEARD SNOW WHITE ASK A DEADLY FAVOR OF CINDERELLA, WHAT NEXT?
SINCE ALL OF THAT HAPPENS IN ABOUT A WEEK FROM NOW, LET'S ABUSE OUR STORYTELLING PREROGATIVE TO WIND THE CLOCK BACK A BIT AND SEE WHAT WE CAN SEE.
DON'T THROW YOUR LIFE AWAY, SNOW!
IF I AM IN FACT THROWING MY LIFE AWAY, YOUR HONOR, IT'S ON A TOSS OF THE DICE.
I'M GAMBLING MY HUSBAND WON'T TRY TO KILL ME, AND PRAYNG TO EVERY GOD I CAN IMAGINE HE WON'T FORCE ME TO KILL HIM.

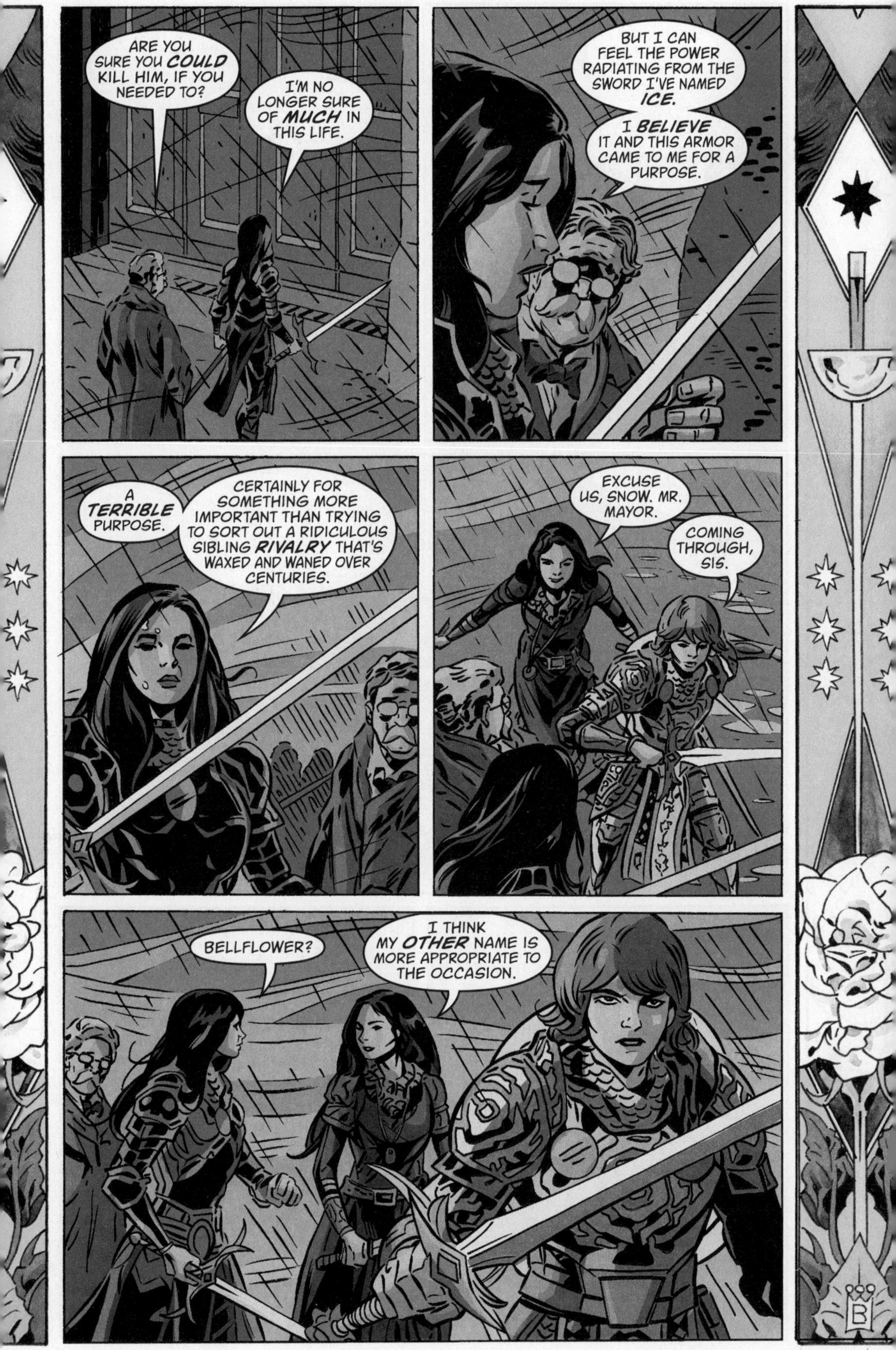
ARE YOU SURE YOU COULD KILL HIM, IF YOU NEEDED TO?
I'M NO LONGER SURE OF MUCH IN THIS LIFE.
BUT I CAN FEEL THE POWER RADIATING FROM THE SWORD I'VE NAMED ICE.
I BELIEVE IT AND THIS ARMOR CAME TO ME FOR A PURPOSE.
A TERRIBLE PURPOSE.
CERTAINLY FOR SOMETHING MORE IMPORTANT THAN TRYING TO SORT OUT A RIDICULOUS SIBLING RIVALRY THAT'S WAXED AND WANED OVER CENTURIES.
EXCUSE US, SNOW. MR. MAYOR.
COMING THROUGH, SIS.
BELLFLOWER?
I THINK MY OTHER NAME IS MORE APPROPRIATE TO THE OCCASION.

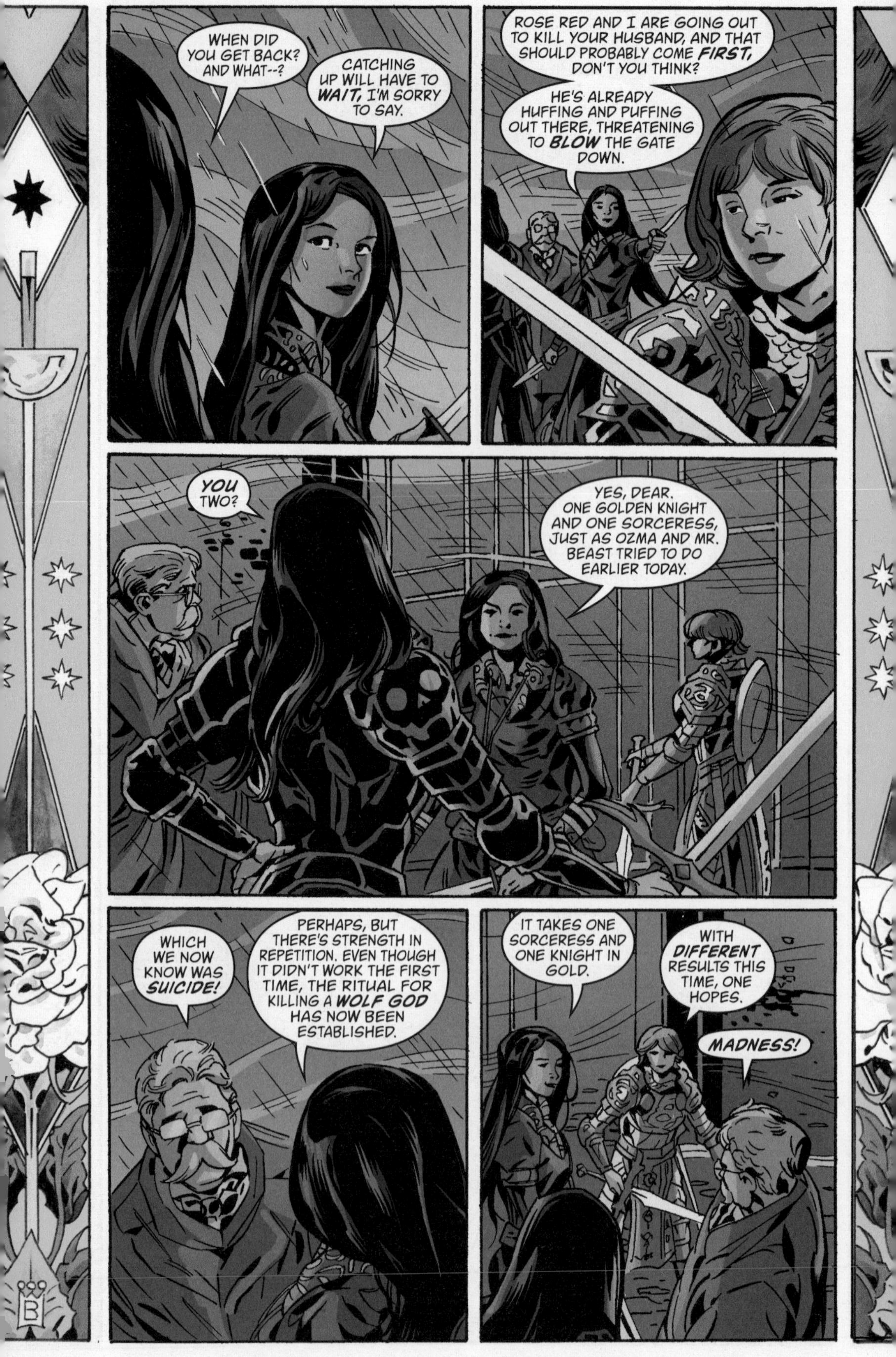
WHEN DID YOU GET BACK? AND WHAT--?
CATCHING UP WILL HAVE TO WAIT, I'M SORRY TO SAY.
ROSE RED AND I ARE GOING OUT TO KILL YOUR HUSBAND, AND THAT SHOULD PROBABLY COME FIRST, DON'T YOU THINK?
HE'S ALREADY HUFFING AND PUFFING OUT THERE, THREATENING TO BLOW THE GATE DOWN.
YOU TWO?
YES, DEAR. ONE GOLDEN KNIGHT AND ONE SORCERESS, JUST AS OZMA AND MR. BEAST TRIED TO DO EARLIER TODAY.
WHICH WE NOW KNOW WAS SUICIDE!
PERHAPS, BUT THERE'S STRENGTH IN REPETITION. EVEN THOUGH IT DIDN'T WORK THE FIRST TIME, THE RITUAL FOR KILLING A WOLF GOD HAS NOW BEEN ESTABLISHED.
IT TAKES ONE SORCERESS AND ONE KNIGHT IN GOLD.
WITH DIFFERENT RESULTS THIS TIME, ONE HOPES.
MADNESS!

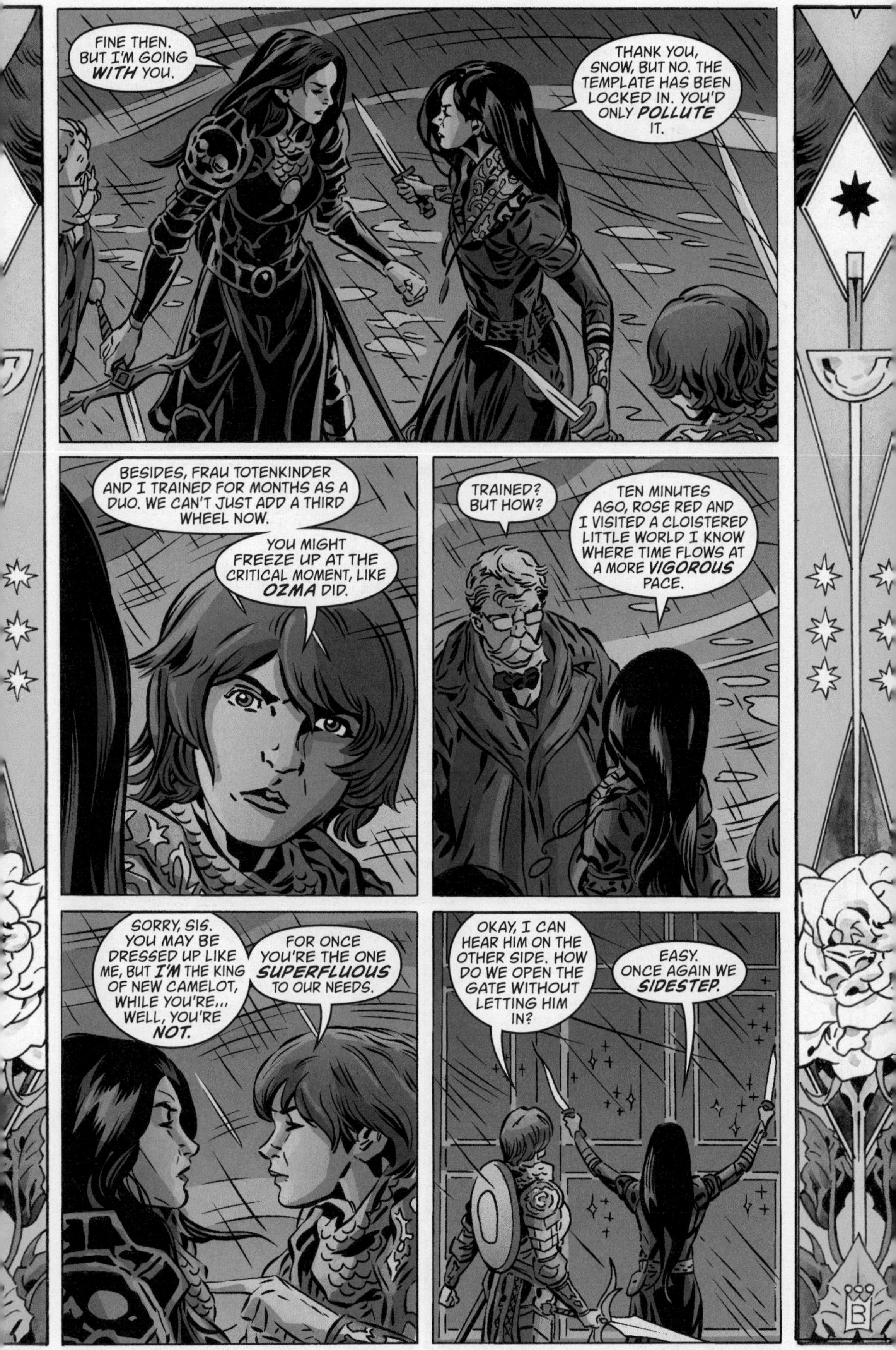
FINE THEN. BUT I'M GOING WITH YOU.
THANK YOU, SNOW, BUT NO. THE TEMPLATE HAS BEEN LOCKED IN. YOU'D ONLY POLLUTE IT.
BESIDES, FRAU TOTENKINDER AND I TRAINED FOR MONTHS AS A DUO. WE CAN'T JUST ADD A THIRD WHEEL NOW.
YOU MIGHT FREEZE UP AT THE CRITICAL MOMENT, LIKE OZMA DID.
TRAINED? BUT HOW?
TEN MINUTES AGO, ROSE RED AND I VISITED A CLOISTERED LITTLE WORLD I KNOW WHERE TIME FLOWS AT A MORE VIGOROUS PACE.
SORRY, SIS. YOU MAY BE DRESSED UP LIKE ME, BUT I'M THE KING OF NEW CAMELOT, WHILE YOU'RE... WELL, YOU'RE NOT.
FOR ONCE YOU'RE THE ONE SUPERFLUOUS TO OUR NEEDS.
OKAY, I CAN HEAR HIM ON THE OTHER SIDE. HOW DO WE OPEN THE GATE WITHOUT LETTING HIM IN?
EASY. ONCE AGAIN WE SIDESTEP.

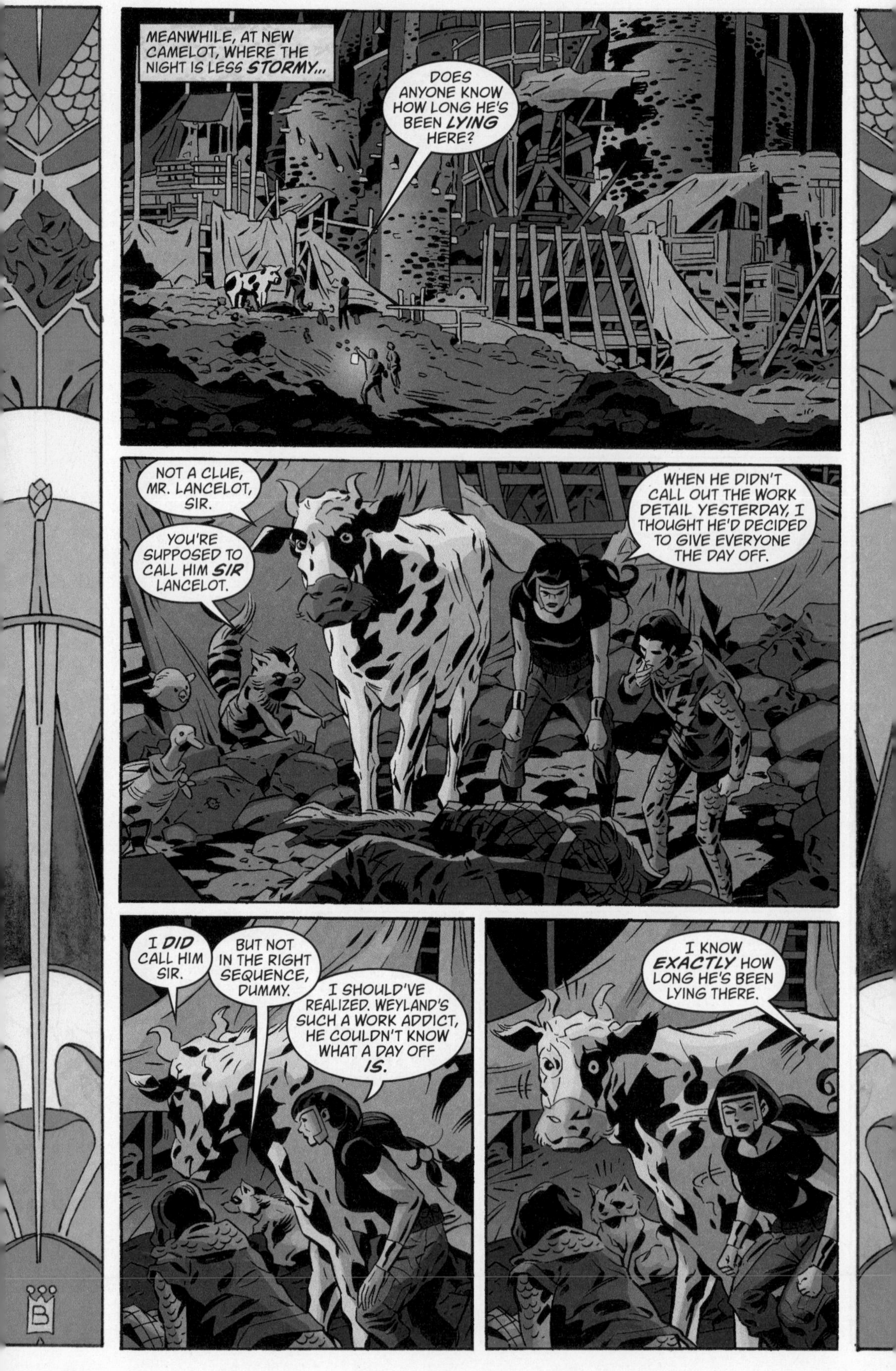
MEANWHILE, AT NEW CAMELOT, WHERE THE NIGHT IS LESS STORMY...
DOES ANYONE KNOW HOW LONG HE'S BEEN LYING HERE?
NOT A CLUE, MR. LANCELOT, SIR.
YOU'RE SUPPOSED TO CALL HIM SIR LANCELOT.
WHEN HE DIDN'T CALL OUT THE WORK DETAIL YESTERDAY, I THOUGHT HE'D DECIDED TO GIVE EVERYONE THE DAY OFF.
I DID CALL HIM SIR.
BUT NOT IN THE RIGHT SEQUENCE, DUMMY.
I SHOULD'VE REALIZED. WEYLAND'S SUCH A WORK ADDICT, HE COULDN'T KNOW WHAT A DAY OFF IS.
I KNOW EXACTLY HOW LONG HE'S BEEN LYING THERE.

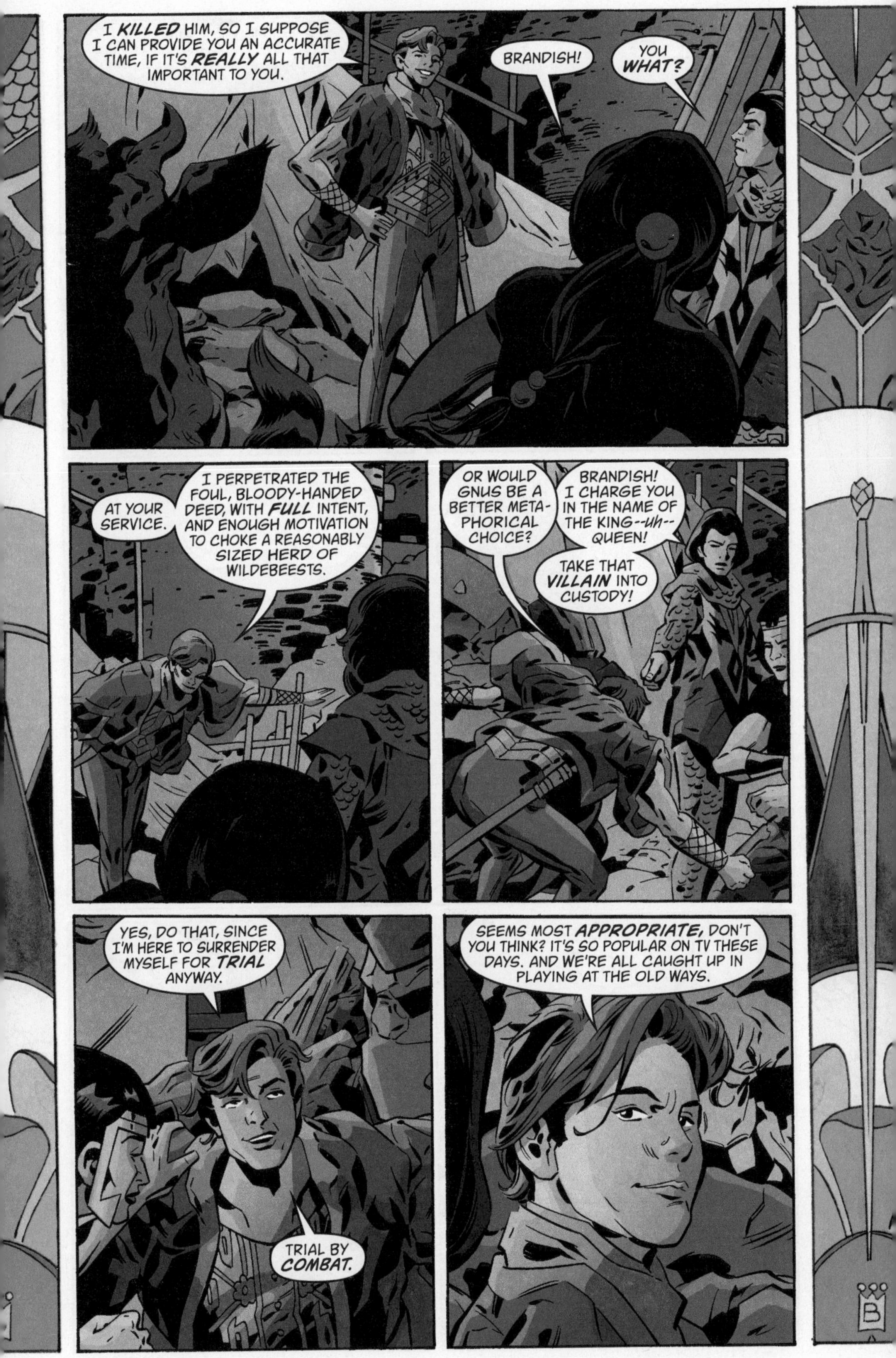
I KILLED HIM, SO I SUPPOSE I CAN PROVIDE YOU AN ACCURATE TIME, IF IT'S REALLY ALL THAT IMPORTANT TO YOU.
BRANDISH!
YOU WHAT?
AT YOUR SERVICE.
I PERPETRATED THE FOUL, BLOODY-HANDED DEED, WITH FULL INTENT, AND ENOUGH MOTIVATION TO CHOKE A REASONABLY SIZED HERD OF WILDEBEESTS.
OR WOULD GNUS BE A BETTER META-PHORICAL CHOICE?
BRANDISH! I CHARGE YOU IN THE NAME OF THE KING--uh--QUEEN!
TAKE THAT VILLAIN INTO CUSTODY!
YES, DO THAT, SINCE I'M HERE TO SURRENDER MYSELF FOR TRIAL ANYWAY.
TRIAL BY COMBAT.
SEEMS MOST APPROPRIATE, DON'T YOU THINK? IT'S SO POPULAR ON TV THESE DAYS. AND WE'RE ALL CAUGHT UP IN PLAYING AT THE OLD WAYS.

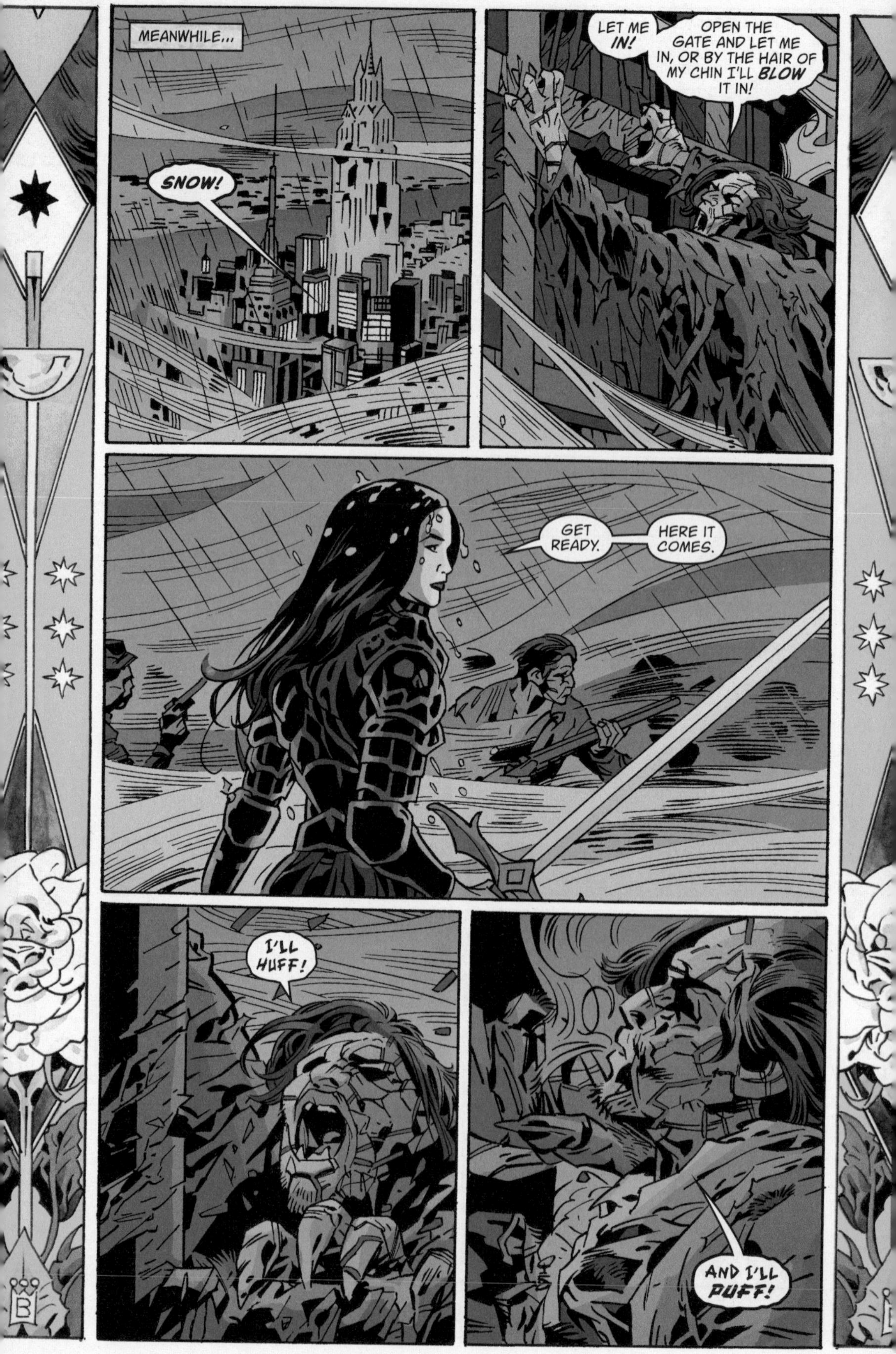
MEANWHILE...
SNOW!
LET ME IN!
OPEN THE GATE AND LET ME IN, OR BY THE HAIR OF MY CHIN I'LL BLOW IT IN!
GET READY.
HERE IT COMES.
I'LL HUFF!
AND I'LL PUFF!

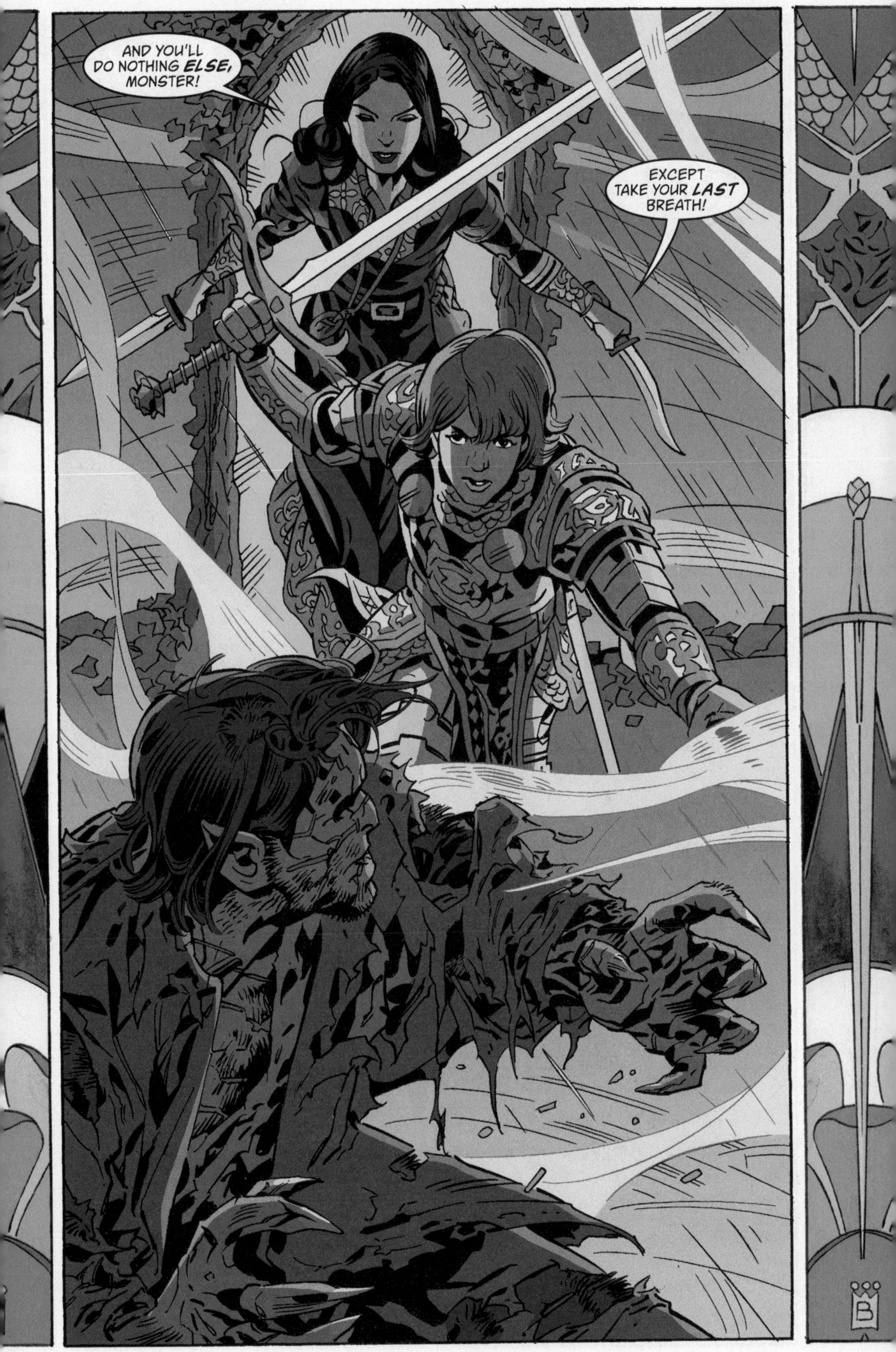
AND YOU'LL DO NOTHING ELSE, MONSTER!
EXCEPT TAKE YOUR LAST BREATH!

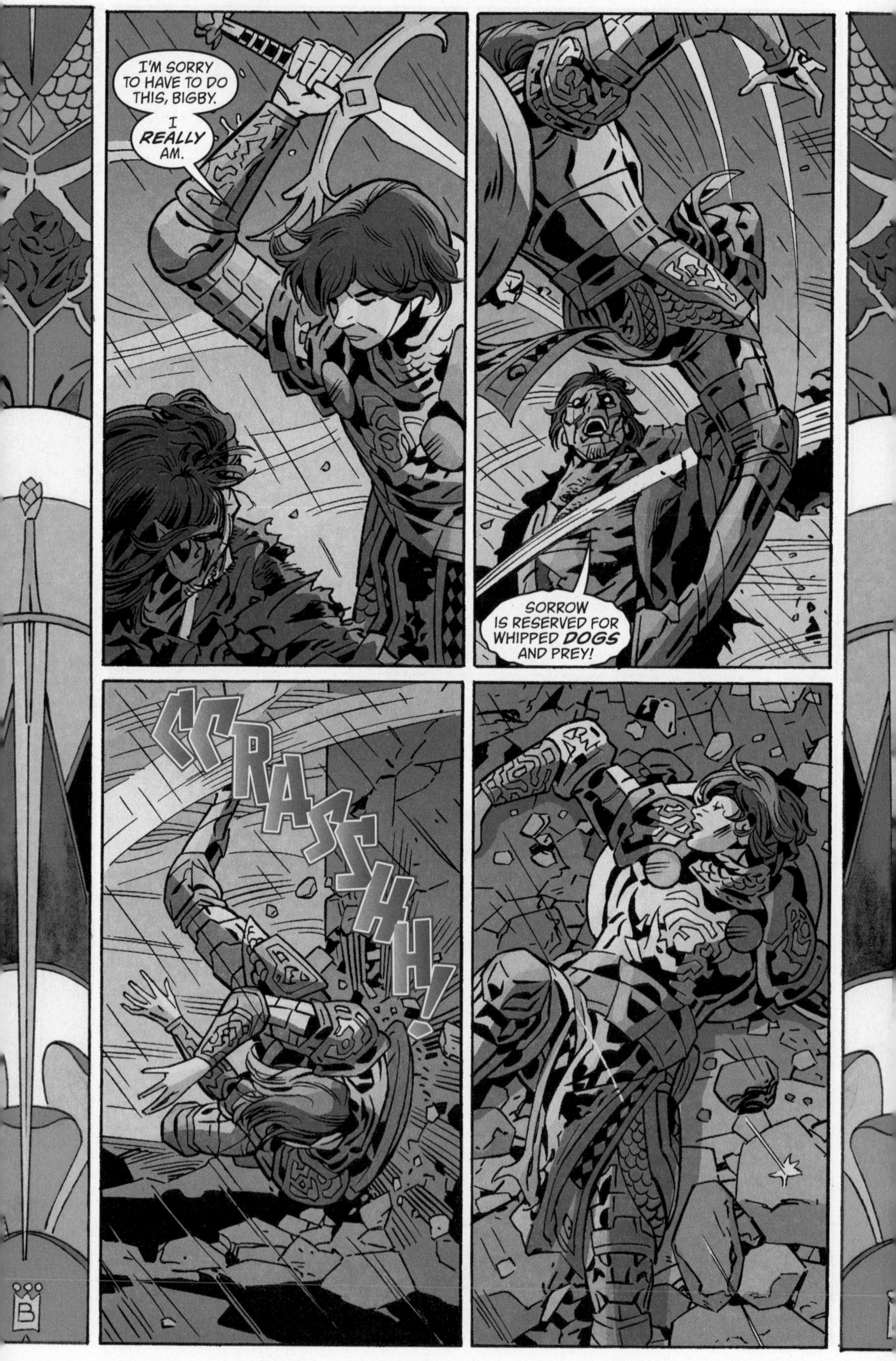
I'M SORRY TO HAVE TO DO THIS, BIGBY.
I *REALLY* AM.
SORROW IS RESERVED FOR WHIPPED *DOGS* AND PREY!
CRASSHH!

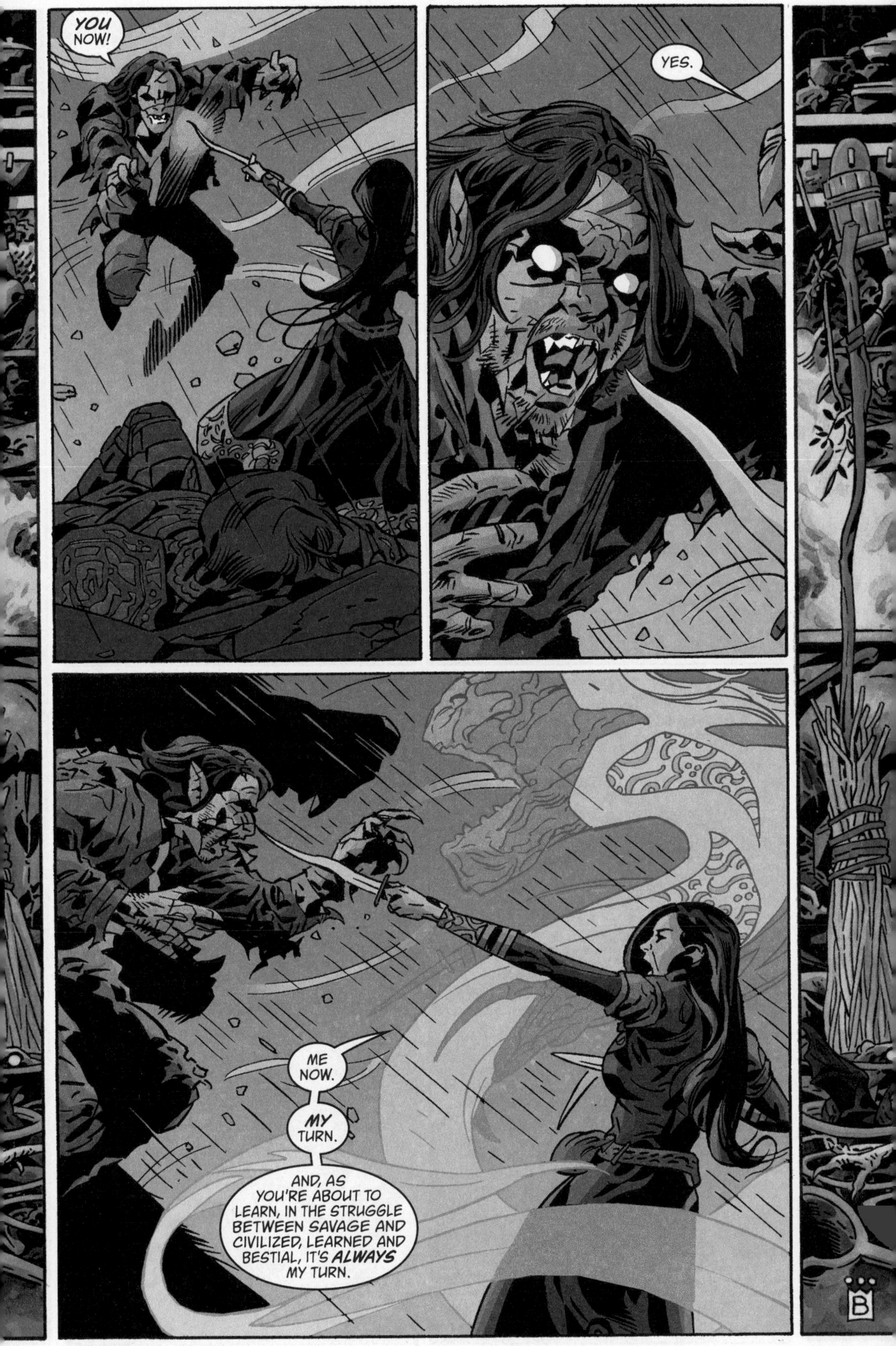
YOU NOW!
YES.
ME NOW.
MY TURN.
AND, AS YOU'RE ABOUT TO LEARN, IN THE STRUGGLE BETWEEN SAVAGE AND CIVILIZED, LEARNED AND BESTIAL, IT'S ALWAYS MY TURN.

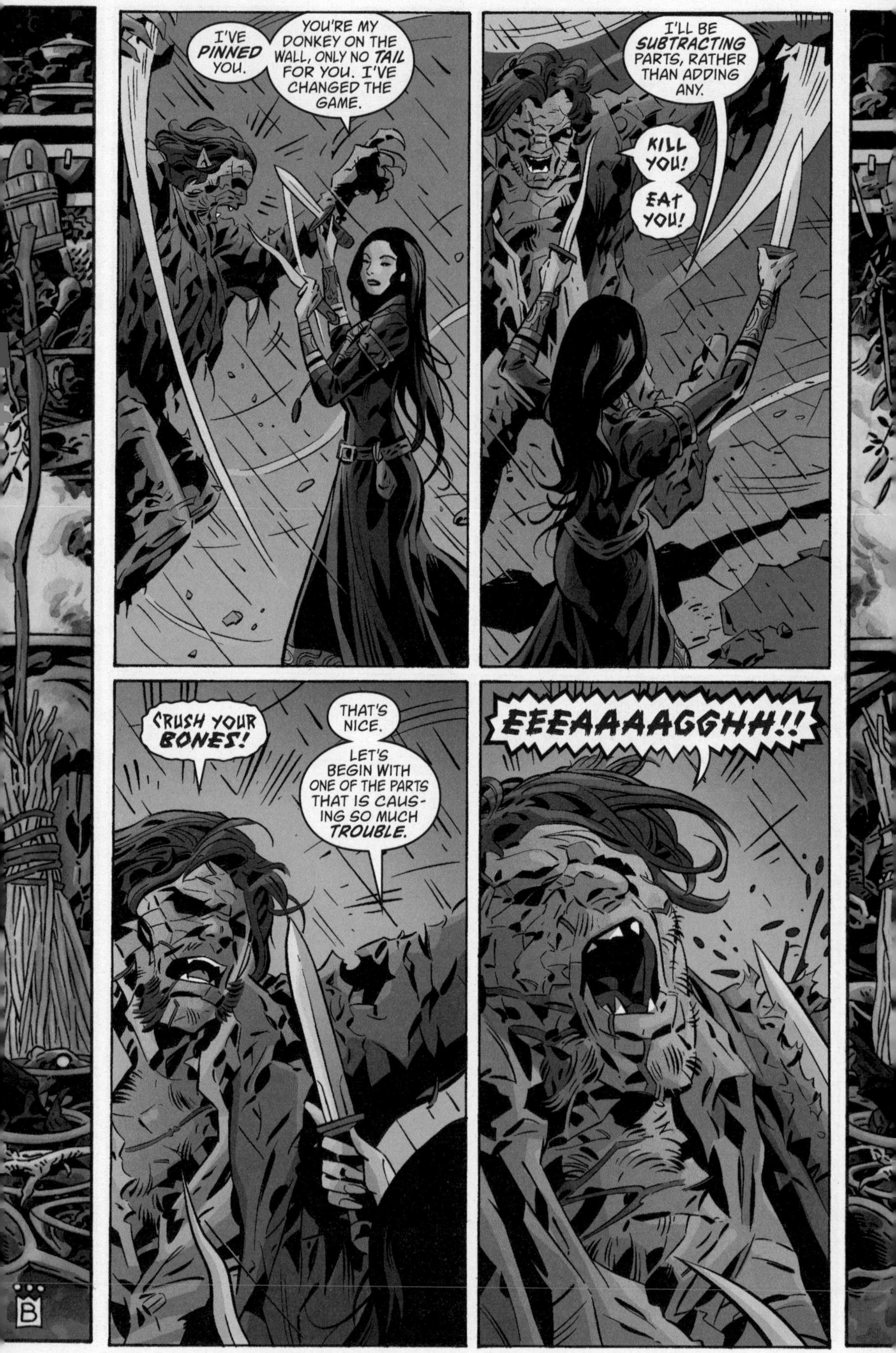

I'VE PINNED YOU.
YOU'RE MY DONKEY ON THE WALL, ONLY NO TAIL FOR YOU. I'VE CHANGED THE GAME.
I'LL BE SUBTRACTING PARTS, RATHER THAN ADDING ANY.
KILL YOU!
EAT YOU!
CRUSH YOUR BONES!
THAT'S NICE.
LET'S BEGIN WITH ONE OF THE PARTS THAT IS CAUSING SO MUCH TROUBLE.
EEEAAAAAGGHH!!

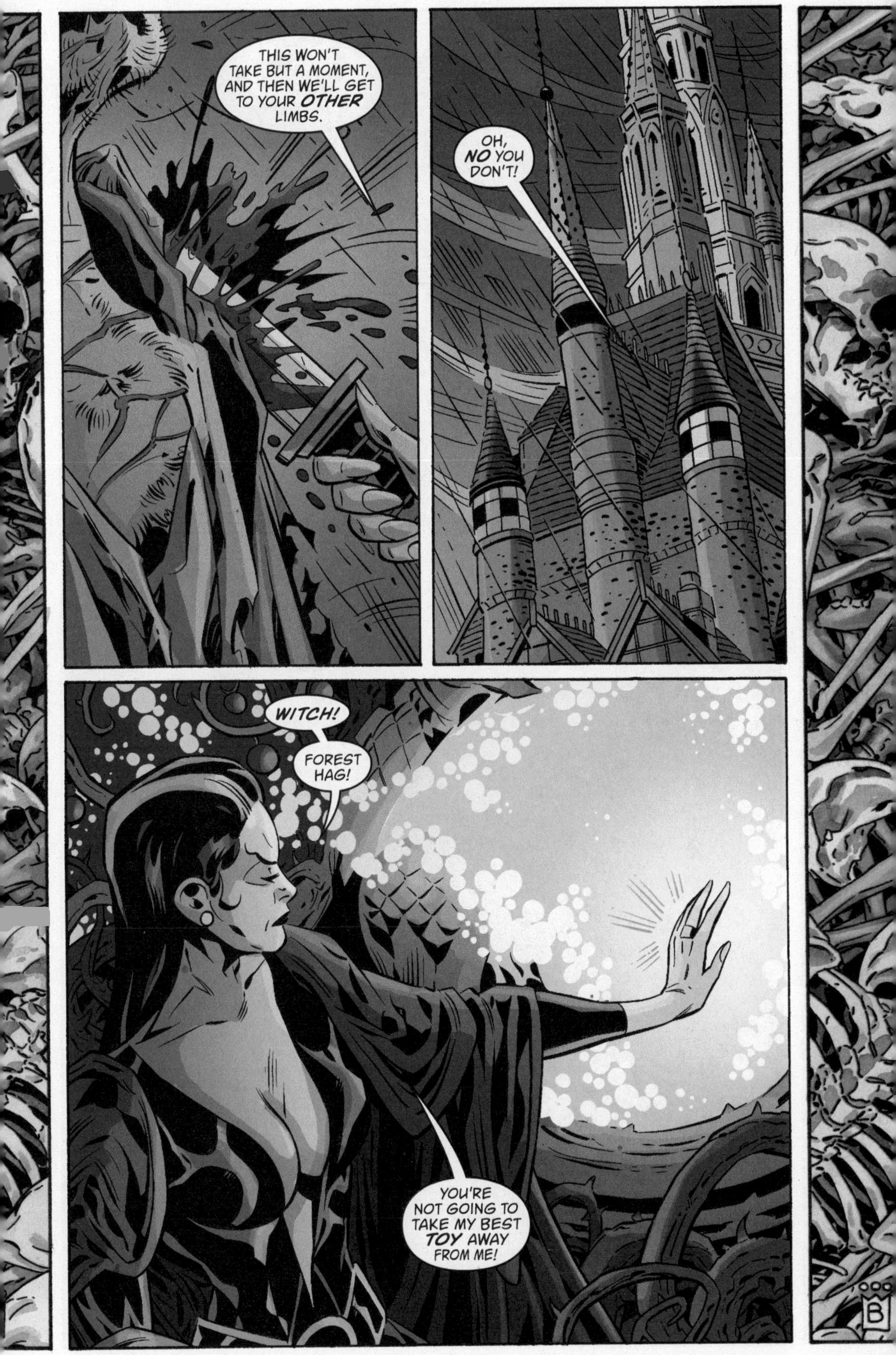

THIS WON'T TAKE BUT A MOMENT, AND THEN WE'LL GET TO YOUR OTHER LIMBS.
OH, NO YOU DON'T!
WITCH!
FOREST HAG!
YOU'RE NOT GOING TO TAKE MY BEST TOY AWAY FROM ME!

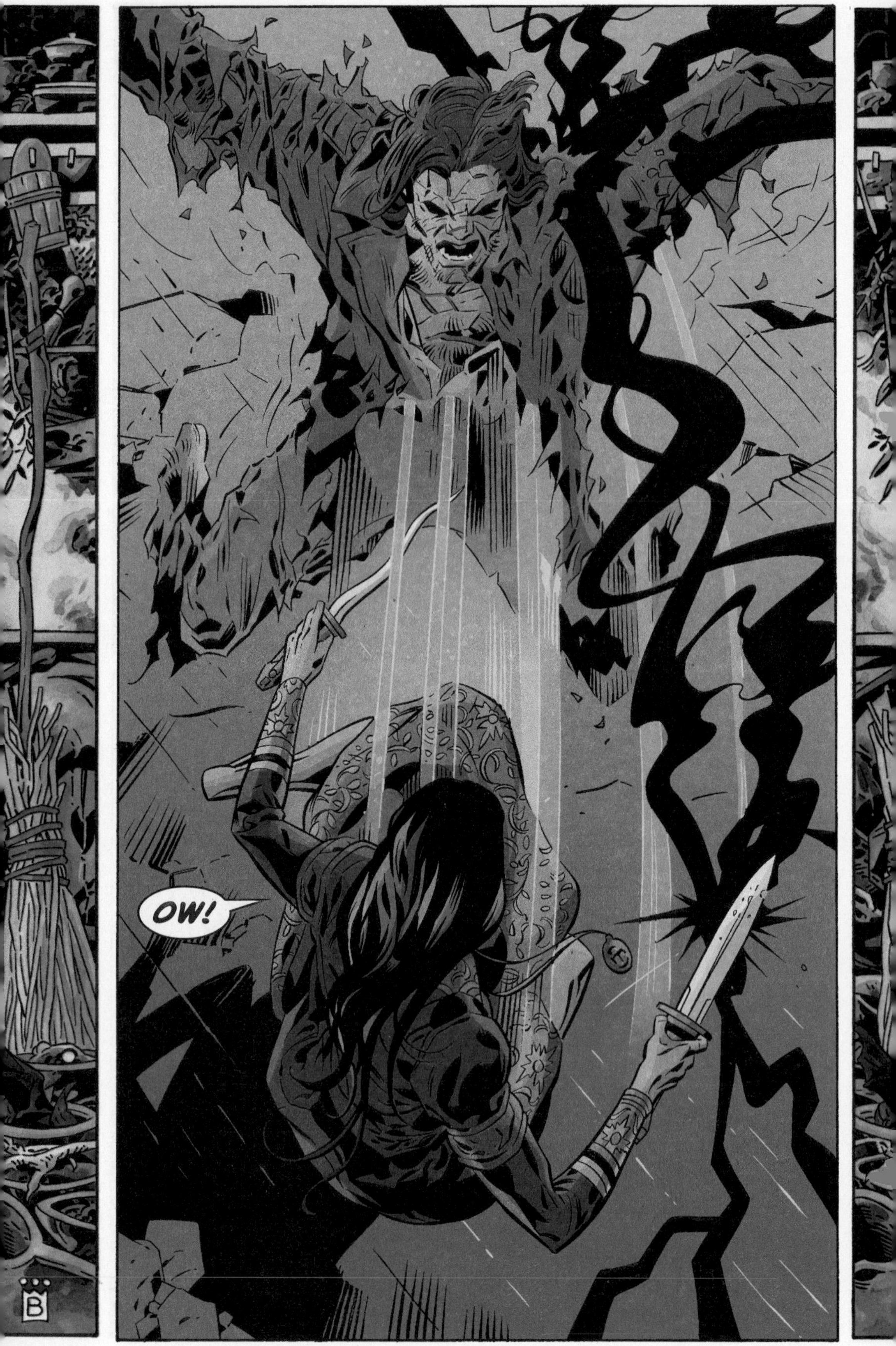
OW!

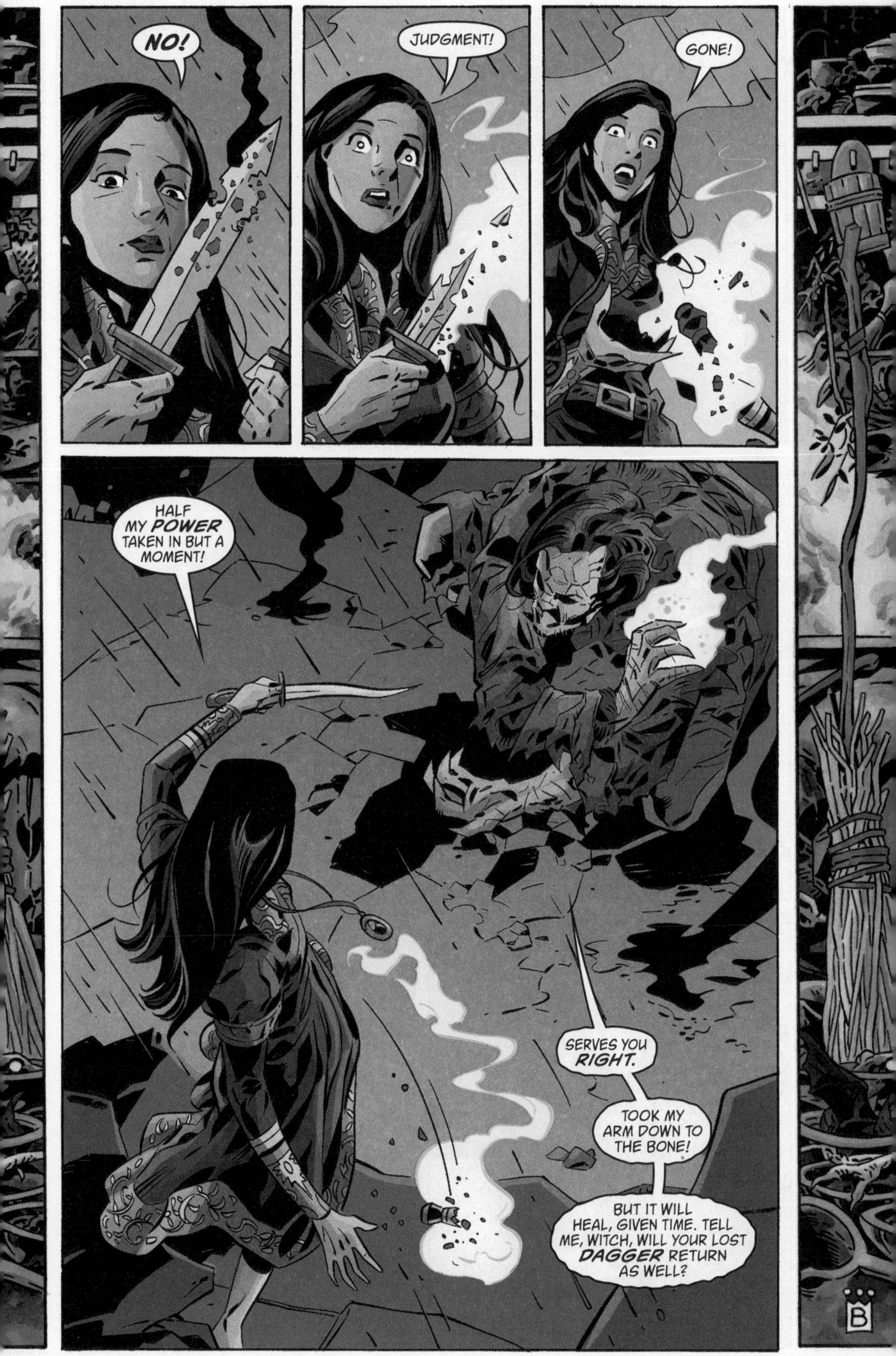
NO!
JUDGMENT!
GONE!
HALF MY POWER TAKEN IN BUT A MOMENT!
SERVES YOU RIGHT.
TOOK MY ARM DOWN TO THE BONE!
BUT IT WILL HEAL, GIVEN TIME. TELL ME, WITCH, WILL YOUR LOST DAGGER RETURN AS WELL?

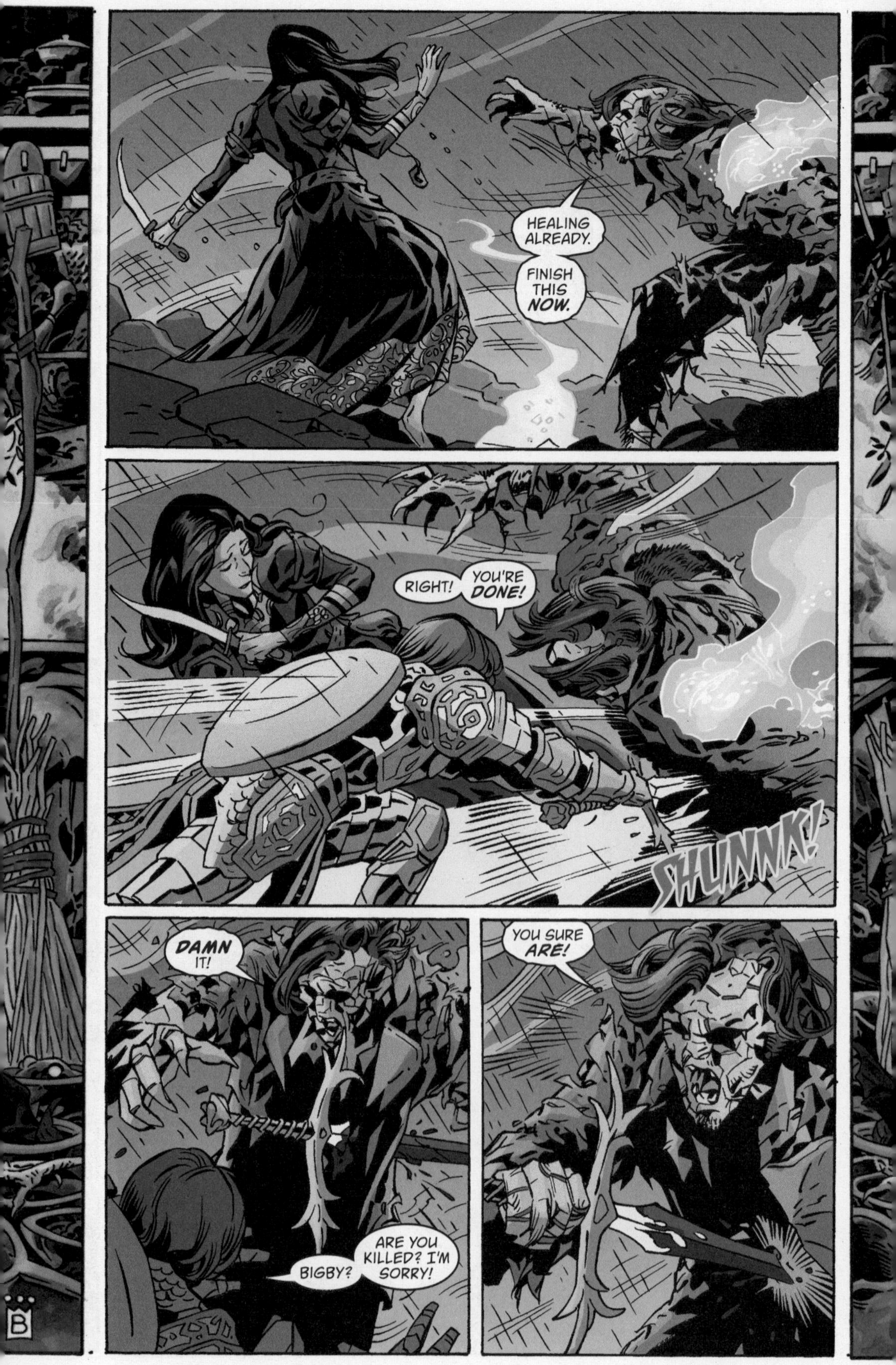
HEALING ALREADY.
FINISH THIS NOW.
RIGHT!
YOU'RE DONE!
SHUNNK!
DAMN IT!
BIGBY?
ARE YOU KILLED? I'M SORRY!
YOU SURE ARE!

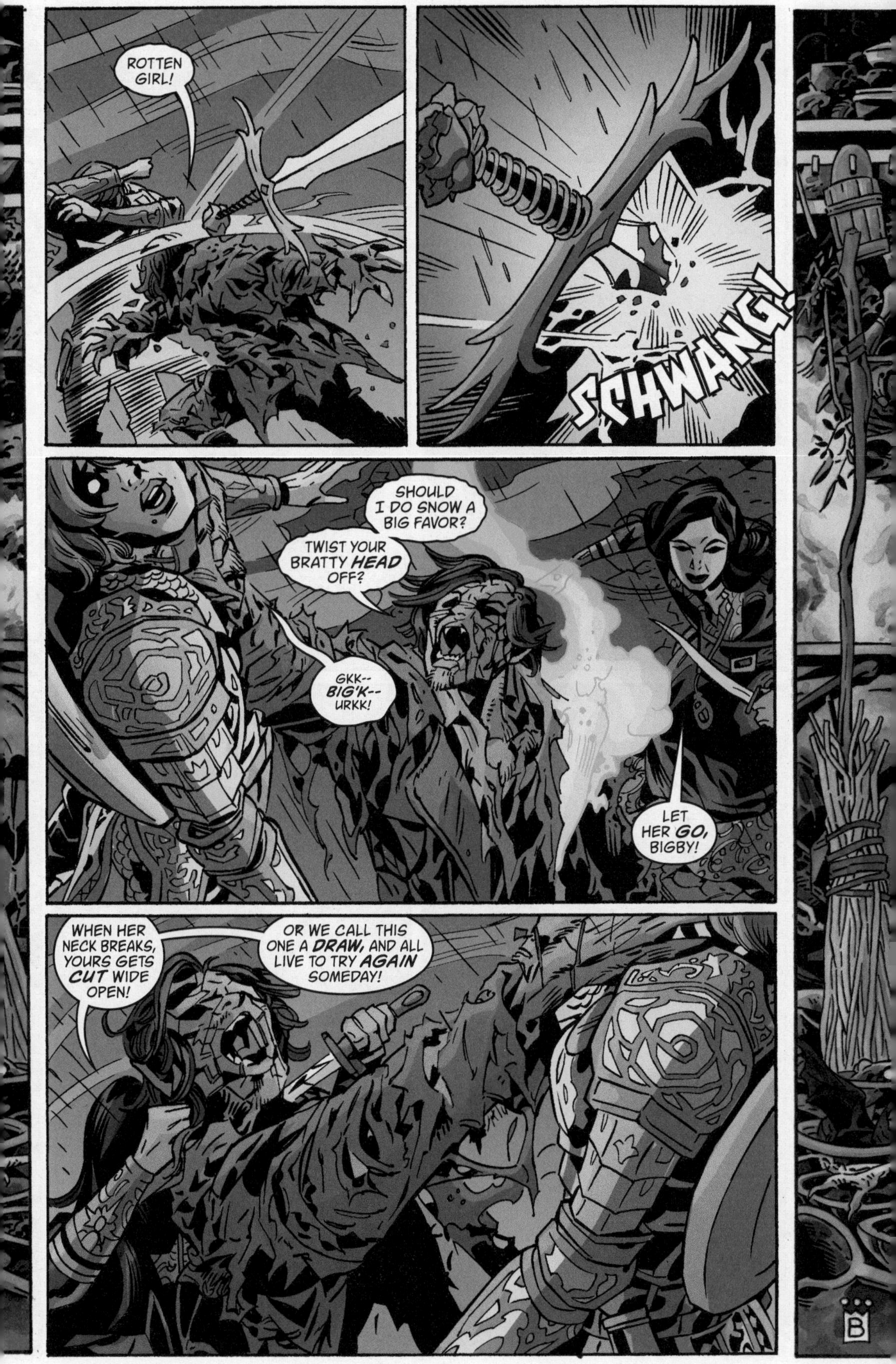

ROTTEN GIRL!
SCHWANG!
SHOULD I DO SNOW A BIG FAVOR?
TWIST YOUR BRATTY HEAD OFF?
GKK-- BIG'K-- URKK!
LET HER GO, BIGBY!
WHEN HER NECK BREAKS, YOURS GETS CUT WIDE OPEN!
OR WE CALL THIS ONE A DRAW, AND ALL LIVE TO TRY AGAIN SOMEDAY!

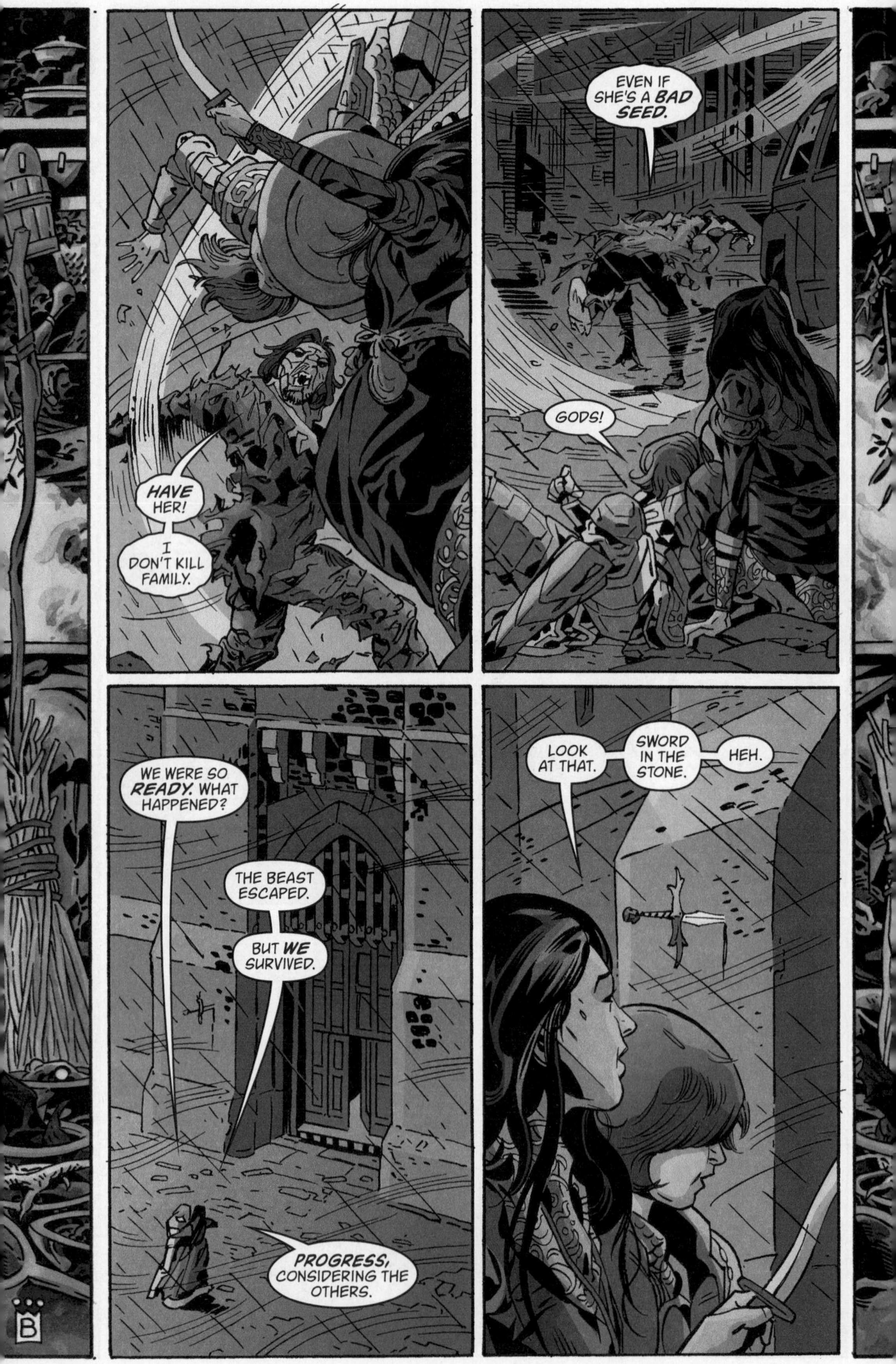
HAVE HER!
I DON'T KILL FAMILY.
EVEN IF SHE'S A BAD SEED.
GODS!
WE WERE SO READY. WHAT HAPPENED?
THE BEAST ESCAPED.
BUT WE SURVIVED.
PROGRESS, CONSIDERING THE OTHERS.
LOOK AT THAT.
SWORD IN THE STONE.
HEH.

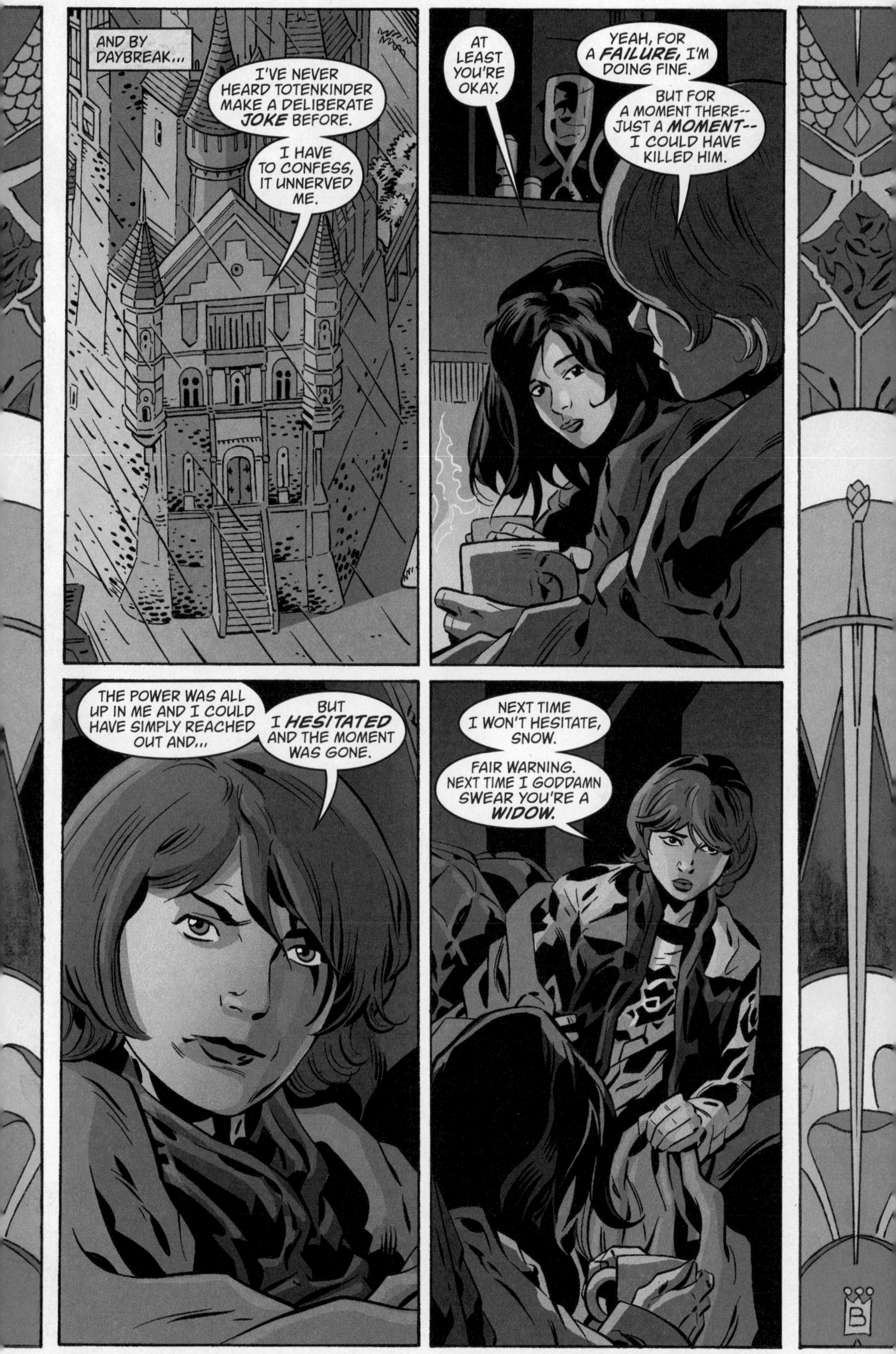
AND BY DAYBREAK...
I'VE NEVER HEARD TOTENKINDER MAKE A DELIBERATE JOKE BEFORE.
I HAVE TO CONFESS, IT UNNERVED ME.
AT LEAST YOU'RE OKAY.
YEAH, FOR A FAILURE, I'M DOING FINE.
BUT FOR A MOMENT THERE-- JUST A MOMENT-- I COULD HAVE KILLED HIM.
THE POWER WAS ALL UP IN ME AND I COULD HAVE SIMPLY REACHED OUT AND...
BUT I HESITATED AND THE MOMENT WAS GONE.
NEXT TIME I WON'T HESITATE, SNOW.
FAIR WARNING. NEXT TIME I GODDAMN SWEAR YOU'RE A WIDOW.

NEXT: LET THIS CUP PASS...

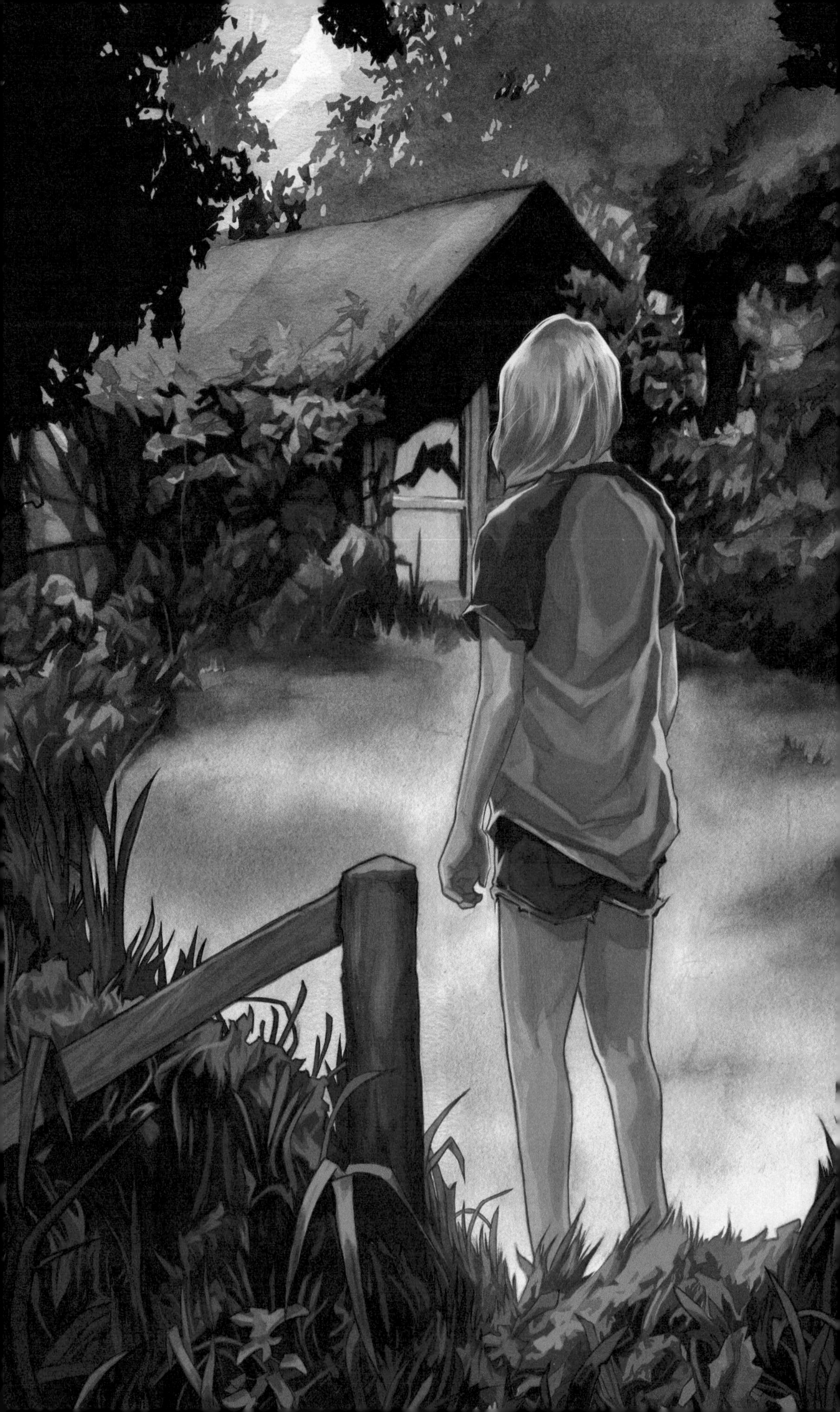

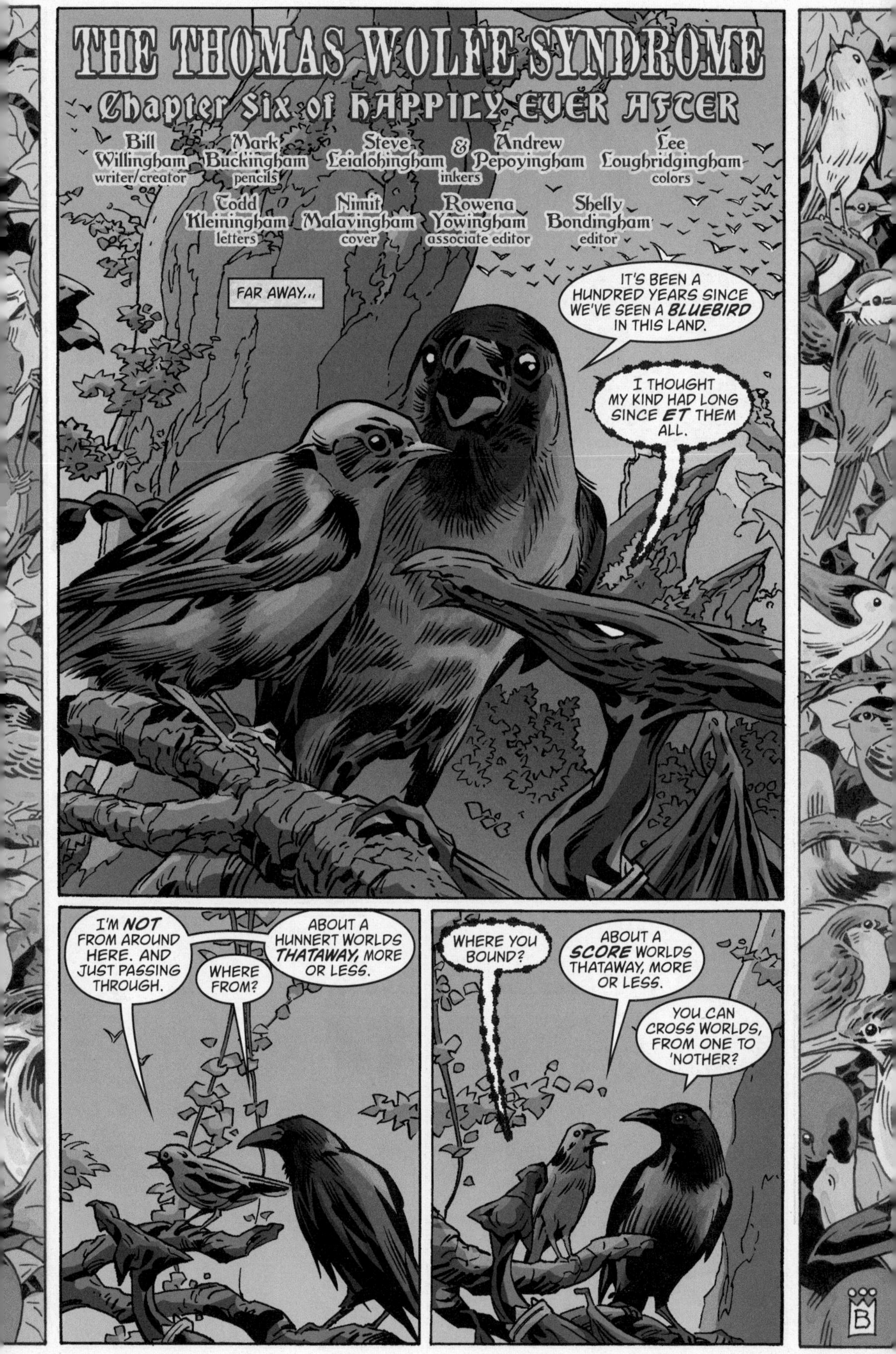
THE THOMAS WOLFE SYNDROME
Chapter Six of HAPPILY EVER AFTER
Bill Willingham writer/creator
Mark Buckingham pencils
Steve Leialohingham & Andrew Pepoyingham inkers
Lee Loughridgingham colors
Todd Kleiningham letters
Nimit Malavingham cover
Rowena Yowingham associate editor
Shelly Bondingham editor
FAR AWAY...
IT'S BEEN A HUNDRED YEARS SINCE WE'VE SEEN A BLUEBIRD IN THIS LAND.
I THOUGHT MY KIND HAD LONG SINCE ET THEM ALL.
I'M NOT FROM AROUND HERE. AND JUST PASSING THROUGH.
WHERE FROM?
ABOUT A HUNNERT WORLDS THATAWAY, MORE OR LESS.
WHERE YOU BOUND?
ABOUT A SCORE WORLDS THATAWAY, MORE OR LESS.
YOU CAN CROSS WORLDS, FROM ONE TO 'NOTHER?

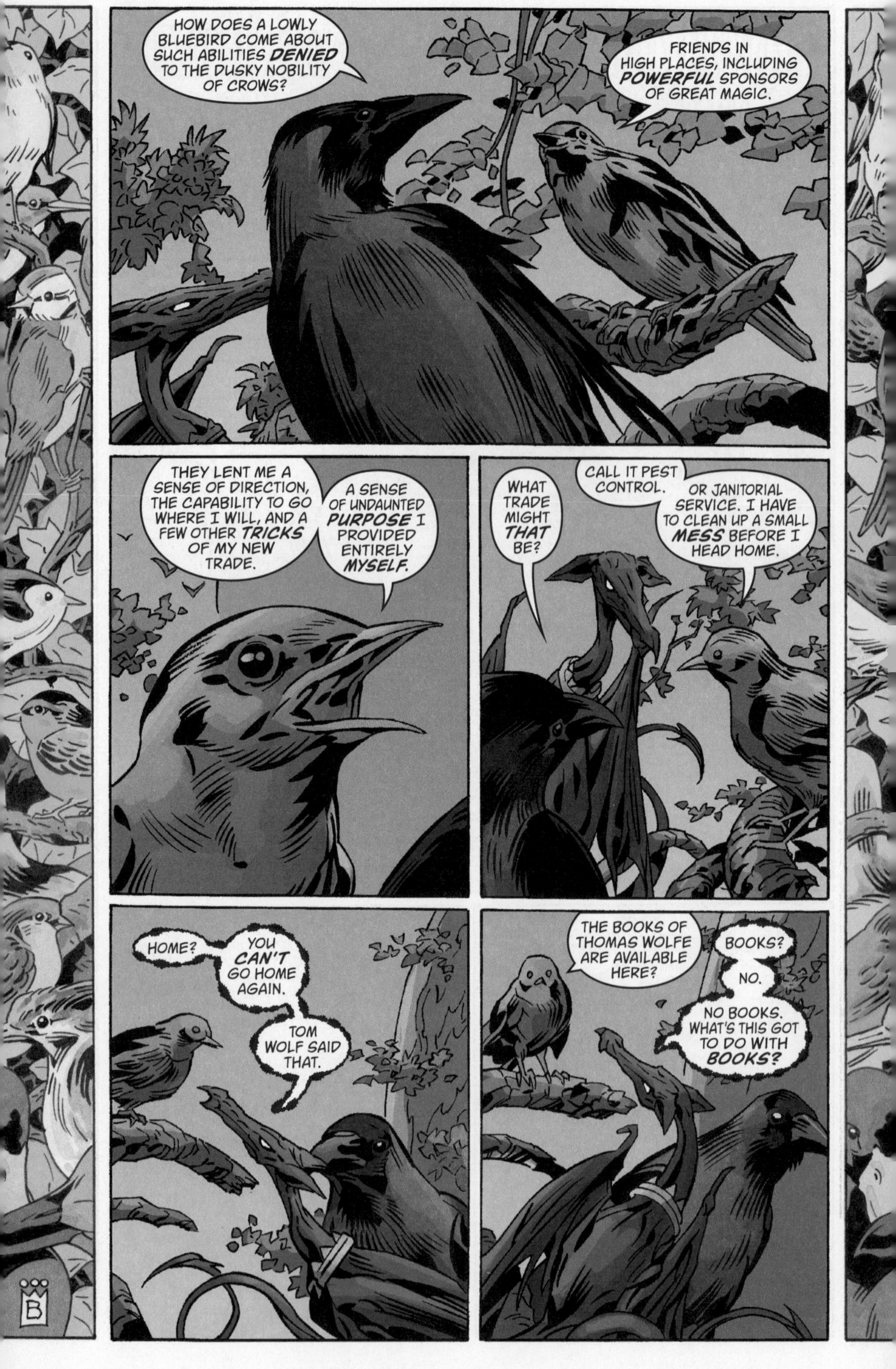
HOW DOES A LOWLY BLUEBIRD COME ABOUT SUCH ABILITIES DENIED TO THE DUSKY NOBILITY OF CROWS?
FRIENDS IN HIGH PLACES, INCLUDING POWERFUL SPONSORS OF GREAT MAGIC.
THEY LENT ME A SENSE OF DIRECTION, THE CAPABILITY TO GO WHERE I WILL, AND A FEW OTHER TRICKS OF MY NEW TRADE.
A SENSE OF UNDAUNTED PURPOSE I PROVIDED ENTIRELY MYSELF.
WHAT TRADE MIGHT THAT BE?
CALL IT PEST CONTROL.
OR JANITORIAL SERVICE. I HAVE TO CLEAN UP A SMALL MESS BEFORE I HEAD HOME.
HOME?
YOU CAN'T GO HOME AGAIN.
TOM WOLF SAID THAT.
THE BOOKS OF THOMAS WOLFE ARE AVAILABLE HERE?
BOOKS?
NO.
NO BOOKS. WHAT'S THIS GOT TO DO WITH BOOKS?

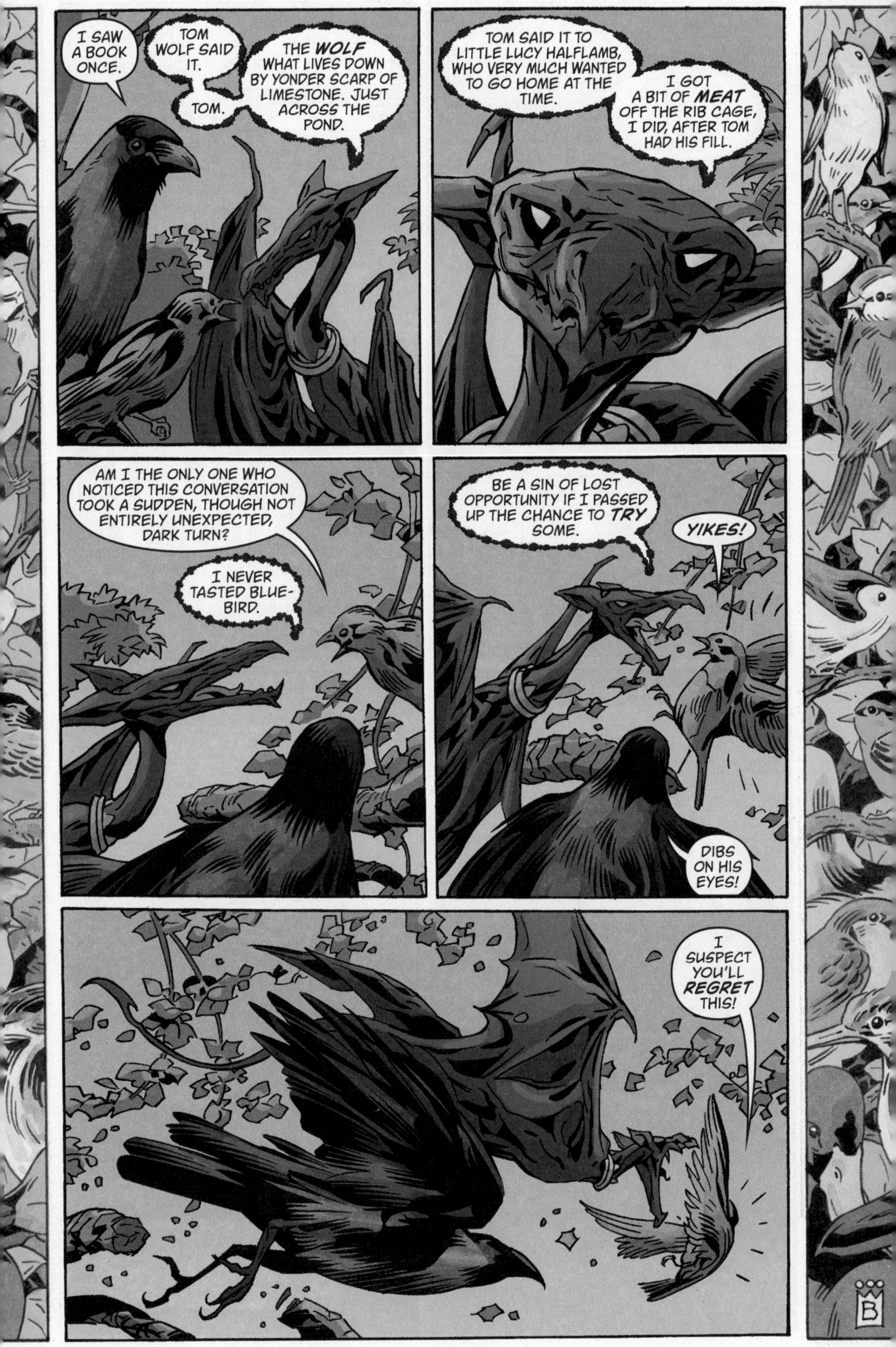
I SAW A BOOK ONCE.
TOM WOLF SAID IT.
TOM.
THE WOLF WHAT LIVES DOWN BY YONDER SCARP OF LIMESTONE. JUST ACROSS THE POND.
TOM SAID IT TO LITTLE LUCY HALFLAMB, WHO VERY MUCH WANTED TO GO HOME AT THE TIME.
I GOT A BIT OF MEAT OFF THE RIB CAGE, I DID, AFTER TOM HAD HIS FILL.
AM I THE ONLY ONE WHO NOTICED THIS CONVERSATION TOOK A SUDDEN, THOUGH NOT ENTIRELY UNEXPECTED, DARK TURN?
I NEVER TASTED BLUE-BIRD.
BE A SIN OF LOST OPPORTUNITY IF I PASSED UP THE CHANCE TO TRY SOME.
YIKES!
DIBS ON HIS EYES!
I SUSPECT YOU'LL REGRET THIS!

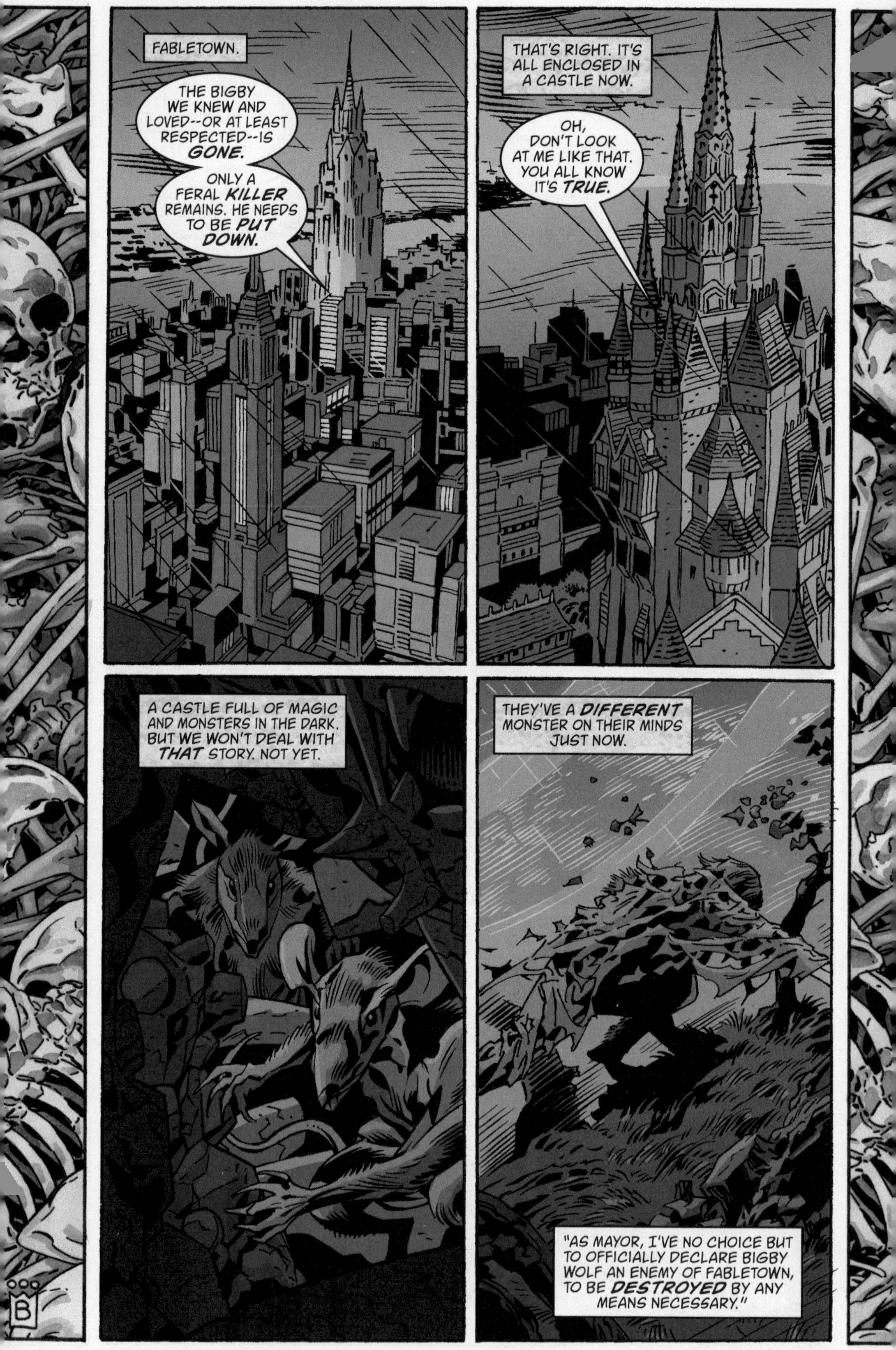
FABLETOWN.
THE BIGBY WE KNEW AND LOVED--OR AT LEAST RESPECTED--IS GONE.
ONLY A FERAL KILLER REMAINS. HE NEEDS TO BE PUT DOWN.
THAT'S RIGHT. IT'S ALL ENCLOSED IN A CASTLE NOW.
OH, DON'T LOOK AT ME LIKE THAT. YOU ALL KNOW IT'S TRUE.
A CASTLE FULL OF MAGIC AND MONSTERS IN THE DARK. BUT WE WON'T DEAL WITH THAT STORY. NOT YET.
THEY'VE A DIFFERENT MONSTER ON THEIR MINDS JUST NOW.
"AS MAYOR, I'VE NO CHOICE BUT TO OFFICIALLY DECLARE BIGBY WOLF AN ENEMY OF FABLETOWN, TO BE DESTROYED BY ANY MEANS NECESSARY."

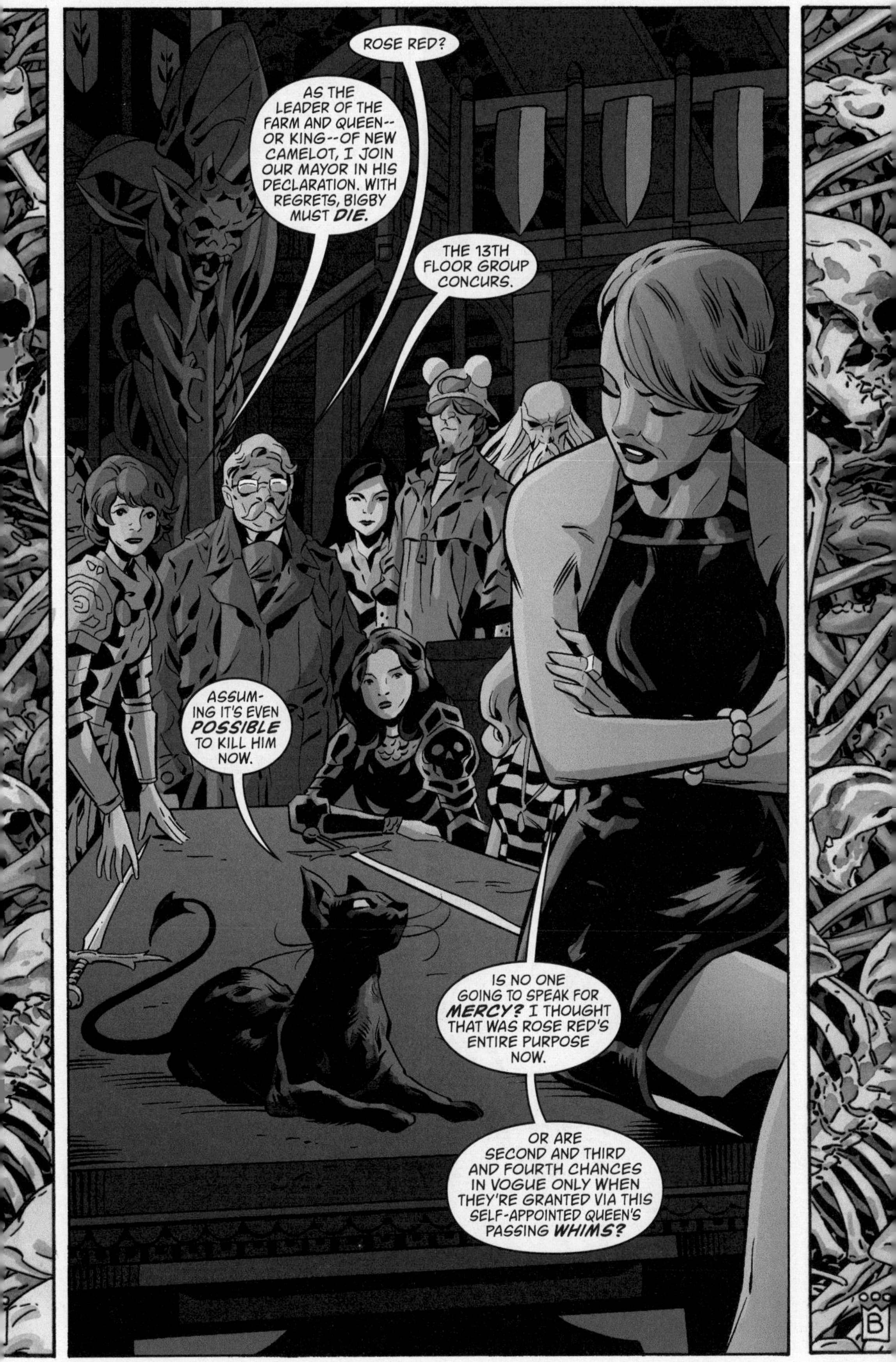
ROSE RED?
AS THE LEADER OF THE FARM AND QUEEN--OR KING--OF NEW CAMELOT, I JOIN OUR MAYOR IN HIS DECLARATION. WITH REGRETS, BIGBY MUST DIE.
THE 13TH FLOOR GROUP CONCURS.
ASSUMING IT'S EVEN POSSIBLE TO KILL HIM NOW.
IS NO ONE GOING TO SPEAK FOR MERCY? I THOUGHT THAT WAS ROSE RED'S ENTIRE PURPOSE NOW.
OR ARE SECOND AND THIRD AND FOURTH CHANCES IN VOGUE ONLY WHEN THEY'RE GRANTED VIA THIS SELF-APPOINTED QUEEN'S PASSING WHIMS?

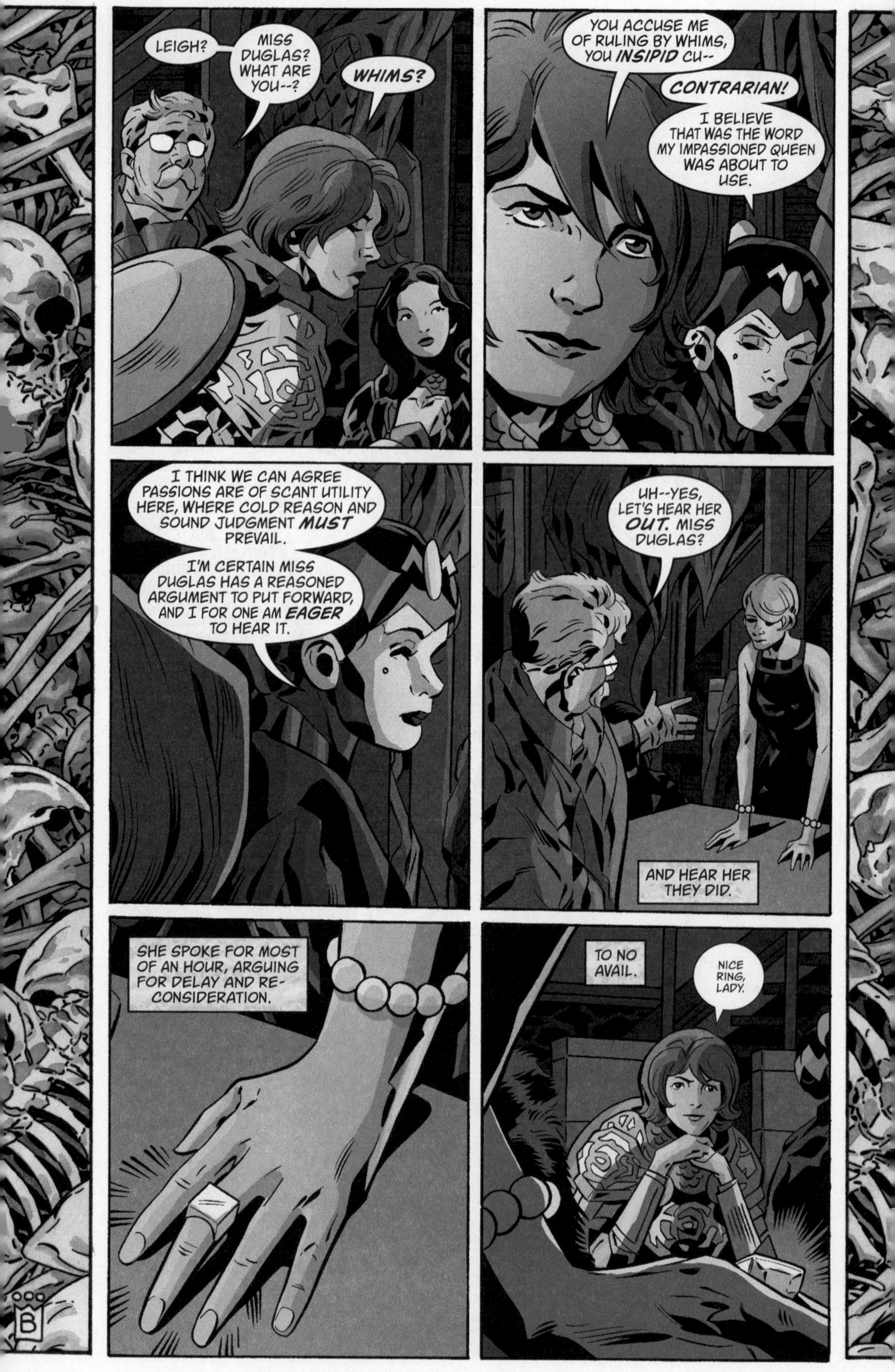

LEIGH?
MISS DUGLAS? WHAT ARE YOU--?
WHIMS?
YOU ACCUSE ME OF RULING BY WHIMS, YOU INSIPID CU--
CONTRARIAN!
I BELIEVE THAT WAS THE WORD MY IMPASSIONED QUEEN WAS ABOUT TO USE.
I THINK WE CAN AGREE PASSIONS ARE OF SCANT UTILITY HERE, WHERE COLD REASON AND SOUND JUDGMENT MUST PREVAIL.
I'M CERTAIN MISS DUGLAS HAS A REASONED ARGUMENT TO PUT FORWARD, AND I FOR ONE AM EAGER TO HEAR IT.
UH--YES, LET'S HEAR HER OUT. MISS DUGLAS?
AND HEAR HER THEY DID.
SHE SPOKE FOR MOST OF AN HOUR, ARGUING FOR DELAY AND RE-CONSIDERATION.
TO NO AVAIL.
NICE RING, LADY.

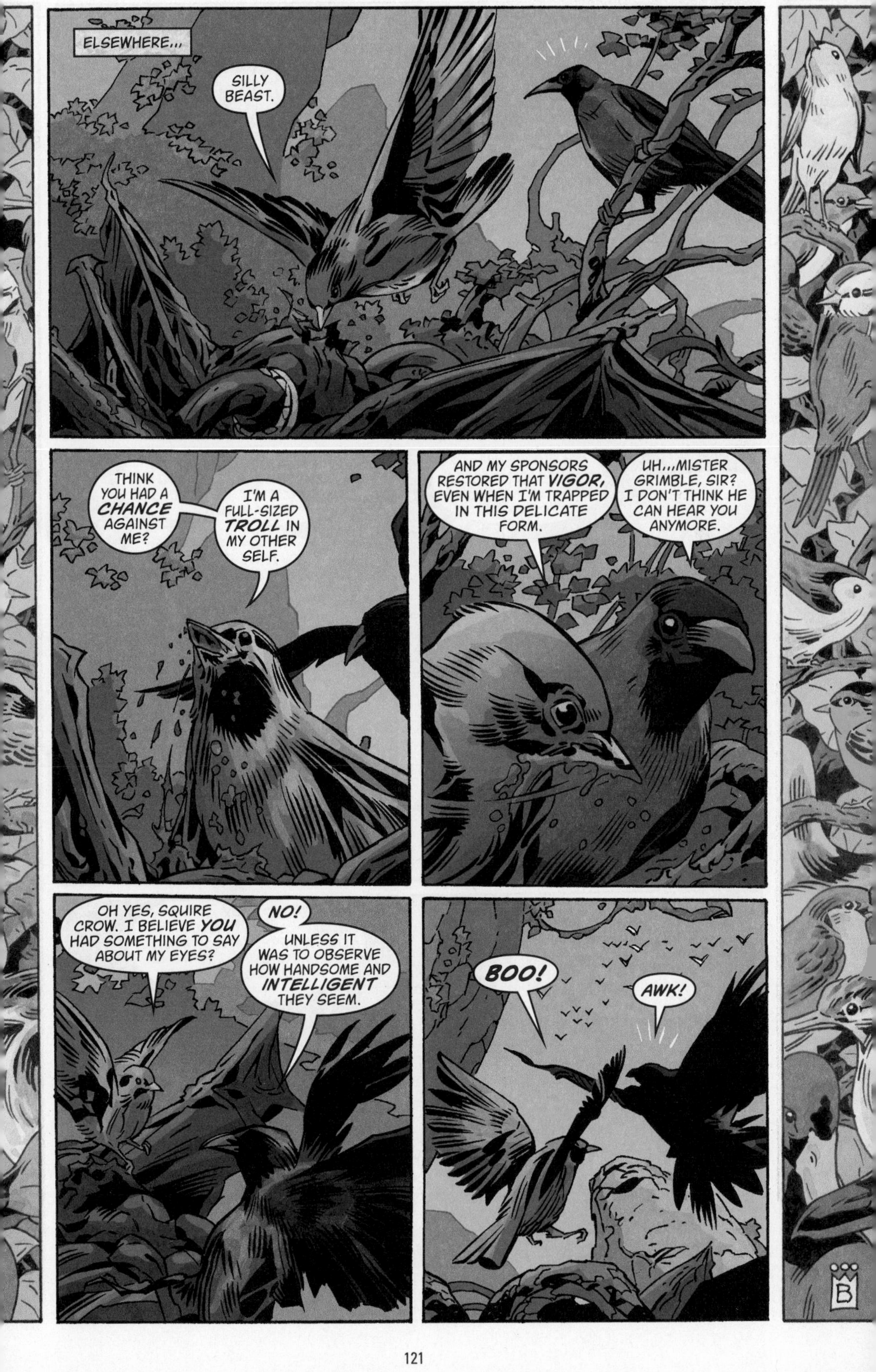
ELSEWHERE...
SILLY BEAST.
THINK YOU HAD A CHANCE AGAINST ME?
I'M A FULL-SIZED TROLL IN MY OTHER SELF.
AND MY SPONSORS RESTORED THAT VIGOR, EVEN WHEN I'M TRAPPED IN THIS DELICATE FORM.
UH...MISTER GRIMBLE, SIR? I DON'T THINK HE CAN HEAR YOU ANYMORE.
OH YES, SQUIRE CROW. I BELIEVE YOU HAD SOMETHING TO SAY ABOUT MY EYES?
NO!
UNLESS IT WAS TO OBSERVE HOW HANDSOME AND INTELLIGENT THEY SEEM.
BOO!
AWK!

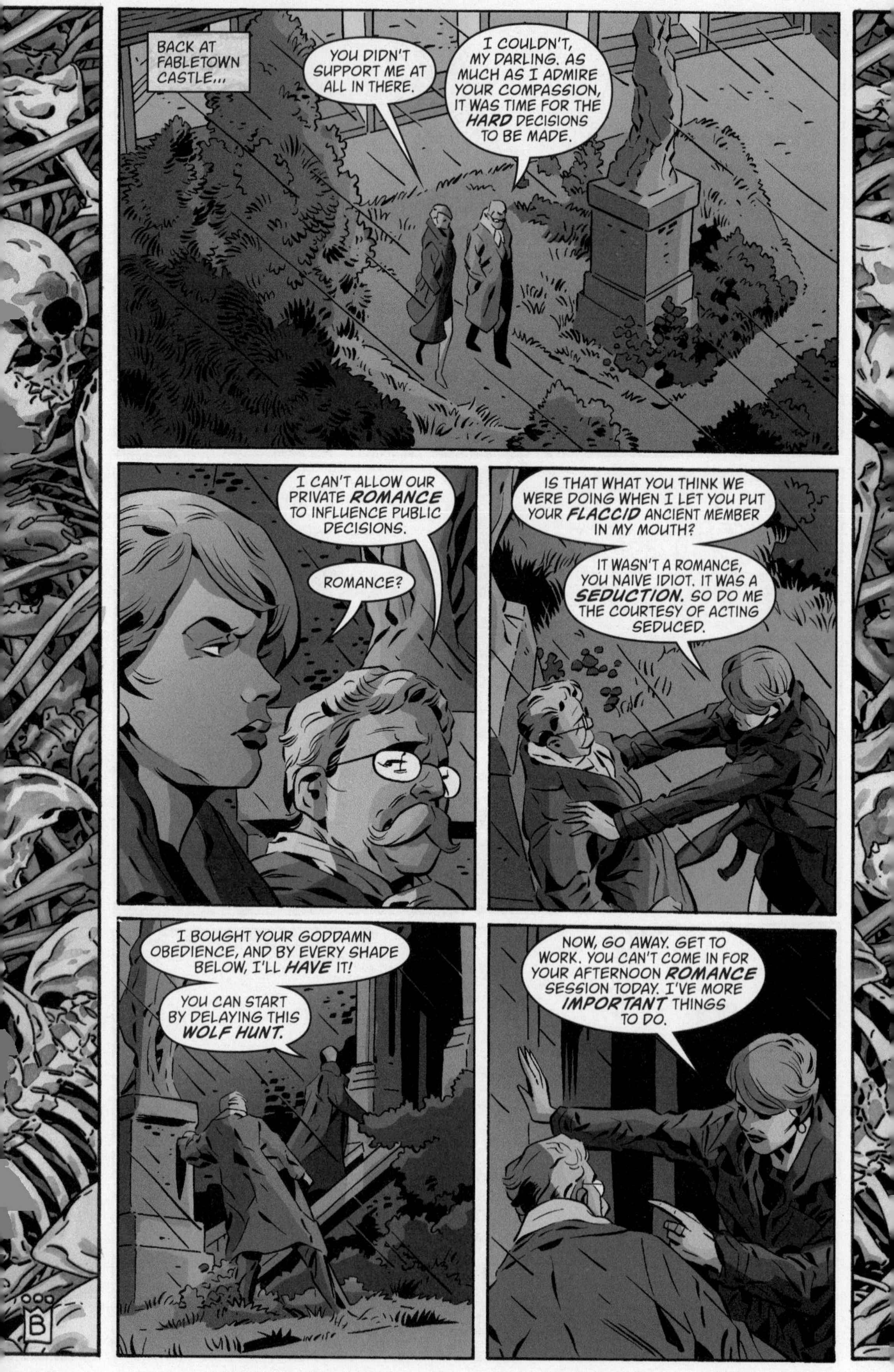

BACK AT FABLETOWN CASTLE...
YOU DIDN'T SUPPORT ME AT ALL IN THERE.
I COULDN'T, MY DARLING. AS MUCH AS I ADMIRE YOUR COMPASSION, IT WAS TIME FOR THE HARD DECISIONS TO BE MADE.
I CAN'T ALLOW OUR PRIVATE ROMANCE TO INFLUENCE PUBLIC DECISIONS.
ROMANCE?
IS THAT WHAT YOU THINK WE WERE DOING WHEN I LET YOU PUT YOUR FLACCID ANCIENT MEMBER IN MY MOUTH?
IT WASN'T A ROMANCE, YOU NAIVE IDIOT. IT WAS A SEDUCTION. SO DO ME THE COURTESY OF ACTING SEDUCED.
I BOUGHT YOUR GODDAMN OBEDIENCE, AND BY EVERY SHADE BELOW, I'LL HAVE IT!
YOU CAN START BY DELAYING THIS WOLF HUNT.
NOW, GO AWAY. GET TO WORK. YOU CAN'T COME IN FOR YOUR AFTERNOON ROMANCE SESSION TODAY. I'VE MORE IMPORTANT THINGS TO DO.

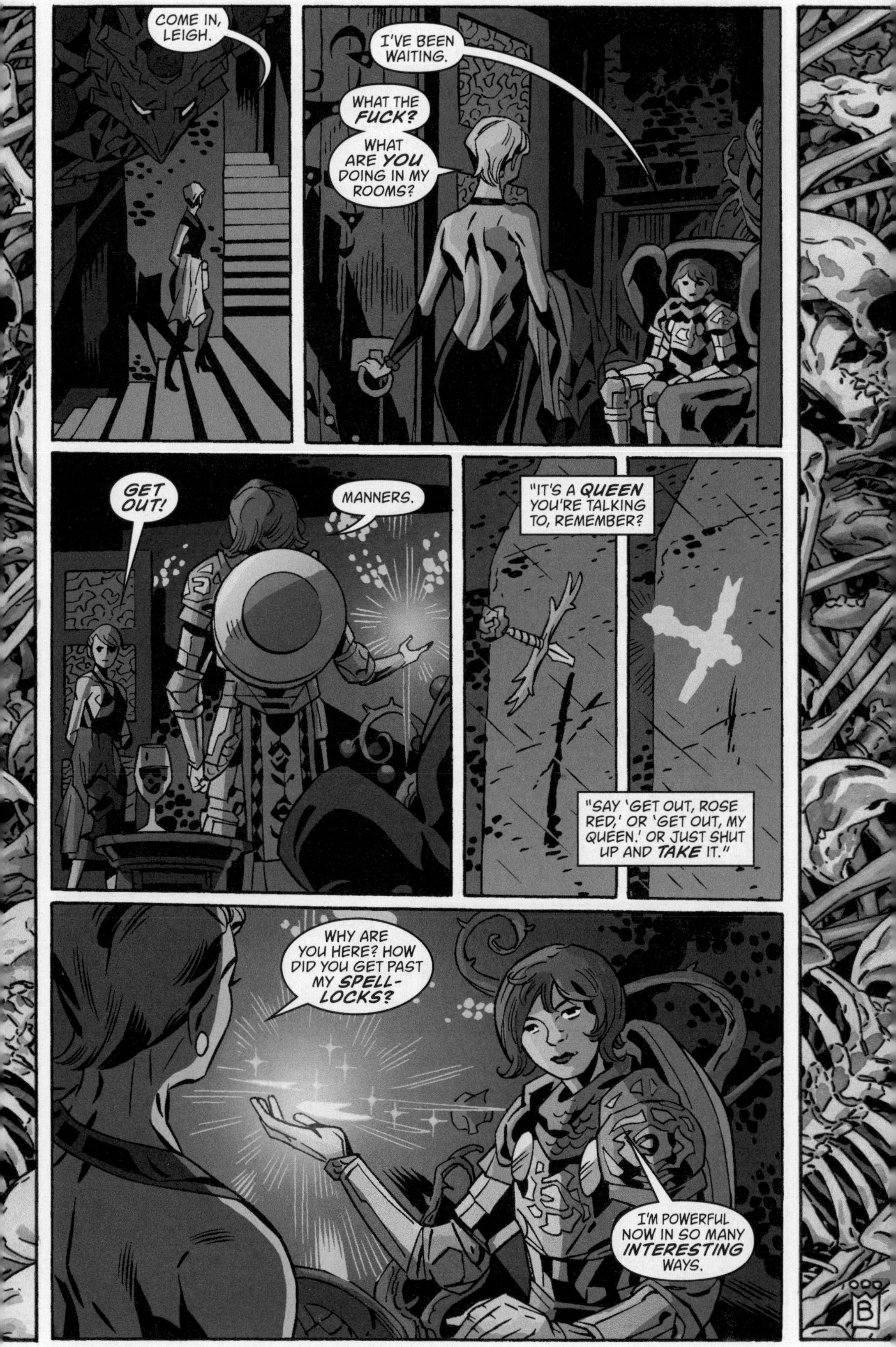
COME IN, LEIGH.
I'VE BEEN WAITING.
WHAT THE FUCK?
WHAT ARE YOU DOING IN MY ROOMS?
GET OUT!
MANNERS.
"IT'S A QUEEN YOU'RE TALKING TO, REMEMBER?
"SAY 'GET OUT, ROSE RED,' OR 'GET OUT, MY QUEEN.' OR JUST SHUT UP AND TAKE IT."
WHY ARE YOU HERE? HOW DID YOU GET PAST MY SPELL-LOCKS?
I'M POWERFUL NOW IN SO MANY INTERESTING WAYS.

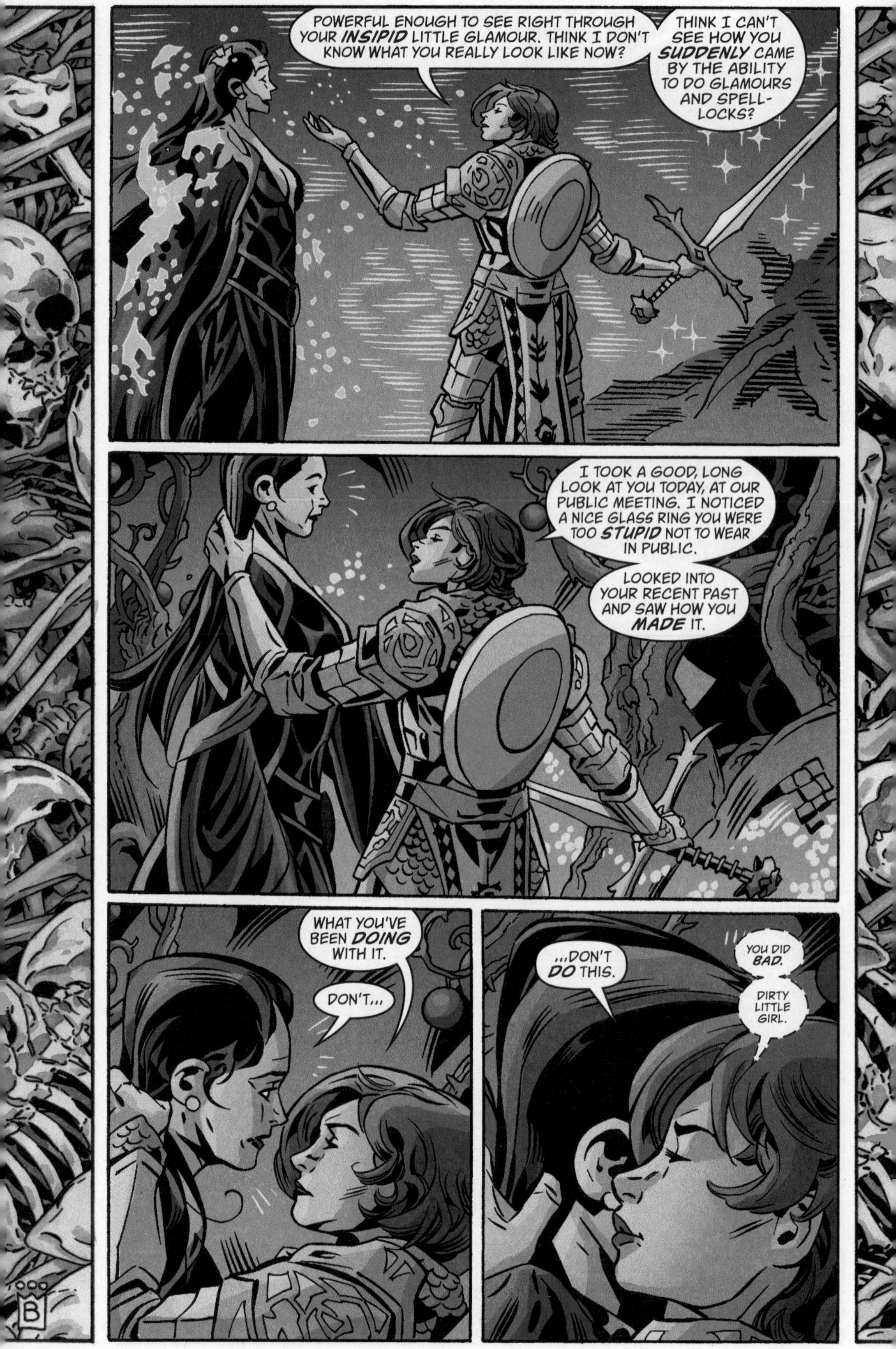

POWERFUL ENOUGH TO SEE RIGHT THROUGH YOUR *INSIPID* LITTLE GLAMOUR. THINK I DON'T KNOW WHAT YOU REALLY LOOK LIKE NOW?
THINK I CAN'T SEE HOW YOU *SUDDENLY* CAME BY THE ABILITY TO DO GLAMOURS AND SPELL-LOCKS?
I TOOK A GOOD, LONG LOOK AT YOU TODAY, AT OUR PUBLIC MEETING. I NOTICED A NICE GLASS RING YOU WERE TOO *STUPID* NOT TO WEAR IN PUBLIC.
LOOKED INTO YOUR RECENT PAST AND SAW HOW YOU *MADE* IT.
WHAT YOU'VE BEEN *DOING* WITH IT.
DON'T...
...DON'T *DO* THIS.
YOU DID *BAD.*
DIRTY LITTLE GIRL.

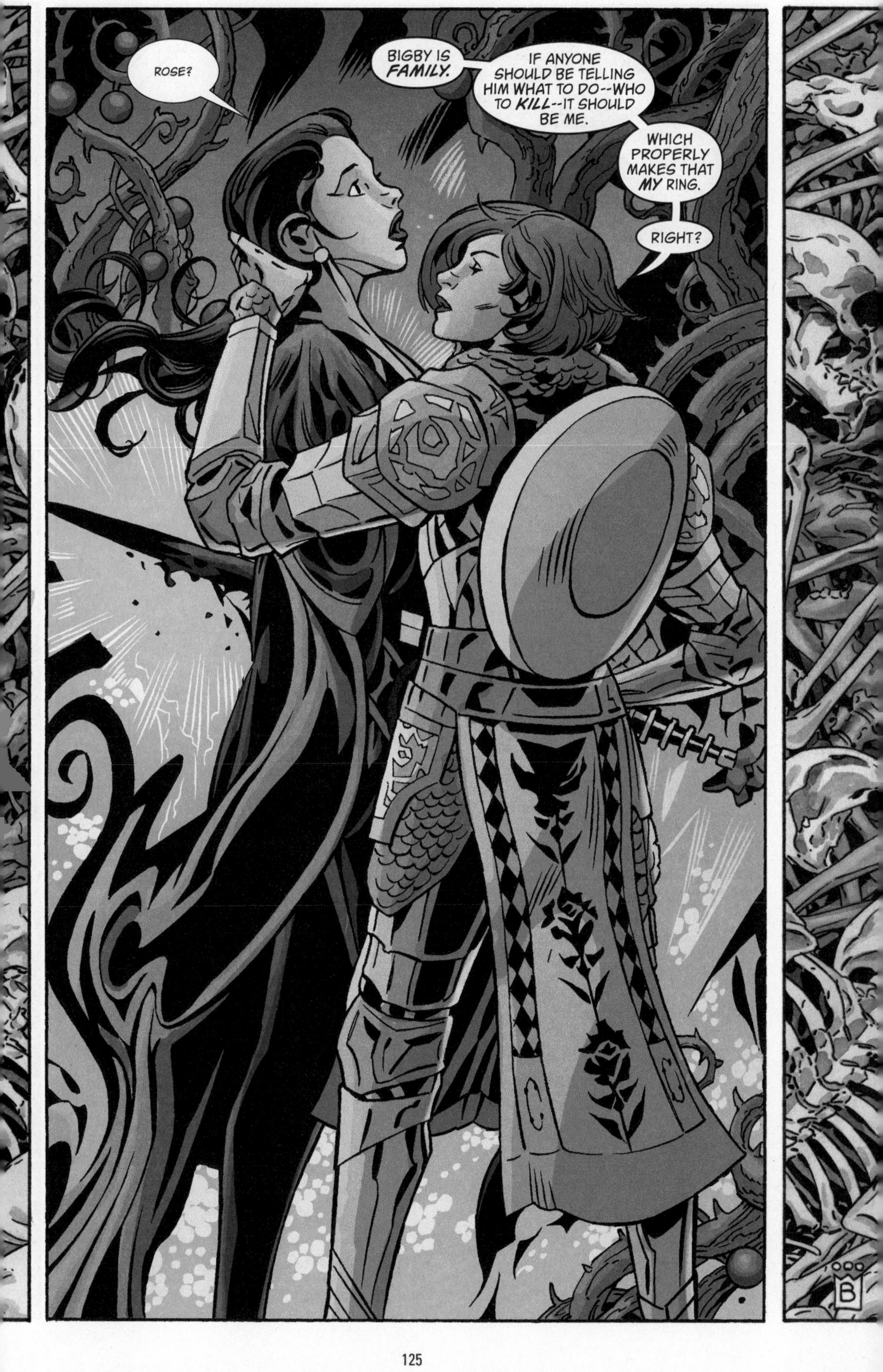
ROSE?
BIGBY IS *FAMILY.*
IF ANYONE SHOULD BE TELLING HIM WHAT TO DO--WHO TO *KILL*--IT SHOULD BE ME.
WHICH PROPERLY MAKES THAT *MY* RING.
RIGHT?

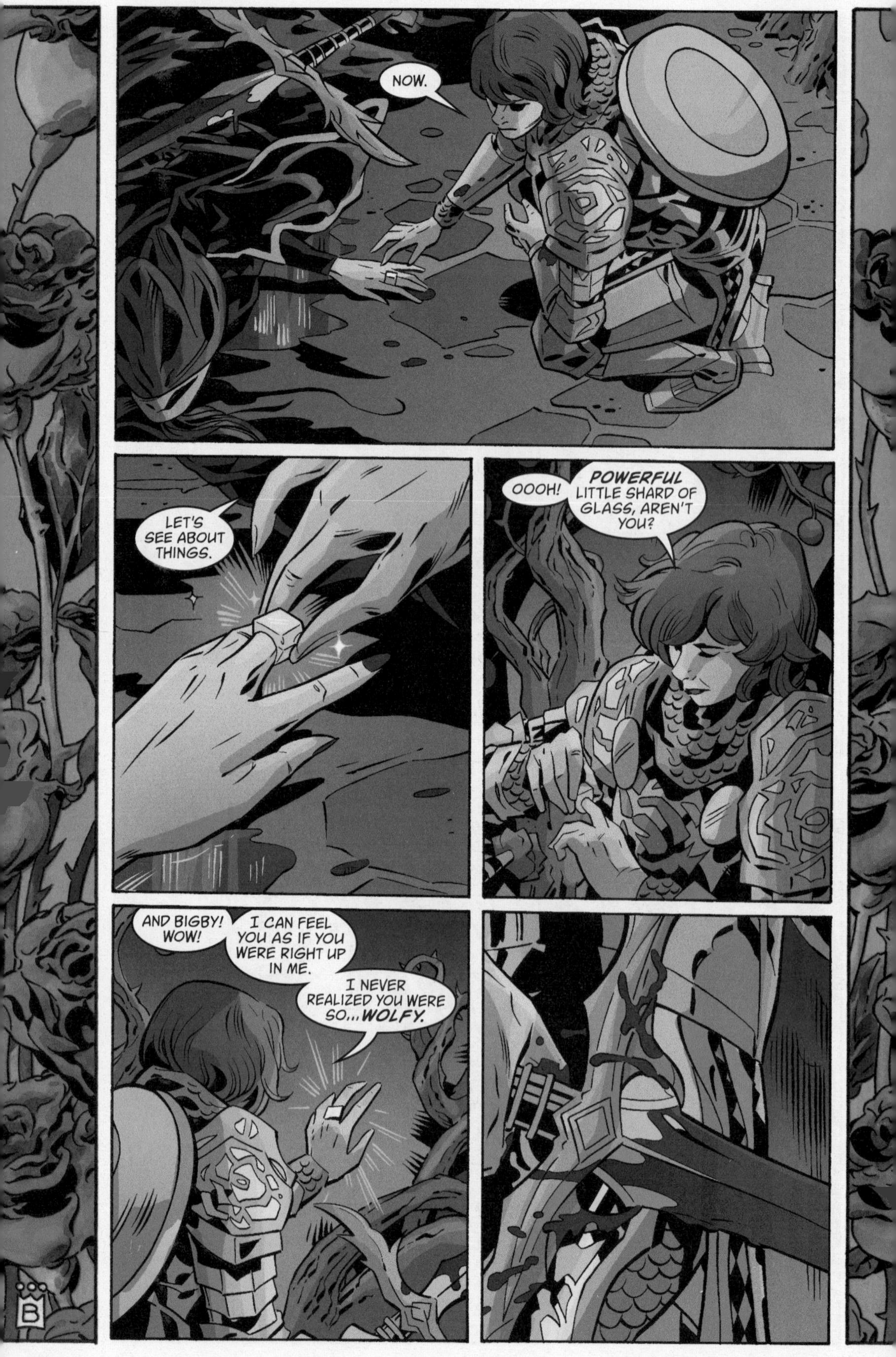
NOW.
LET'S SEE ABOUT THINGS.
OOOH!
POWERFUL LITTLE SHARD OF GLASS, AREN'T YOU?
AND BIGBY! WOW!
I CAN FEEL YOU AS IF YOU WERE RIGHT UP IN ME.
I NEVER REALIZED YOU WERE SO...WOLFY.

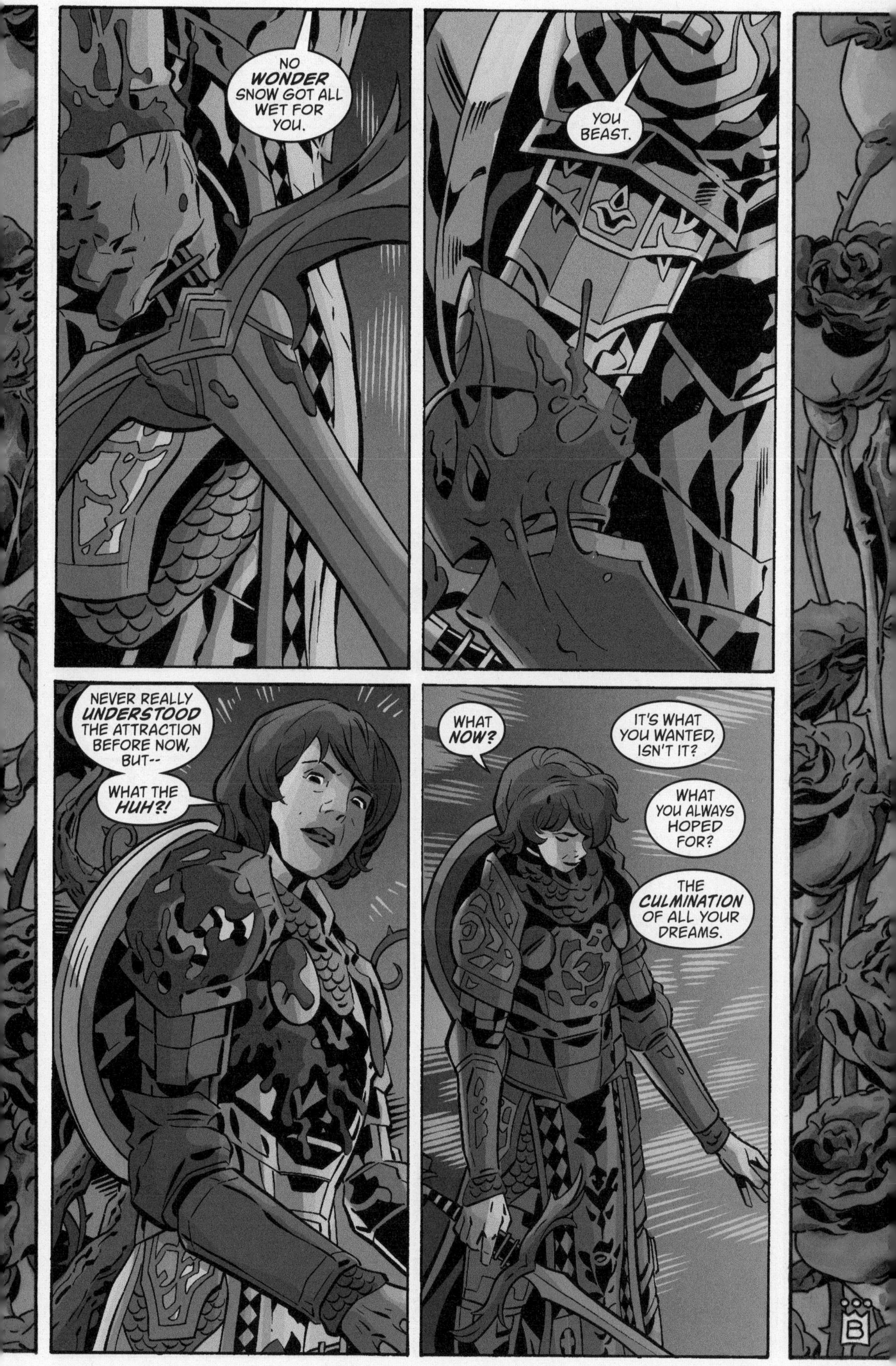
NO WONDER SNOW GOT ALL WET FOR YOU.
YOU BEAST.
NEVER REALLY UNDERSTOOD THE ATTRACTION BEFORE NOW, BUT--
WHAT THE HUH?!
WHAT NOW?
IT'S WHAT YOU WANTED, ISN'T IT?
WHAT YOU ALWAYS HOPED FOR?
THE CULMINATION OF ALL YOUR DREAMS.

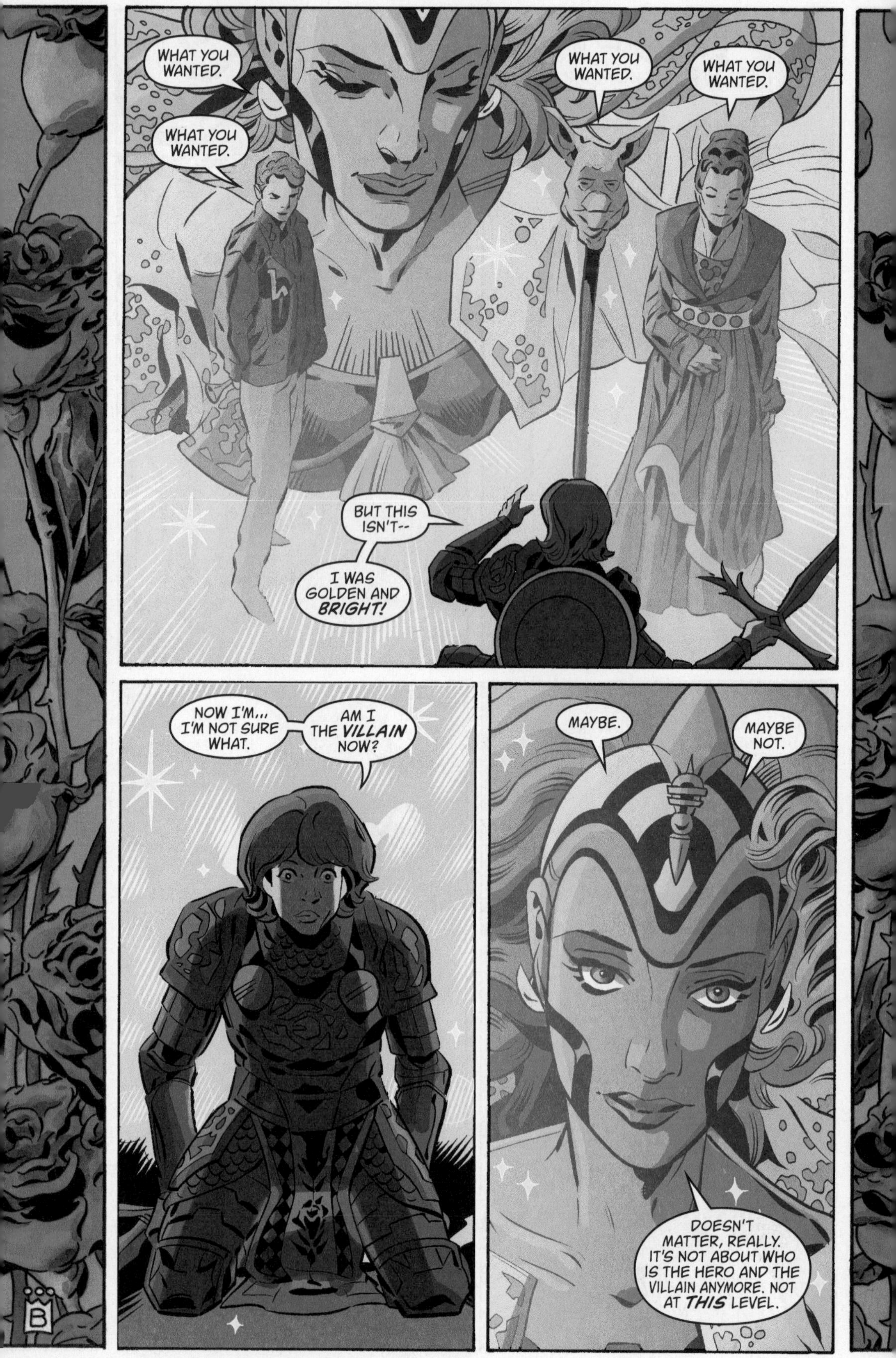
WHAT YOU WANTED.
WHAT YOU WANTED.
WHAT YOU WANTED.
WHAT YOU WANTED.
BUT THIS ISN'T--
I WAS GOLDEN AND BRIGHT!
NOW I'M... I'M NOT SURE WHAT.
AM I THE VILLAIN NOW?
MAYBE.
MAYBE NOT.
DOESN'T MATTER, REALLY. IT'S NOT ABOUT WHO IS THE HERO AND THE VILLAIN ANYMORE. NOT AT THIS LEVEL.

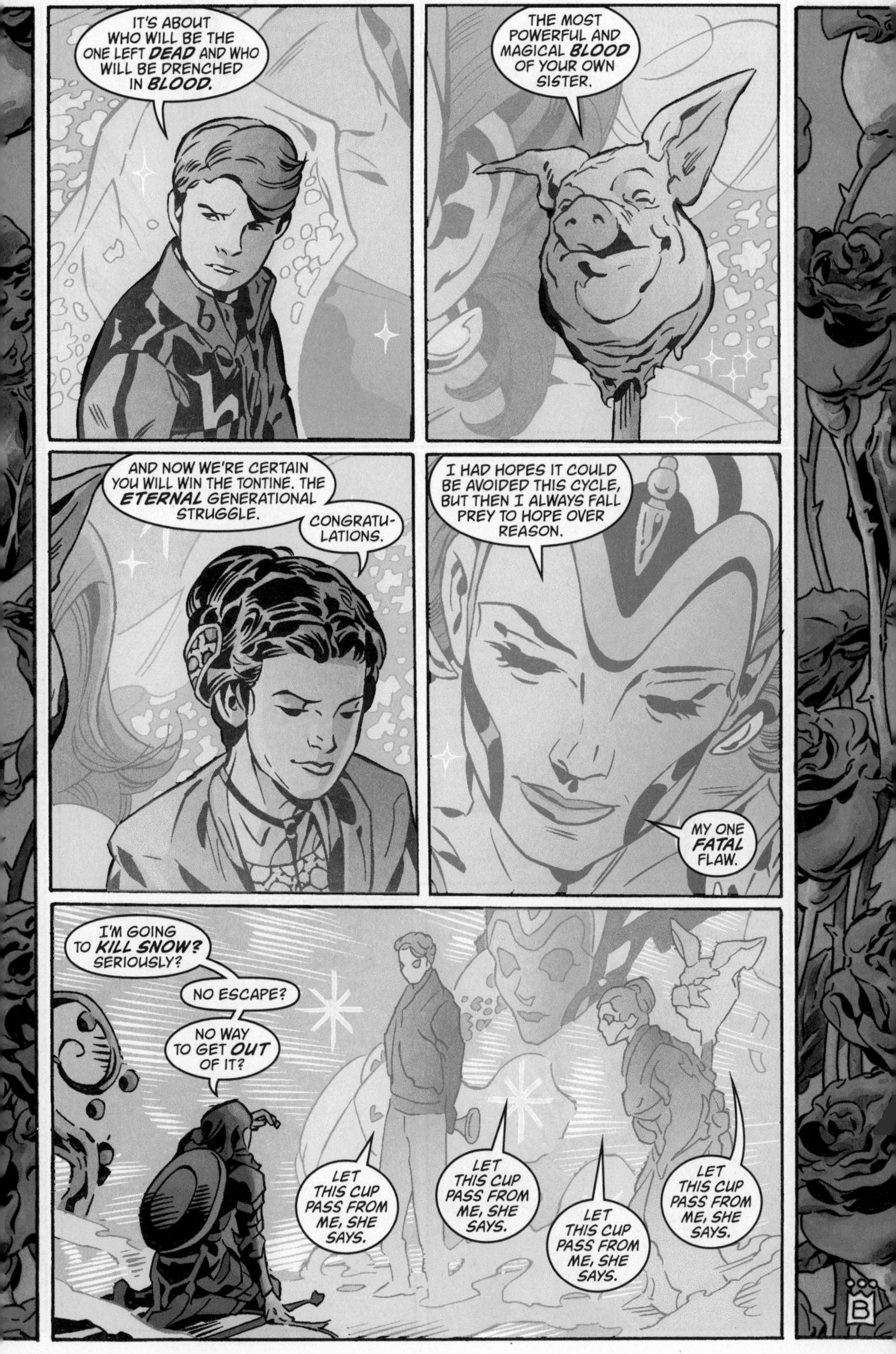
IT'S ABOUT WHO WILL BE THE ONE LEFT DEAD AND WHO WILL BE DRENCHED IN BLOOD.
THE MOST POWERFUL AND MAGICAL BLOOD OF YOUR OWN SISTER.
AND NOW WE'RE CERTAIN YOU WILL WIN THE TONTINE. THE ETERNAL GENERATIONAL STRUGGLE.
CONGRATU-LATIONS.
I HAD HOPES IT COULD BE AVOIDED THIS CYCLE, BUT THEN I ALWAYS FALL PREY TO HOPE OVER REASON.
MY ONE FATAL FLAW.
I'M GOING TO KILL SNOW? SERIOUSLY?
NO ESCAPE?
NO WAY TO GET OUT OF IT?
LET THIS CUP PASS FROM ME, SHE SAYS.
LET THIS CUP PASS FROM ME, SHE SAYS.
LET THIS CUP PASS FROM ME, SHE SAYS.
LET THIS CUP PASS FROM ME, SHE SAYS.

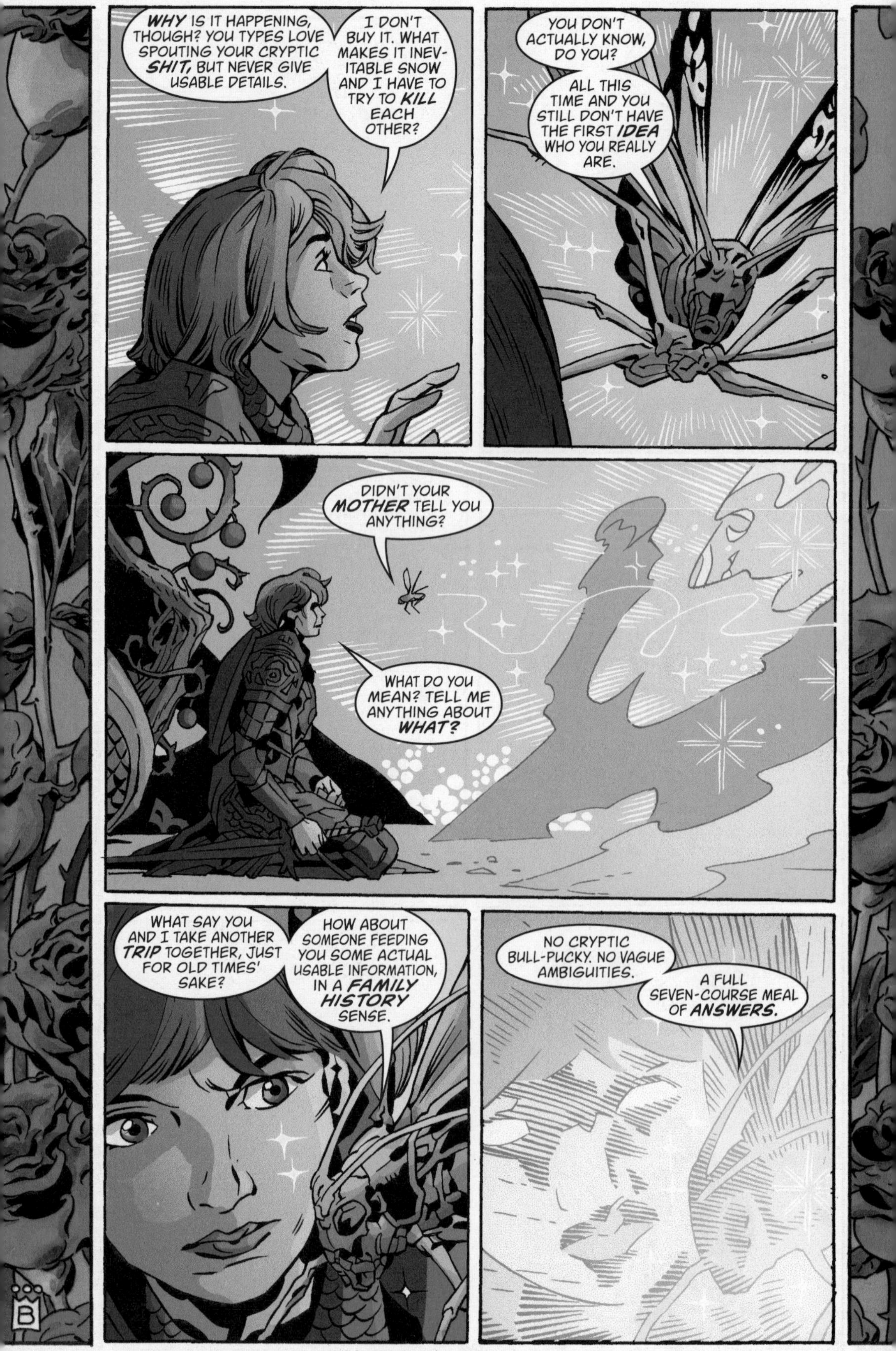
WHY IS IT HAPPENING, THOUGH? YOU TYPES LOVE SPOUTING YOUR CRYPTIC SHIT, BUT NEVER GIVE USABLE DETAILS.
I DON'T BUY IT. WHAT MAKES IT INEVITABLE SNOW AND I HAVE TO TRY TO KILL EACH OTHER?
YOU DON'T ACTUALLY KNOW, DO YOU?
ALL THIS TIME AND YOU STILL DON'T HAVE THE FIRST IDEA WHO YOU REALLY ARE.
DIDN'T YOUR MOTHER TELL YOU ANYTHING?
WHAT DO YOU MEAN? TELL ME ANYTHING ABOUT WHAT?
WHAT SAY YOU AND I TAKE ANOTHER TRIP TOGETHER, JUST FOR OLD TIMES' SAKE?
HOW ABOUT SOMEONE FEEDING YOU SOME ACTUAL USABLE INFORMATION, IN A FAMILY HISTORY SENSE.
NO CRYPTIC BULL-PUCKY. NO VAGUE AMBIGUITIES.
A FULL SEVEN-COURSE MEAL OF ANSWERS.

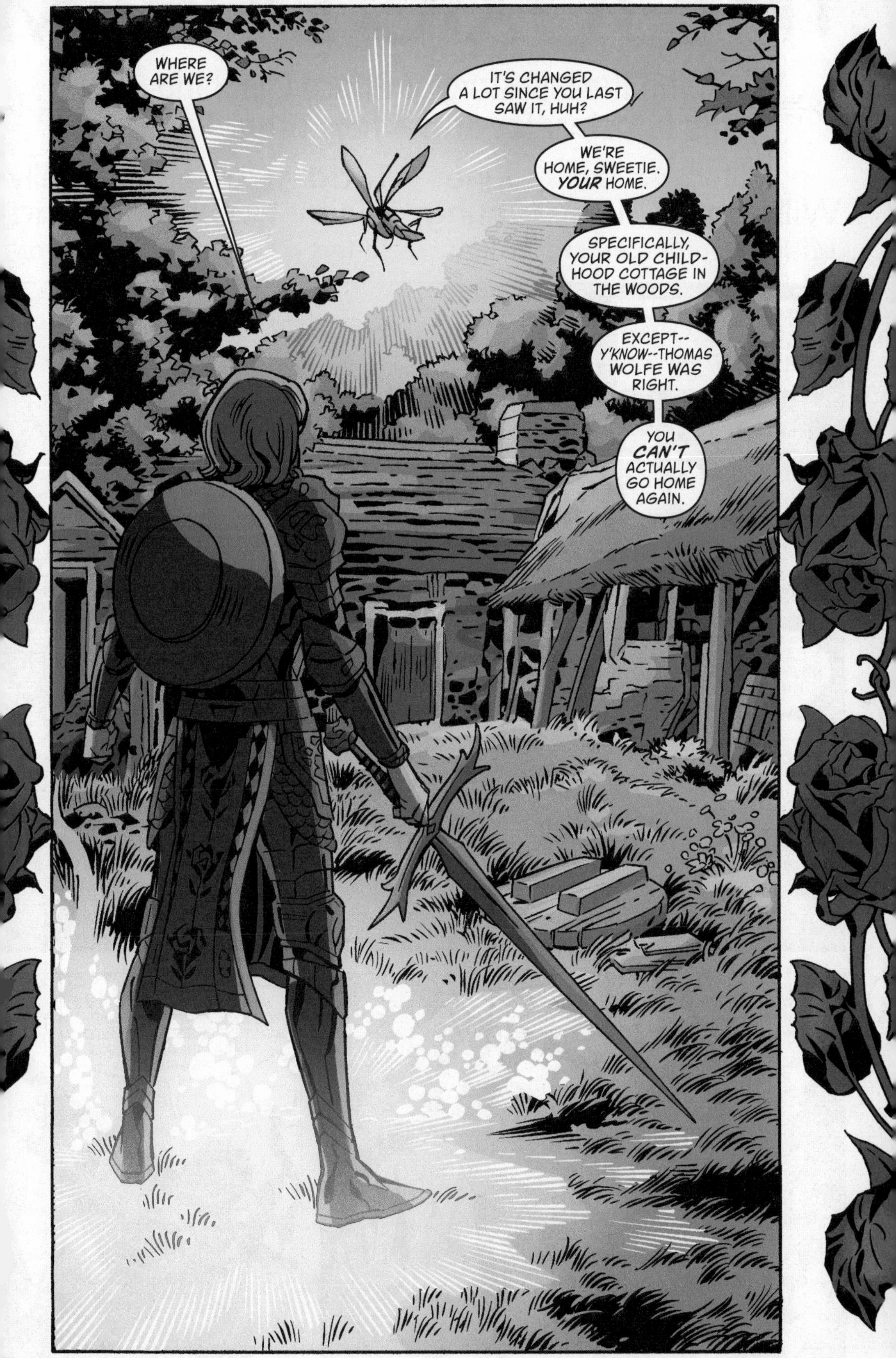
WHERE ARE WE?
IT'S CHANGED A LOT SINCE YOU LAST SAW IT, HUH?
WE'RE HOME, SWEETIE. YOUR HOME.
SPECIFICALLY, YOUR OLD CHILD-HOOD COTTAGE IN THE WOODS.
EXCEPT--Y'KNOW--THOMAS WOLFE WAS RIGHT.
YOU CAN'T ACTUALLY GO HOME AGAIN.

NEXT: TONTINE!

THE TOXIC DREAM

Being the last story of Prince Charming, of his latest wife, and a few other Fables.

Bill Willingham writer/creator — Jae Lee artist — June Chung colors — Todd Klein letters — Rowena Yow assoc. ed. — Shelly Bond editor

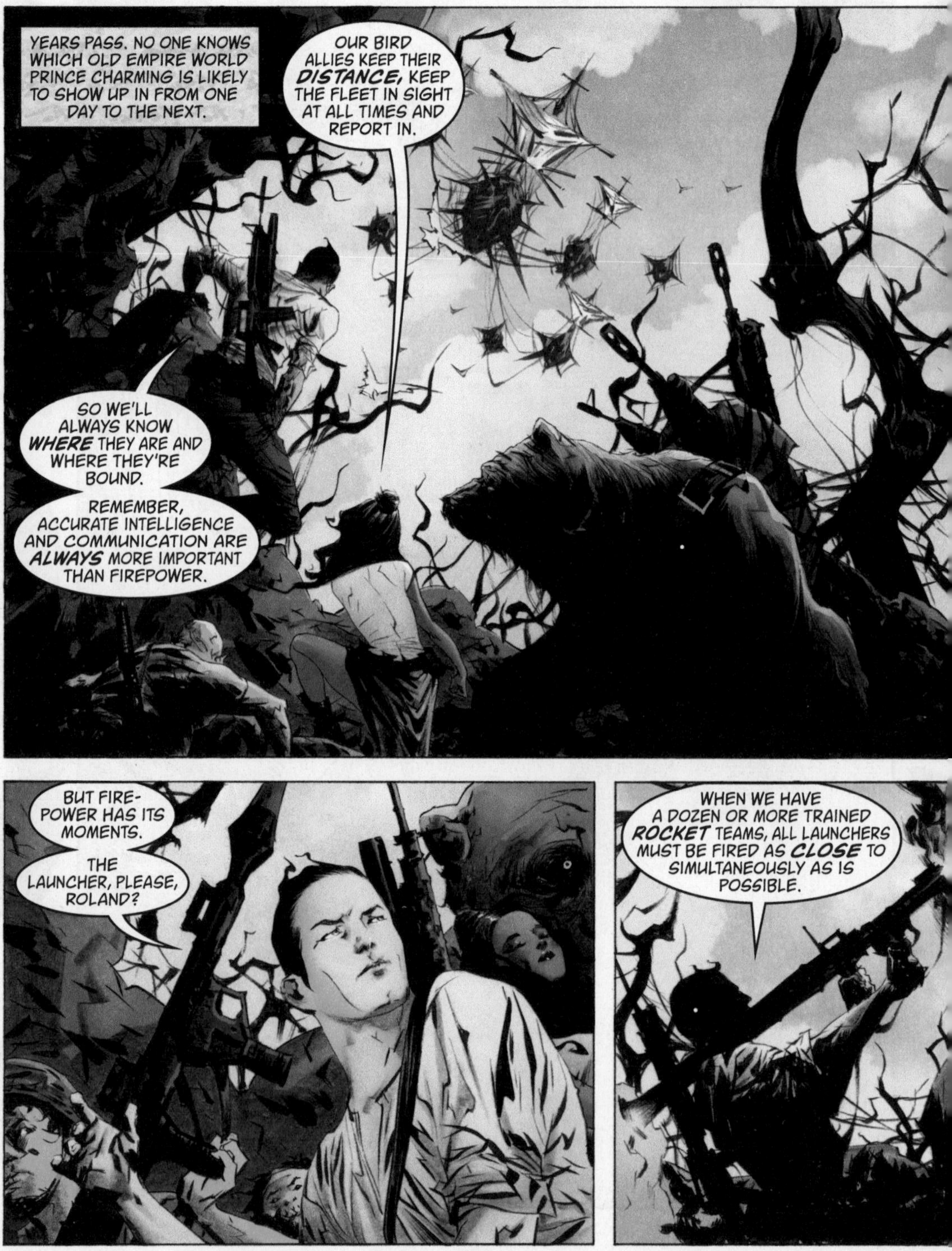

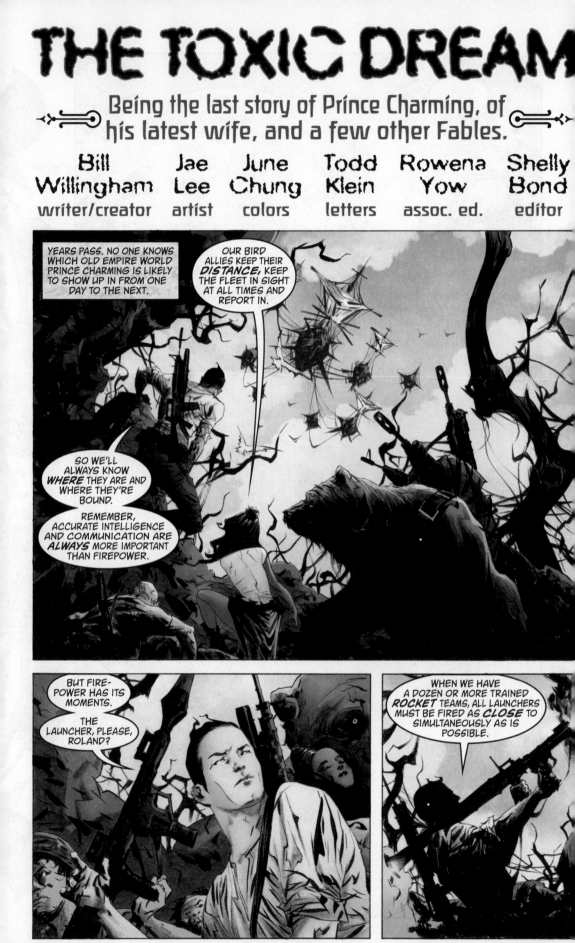

YEARS PASS. NO ONE KNOWS WHICH OLD EMPIRE WORLD PRINCE CHARMING IS LIKELY TO SHOW UP IN FROM ONE DAY TO THE NEXT.
OUR BIRD ALLIES KEEP THEIR DISTANCE, KEEP THE FLEET IN SIGHT AT ALL TIMES AND REPORT IN.
SO WE'LL ALWAYS KNOW WHERE THEY ARE AND WHERE THEY'RE BOUND.
REMEMBER, ACCURATE INTELLIGENCE AND COMMUNICATION ARE ALWAYS MORE IMPORTANT THAN FIREPOWER.
BUT FIRE-POWER HAS ITS MOMENTS.
THE LAUNCHER, PLEASE, ROLAND?
WHEN WE HAVE A DOZEN OR MORE TRAINED ROCKET TEAMS, ALL LAUNCHERS MUST BE FIRED AS CLOSE TO SIMULTANEOUSLY AS IS POSSIBLE.

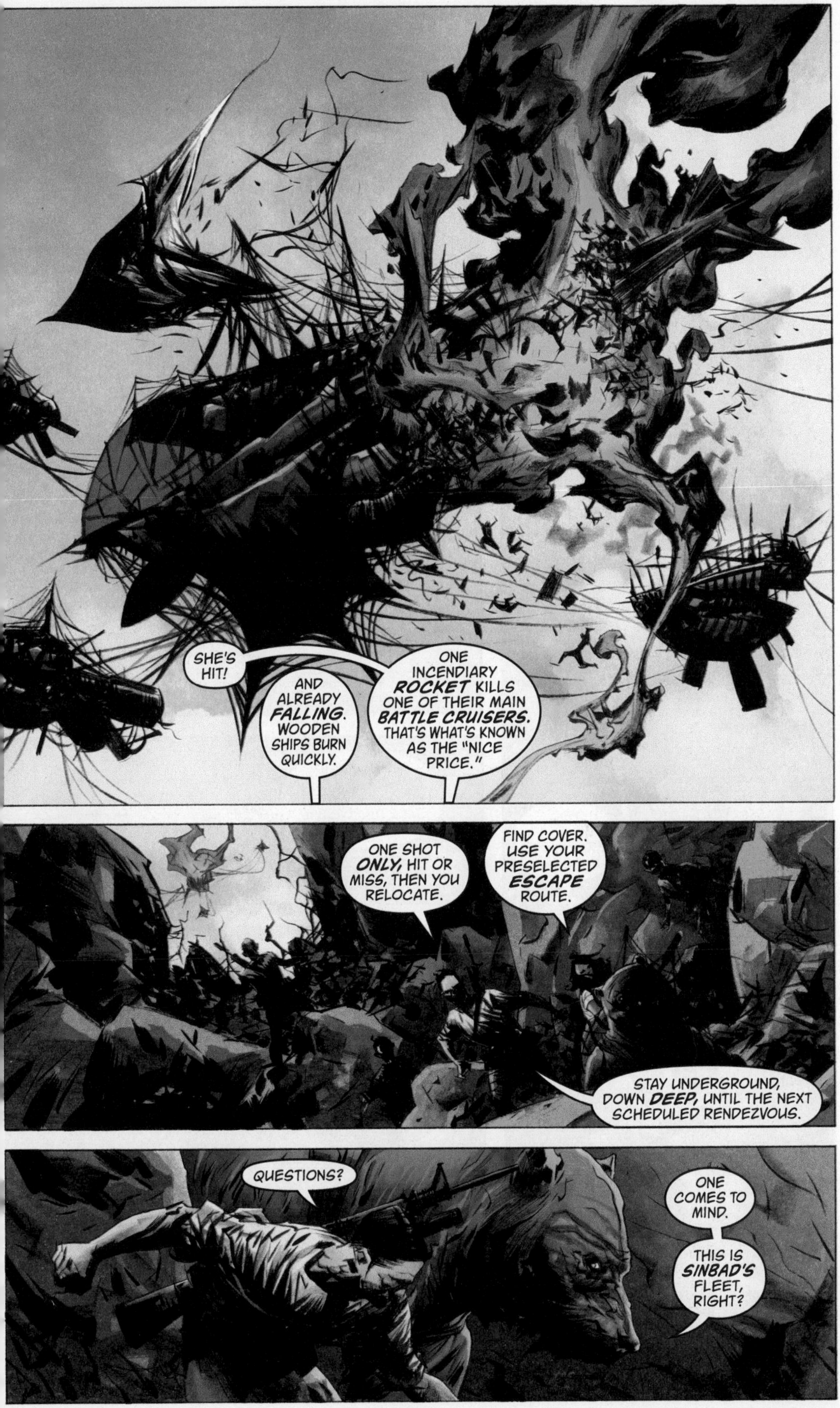
SHE'S HIT!
AND ALREADY FALLING. WOODEN SHIPS BURN QUICKLY.
ONE INCENDIARY ROCKET KILLS ONE OF THEIR MAIN BATTLE CRUISERS. THAT'S WHAT'S KNOWN AS THE "NICE PRICE."
ONE SHOT ONLY, HIT OR MISS, THEN YOU RELOCATE.
FIND COVER. USE YOUR PRESELECTED ESCAPE ROUTE.
STAY UNDERGROUND, DOWN DEEP, UNTIL THE NEXT SCHEDULED RENDEZVOUS.
QUESTIONS?
ONE COMES TO MIND.
THIS IS SINBAD'S FLEET, RIGHT?

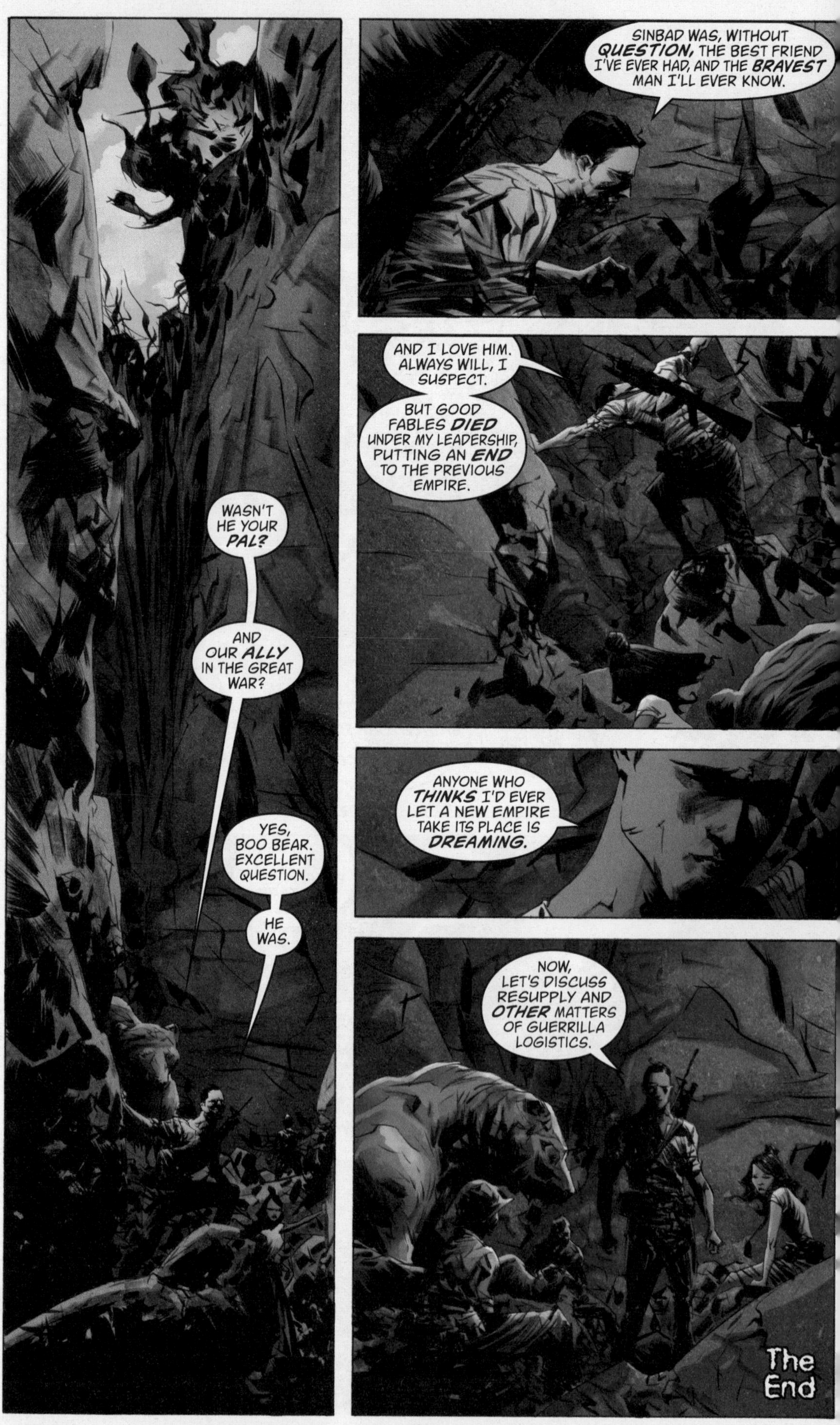

WASN'T HE YOUR PAL?
AND OUR ALLY IN THE GREAT WAR?
YES, BOO BEAR. EXCELLENT QUESTION.
HE WAS.
SINBAD WAS, WITHOUT QUESTION, THE BEST FRIEND I'VE EVER HAD, AND THE BRAVEST MAN I'LL EVER KNOW.
AND I LOVE HIM. ALWAYS WILL, I SUSPECT.
BUT GOOD FABLES DIED UNDER MY LEADERSHIP, PUTTING AN END TO THE PREVIOUS EMPIRE.
ANYONE WHO THINKS I'D EVER LET A NEW EMPIRE TAKE ITS PLACE IS DREAMING.
NOW, LET'S DISCUSS RESUPPLY AND OTHER MATTERS OF GUERRILLA LOGISTICS.
The End

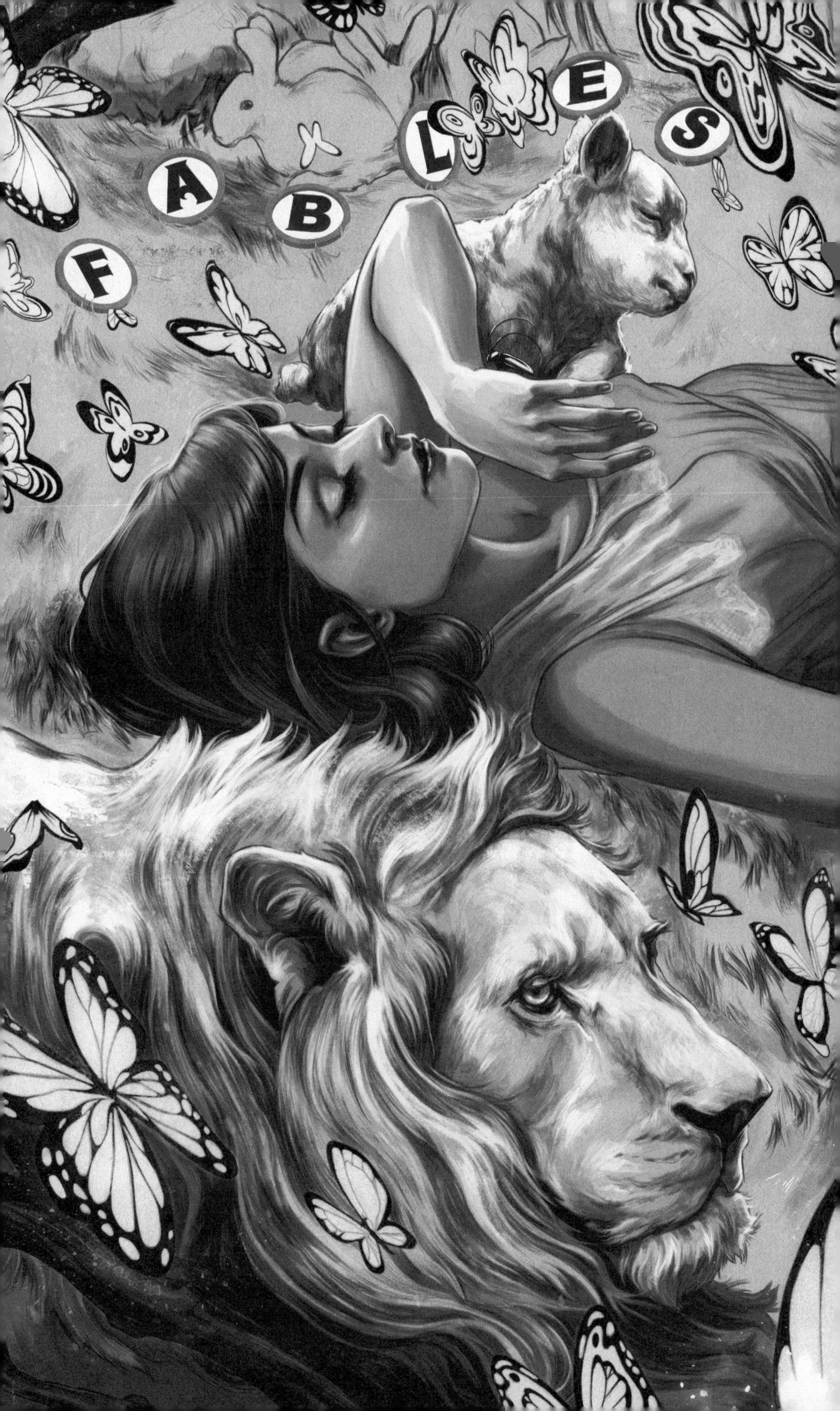
FABLES

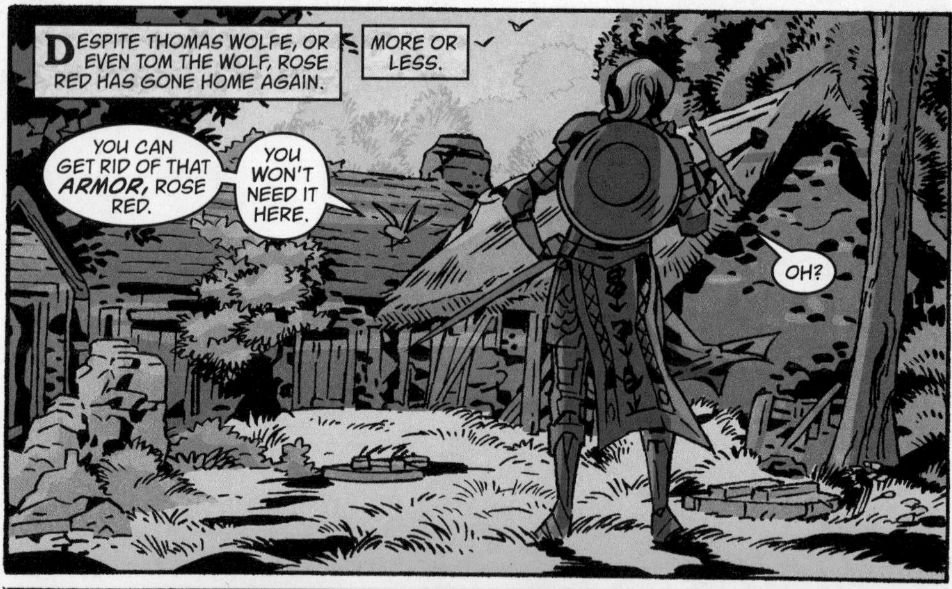
DESPITE THOMAS WOLFE, OR EVEN TOM THE WOLF, ROSE RED HAS GONE HOME AGAIN.
MORE OR LESS.
YOU CAN GET RID OF THAT ARMOR, ROSE RED.
YOU WON'T NEED IT HERE.
OH?

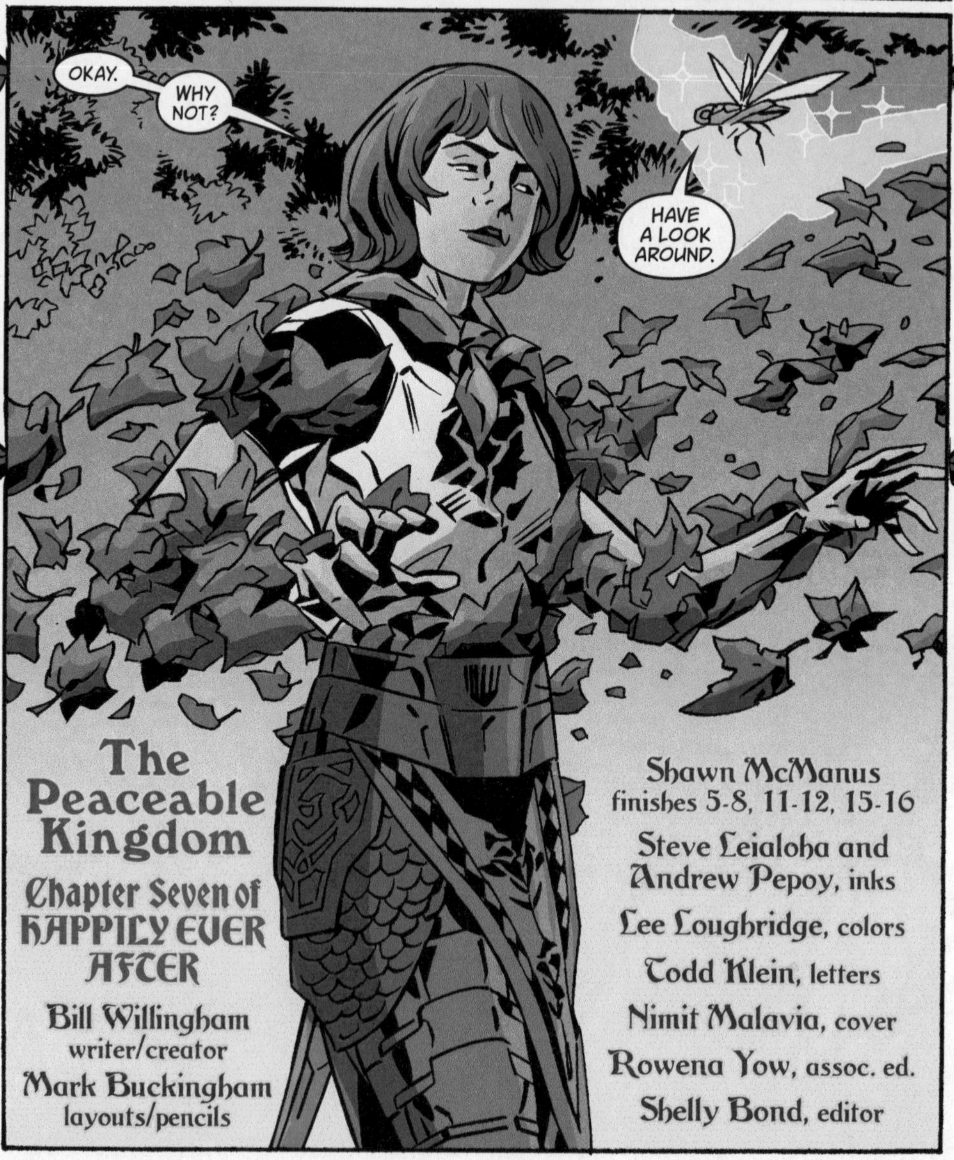
OKAY.
WHY NOT?
HAVE A LOOK AROUND.
The Peaceable Kingdom
Chapter Seven of HAPPILY EVER AFTER
Bill Willingham writer/creator
Mark Buckingham layouts/pencils
Shawn McManus finishes 5-8, 11-12, 15-16
Steve Leialoha and Andrew Pepoy, inks
Lee Loughridge, colors
Todd Klein, letters
Nimit Malavia, cover
Rowena Yow, assoc. ed.
Shelly Bond, editor

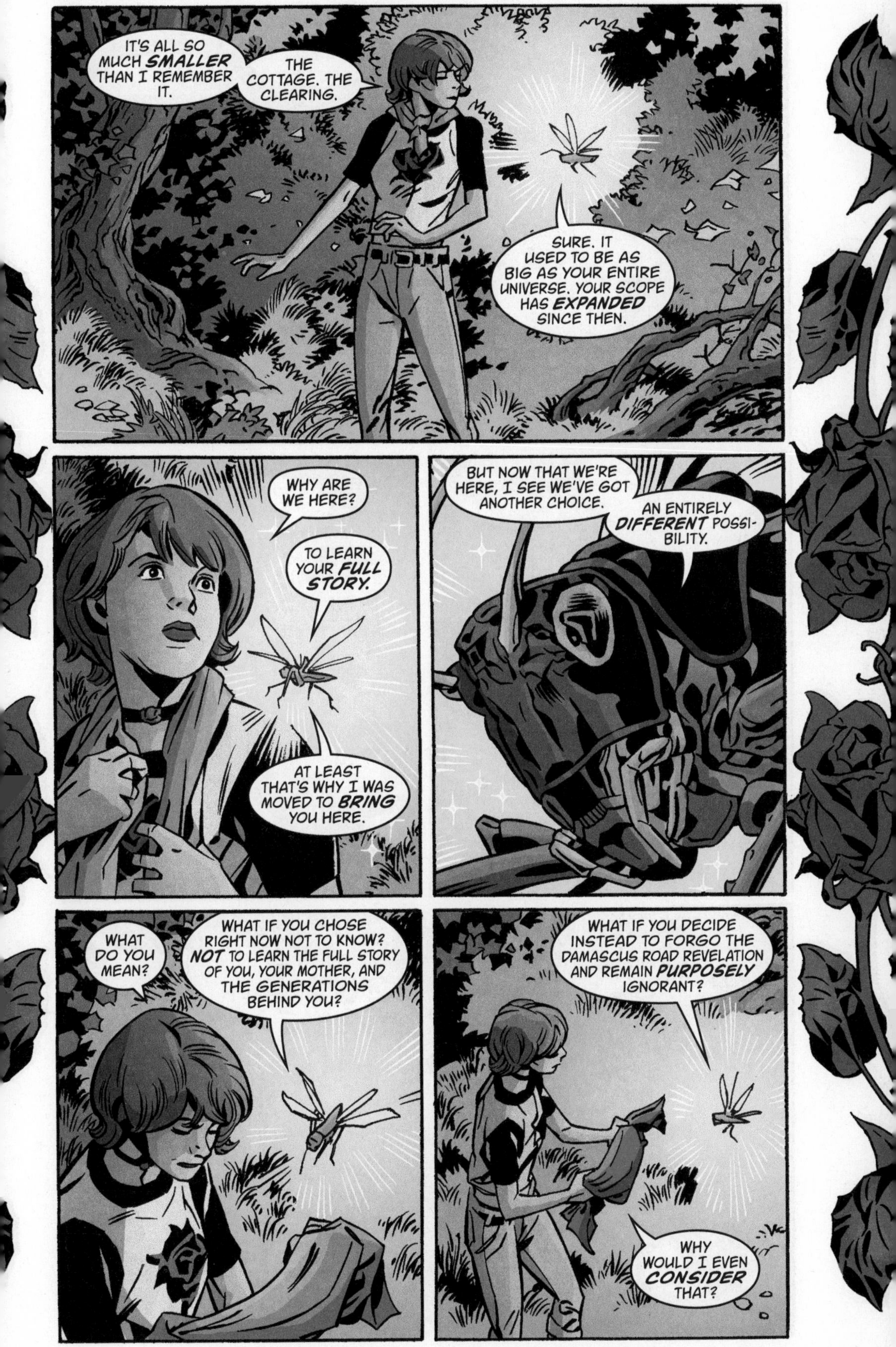
IT'S ALL SO MUCH SMALLER THAN I REMEMBER IT.
THE COTTAGE. THE CLEARING.
SURE. IT USED TO BE AS BIG AS YOUR ENTIRE UNIVERSE. YOUR SCOPE HAS EXPANDED SINCE THEN.
WHY ARE WE HERE?
TO LEARN YOUR FULL STORY.
AT LEAST THAT'S WHY I WAS MOVED TO BRING YOU HERE.
BUT NOW THAT WE'RE HERE, I SEE WE'VE GOT ANOTHER CHOICE.
AN ENTIRELY DIFFERENT POSSIBILITY.
WHAT DO YOU MEAN?
WHAT IF YOU CHOSE RIGHT NOW NOT TO KNOW? NOT TO LEARN THE FULL STORY OF YOU, YOUR MOTHER, AND THE GENERATIONS BEHIND YOU?
WHAT IF YOU DECIDE INSTEAD TO FORGO THE DAMASCUS ROAD REVELATION AND REMAIN PURPOSELY IGNORANT?
WHY WOULD I EVEN CONSIDER THAT?

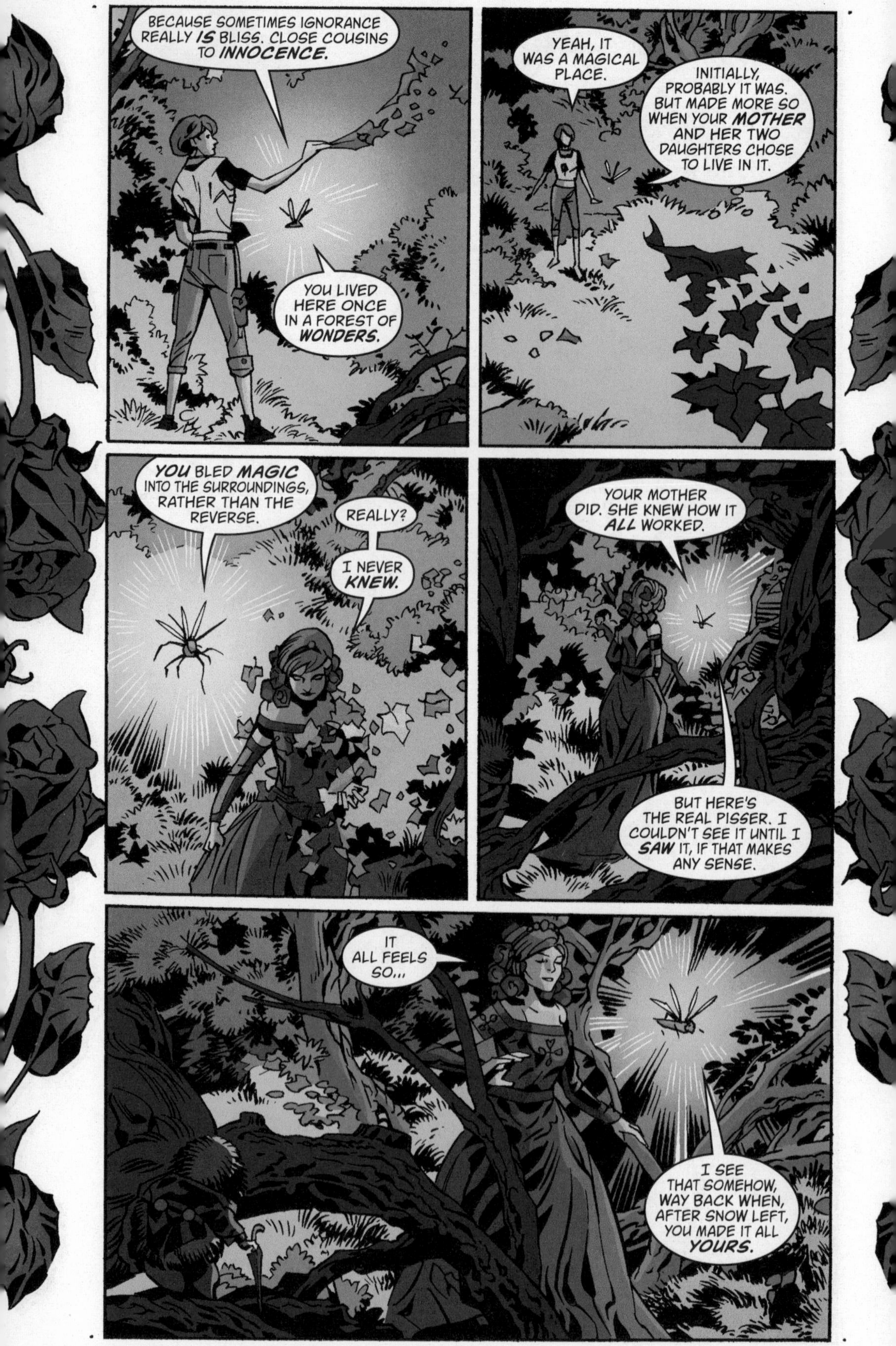
BECAUSE SOMETIMES IGNORANCE REALLY IS BLISS. CLOSE COUSINS TO INNOCENCE.
YOU LIVED HERE ONCE IN A FOREST OF WONDERS.
YEAH, IT WAS A MAGICAL PLACE.
INITIALLY, PROBABLY IT WAS. BUT MADE MORE SO WHEN YOUR MOTHER AND HER TWO DAUGHTERS CHOSE TO LIVE IN IT.
YOU BLED MAGIC INTO THE SURROUNDINGS, RATHER THAN THE REVERSE.
REALLY?
I NEVER KNEW.
YOUR MOTHER DID. SHE KNEW HOW IT ALL WORKED.
BUT HERE'S THE REAL PISSER. I COULDN'T SEE IT UNTIL I SAW IT, IF THAT MAKES ANY SENSE.
IT ALL FEELS SO...
I SEE THAT SOMEHOW, WAY BACK WHEN, AFTER SNOW LEFT, YOU MADE IT ALL YOURS.

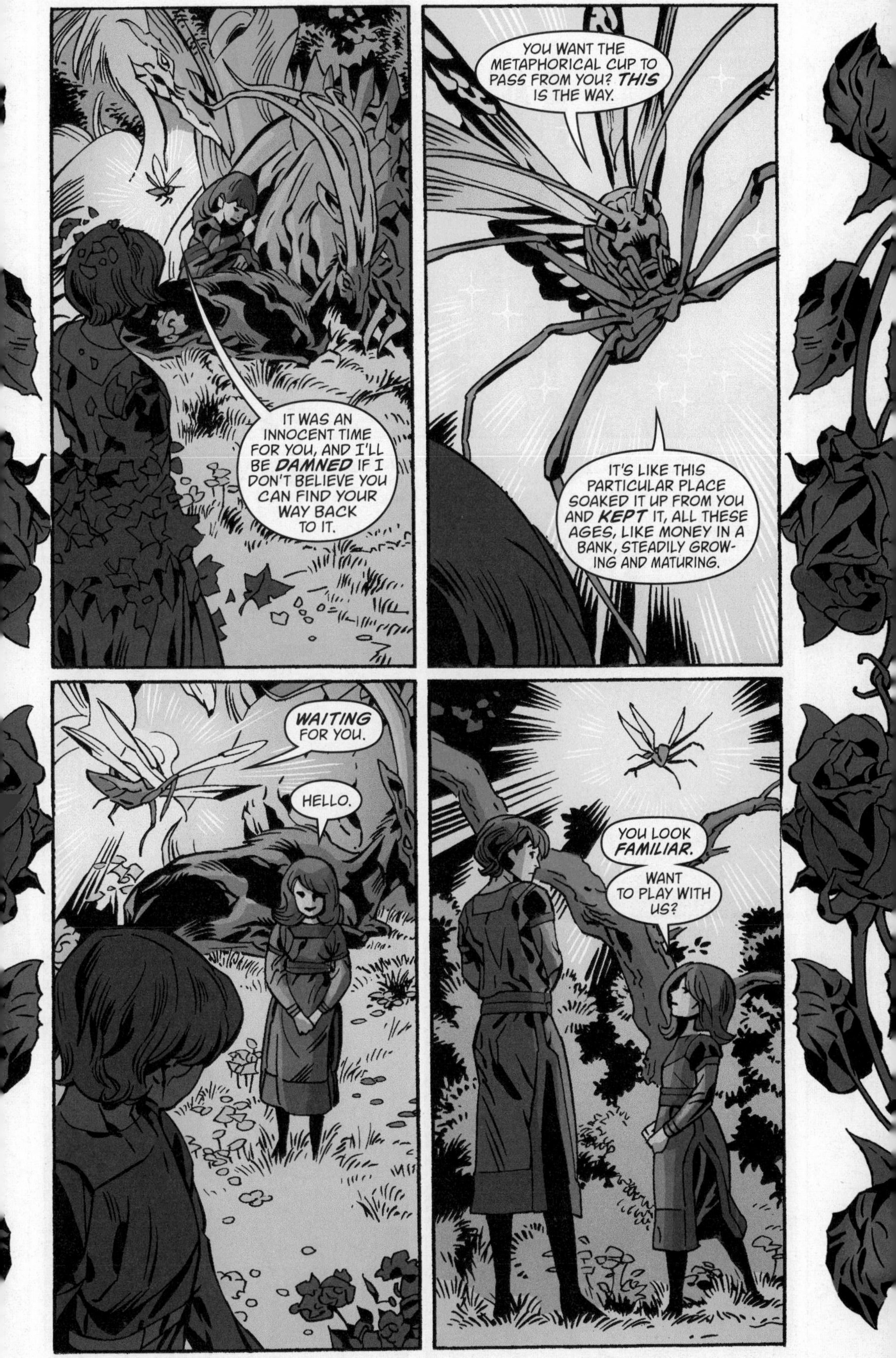
IT WAS AN INNOCENT TIME FOR YOU, AND I'LL BE DAMNED IF I DON'T BELIEVE YOU CAN FIND YOUR WAY BACK TO IT.
YOU WANT THE METAPHORICAL CUP TO PASS FROM YOU? THIS IS THE WAY.
IT'S LIKE THIS PARTICULAR PLACE SOAKED IT UP FROM YOU AND KEPT IT, ALL THESE AGES, LIKE MONEY IN A BANK, STEADILY GROWING AND MATURING.
WAITING FOR YOU.
HELLO.
YOU LOOK FAMILIAR.
WANT TO PLAY WITH US?

AT THAT MOMENT, IN THE AREA OF THE FARM KNOWN AS NEW CAMELOT...

DID YOU REACH HER?

NO. NO ONE'S SEEN HER FOR A DAY OR MORE.

I CAN'T SEE HOW WE CAN DELAY THIS TRIAL ANY LONGER. WE SHOULD PROCEED.

OKAY, LANCE, IF YOU THINK IT'S BEST, BUT ABOUT THAT...

WEYLAND WAS MY FRIEND AND MY SUBJECT. AS HIS KING, IT'S MY DUTY TO FIGHT BRANDISH.

BUT IT'S MY DUTY AS THE QUEEN'S OFFICIAL CHAMPION AND FUTURE CONSORT, KING AMBROSE.

AND, IF I CAN BE FORGIVEN THE FAMILIARITY, SIRE, I'VE SEEN YOU IN COMBAT. LACKING EXCALIBUR AND MAGIC ARMOR, I DOUBT YOU'D PREVAIL.

BEST IF I DO IT AND WE END THIS FARCE QUICKLY, HMM?

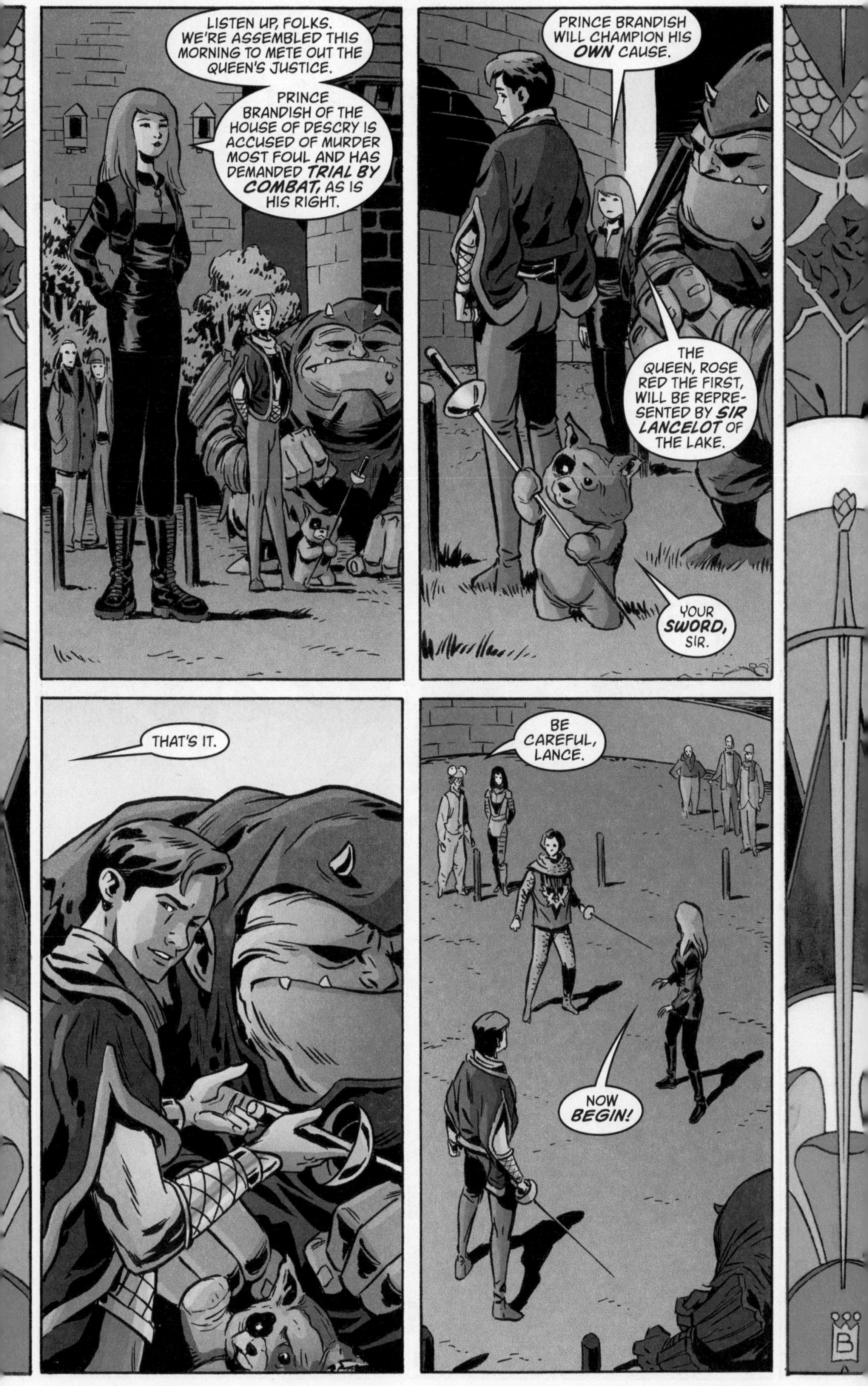
LISTEN UP, FOLKS. WE'RE ASSEMBLED THIS MORNING TO METE OUT THE QUEEN'S JUSTICE.
PRINCE BRANDISH OF THE HOUSE OF DESCRY IS ACCUSED OF MURDER MOST FOUL AND HAS DEMANDED **TRIAL BY COMBAT,** AS IS HIS RIGHT.
PRINCE BRANDISH WILL CHAMPION HIS **OWN** CAUSE.
THE QUEEN, ROSE RED THE FIRST, WILL BE REPRE-SENTED BY **SIR LANCELOT** OF THE LAKE.
YOUR **SWORD,** SIR.
THAT'S IT.
BE CAREFUL, LANCE.
NOW **BEGIN!**

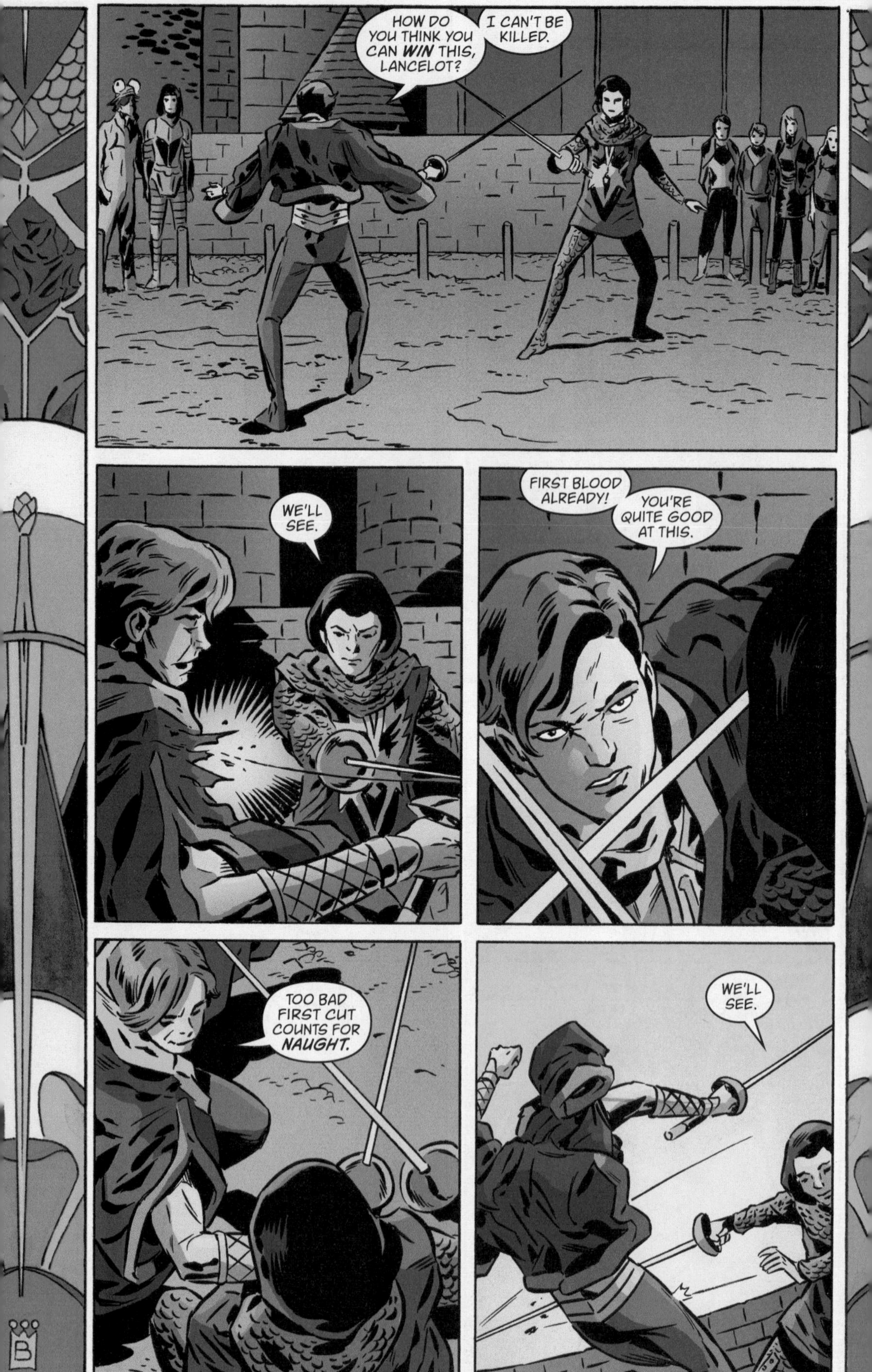
HOW DO YOU THINK YOU CAN **WIN** THIS, LANCELOT?
I CAN'T BE KILLED.
WE'LL SEE.
FIRST BLOOD ALREADY!
YOU'RE QUITE GOOD AT THIS.
TOO BAD FIRST CUT COUNTS FOR **NAUGHT.**
WE'LL SEE.

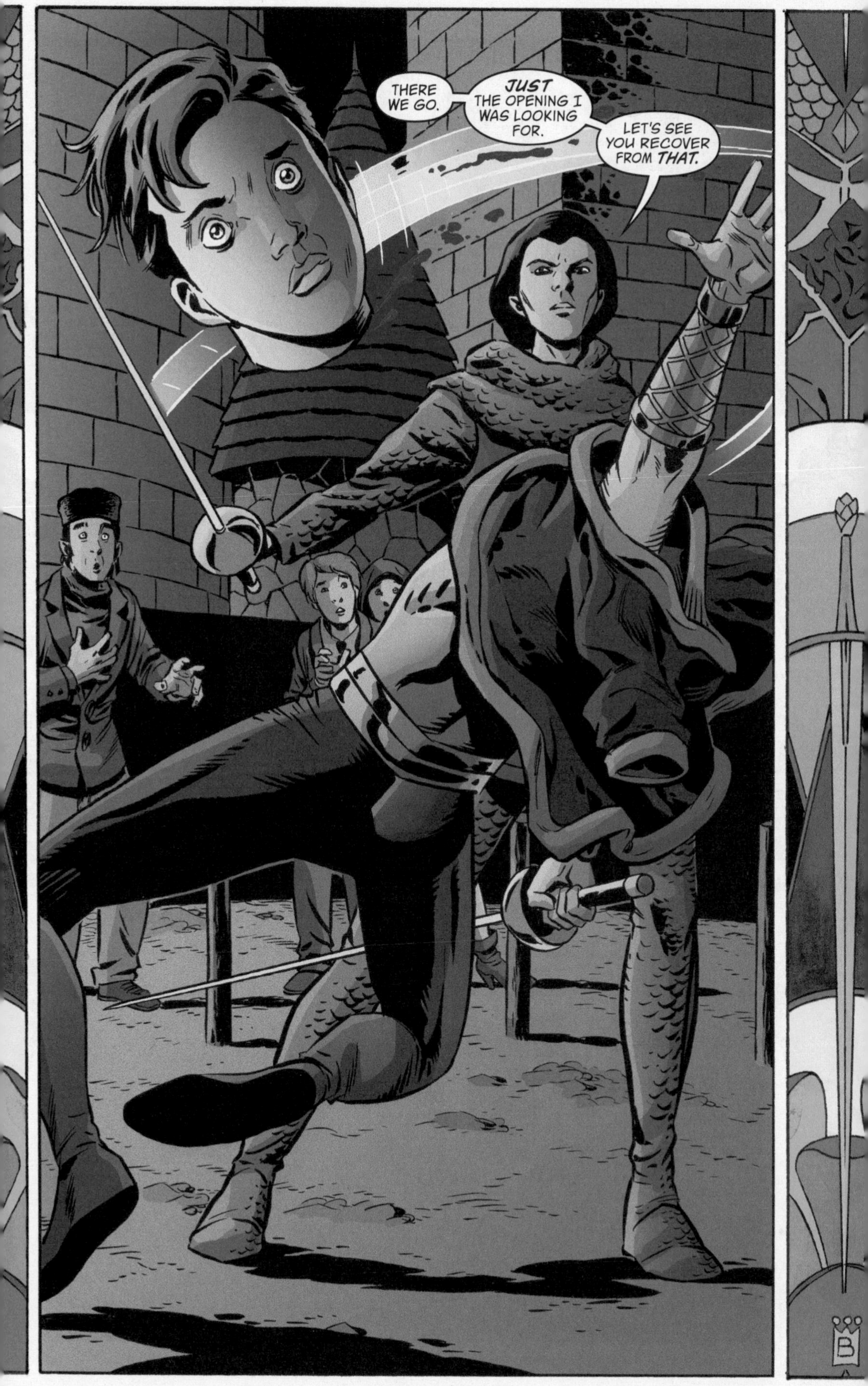
THERE WE GO.
JUST THE OPENING I WAS LOOKING FOR.
LET'S SEE YOU RECOVER FROM THAT.

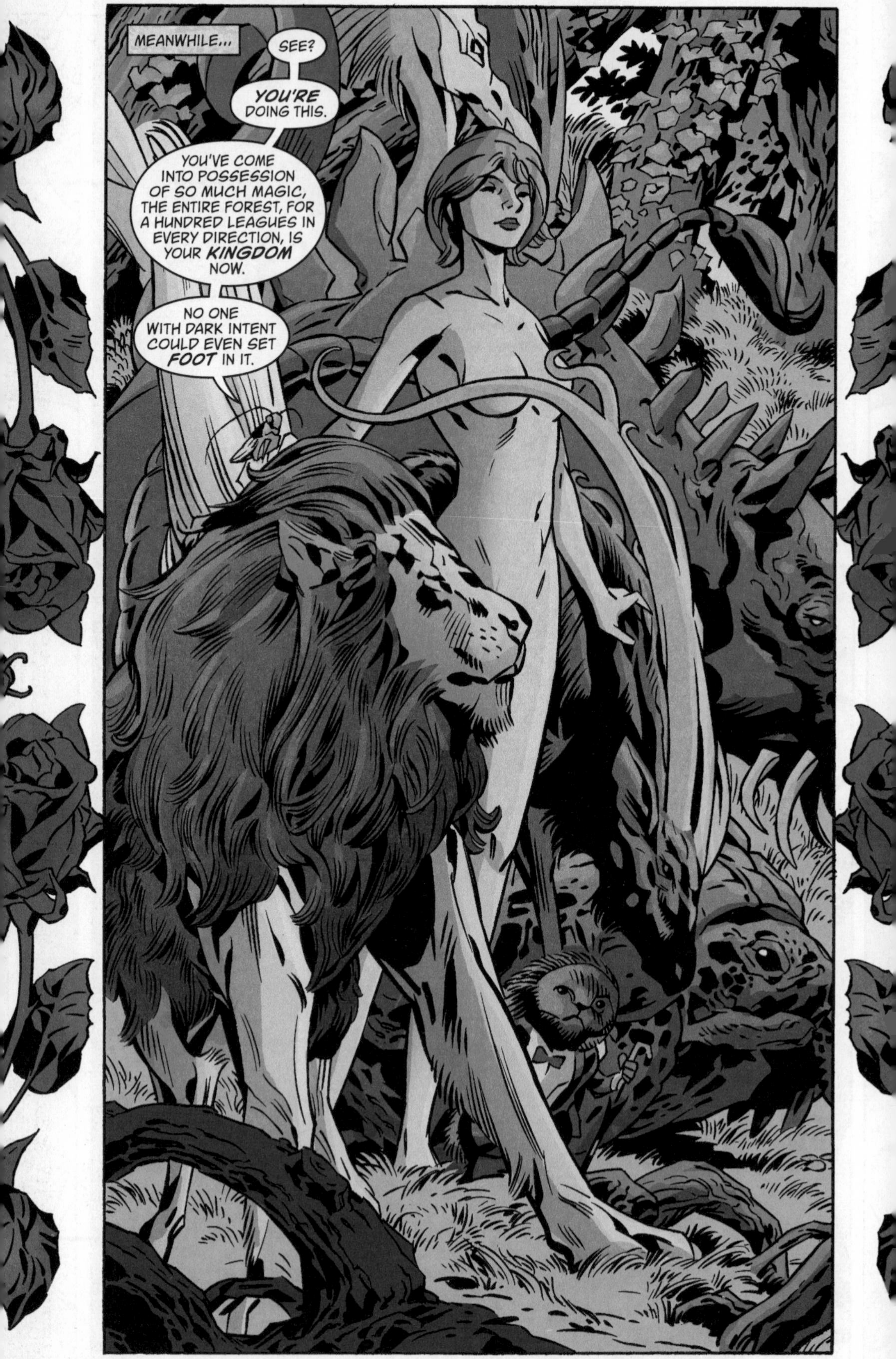

MEANWHILE...
SEE?
YOU'RE DOING THIS.
YOU'VE COME INTO POSSESSION OF SO MUCH MAGIC, THE ENTIRE FOREST, FOR A HUNDRED LEAGUES IN EVERY DIRECTION, IS YOUR KINGDOM NOW.
NO ONE WITH DARK INTENT COULD EVEN SET FOOT IN IT.

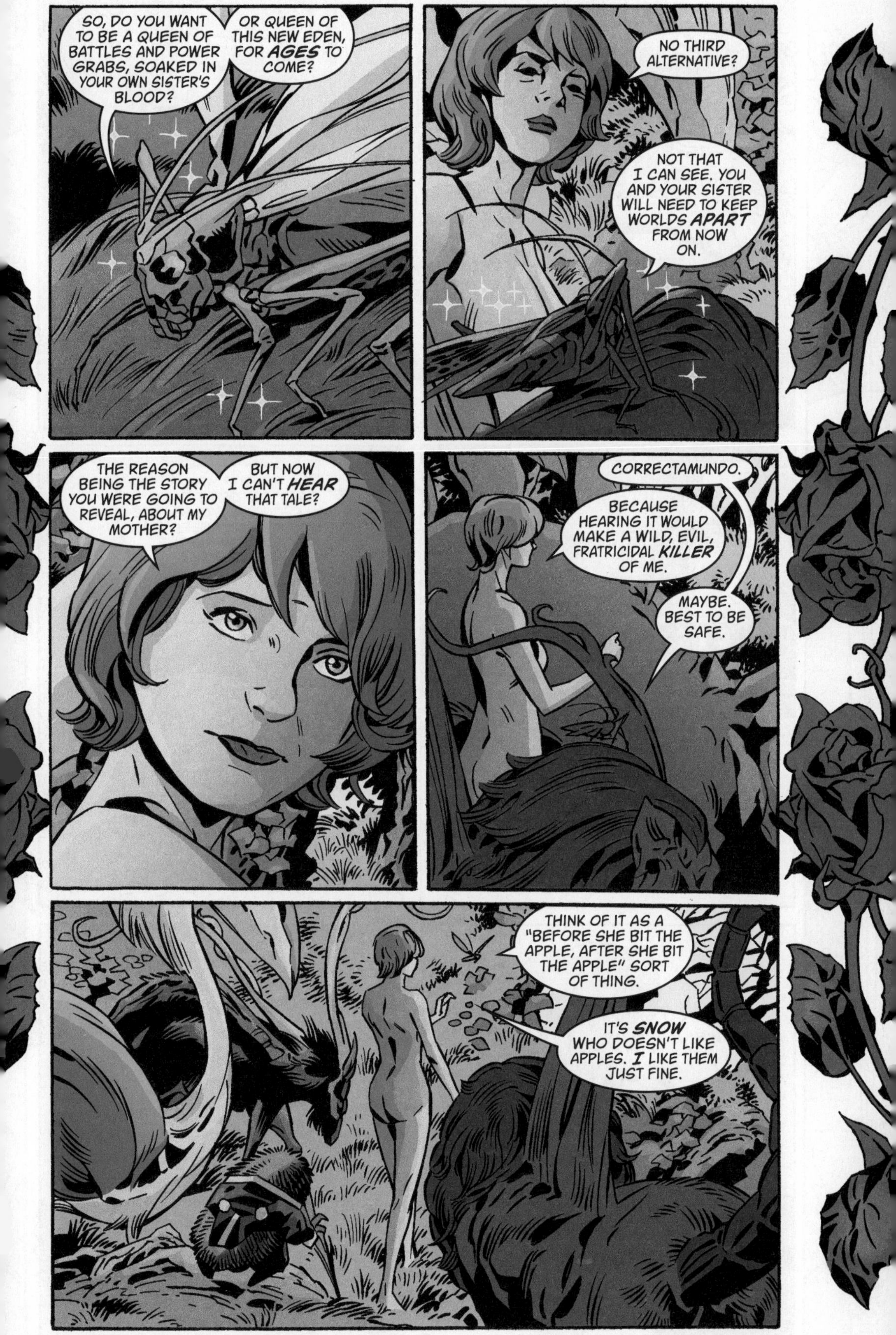
SO, DO YOU WANT TO BE A QUEEN OF BATTLES AND POWER GRABS, SOAKED IN YOUR OWN SISTER'S BLOOD?
OR QUEEN OF THIS NEW EDEN, FOR AGES TO COME?
NO THIRD ALTERNATIVE?
NOT THAT I CAN SEE. YOU AND YOUR SISTER WILL NEED TO KEEP WORLDS APART FROM NOW ON.
THE REASON BEING THE STORY YOU WERE GOING TO REVEAL, ABOUT MY MOTHER?
BUT NOW I CAN'T HEAR THAT TALE?
CORRECTAMUNDO.
BECAUSE HEARING IT WOULD MAKE A WILD, EVIL, FRATRICIDAL KILLER OF ME.
MAYBE. BEST TO BE SAFE.
THINK OF IT AS A "BEFORE SHE BIT THE APPLE, AFTER SHE BIT THE APPLE" SORT OF THING.
IT'S SNOW WHO DOESN'T LIKE APPLES. I LIKE THEM JUST FINE.

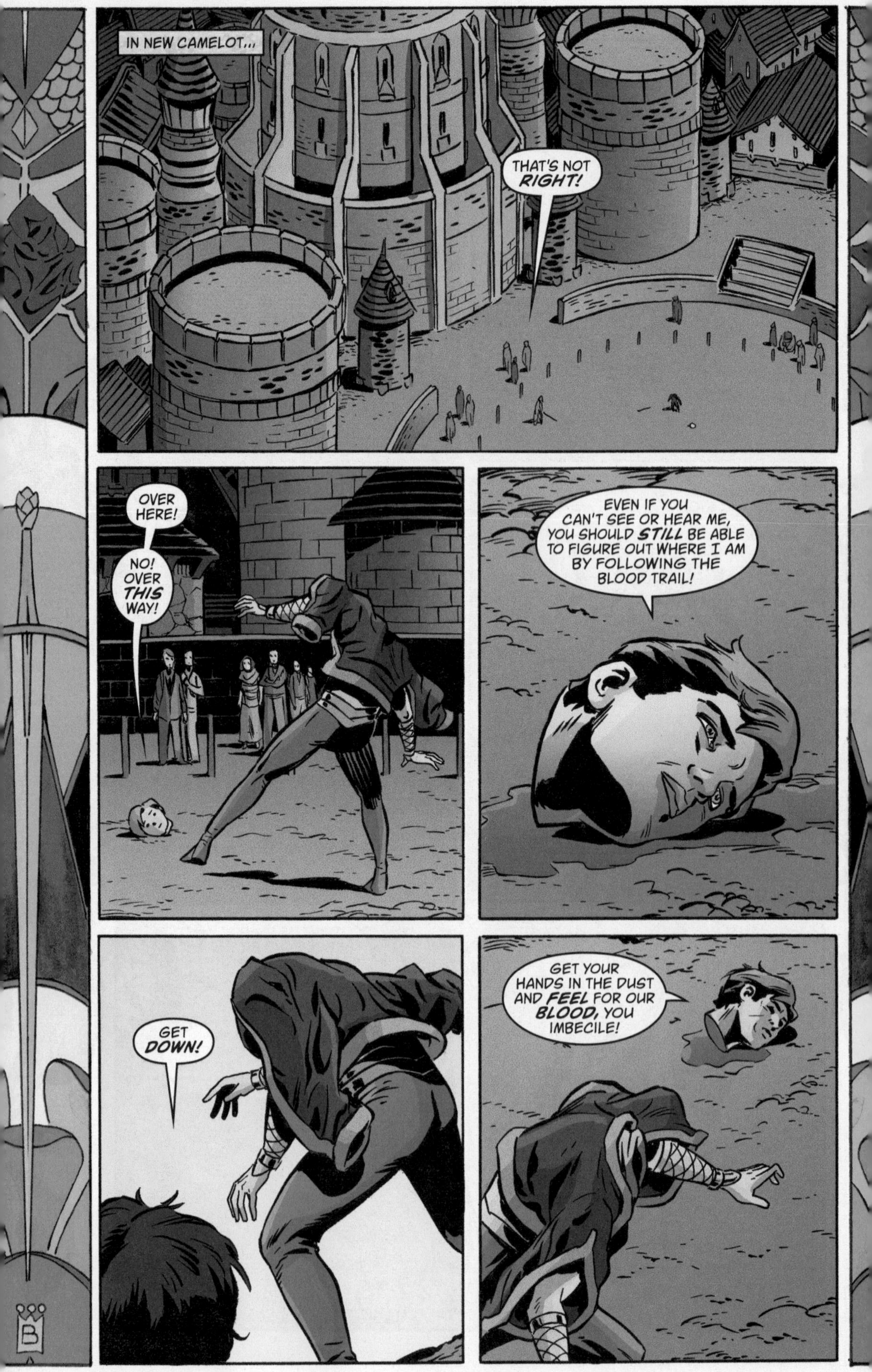
IN NEW CAMELOT...
THAT'S NOT RIGHT!
OVER HERE!
NO! OVER THIS WAY!
EVEN IF YOU CAN'T SEE OR HEAR ME, YOU SHOULD STILL BE ABLE TO FIGURE OUT WHERE I AM BY FOLLOWING THE BLOOD TRAIL!
GET DOWN!
GET YOUR HANDS IN THE DUST AND FEEL FOR OUR BLOOD, YOU IMBECILE!

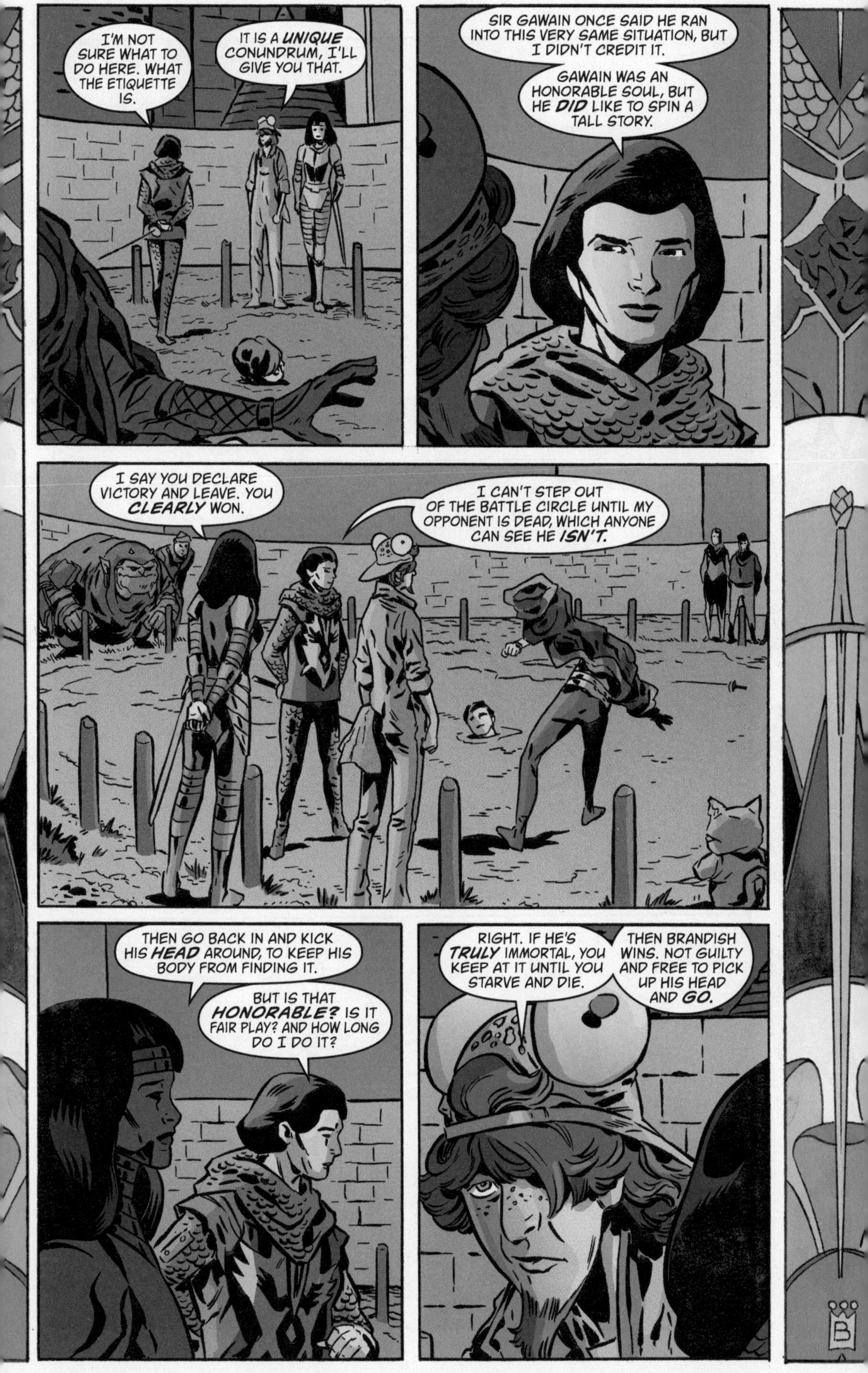
I'M NOT SURE WHAT TO DO HERE. WHAT THE ETIQUETTE IS.
IT IS A *UNIQUE* CONUNDRUM, I'LL GIVE YOU THAT.
SIR GAWAIN ONCE SAID HE RAN INTO THIS VERY SAME SITUATION, BUT I DIDN'T CREDIT IT.
GAWAIN WAS AN HONORABLE SOUL, BUT HE *DID* LIKE TO SPIN A TALL STORY.
I SAY YOU DECLARE VICTORY AND LEAVE. YOU *CLEARLY* WON.
I CAN'T STEP OUT OF THE BATTLE CIRCLE UNTIL MY OPPONENT IS DEAD, WHICH ANYONE CAN SEE HE *ISN'T*.
THEN GO BACK IN AND KICK HIS *HEAD* AROUND, TO KEEP HIS BODY FROM FINDING IT.
BUT IS THAT *HONORABLE?* IS IT FAIR PLAY? AND HOW LONG DO I DO IT?
RIGHT. IF HE'S *TRULY* IMMORTAL, YOU KEEP AT IT UNTIL YOU STARVE AND DIE.
THEN BRANDISH WINS. NOT GUILTY AND FREE TO PICK UP HIS HEAD AND *GO*.

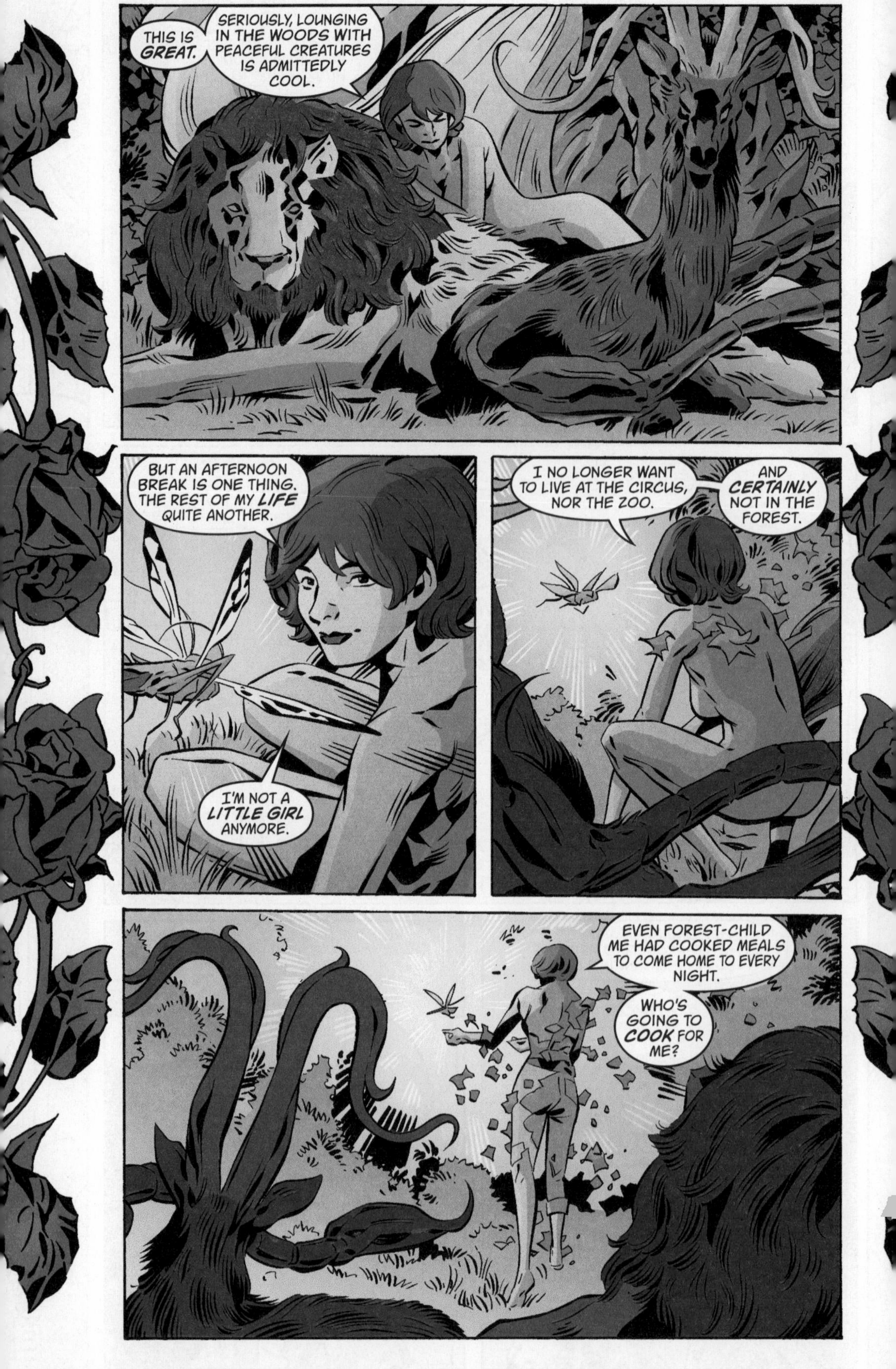
THIS IS GREAT.
SERIOUSLY, LOUNGING IN THE WOODS WITH PEACEFUL CREATURES IS ADMITTEDLY COOL.
BUT AN AFTERNOON BREAK IS ONE THING. THE REST OF MY LIFE QUITE ANOTHER.
I'M NOT A LITTLE GIRL ANYMORE.
I NO LONGER WANT TO LIVE AT THE CIRCUS, NOR THE ZOO.
AND CERTAINLY NOT IN THE FOREST.
EVEN FOREST-CHILD ME HAD COOKED MEALS TO COME HOME TO EVERY NIGHT.
WHO'S GOING TO COOK FOR ME?

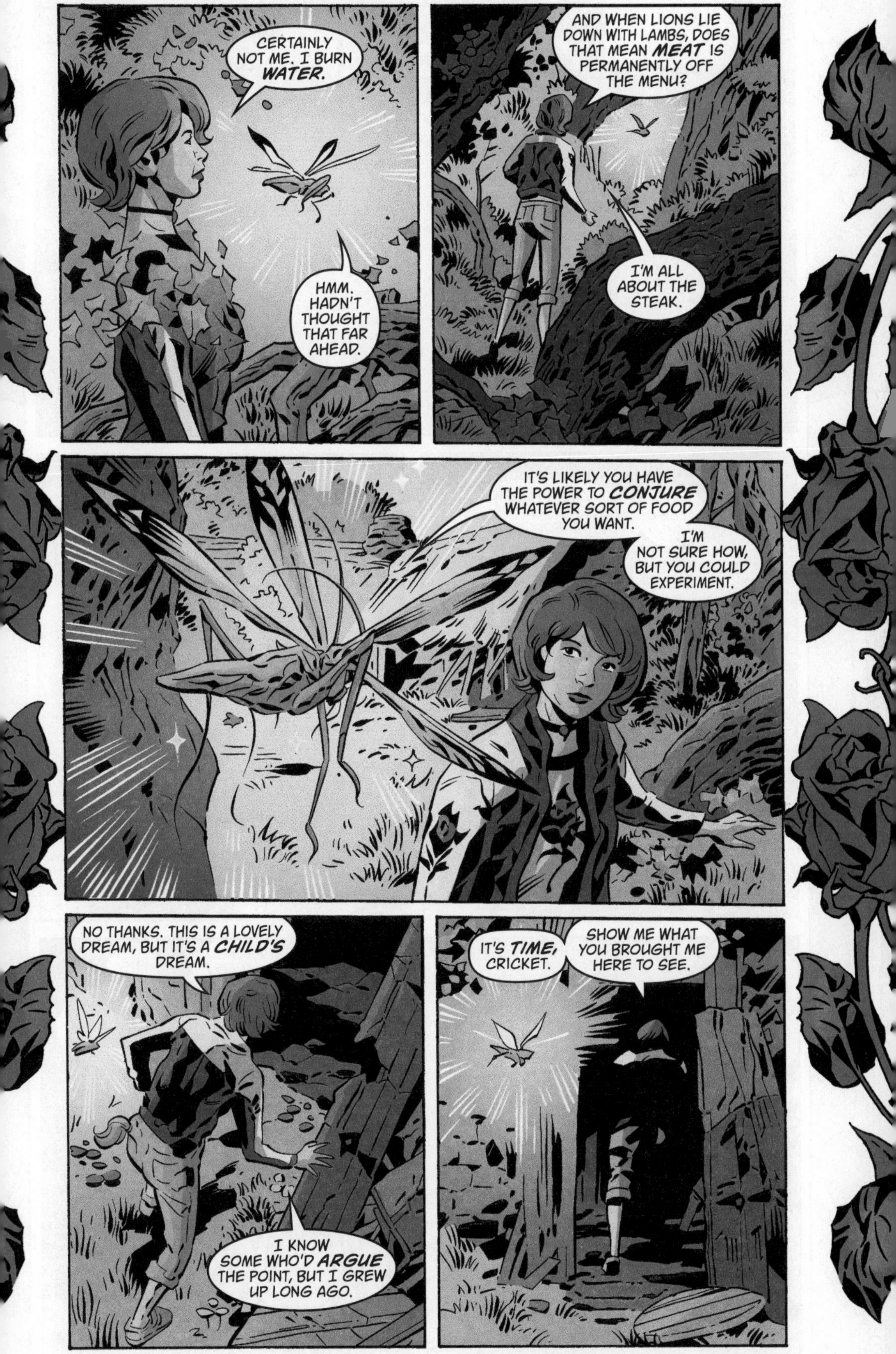
CERTAINLY NOT ME. I BURN WATER.
HMM. HADN'T THOUGHT THAT FAR AHEAD.
AND WHEN LIONS LIE DOWN WITH LAMBS, DOES THAT MEAN MEAT IS PERMANENTLY OFF THE MENU?
I'M ALL ABOUT THE STEAK.
IT'S LIKELY YOU HAVE THE POWER TO CONJURE WHATEVER SORT OF FOOD YOU WANT.
I'M NOT SURE HOW, BUT YOU COULD EXPERIMENT.
NO THANKS. THIS IS A LOVELY DREAM, BUT IT'S A CHILD'S DREAM.
I KNOW SOME WHO'D ARGUE THE POINT, BUT I GREW UP LONG AGO.
IT'S TIME, CRICKET.
SHOW ME WHAT YOU BROUGHT ME HERE TO SEE.

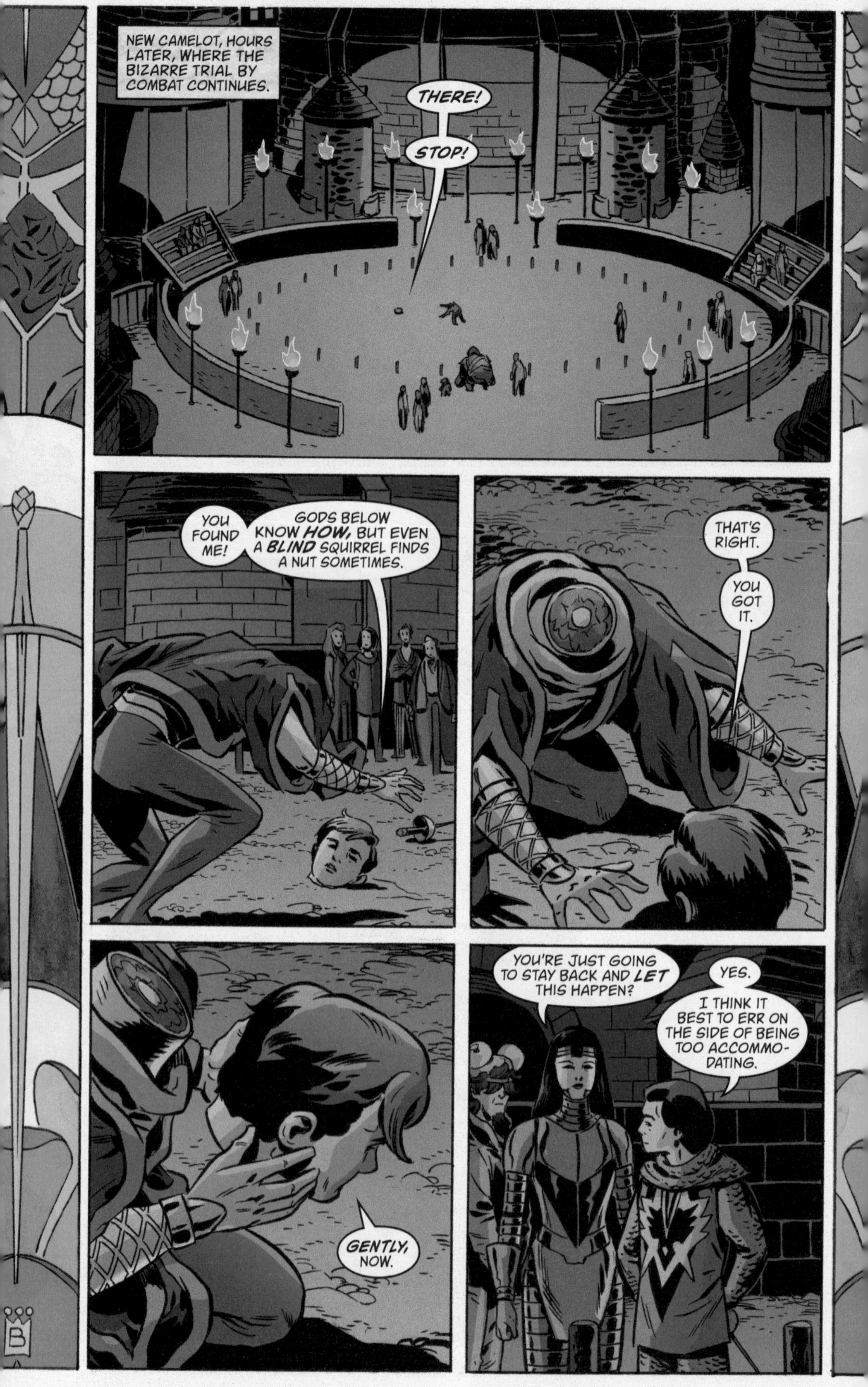
NEW CAMELOT, HOURS LATER, WHERE THE BIZARRE TRIAL BY COMBAT CONTINUES.
THERE!
STOP!
YOU FOUND ME!
GODS BELOW KNOW HOW, BUT EVEN A BLIND SQUIRREL FINDS A NUT SOMETIMES.
THAT'S RIGHT.
YOU GOT IT.
GENTLY, NOW.
YOU'RE JUST GOING TO STAY BACK AND LET THIS HAPPEN?
YES.
I THINK IT BEST TO ERR ON THE SIDE OF BEING TOO ACCOMMO-DATING.

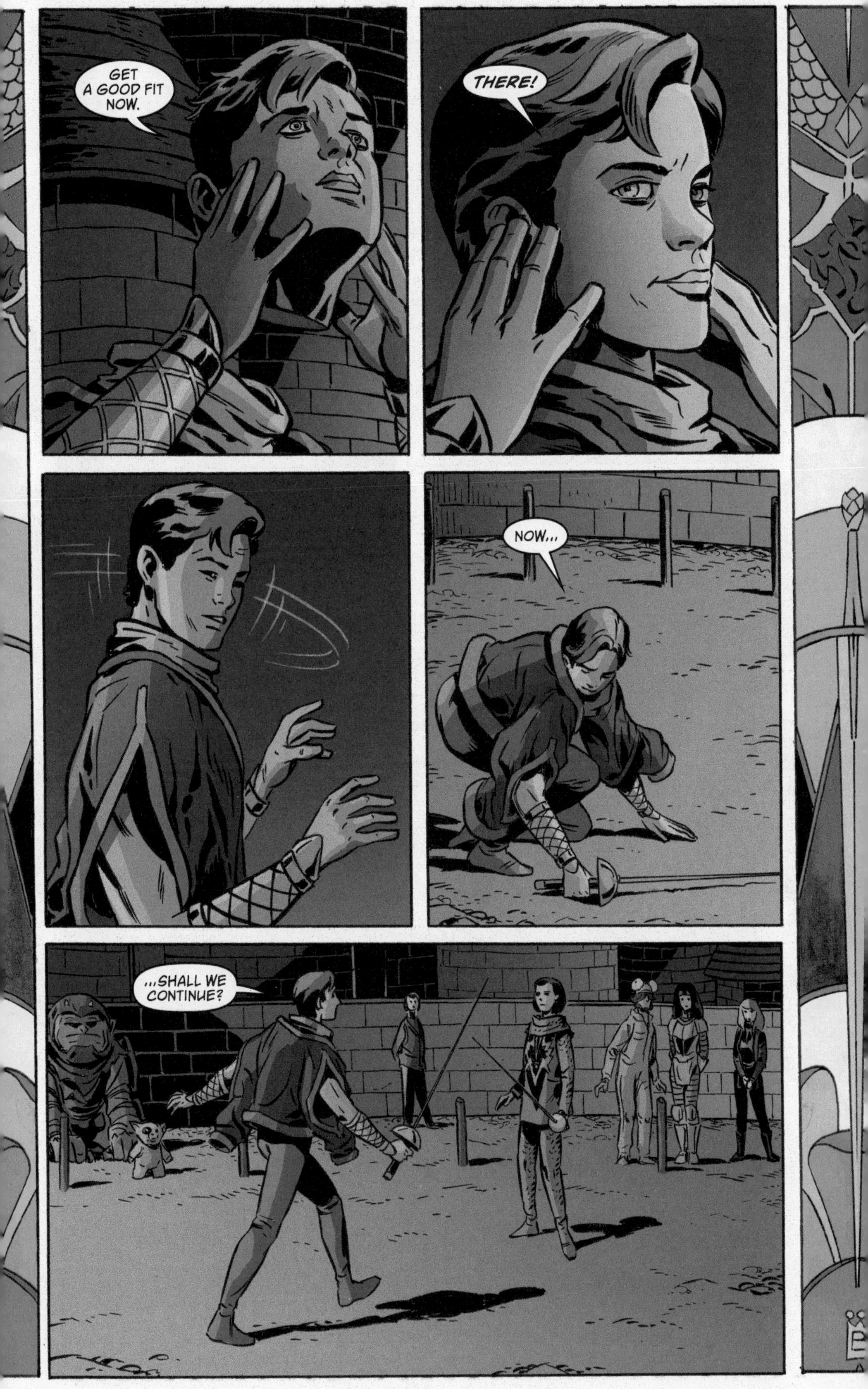
GET A GOOD FIT NOW.
THERE!
NOW...
...SHALL WE CONTINUE?

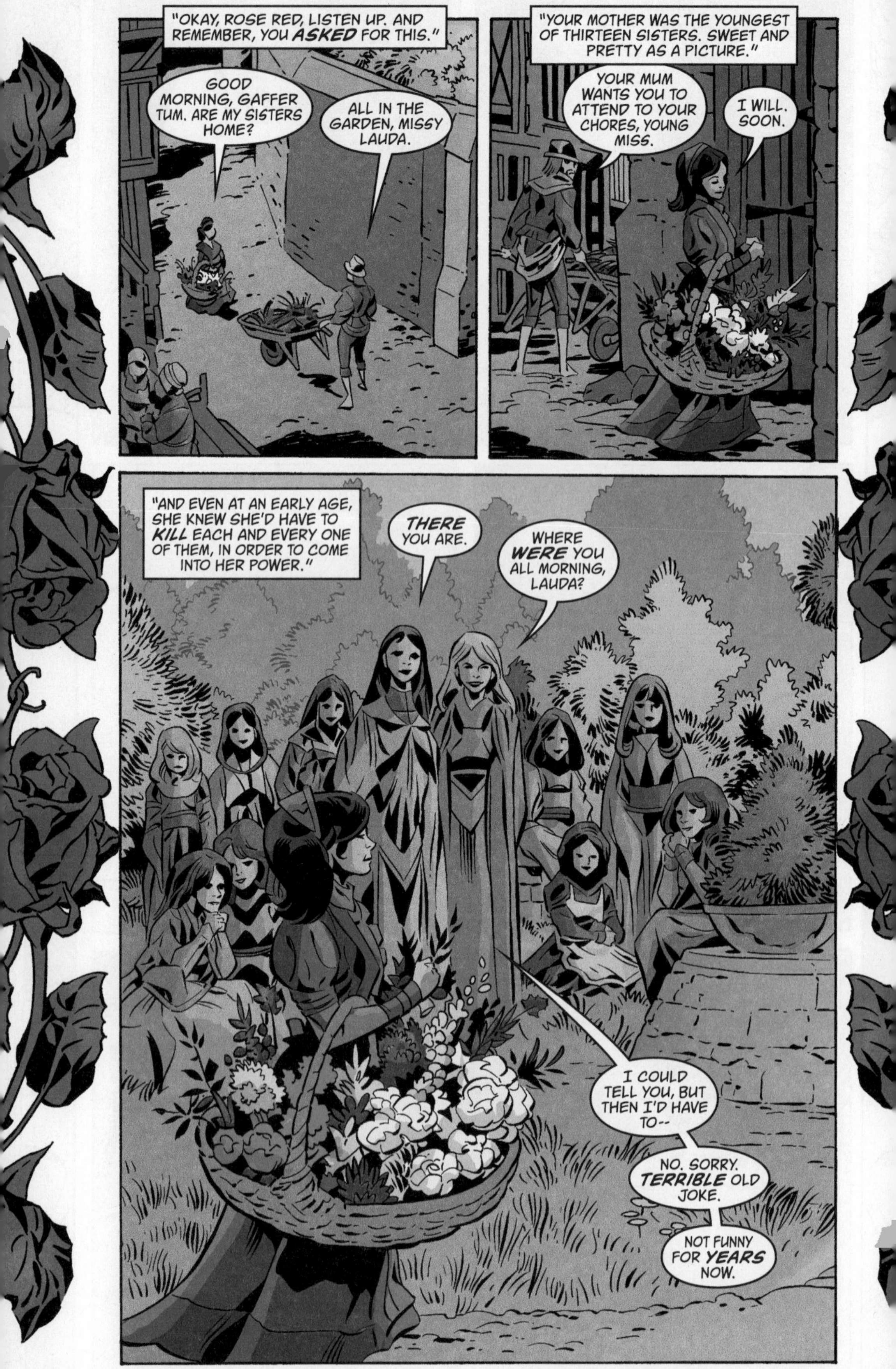
"OKAY, ROSE RED, LISTEN UP. AND REMEMBER, YOU ASKED FOR THIS."
GOOD MORNING, GAFFER TUM. ARE MY SISTERS HOME?
ALL IN THE GARDEN, MISSY LAUDA.
"YOUR MOTHER WAS THE YOUNGEST OF THIRTEEN SISTERS. SWEET AND PRETTY AS A PICTURE."
YOUR MUM WANTS YOU TO ATTEND TO YOUR CHORES, YOUNG MISS.
I WILL. SOON.
"AND EVEN AT AN EARLY AGE, SHE KNEW SHE'D HAVE TO KILL EACH AND EVERY ONE OF THEM, IN ORDER TO COME INTO HER POWER."
THERE YOU ARE.
WHERE WERE YOU ALL MORNING, LAUDA?
I COULD TELL YOU, BUT THEN I'D HAVE TO--
NO. SORRY. TERRIBLE OLD JOKE.
NOT FUNNY FOR YEARS NOW.

NEXT: WHAT ARE LITTLE GIRLS MADE OF?

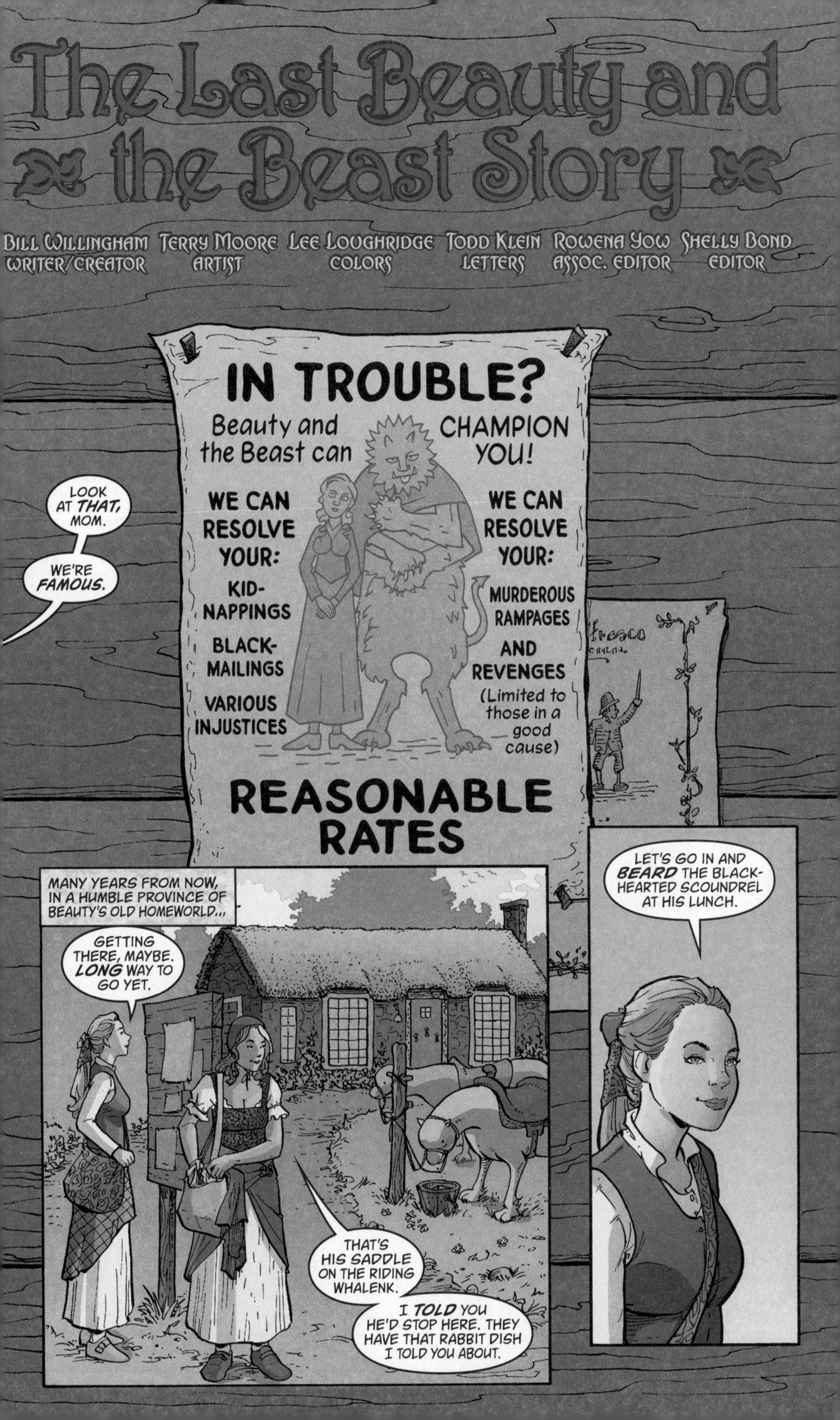
The Last Beauty and the Beast Story
Bill Willingham Writer/Creator
Terry Moore Artist
Lee Loughridge Colors
Todd Klein Letters
Rowena Yow Assoc. Editor
Shelly Bond Editor
IN TROUBLE?
Beauty and the Beast can CHAMPION YOU!
WE CAN RESOLVE YOUR: KID-NAPPINGS BLACK-MAILINGS VARIOUS INJUSTICES
WE CAN RESOLVE YOUR: MURDEROUS RAMPAGES AND REVENGES (Limited to those in a good cause)
REASONABLE RATES
LOOK AT THAT, MOM.
WE'RE FAMOUS.
MANY YEARS FROM NOW, IN A HUMBLE PROVINCE OF BEAUTY'S OLD HOMEWORLD...
GETTING THERE, MAYBE. LONG WAY TO GO YET.
THAT'S HIS SADDLE ON THE RIDING WHALENK.
I TOLD YOU HE'D STOP HERE. THEY HAVE THAT RABBIT DISH I TOLD YOU ABOUT.
LET'S GO IN AND BEARD THE BLACK-HEARTED SCOUNDREL AT HIS LUNCH.

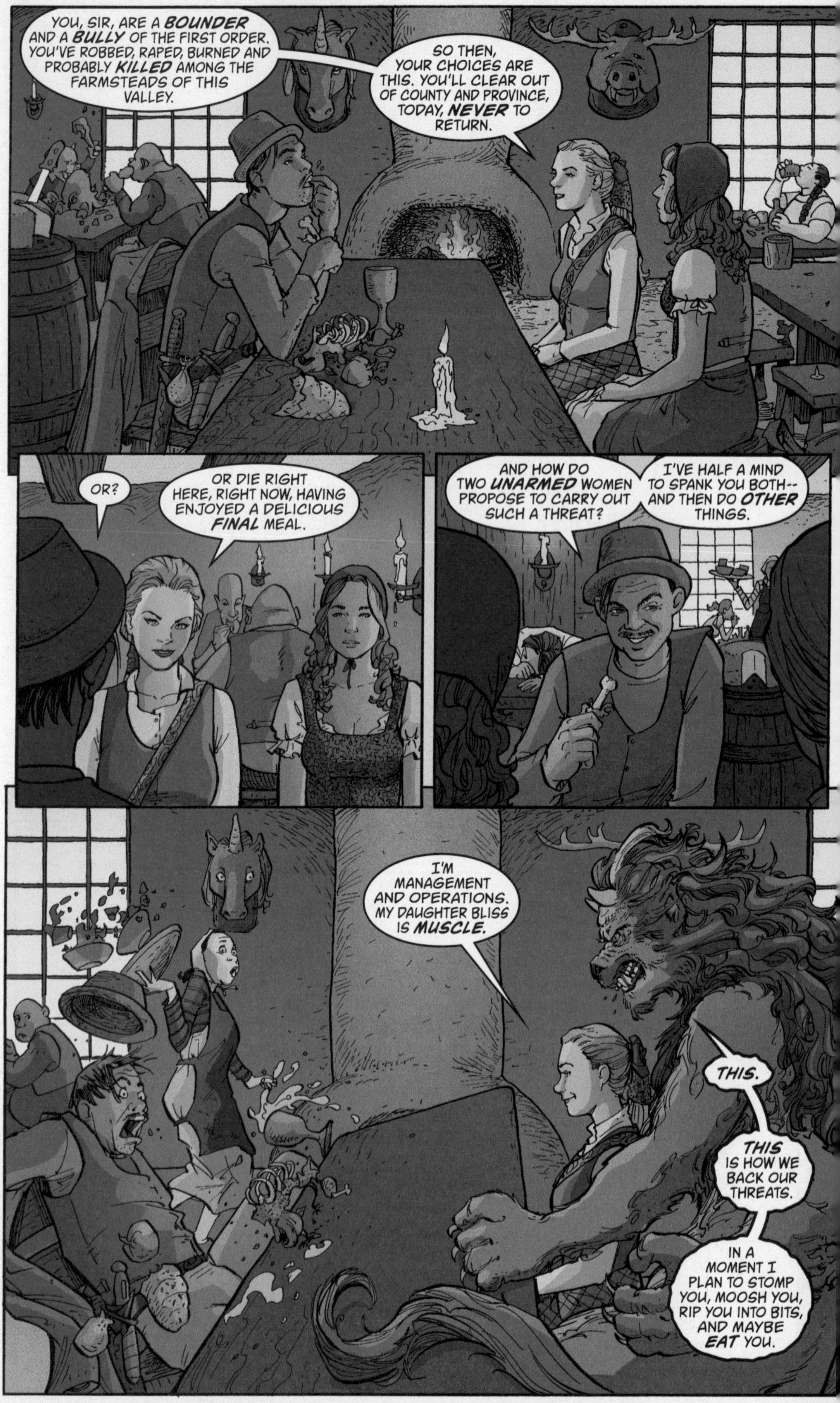
YOU, SIR, ARE A **BOUNDER** AND A **BULLY** OF THE FIRST ORDER. YOU'VE ROBBED, RAPED, BURNED AND PROBABLY **KILLED** AMONG THE FARMSTEADS OF THIS VALLEY.
SO THEN, YOUR CHOICES ARE THIS. YOU'LL CLEAR OUT OF COUNTY AND PROVINCE, TODAY, **NEVER** TO RETURN.
OR?
OR DIE RIGHT HERE, RIGHT NOW, HAVING ENJOYED A DELICIOUS **FINAL** MEAL.
AND HOW DO TWO **UNARMED** WOMEN PROPOSE TO CARRY OUT SUCH A THREAT?
I'VE HALF A MIND TO SPANK YOU BOTH-- AND THEN DO **OTHER** THINGS.
I'M MANAGEMENT AND OPERATIONS. MY DAUGHTER BLISS IS **MUSCLE.**
THIS.
THIS IS HOW WE BACK OUR THREATS.
IN A MOMENT I PLAN TO STOMP YOU, MOOSH YOU, RIP YOU INTO BITS, AND MAYBE **EAT** YOU.

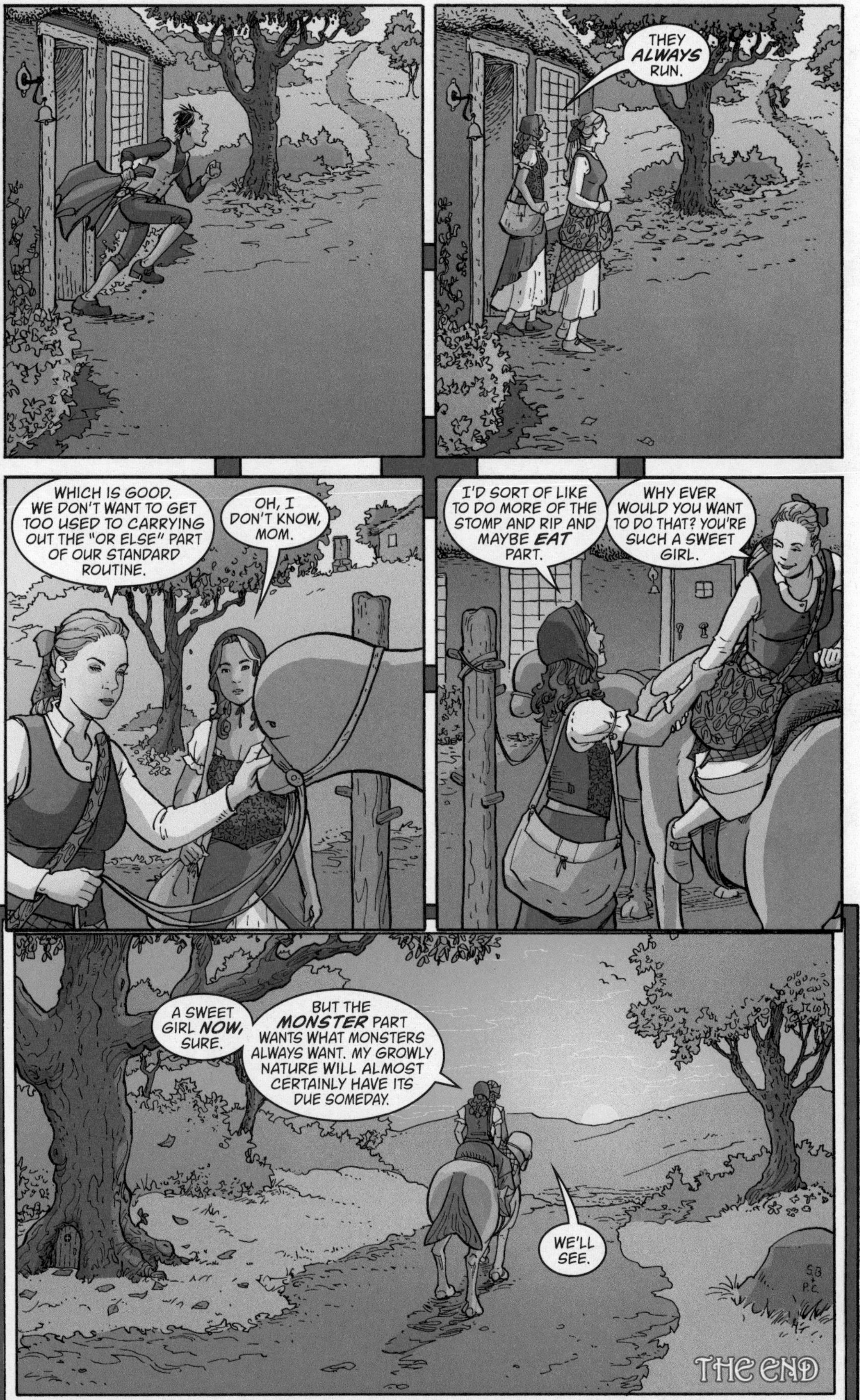

THEY ALWAYS RUN.
WHICH IS GOOD. WE DON'T WANT TO GET TOO USED TO CARRYING OUT THE "OR ELSE" PART OF OUR STANDARD ROUTINE.
OH, I DON'T KNOW, MOM.
I'D SORT OF LIKE TO DO MORE OF THE STOMP AND RIP AND MAYBE EAT PART.
WHY EVER WOULD YOU WANT TO DO THAT? YOU'RE SUCH A SWEET GIRL.
A SWEET GIRL NOW, SURE.
BUT THE MONSTER PART WANTS WHAT MONSTERS ALWAYS WANT. MY GROWLY NATURE WILL ALMOST CERTAINLY HAVE ITS DUE SOMEDAY.
WE'LL SEE.
S.B. + P.C.
THE END

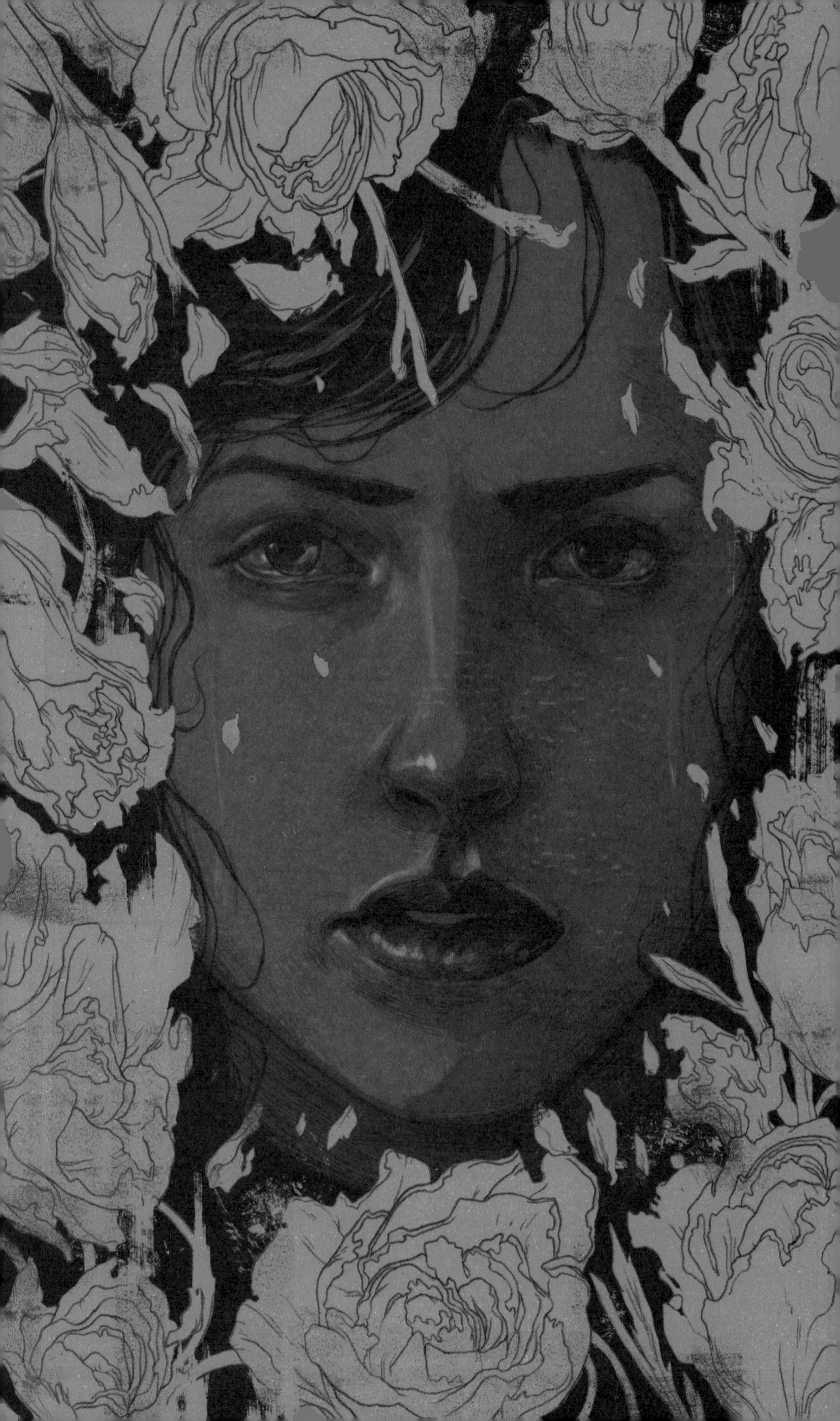

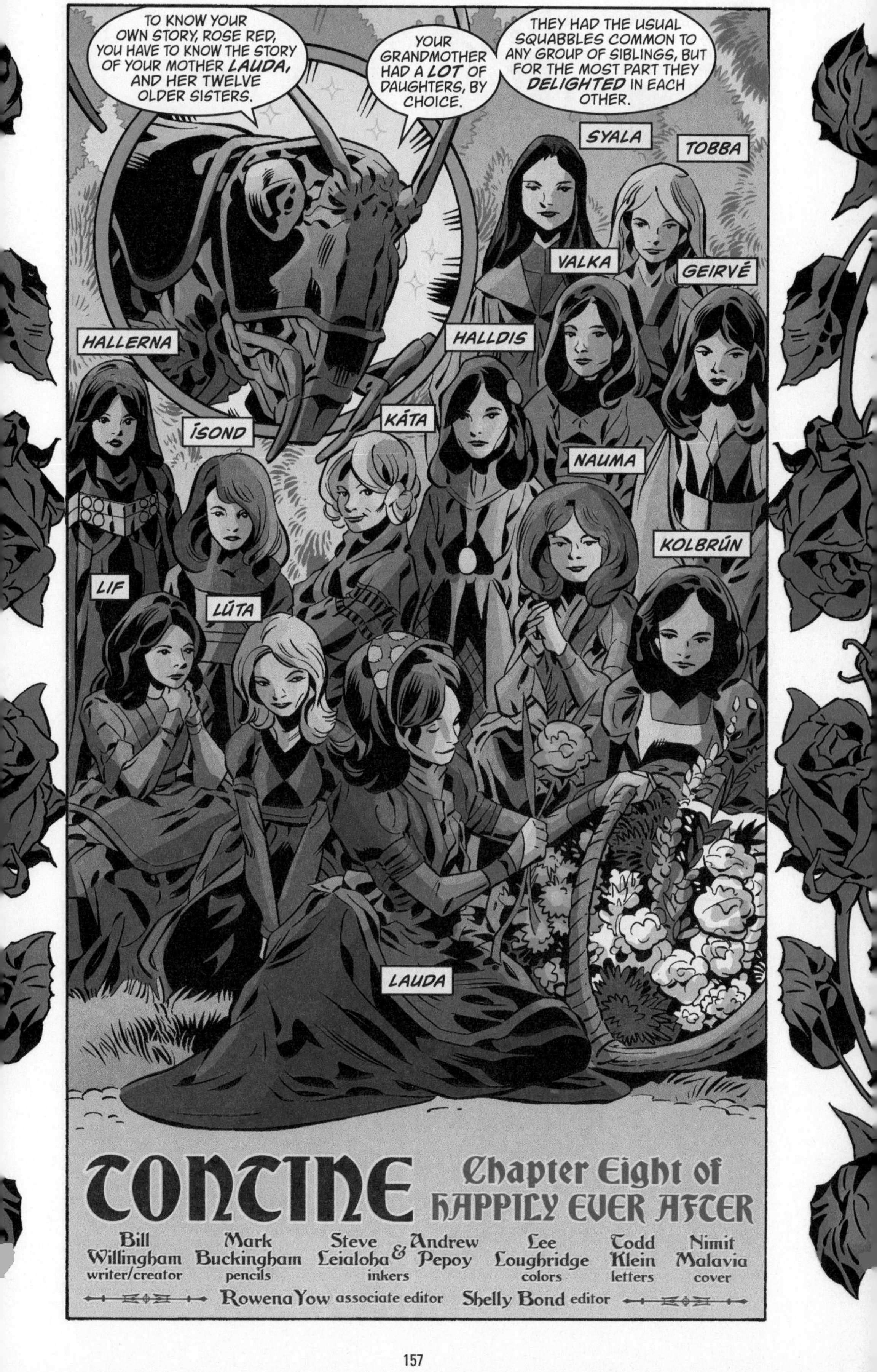

TO KNOW YOUR OWN STORY, ROSE RED, YOU HAVE TO KNOW THE STORY OF YOUR MOTHER LAUDA, AND HER TWELVE OLDER SISTERS.
YOUR GRANDMOTHER HAD A LOT OF DAUGHTERS, BY CHOICE.
THEY HAD THE USUAL SQUABBLES COMMON TO ANY GROUP OF SIBLINGS, BUT FOR THE MOST PART THEY DELIGHTED IN EACH OTHER.
SYALA
TOBBA
VALKA
GEIRVÉ
HALLERNA
HALLDIS
ÍSOND
KÁTA
NAUMA
KOLBRÚN
LIF
LŪTA
LAUDA
TONTINE
Chapter Eight of HAPPILY EVER AFTER
Bill Willingham writer/creator
Mark Buckingham pencils
Steve Leialoha & Andrew Pepoy inkers
Lee Loughridge colors
Todd Klein letters
Nimit Malavia cover
Rowena Yow associate editor
Shelly Bond editor

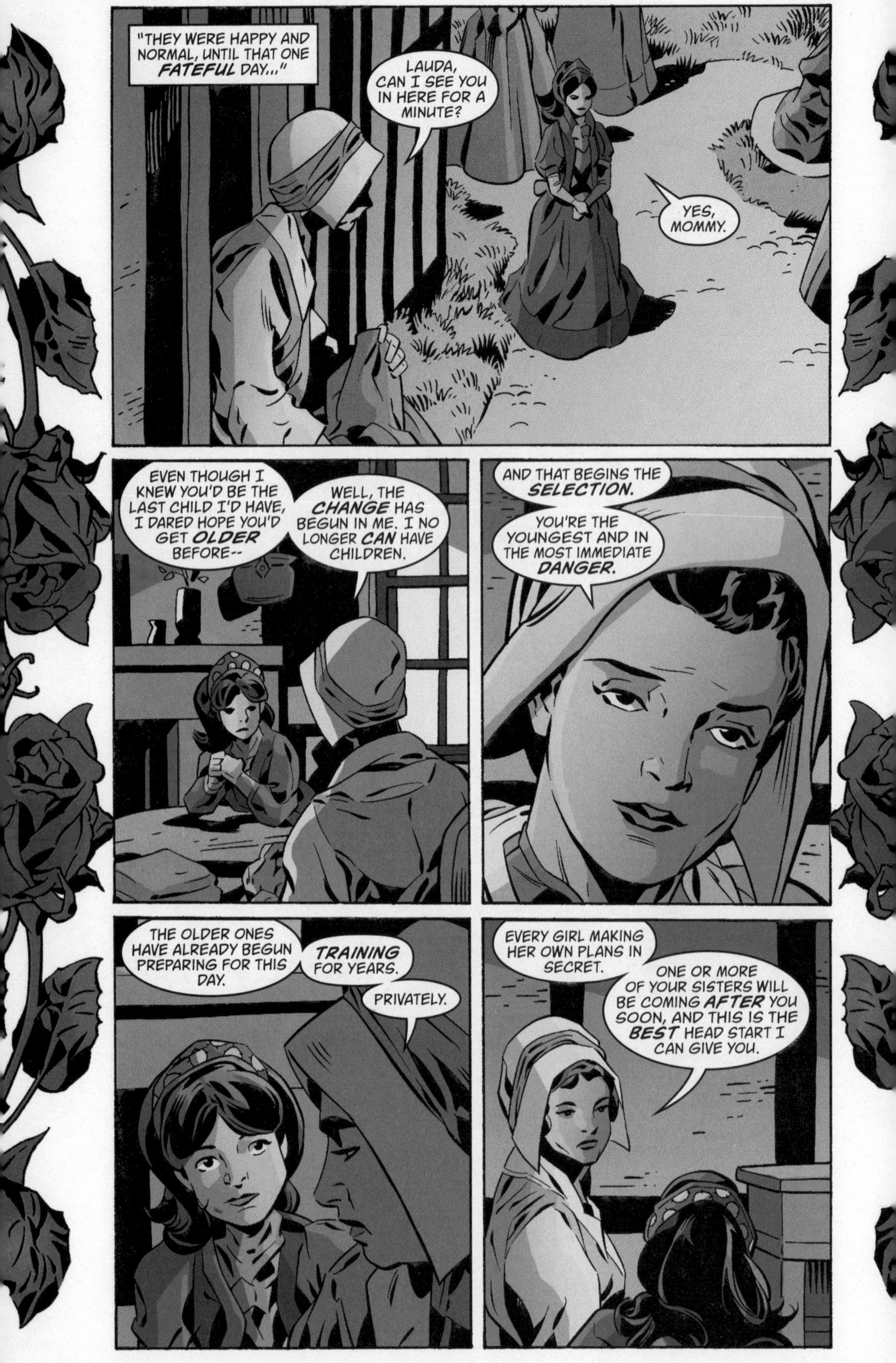
"THEY WERE HAPPY AND NORMAL, UNTIL THAT ONE FATEFUL DAY..."
LAUDA, CAN I SEE YOU IN HERE FOR A MINUTE?
YES, MOMMY.
EVEN THOUGH I KNEW YOU'D BE THE LAST CHILD I'D HAVE, I DARED HOPE YOU'D GET OLDER BEFORE--
WELL, THE CHANGE HAS BEGUN IN ME. I NO LONGER CAN HAVE CHILDREN.
AND THAT BEGINS THE SELECTION.
YOU'RE THE YOUNGEST AND IN THE MOST IMMEDIATE DANGER.
THE OLDER ONES HAVE ALREADY BEGUN PREPARING FOR THIS DAY.
TRAINING FOR YEARS.
PRIVATELY.
EVERY GIRL MAKING HER OWN PLANS IN SECRET.
ONE OR MORE OF YOUR SISTERS WILL BE COMING AFTER YOU SOON, AND THIS IS THE BEST HEAD START I CAN GIVE YOU.

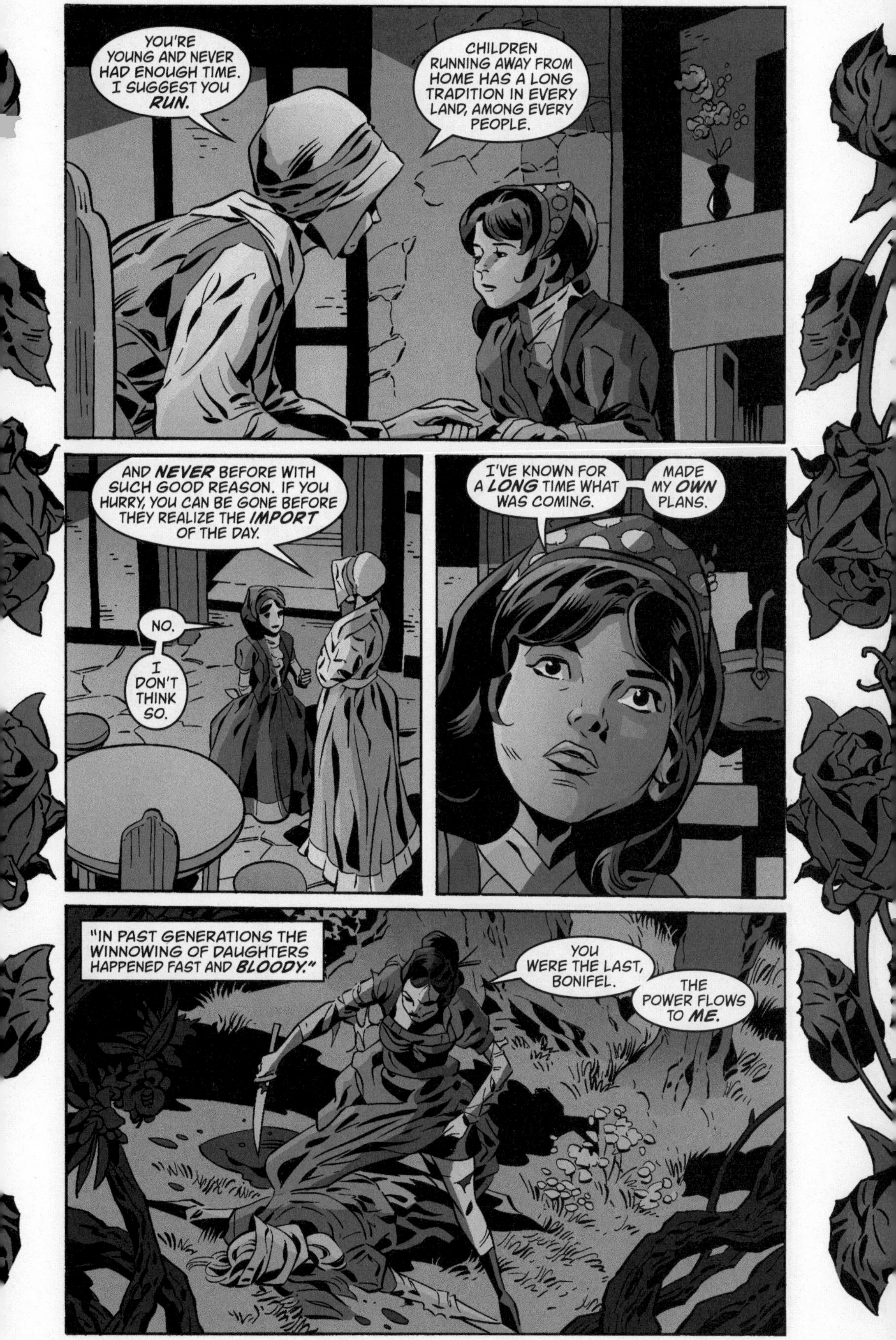
YOU'RE YOUNG AND NEVER HAD ENOUGH TIME. I SUGGEST YOU RUN.
CHILDREN RUNNING AWAY FROM HOME HAS A LONG TRADITION IN EVERY LAND, AMONG EVERY PEOPLE.
AND NEVER BEFORE WITH SUCH GOOD REASON. IF YOU HURRY, YOU CAN BE GONE BEFORE THEY REALIZE THE IMPORT OF THE DAY.
NO.
I DON'T THINK SO.
I'VE KNOWN FOR A LONG TIME WHAT WAS COMING.
MADE MY OWN PLANS.
"IN PAST GENERATIONS THE WINNOWING OF DAUGHTERS HAPPENED FAST AND BLOODY."
YOU WERE THE LAST, BONIFEL.
THE POWER FLOWS TO ME.

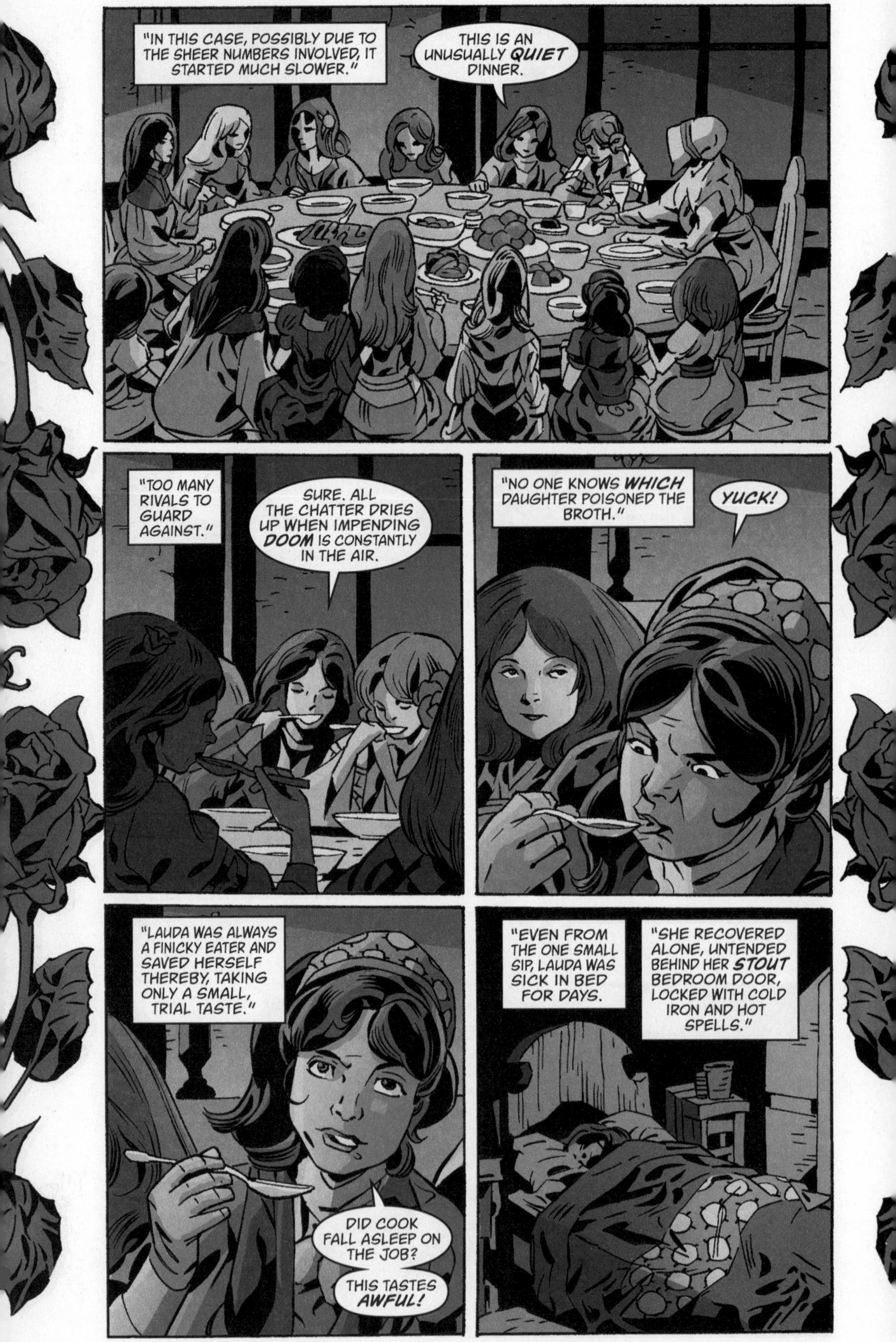
"IN THIS CASE, POSSIBLY DUE TO THE SHEER NUMBERS INVOLVED, IT STARTED MUCH SLOWER."
THIS IS AN UNUSUALLY QUIET DINNER.
"TOO MANY RIVALS TO GUARD AGAINST."
SURE. ALL THE CHATTER DRIES UP WHEN IMPENDING DOOM IS CONSTANTLY IN THE AIR.
"NO ONE KNOWS WHICH DAUGHTER POISONED THE BROTH."
YUCK!
"LAUDA WAS ALWAYS A FINICKY EATER AND SAVED HERSELF THEREBY, TAKING ONLY A SMALL, TRIAL TASTE."
DID COOK FALL ASLEEP ON THE JOB?
THIS TASTES AWFUL!
"EVEN FROM THE ONE SMALL SIP, LAUDA WAS SICK IN BED FOR DAYS.
"SHE RECOVERED ALONE, UNTENDED BEHIND HER STOUT BEDROOM DOOR, LOCKED WITH COLD IRON AND HOT SPELLS."

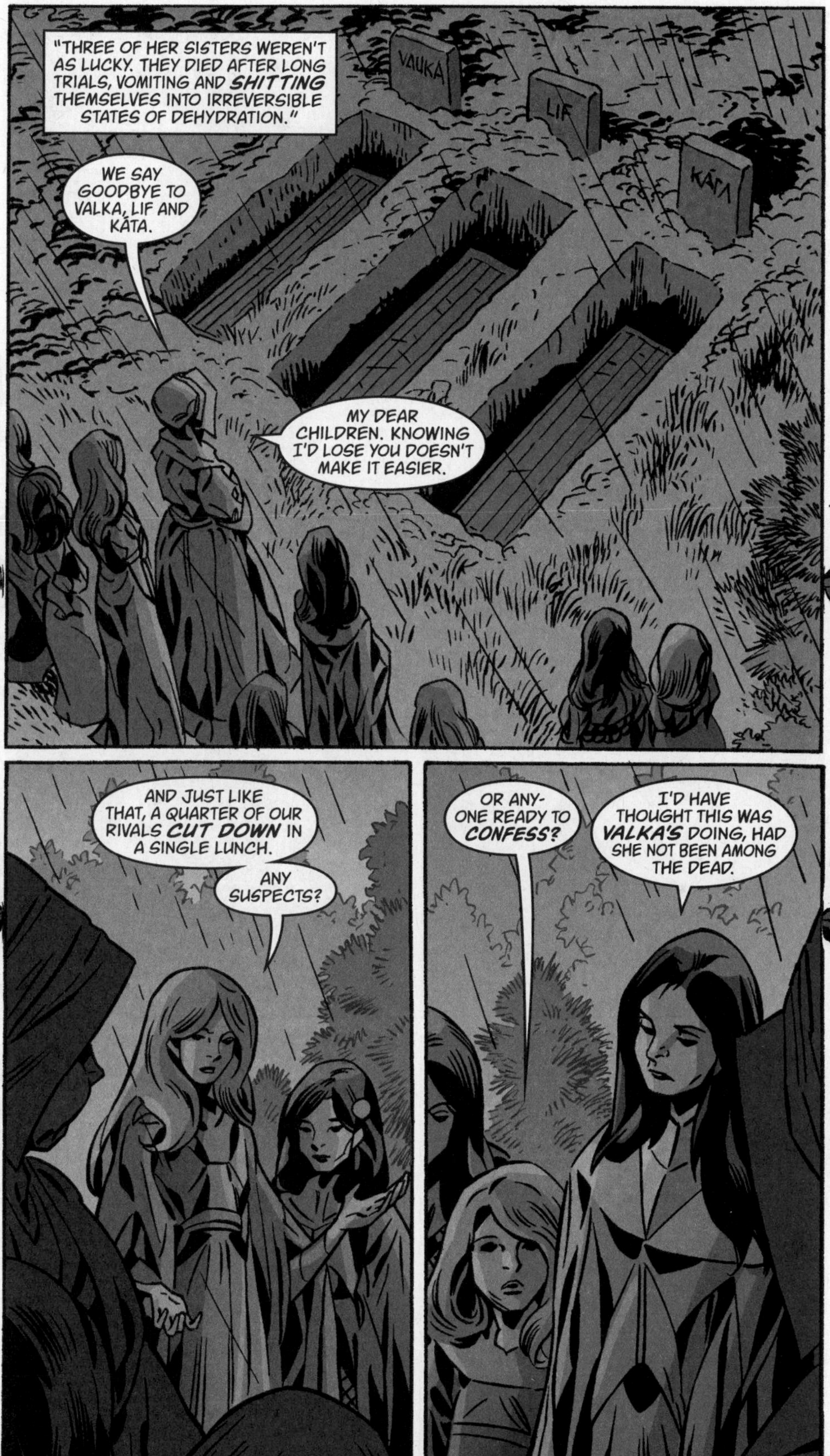
"THREE OF HER SISTERS WEREN'T AS LUCKY. THEY DIED AFTER LONG TRIALS, VOMITING AND SHITTING THEMSELVES INTO IRREVERSIBLE STATES OF DEHYDRATION."
WE SAY GOODBYE TO VALKA, LIF AND KÁTA.
MY DEAR CHILDREN. KNOWING I'D LOSE YOU DOESN'T MAKE IT EASIER.
AND JUST LIKE THAT, A QUARTER OF OUR RIVALS CUT DOWN IN A SINGLE LUNCH.
ANY SUSPECTS?
OR ANY-ONE READY TO CONFESS?
I'D HAVE THOUGHT THIS WAS VALKA'S DOING, HAD SHE NOT BEEN AMONG THE DEAD.

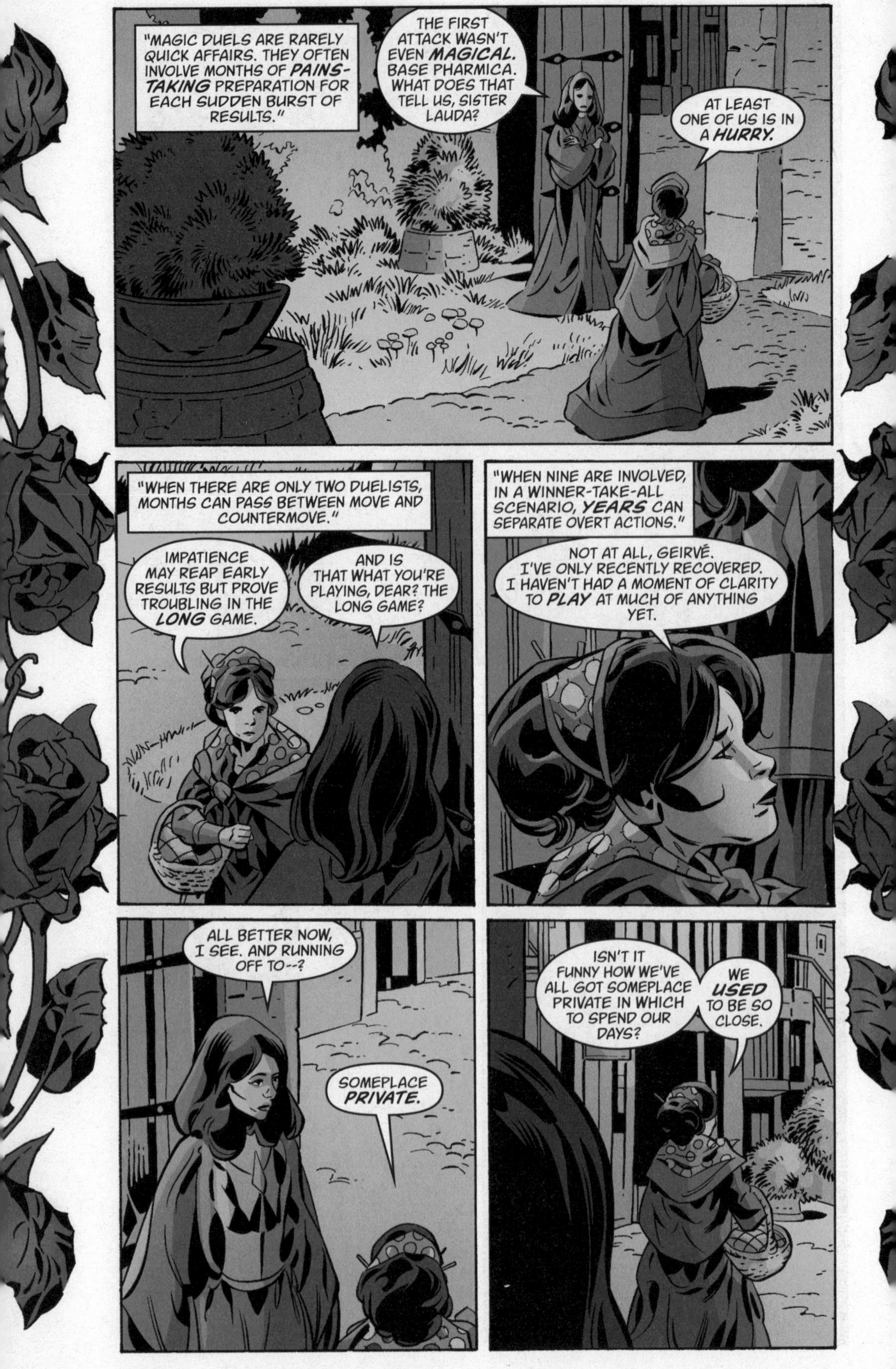
"MAGIC DUELS ARE RARELY QUICK AFFAIRS. THEY OFTEN INVOLVE MONTHS OF PAINS-TAKING PREPARATION FOR EACH SUDDEN BURST OF RESULTS."
THE FIRST ATTACK WASN'T EVEN MAGICAL. BASE PHARMICA. WHAT DOES THAT TELL US, SISTER LAUDA?
AT LEAST ONE OF US IS IN A HURRY.
"WHEN THERE ARE ONLY TWO DUELISTS, MONTHS CAN PASS BETWEEN MOVE AND COUNTERMOVE."
IMPATIENCE MAY REAP EARLY RESULTS BUT PROVE TROUBLING IN THE LONG GAME.
AND IS THAT WHAT YOU'RE PLAYING, DEAR? THE LONG GAME?
"WHEN NINE ARE INVOLVED, IN A WINNER-TAKE-ALL SCENARIO, YEARS CAN SEPARATE OVERT ACTIONS."
NOT AT ALL, GEIRVÉ. I'VE ONLY RECENTLY RECOVERED. I HAVEN'T HAD A MOMENT OF CLARITY TO PLAY AT MUCH OF ANYTHING YET.
ALL BETTER NOW, I SEE. AND RUNNING OFF TO--?
SOMEPLACE PRIVATE.
ISN'T IT FUNNY HOW WE'VE ALL GOT SOMEPLACE PRIVATE IN WHICH TO SPEND OUR DAYS?
WE USED TO BE SO CLOSE.

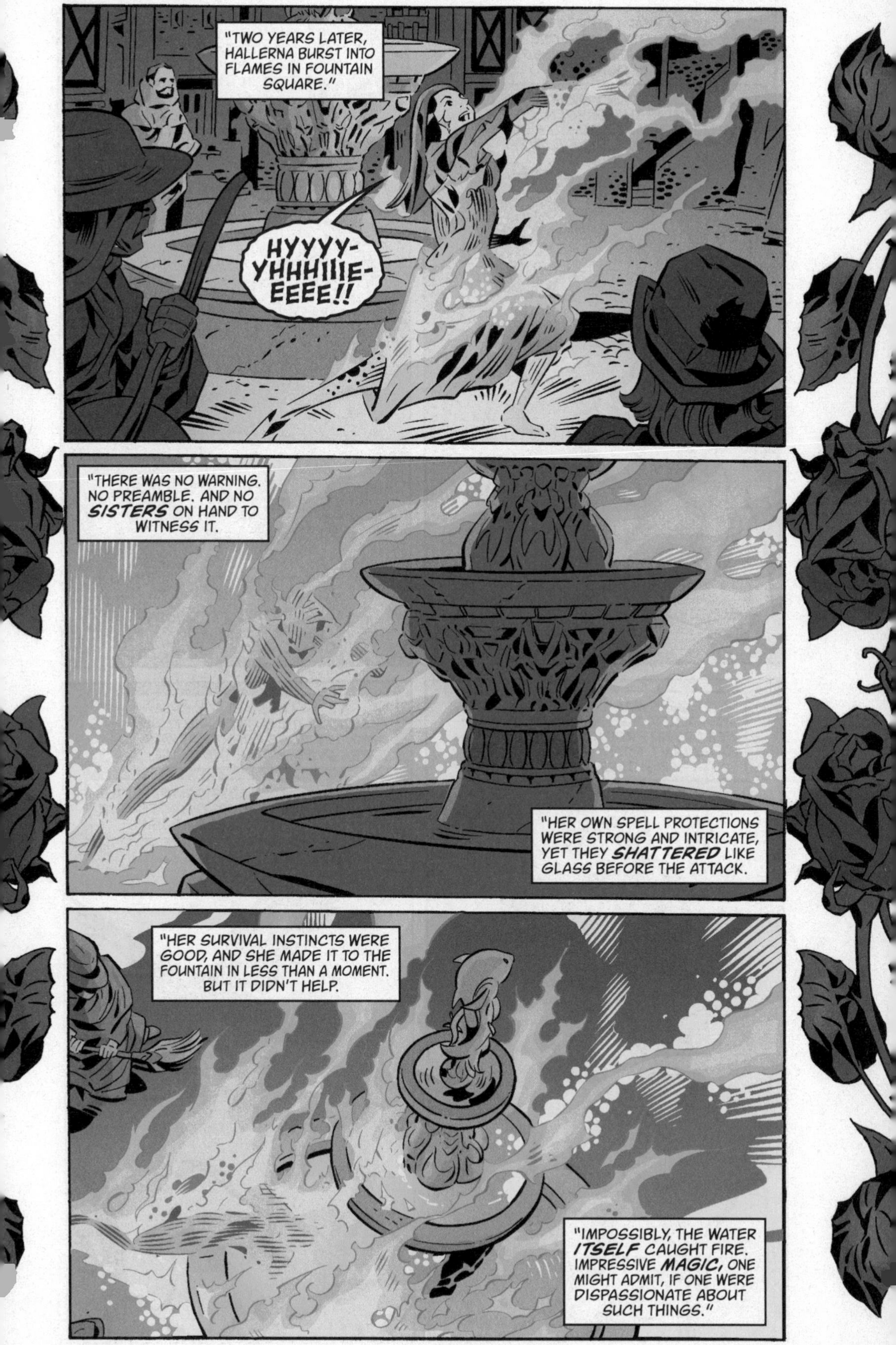
"TWO YEARS LATER, HALLERNA BURST INTO FLAMES IN FOUNTAIN SQUARE."
HYYYY-YHHHIIIE-EEEE!!
"THERE WAS NO WARNING. NO PREAMBLE. AND NO SISTERS ON HAND TO WITNESS IT.
"HER OWN SPELL PROTECTIONS WERE STRONG AND INTRICATE, YET THEY SHATTERED LIKE GLASS BEFORE THE ATTACK.
"HER SURVIVAL INSTINCTS WERE GOOD, AND SHE MADE IT TO THE FOUNTAIN IN LESS THAN A MOMENT. BUT IT DIDN'T HELP.
"IMPOSSIBLY, THE WATER ITSELF CAUGHT FIRE. IMPRESSIVE MAGIC, ONE MIGHT ADMIT, IF ONE WERE DISPASSIONATE ABOUT SUCH THINGS."

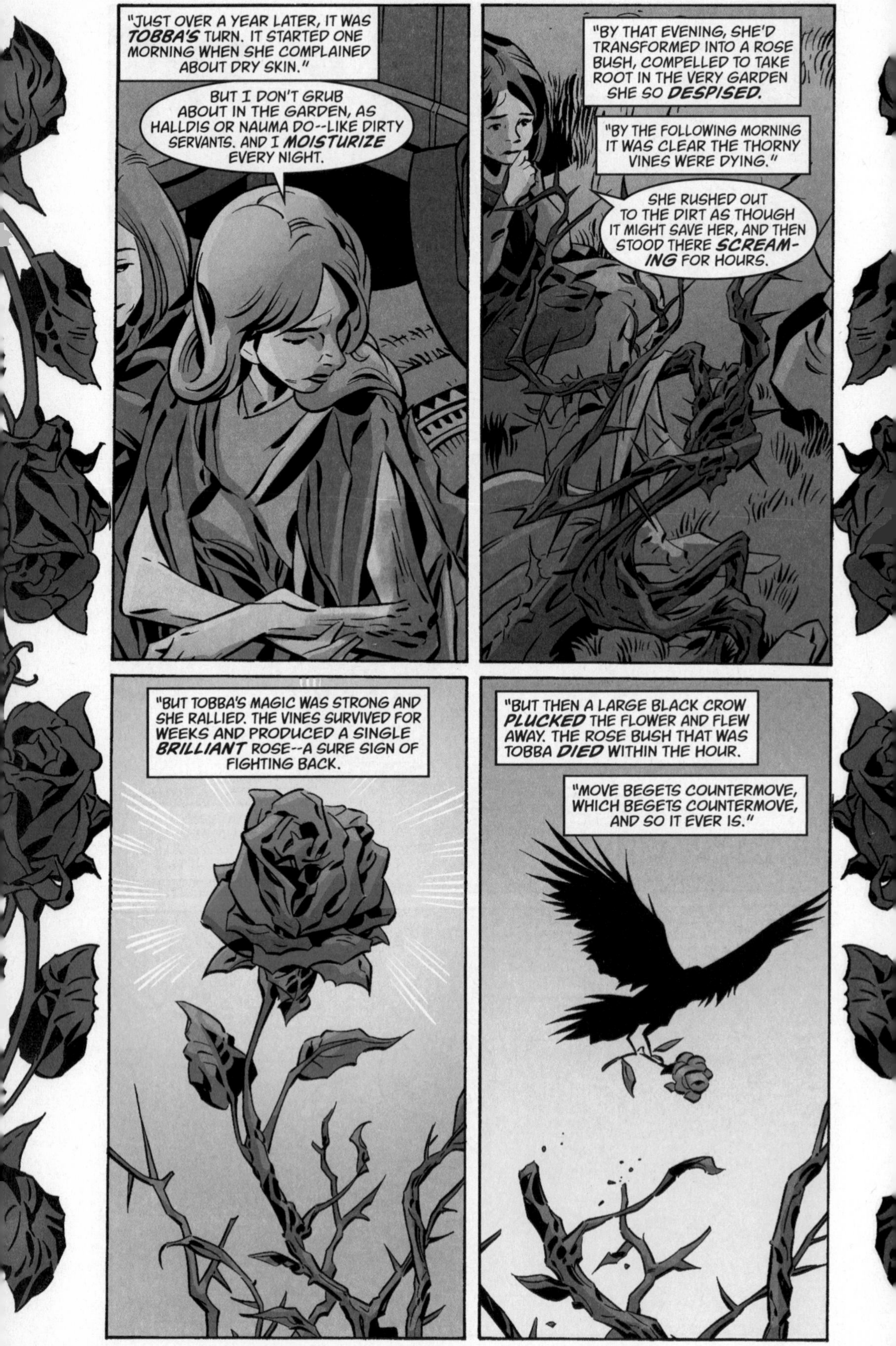
"JUST OVER A YEAR LATER, IT WAS TOBBA'S TURN. IT STARTED ONE MORNING WHEN SHE COMPLAINED ABOUT DRY SKIN."
BUT I DON'T GRUB ABOUT IN THE GARDEN, AS HALLDIS OR NAUMA DO--LIKE DIRTY SERVANTS. AND I MOISTURIZE EVERY NIGHT.
"BY THAT EVENING, SHE'D TRANSFORMED INTO A ROSE BUSH, COMPELLED TO TAKE ROOT IN THE VERY GARDEN SHE SO DESPISED.
"BY THE FOLLOWING MORNING IT WAS CLEAR THE THORNY VINES WERE DYING."
SHE RUSHED OUT TO THE DIRT AS THOUGH IT MIGHT SAVE HER, AND THEN STOOD THERE SCREAMING FOR HOURS.
"BUT TOBBA'S MAGIC WAS STRONG AND SHE RALLIED. THE VINES SURVIVED FOR WEEKS AND PRODUCED A SINGLE BRILLIANT ROSE--A SURE SIGN OF FIGHTING BACK.
"BUT THEN A LARGE BLACK CROW PLUCKED THE FLOWER AND FLEW AWAY. THE ROSE BUSH THAT WAS TOBBA DIED WITHIN THE HOUR.
"MOVE BEGETS COUNTERMOVE, WHICH BEGETS COUNTERMOVE, AND SO IT EVER IS."

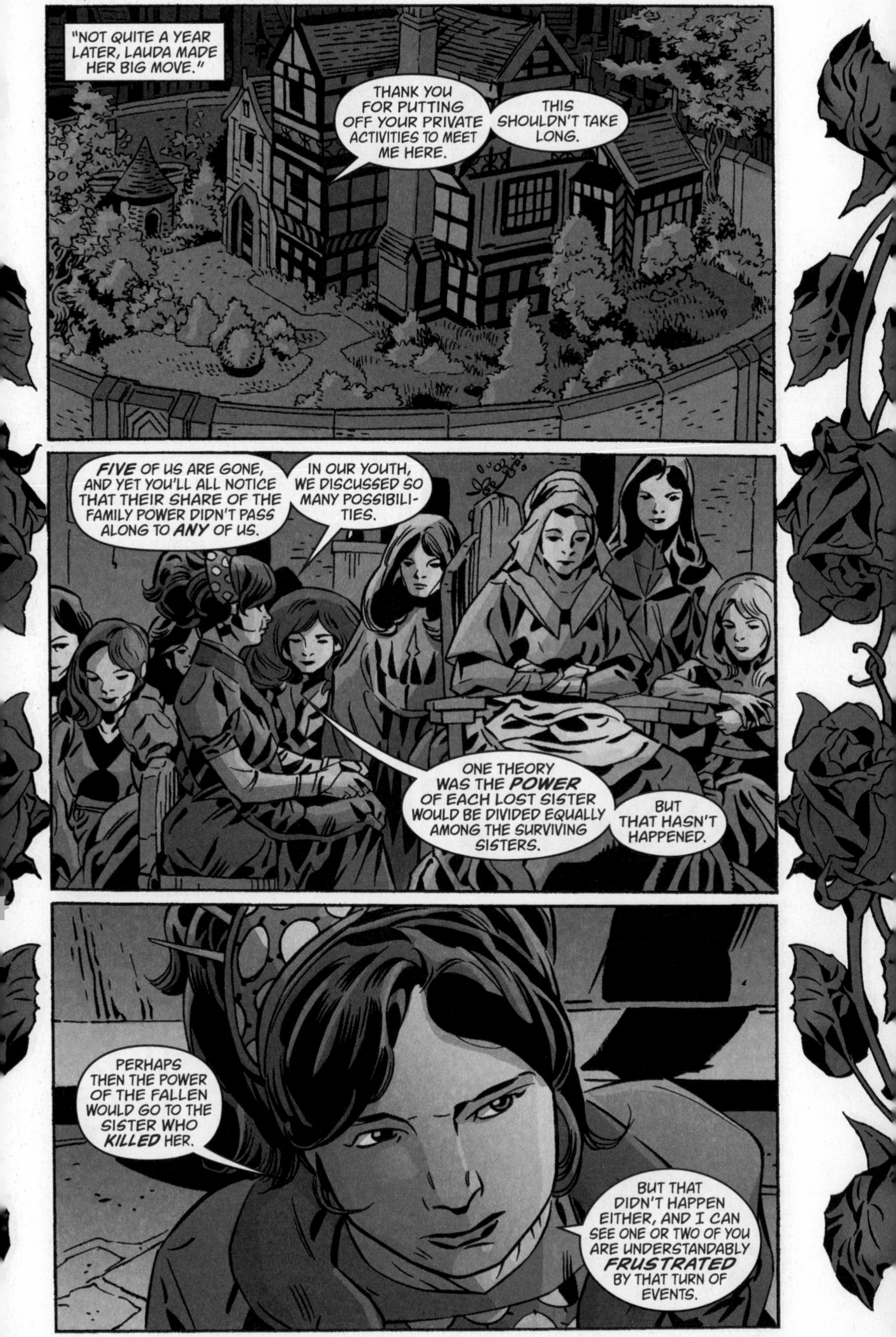
"NOT QUITE A YEAR LATER, LAUDA MADE HER BIG MOVE."
THANK YOU FOR PUTTING OFF YOUR PRIVATE ACTIVITIES TO MEET ME HERE.
THIS SHOULDN'T TAKE LONG.
FIVE OF US ARE GONE, AND YET YOU'LL ALL NOTICE THAT THEIR SHARE OF THE FAMILY POWER DIDN'T PASS ALONG TO ANY OF US.
IN OUR YOUTH, WE DISCUSSED SO MANY POSSIBILITIES.
ONE THEORY WAS THE POWER OF EACH LOST SISTER WOULD BE DIVIDED EQUALLY AMONG THE SURVIVING SISTERS.
BUT THAT HASN'T HAPPENED.
PERHAPS THEN THE POWER OF THE FALLEN WOULD GO TO THE SISTER WHO KILLED HER.
BUT THAT DIDN'T HAPPEN EITHER, AND I CAN SEE ONE OR TWO OF YOU ARE UNDERSTANDABLY FRUSTRATED BY THAT TURN OF EVENTS.

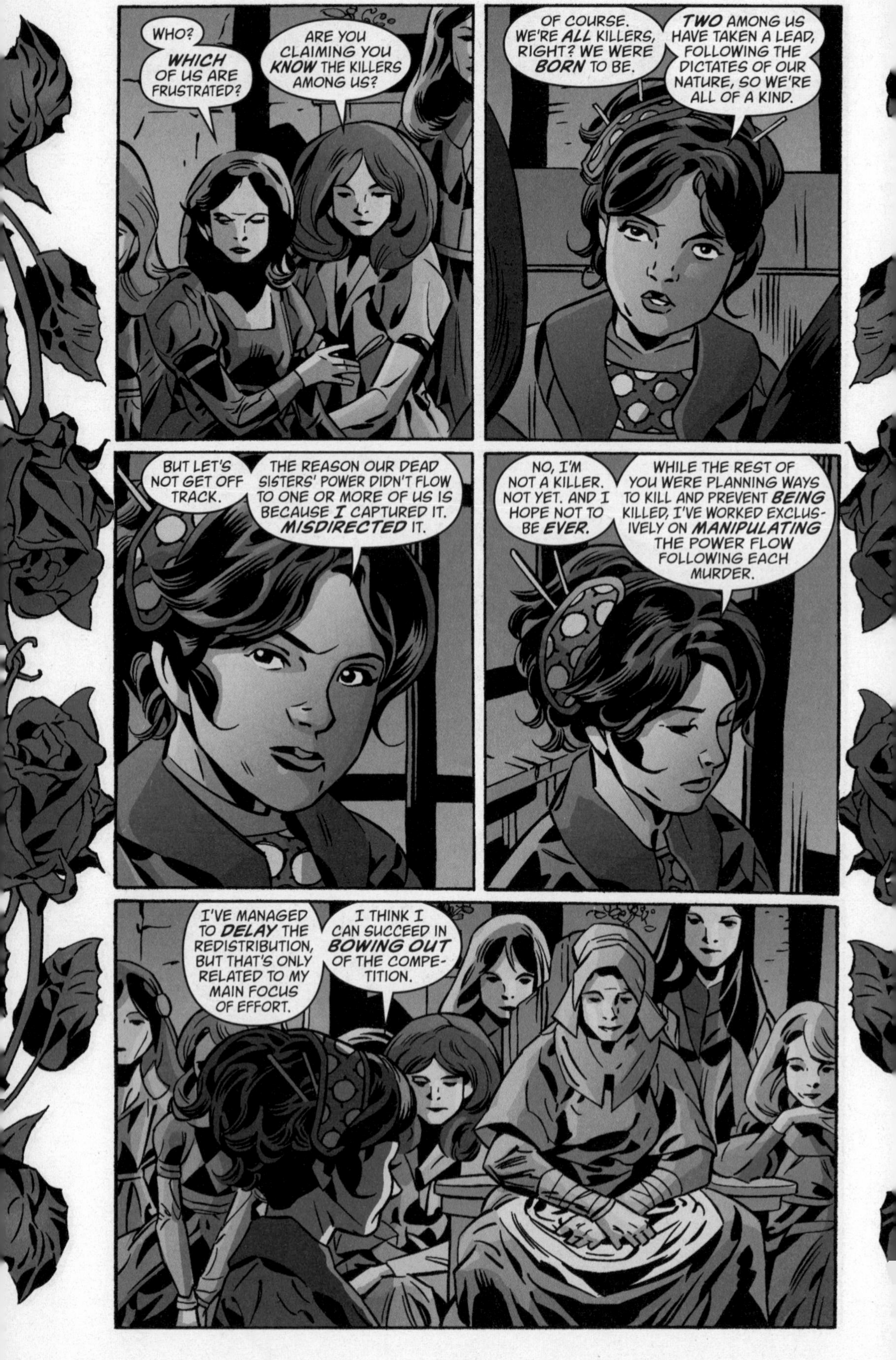
WHO? WHICH OF US ARE FRUSTRATED?
ARE YOU CLAIMING YOU KNOW THE KILLERS AMONG US?
OF COURSE. WE'RE ALL KILLERS, RIGHT? WE WERE BORN TO BE.
TWO AMONG US HAVE TAKEN A LEAD, FOLLOWING THE DICTATES OF OUR NATURE, SO WE'RE ALL OF A KIND.
BUT LET'S NOT GET OFF TRACK.
THE REASON OUR DEAD SISTERS' POWER DIDN'T FLOW TO ONE OR MORE OF US IS BECAUSE I CAPTURED IT. MISDIRECTED IT.
NO, I'M NOT A KILLER. NOT YET. AND I HOPE NOT TO BE EVER.
WHILE THE REST OF YOU WERE PLANNING WAYS TO KILL AND PREVENT BEING KILLED, I'VE WORKED EXCLUSIVELY ON MANIPULATING THE POWER FLOW FOLLOWING EACH MURDER.
I'VE MANAGED TO DELAY THE REDISTRIBUTION, BUT THAT'S ONLY RELATED TO MY MAIN FOCUS OF EFFORT.
I THINK I CAN SUCCEED IN BOWING OUT OF THE COMPETITION.

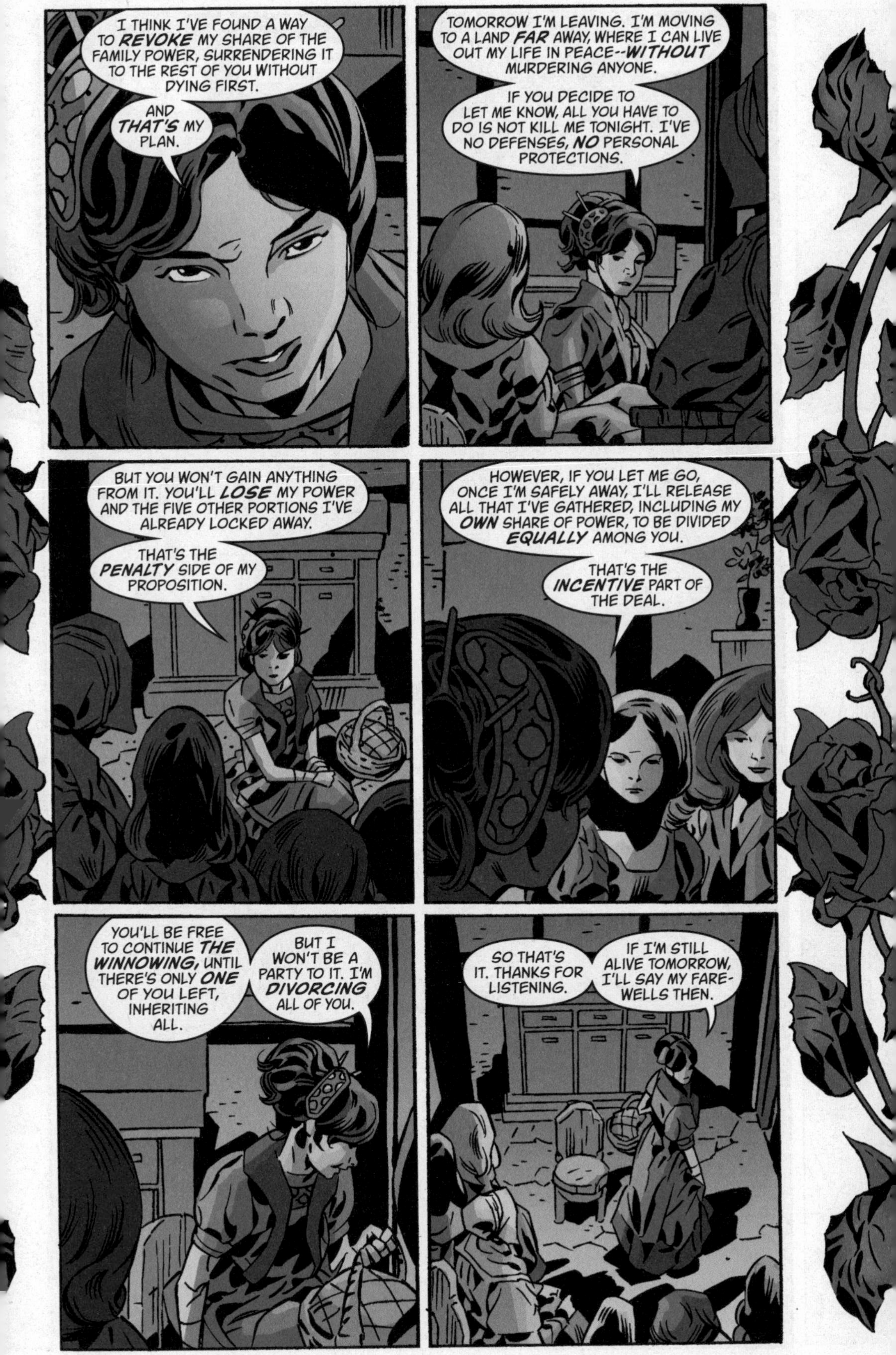

I THINK I'VE FOUND A WAY TO REVOKE MY SHARE OF THE FAMILY POWER, SURRENDERING IT TO THE REST OF YOU WITHOUT DYING FIRST.
AND THAT'S MY PLAN.
TOMORROW I'M LEAVING. I'M MOVING TO A LAND FAR AWAY, WHERE I CAN LIVE OUT MY LIFE IN PEACE--WITHOUT MURDERING ANYONE.
IF YOU DECIDE TO LET ME KNOW, ALL YOU HAVE TO DO IS NOT KILL ME TONIGHT. I'VE NO DEFENSES, NO PERSONAL PROTECTIONS.
BUT YOU WON'T GAIN ANYTHING FROM IT. YOU'LL LOSE MY POWER AND THE FIVE OTHER PORTIONS I'VE ALREADY LOCKED AWAY.
THAT'S THE PENALTY SIDE OF MY PROPOSITION.
HOWEVER, IF YOU LET ME GO, ONCE I'M SAFELY AWAY, I'LL RELEASE ALL THAT I'VE GATHERED, INCLUDING MY OWN SHARE OF POWER, TO BE DIVIDED EQUALLY AMONG YOU.
THAT'S THE INCENTIVE PART OF THE DEAL.
YOU'LL BE FREE TO CONTINUE THE WINNOWING, UNTIL THERE'S ONLY ONE OF YOU LEFT, INHERITING ALL.
BUT I WON'T BE A PARTY TO IT. I'M DIVORCING ALL OF YOU.
SO THAT'S IT. THANKS FOR LISTENING.
IF I'M STILL ALIVE TOMORROW, I'LL SAY MY FAREWELLS THEN.

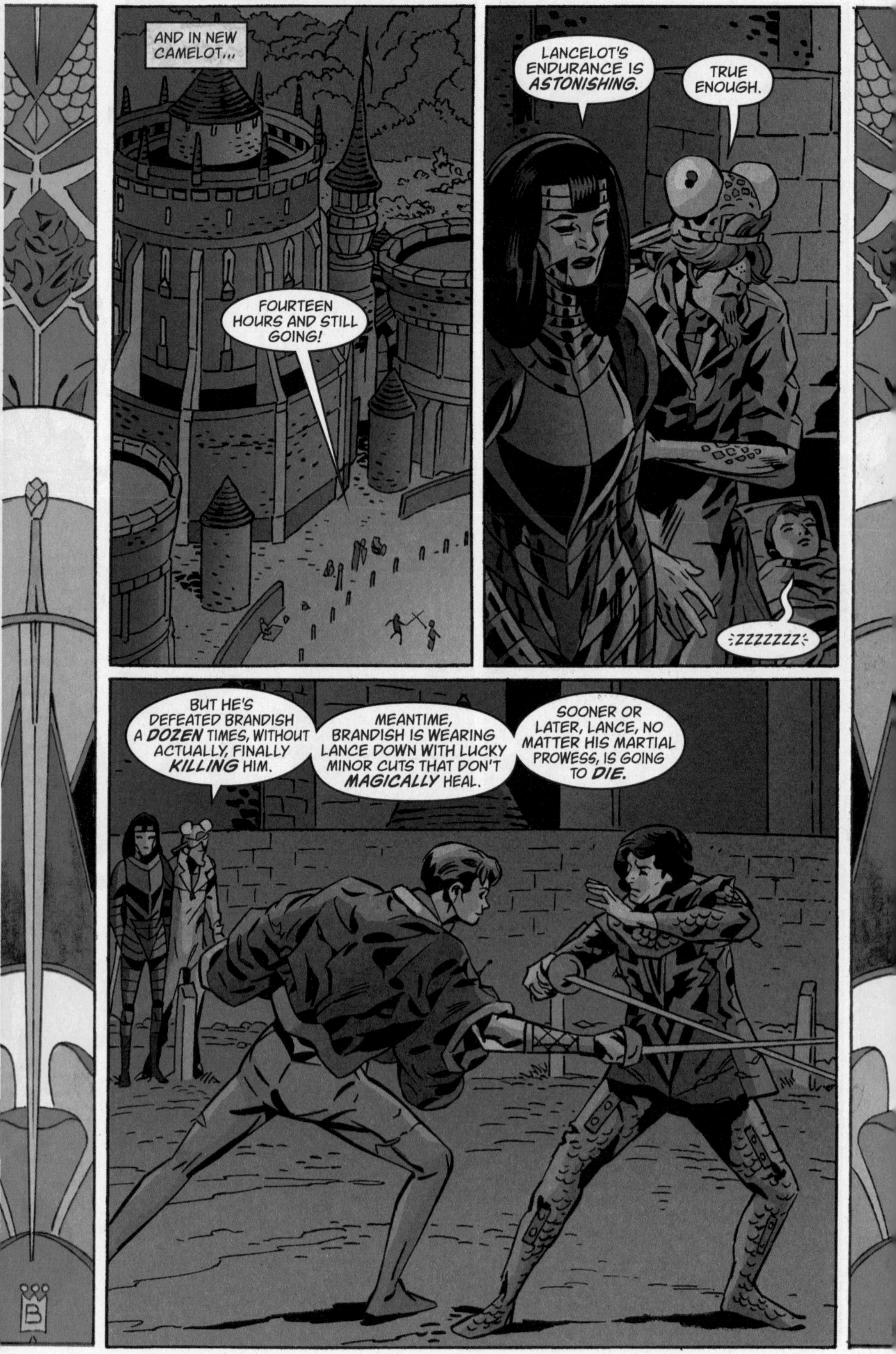
AND IN NEW CAMELOT...
FOURTEEN HOURS AND STILL GOING!
LANCELOT'S ENDURANCE IS ASTONISHING.
TRUE ENOUGH.
ZZZZZZZ
BUT HE'S DEFEATED BRANDISH A DOZEN TIMES, WITHOUT ACTUALLY, FINALLY KILLING HIM.
MEANTIME, BRANDISH IS WEARING LANCE DOWN WITH LUCKY MINOR CUTS THAT DON'T MAGICALLY HEAL.
SOONER OR LATER, LANCE, NO MATTER HIS MARTIAL PROWESS, IS GOING TO DIE.

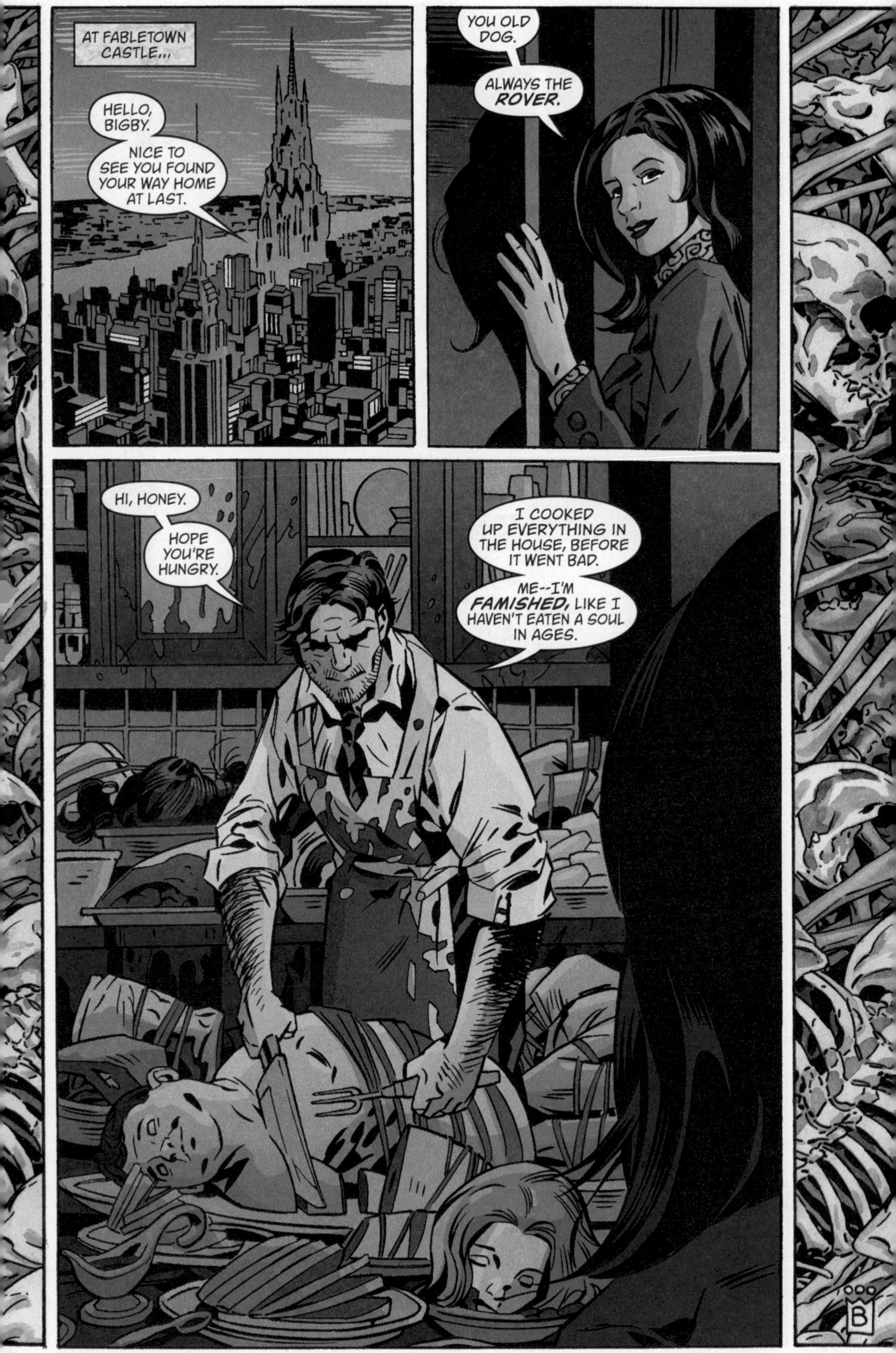
AT FABLETOWN CASTLE...
HELLO, BIGBY.
NICE TO SEE YOU FOUND YOUR WAY HOME AT LAST.
YOU OLD DOG.
ALWAYS THE ROVER.
HI, HONEY.
HOPE YOU'RE HUNGRY.
I COOKED UP EVERYTHING IN THE HOUSE, BEFORE IT WENT BAD.
ME--I'M FAMISHED, LIKE I HAVEN'T EATEN A SOUL IN AGES.

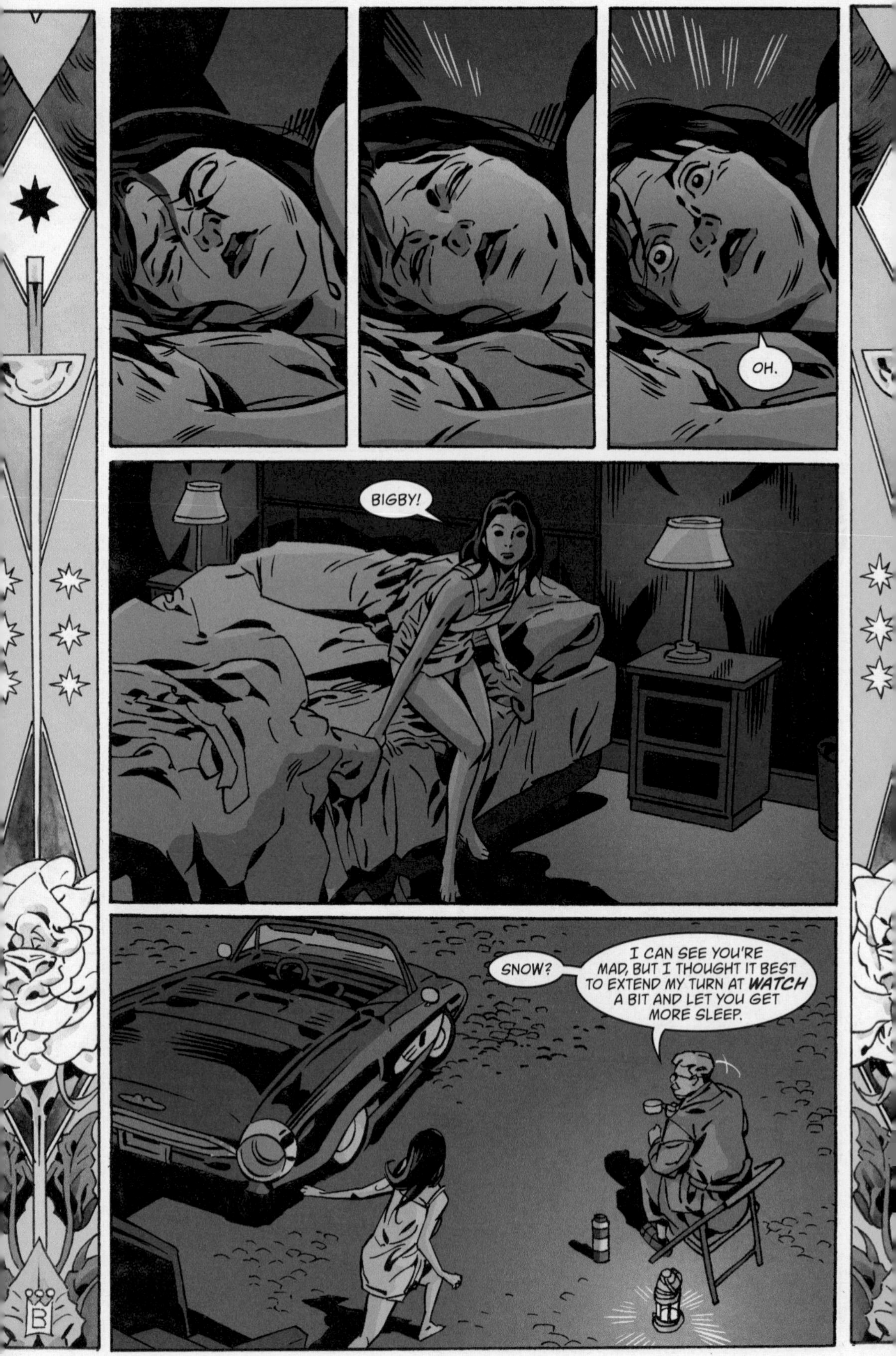
OH.
BIGBY!
SNOW?
I CAN SEE YOU'RE MAD, BUT I THOUGHT IT BEST TO EXTEND MY TURN AT WATCH A BIT AND LET YOU GET MORE SLEEP.

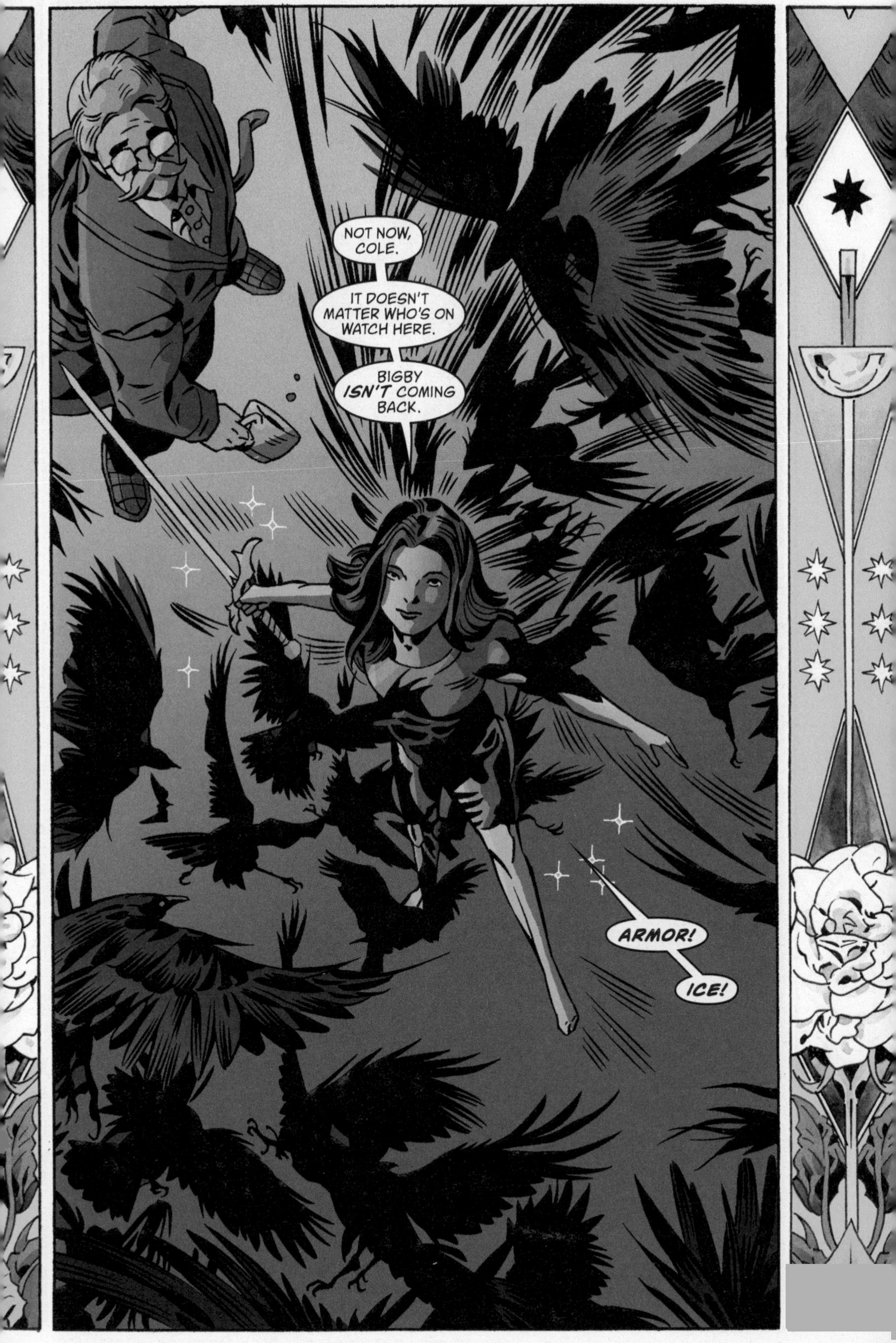
NOT NOW, COLE.
IT DOESN'T MATTER WHO'S ON WATCH HERE.
BIGBY *ISN'T* COMING BACK.
ARMOR!
ICE!

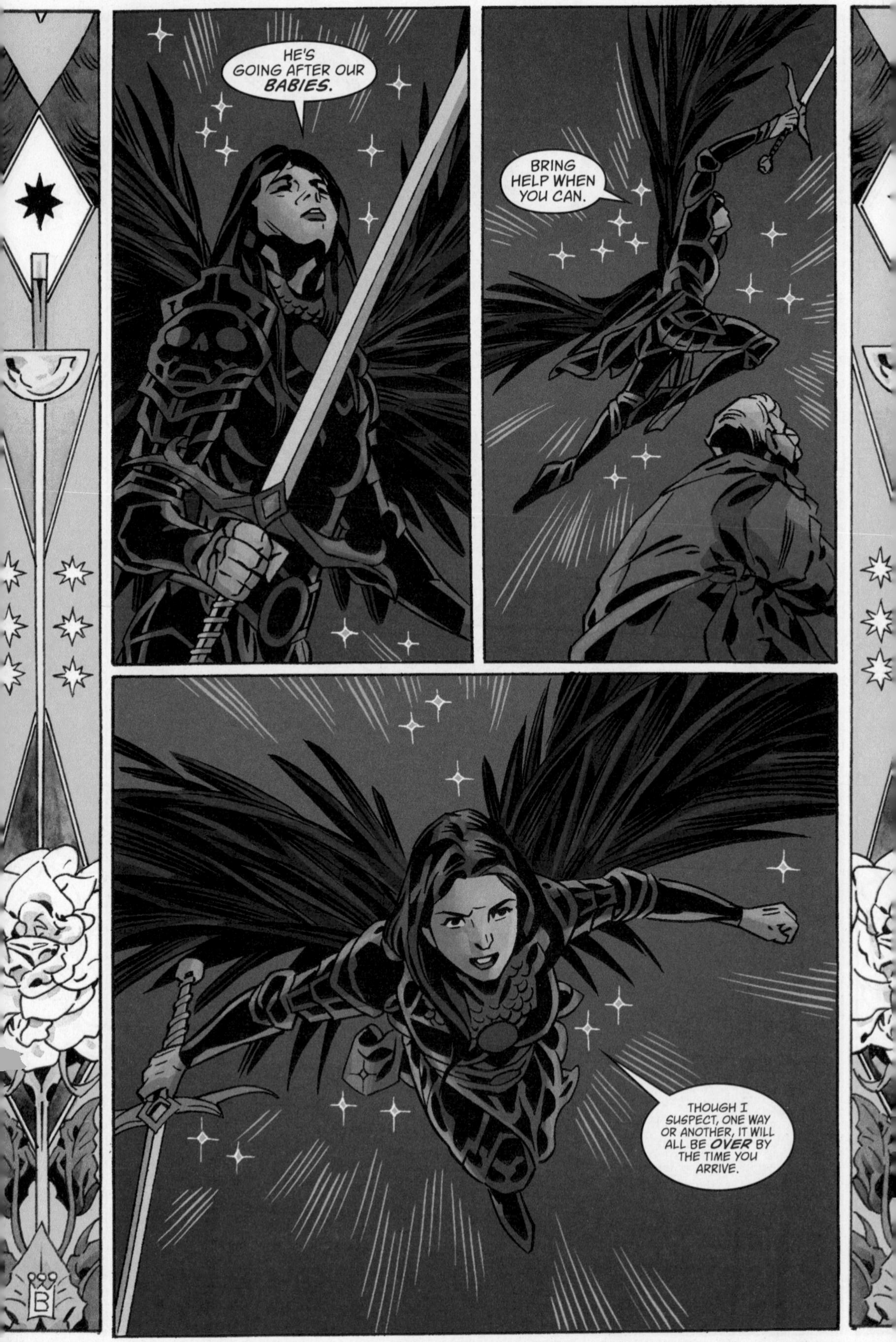
HE'S GOING AFTER OUR *BABIES.*
BRING HELP WHEN YOU CAN.
THOUGH I SUSPECT, ONE WAY OR ANOTHER, IT WILL ALL BE *OVER* BY THE TIME YOU ARRIVE.

NEXT: THE LEGEND OF THE DARK ANGEL OF VENGEANCE.

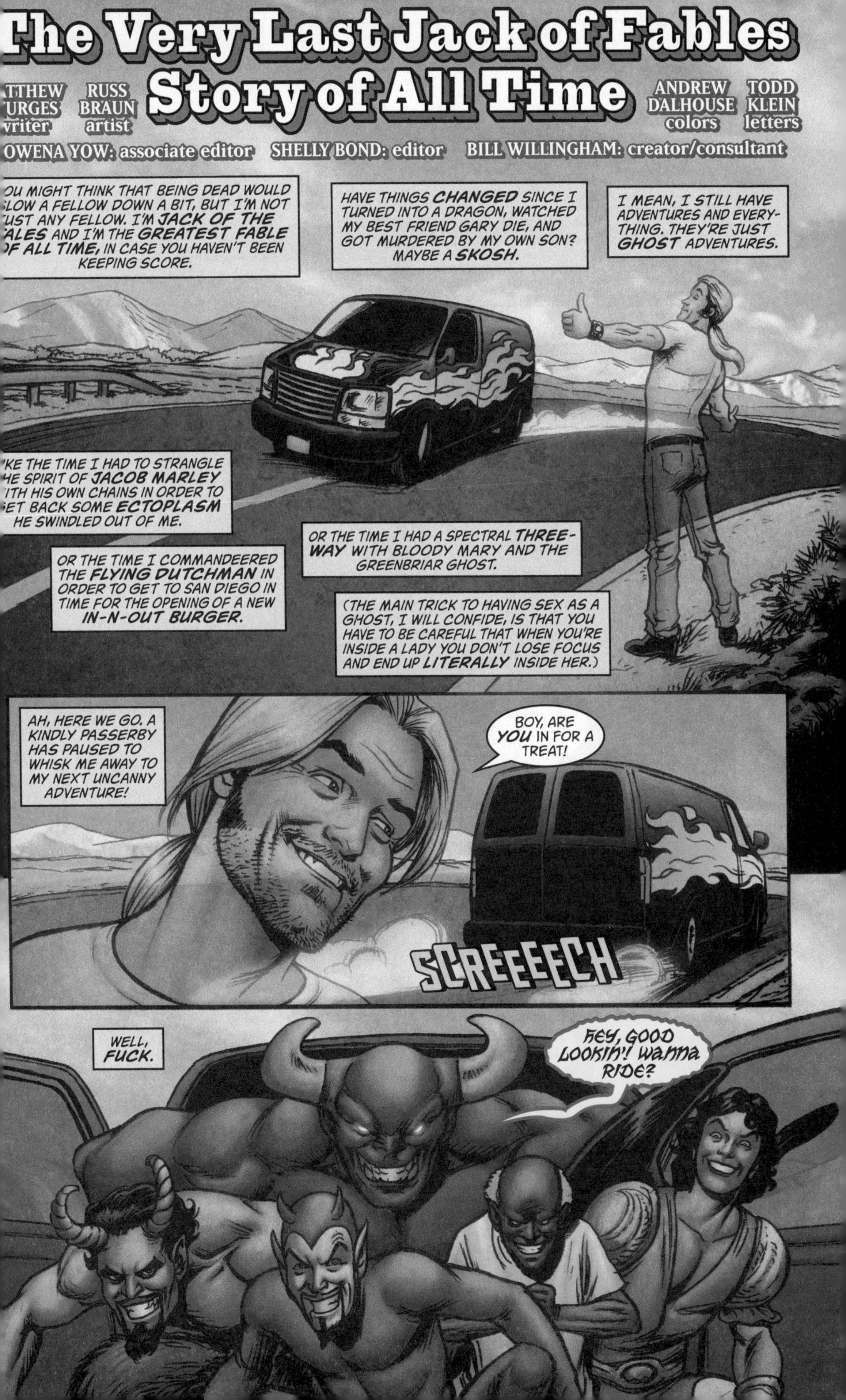
The Very Last Jack of Fables Story of All Time
TTHEW URGES writer
RUSS BRAUN artist
ANDREW DALHOUSE colors
TODD KLEIN letters
OWENA YOW: associate editor
SHELLY BOND: editor
BILL WILLINGHAM: creator/consultant
OU MIGHT THINK THAT BEING DEAD WOULD LOW A FELLOW DOWN A BIT, BUT I'M NOT UST ANY FELLOW. I'M JACK OF THE ALES AND I'M THE GREATEST FABLE F ALL TIME, IN CASE YOU HAVEN'T BEEN KEEPING SCORE.
HAVE THINGS CHANGED SINCE I TURNED INTO A DRAGON, WATCHED MY BEST FRIEND GARY DIE, AND GOT MURDERED BY MY OWN SON? MAYBE A SKOSH.
I MEAN, I STILL HAVE ADVENTURES AND EVERYTHING. THEY'RE JUST GHOST ADVENTURES.
KE THE TIME I HAD TO STRANGLE HE SPIRIT OF JACOB MARLEY ITH HIS OWN CHAINS IN ORDER TO ET BACK SOME ECTOPLASM HE SWINDLED OUT OF ME.
OR THE TIME I COMMANDEERED THE FLYING DUTCHMAN IN ORDER TO GET TO SAN DIEGO IN TIME FOR THE OPENING OF A NEW IN-N-OUT BURGER.
OR THE TIME I HAD A SPECTRAL THREE-WAY WITH BLOODY MARY AND THE GREENBRIAR GHOST.
(THE MAIN TRICK TO HAVING SEX AS A GHOST, I WILL CONFIDE, IS THAT YOU HAVE TO BE CAREFUL THAT WHEN YOU'RE INSIDE A LADY YOU DON'T LOSE FOCUS AND END UP LITERALLY INSIDE HER.)
AH, HERE WE GO. A KINDLY PASSERBY HAS PAUSED TO WHISK ME AWAY TO MY NEXT UNCANNY ADVENTURE!
BOY, ARE YOU IN FOR A TREAT!
SCREEEECH
WELL, FUCK.
HEY, GOOD LOOKIN'! WANNA RIDE?

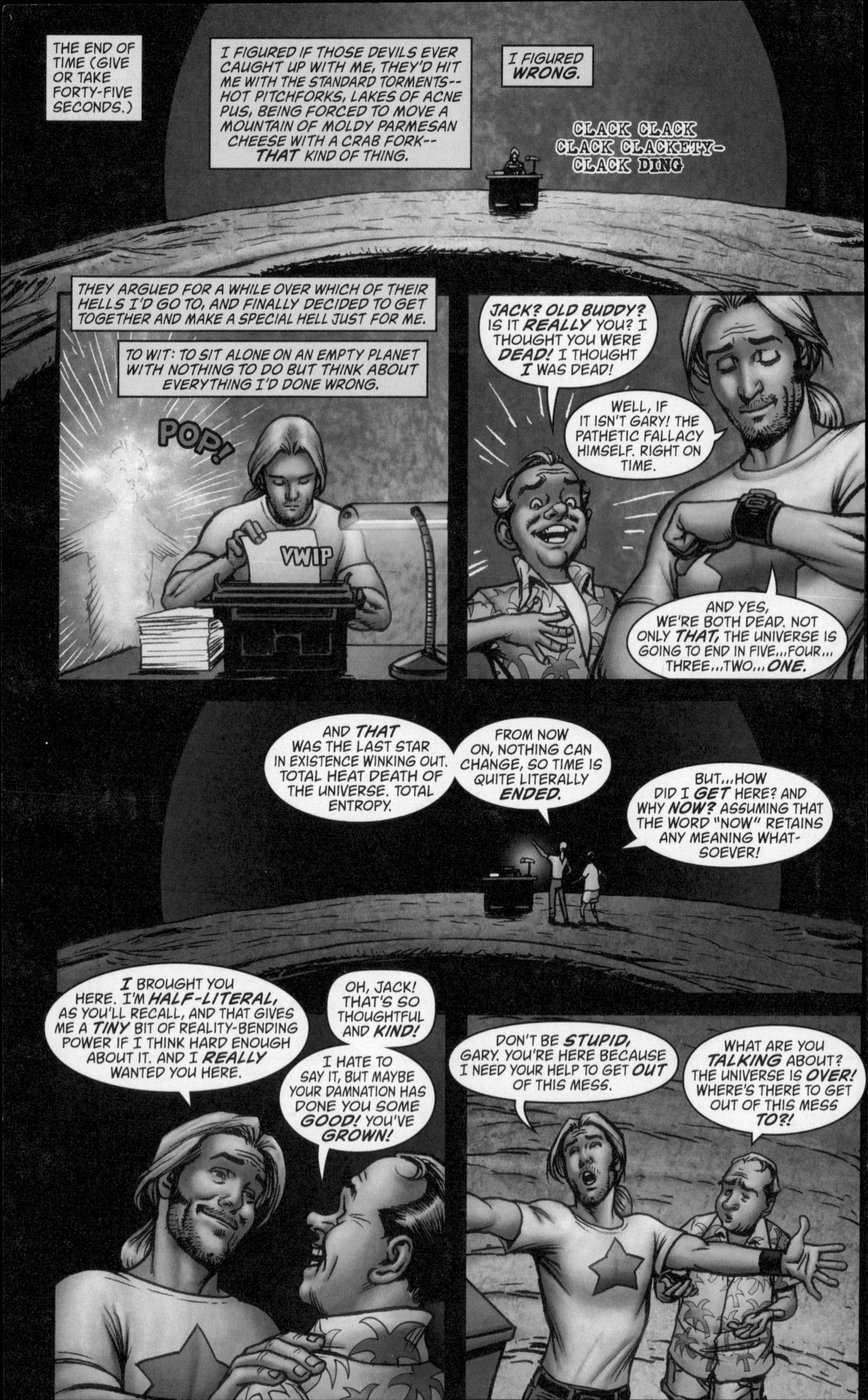
THE END OF TIME (GIVE OR TAKE FORTY-FIVE SECONDS.)
I FIGURED IF THOSE DEVILS EVER CAUGHT UP WITH ME, THEY'D HIT ME WITH THE STANDARD TORMENTS-- HOT PITCHFORKS, LAKES OF ACNE PUS, BEING FORCED TO MOVE A MOUNTAIN OF MOLDY PARMESAN CHEESE WITH A CRAB FORK-- THAT KIND OF THING.
I FIGURED WRONG.
CLACK CLACK CLACK CLACKETY-CLACK DING
THEY ARGUED FOR A WHILE OVER WHICH OF THEIR HELLS I'D GO TO, AND FINALLY DECIDED TO GET TOGETHER AND MAKE A SPECIAL HELL JUST FOR ME.
TO WIT: TO SIT ALONE ON AN EMPTY PLANET WITH NOTHING TO DO BUT THINK ABOUT EVERYTHING I'D DONE WRONG.
POP!
VWIP
JACK? OLD BUDDY? IS IT REALLY YOU? I THOUGHT YOU WERE DEAD! I THOUGHT I WAS DEAD!
WELL, IF IT ISN'T GARY! THE PATHETIC FALLACY HIMSELF. RIGHT ON TIME.
AND YES, WE'RE BOTH DEAD. NOT ONLY THAT, THE UNIVERSE IS GOING TO END IN FIVE...FOUR... THREE...TWO...ONE.
AND THAT WAS THE LAST STAR IN EXISTENCE WINKING OUT. TOTAL HEAT DEATH OF THE UNIVERSE. TOTAL ENTROPY.
FROM NOW ON, NOTHING CAN CHANGE, SO TIME IS QUITE LITERALLY ENDED.
BUT...HOW DID I GET HERE? AND WHY NOW? ASSUMING THAT THE WORD "NOW" RETAINS ANY MEANING WHAT-SOEVER!
I BROUGHT YOU HERE. I'M HALF-LITERAL, AS YOU'LL RECALL, AND THAT GIVES ME A TINY BIT OF REALITY-BENDING POWER IF I THINK HARD ENOUGH ABOUT IT. AND I REALLY WANTED YOU HERE.
OH, JACK! THAT'S SO THOUGHTFUL AND KIND!
I HATE TO SAY IT, BUT MAYBE YOUR DAMNATION HAS DONE YOU SOME GOOD! YOU'VE GROWN!
DON'T BE STUPID, GARY. YOU'RE HERE BECAUSE I NEED YOUR HELP TO GET OUT OF THIS MESS.
WHAT ARE YOU TALKING ABOUT? THE UNIVERSE IS OVER! WHERE'S THERE TO GET OUT OF THIS MESS TO?!

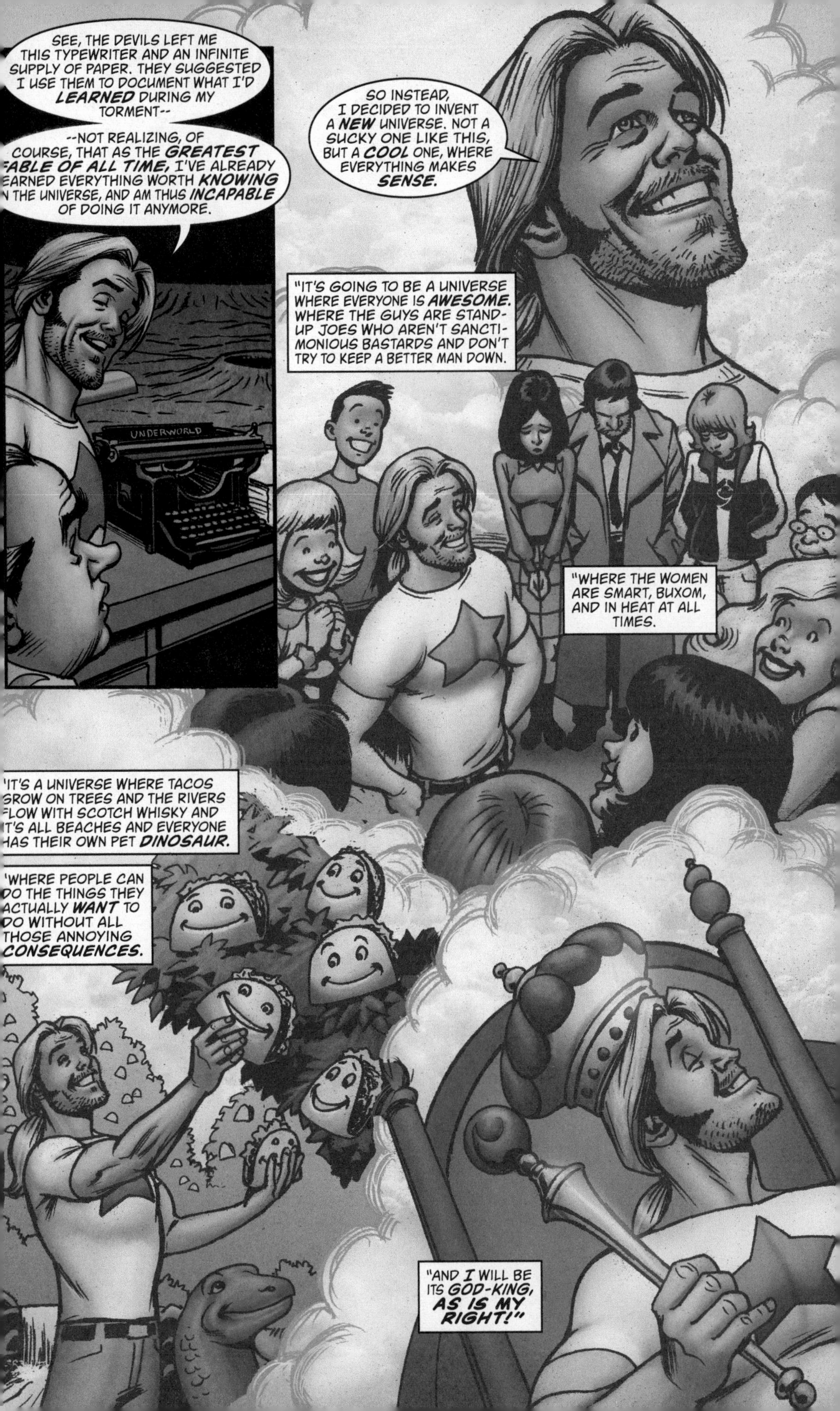

SEE, THE DEVILS LEFT ME THIS TYPEWRITER AND AN INFINITE SUPPLY OF PAPER. THEY SUGGESTED I USE THEM TO DOCUMENT WHAT I'D LEARNED DURING MY TORMENT--
--NOT REALIZING, OF COURSE, THAT AS THE GREATEST FABLE OF ALL TIME, I'VE ALREADY LEARNED EVERYTHING WORTH KNOWING IN THE UNIVERSE, AND AM THUS INCAPABLE OF DOING IT ANYMORE.
UNDERWORLD
SO INSTEAD, I DECIDED TO INVENT A NEW UNIVERSE. NOT A SUCKY ONE LIKE THIS, BUT A COOL ONE, WHERE EVERYTHING MAKES SENSE.
"IT'S GOING TO BE A UNIVERSE WHERE EVERYONE IS AWESOME. WHERE THE GUYS ARE STAND-UP JOES WHO AREN'T SANCTIMONIOUS BASTARDS AND DON'T TRY TO KEEP A BETTER MAN DOWN.
"WHERE THE WOMEN ARE SMART, BUXOM, AND IN HEAT AT ALL TIMES.
"IT'S A UNIVERSE WHERE TACOS GROW ON TREES AND THE RIVERS FLOW WITH SCOTCH WHISKY AND IT'S ALL BEACHES AND EVERYONE HAS THEIR OWN PET DINOSAUR.
"WHERE PEOPLE CAN DO THE THINGS THEY ACTUALLY WANT TO DO WITHOUT ALL THOSE ANNOYING CONSEQUENCES.
"AND I WILL BE ITS GOD-KING, AS IS MY RIGHT!"

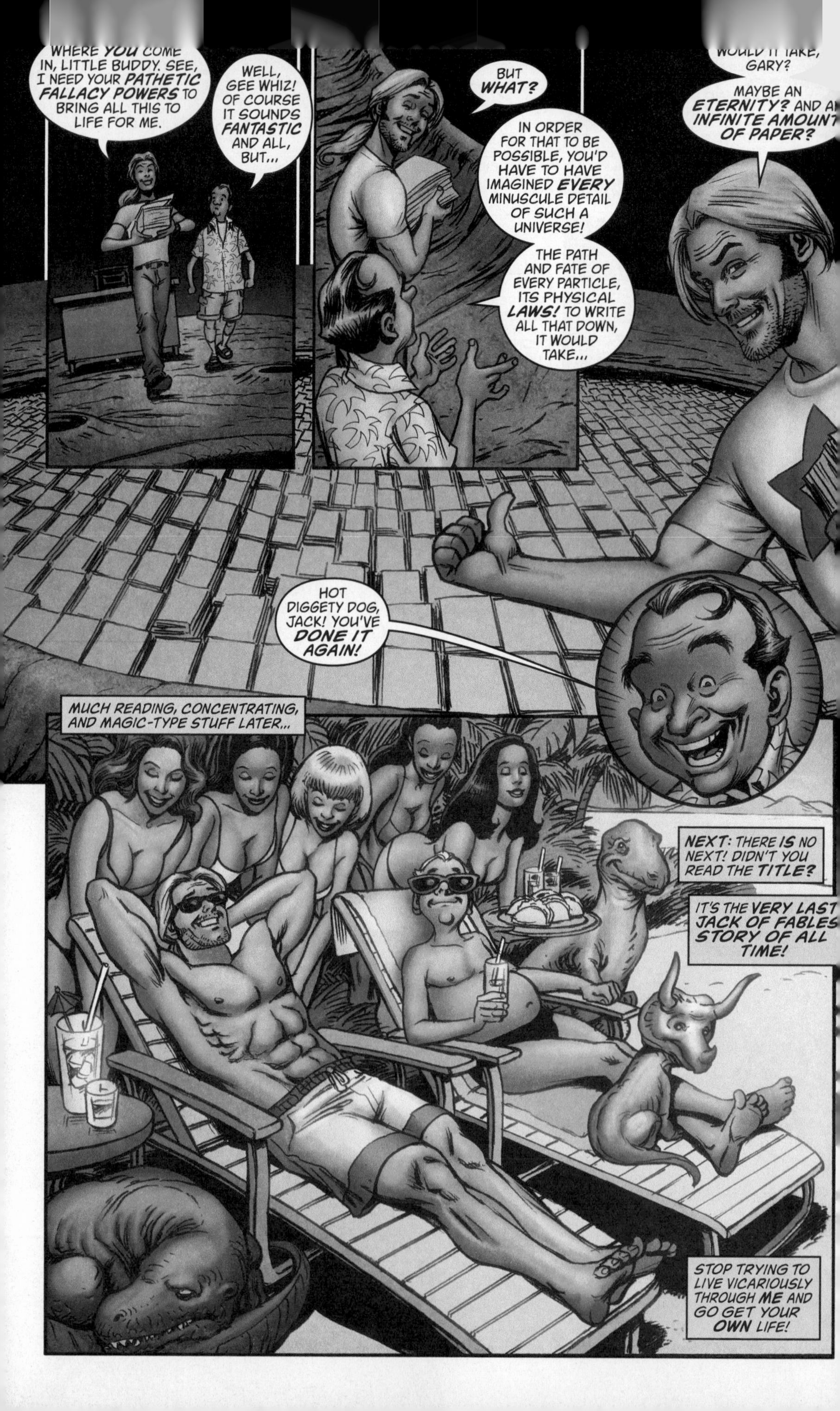

WHERE YOU COME IN, LITTLE BUDDY. SEE, I NEED YOUR PATHETIC FALLACY POWERS TO BRING ALL THIS TO LIFE FOR ME.
WELL, GEE WHIZ! OF COURSE IT SOUNDS FANTASTIC AND ALL, BUT...
BUT WHAT?
IN ORDER FOR THAT TO BE POSSIBLE, YOU'D HAVE TO HAVE IMAGINED EVERY MINUSCULE DETAIL OF SUCH A UNIVERSE!
THE PATH AND FATE OF EVERY PARTICLE, ITS PHYSICAL LAWS! TO WRITE ALL THAT DOWN, IT WOULD TAKE...
GARY?
MAYBE AN ETERNITY? AND AN INFINITE AMOUNT OF PAPER?
HOT DIGGETY DOG, JACK! YOU'VE DONE IT AGAIN!
MUCH READING, CONCENTRATING, AND MAGIC-TYPE STUFF LATER...
NEXT: THERE IS NO NEXT! DIDN'T YOU READ THE TITLE?
IT'S THE VERY LAST JACK OF FABLES STORY OF ALL TIME!
STOP TRYING TO LIVE VICARIOUSLY THROUGH ME AND GO GET YOUR OWN LIFE!

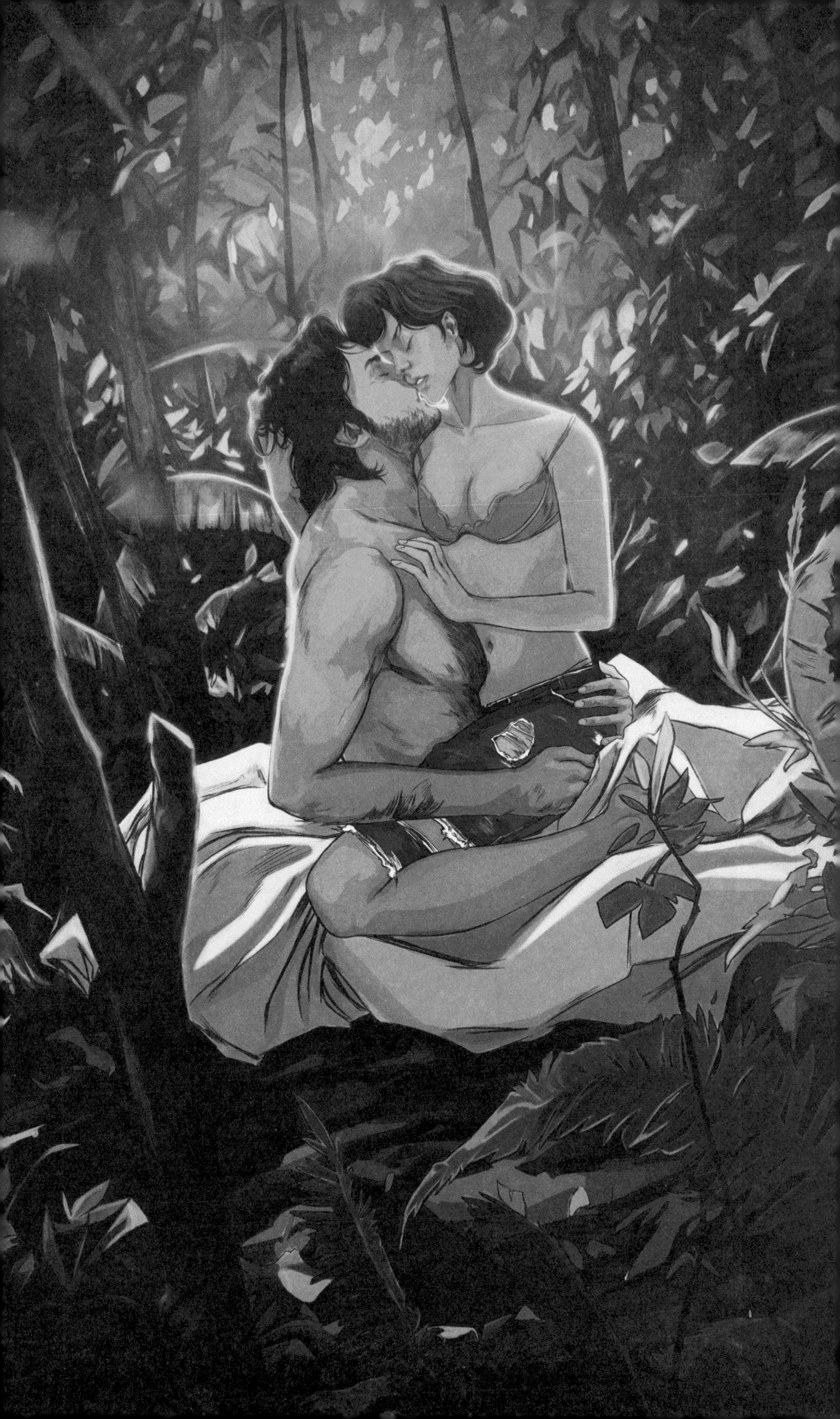

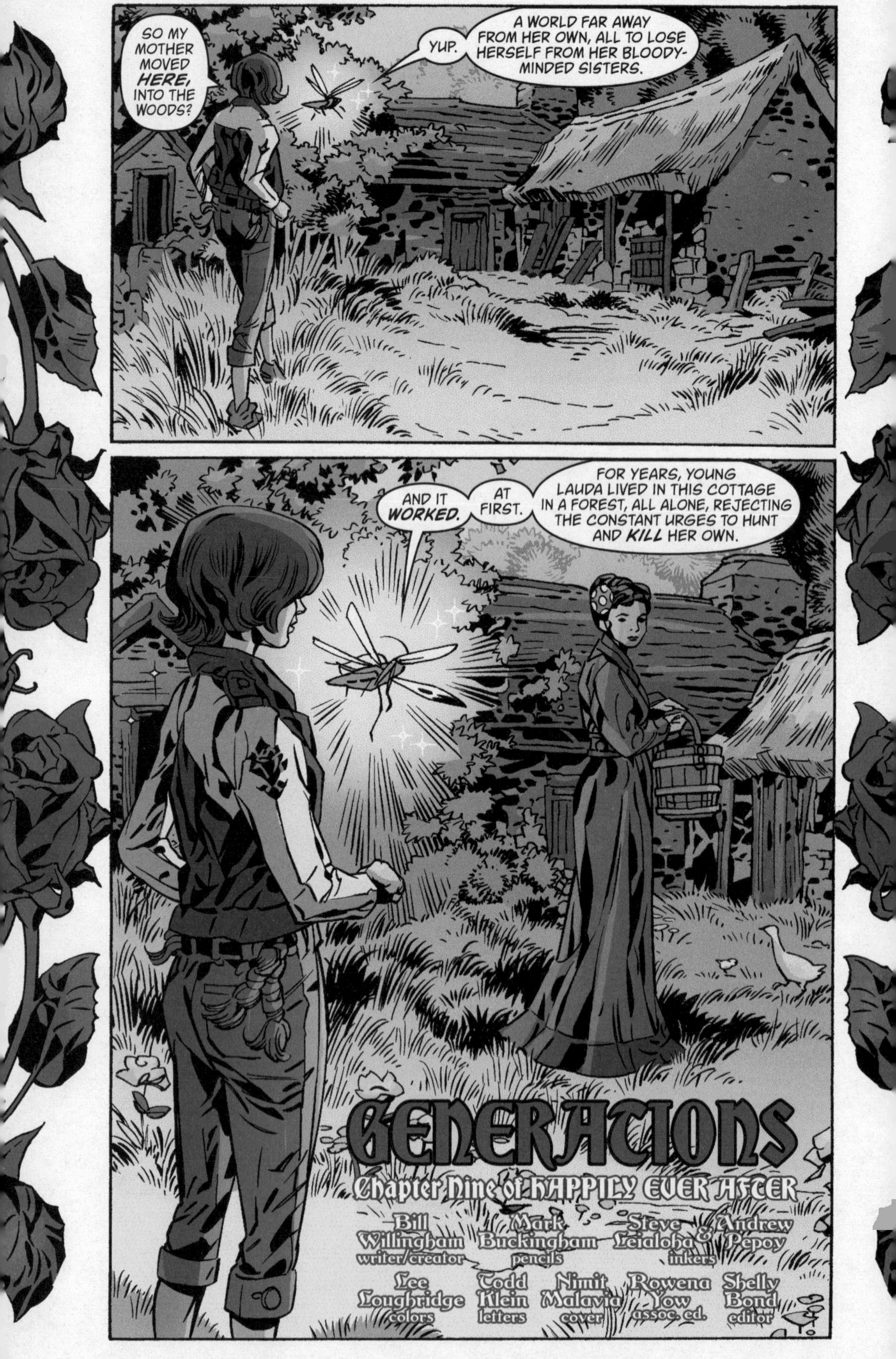
SO MY MOTHER MOVED **HERE,** INTO THE WOODS?
YUP.
A WORLD FAR AWAY FROM HER OWN, ALL TO LOSE HERSELF FROM HER BLOODY-MINDED SISTERS.
AND IT **WORKED.**
AT FIRST.
FOR YEARS, YOUNG LAUDA LIVED IN THIS COTTAGE IN A FOREST, ALL ALONE, REJECTING THE CONSTANT URGES TO HUNT AND **KILL** HER OWN.
GENERATIONS
Chapter Nine of HAPPILY EVER AFTER
Bill Willingham writer/creator
Mark Buckingham pencils
Steve Leialoha & Andrew Pepoy inkers
Lee Loughridge colors
Todd Klein letters
Nimit Malavia cover
Rowena Yow assoc. ed.
Shelly Bond editor

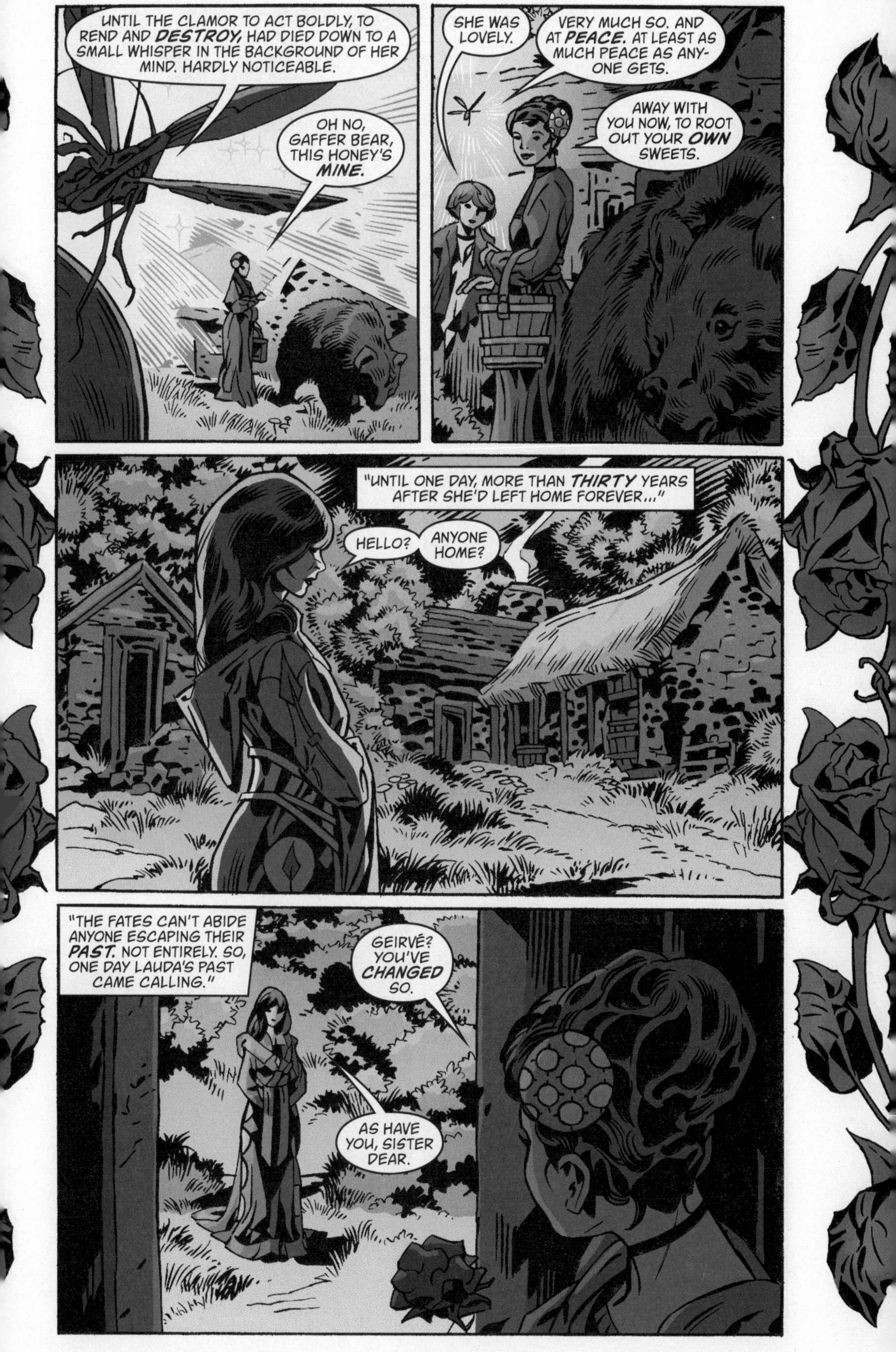
UNTIL THE CLAMOR TO ACT BOLDLY, TO REND AND DESTROY, HAD DIED DOWN TO A SMALL WHISPER IN THE BACKGROUND OF HER MIND. HARDLY NOTICEABLE.
OH NO, GAFFER BEAR, THIS HONEY'S MINE.
SHE WAS LOVELY.
VERY MUCH SO. AND AT PEACE. AT LEAST AS MUCH PEACE AS ANY-ONE GETS.
AWAY WITH YOU NOW, TO ROOT OUT YOUR OWN SWEETS.
"UNTIL ONE DAY, MORE THAN THIRTY YEARS AFTER SHE'D LEFT HOME FOREVER..."
HELLO?
ANYONE HOME?
"THE FATES CAN'T ABIDE ANYONE ESCAPING THEIR PAST. NOT ENTIRELY. SO, ONE DAY LAUDA'S PAST CAME CALLING."
GEIRVÉ? YOU'VE CHANGED SO.
AS HAVE YOU, SISTER DEAR.

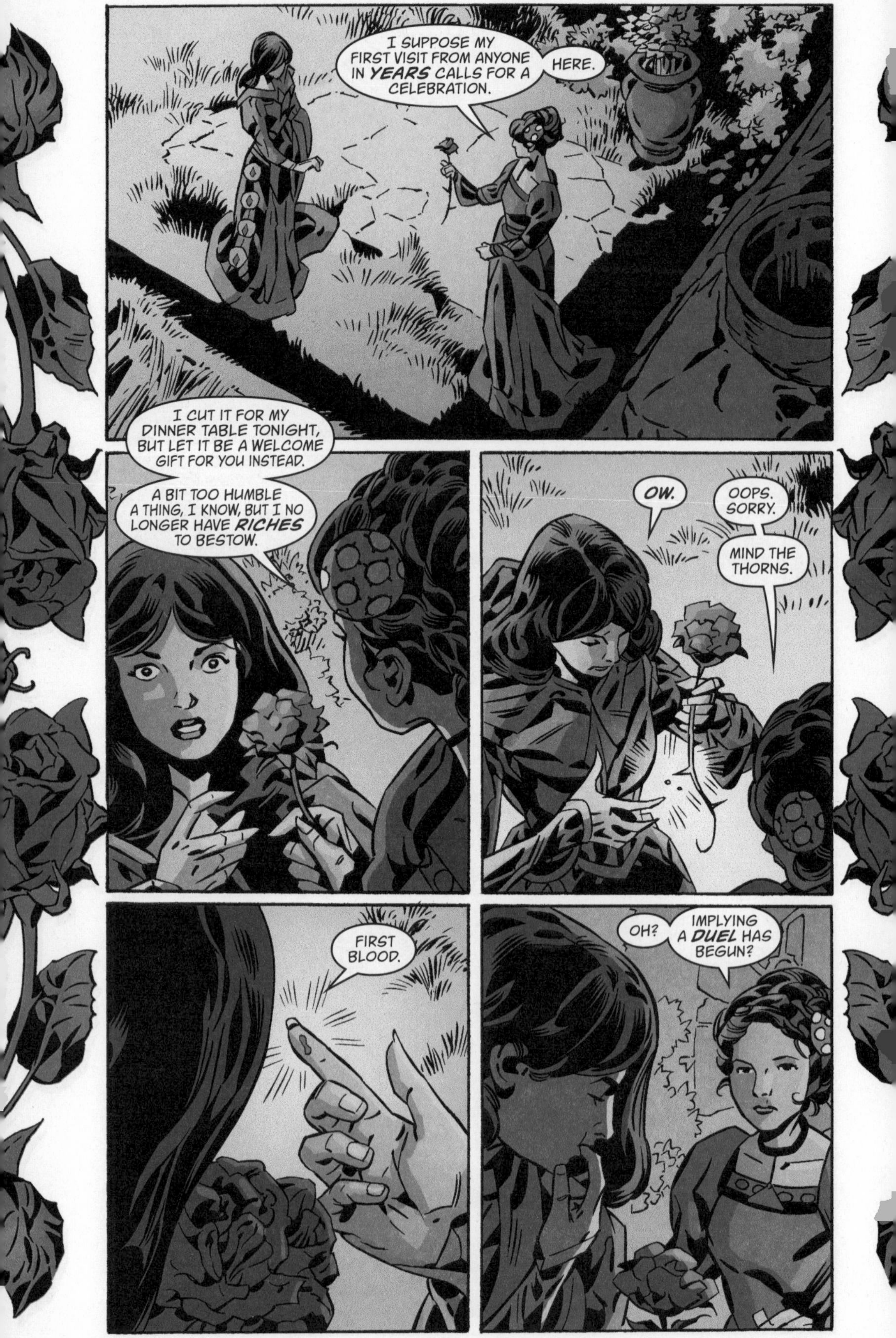
I SUPPOSE MY FIRST VISIT FROM ANYONE IN YEARS CALLS FOR A CELEBRATION.
HERE.
I CUT IT FOR MY DINNER TABLE TONIGHT, BUT LET IT BE A WELCOME GIFT FOR YOU INSTEAD.
A BIT TOO HUMBLE A THING, I KNOW, BUT I NO LONGER HAVE RICHES TO BESTOW.
OW.
OOPS. SORRY.
MIND THE THORNS.
FIRST BLOOD.
OH?
IMPLYING A DUEL HAS BEGUN?

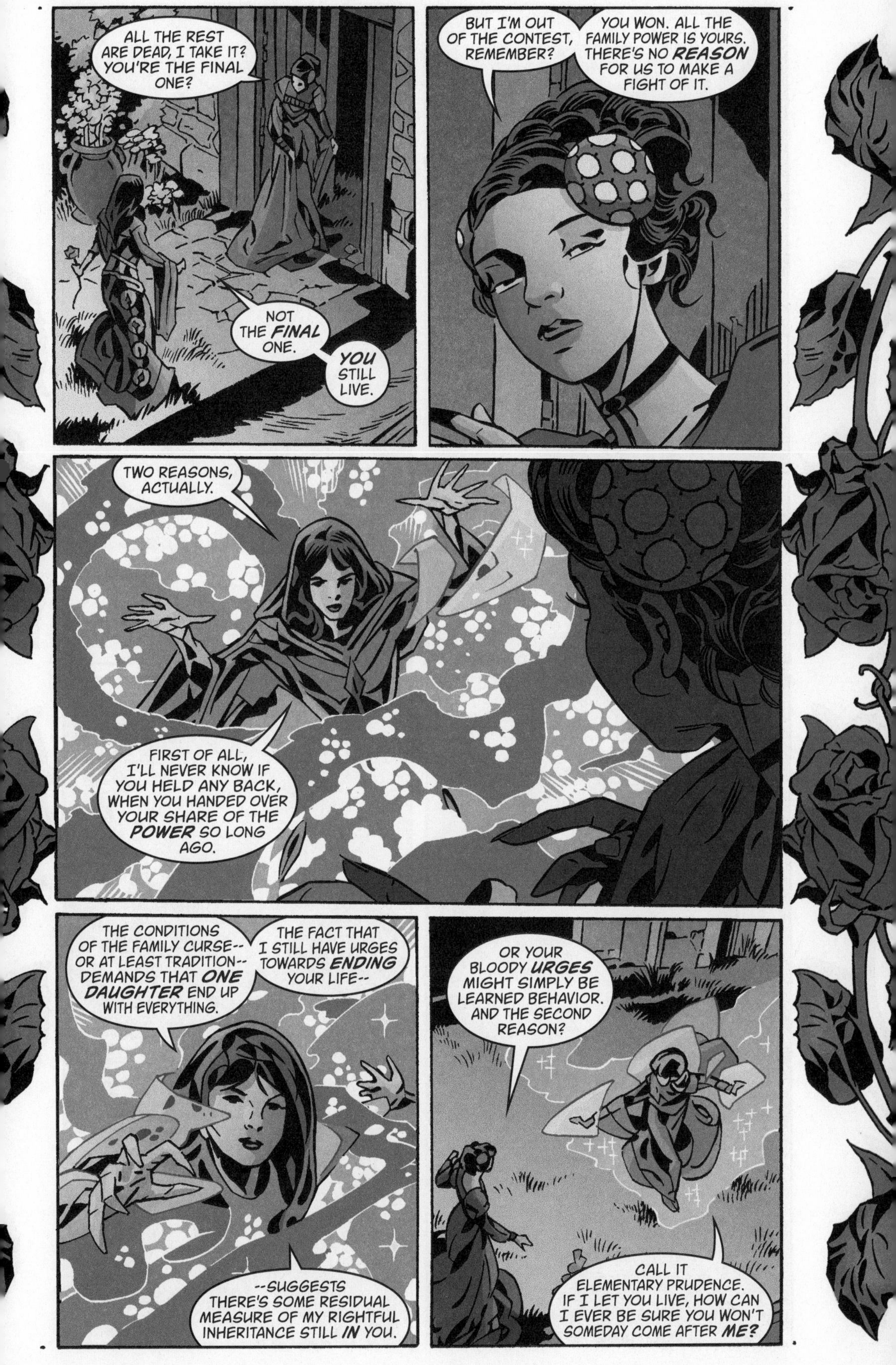
ALL THE REST ARE DEAD, I TAKE IT? YOU'RE THE FINAL ONE?
NOT THE FINAL ONE.
YOU STILL LIVE.
BUT I'M OUT OF THE CONTEST, REMEMBER?
YOU WON. ALL THE FAMILY POWER IS YOURS. THERE'S NO REASON FOR US TO MAKE A FIGHT OF IT.
TWO REASONS, ACTUALLY.
FIRST OF ALL, I'LL NEVER KNOW IF YOU HELD ANY BACK, WHEN YOU HANDED OVER YOUR SHARE OF THE POWER SO LONG AGO.
THE CONDITIONS OF THE FAMILY CURSE-- OR AT LEAST TRADITION-- DEMANDS THAT ONE DAUGHTER END UP WITH EVERYTHING.
THE FACT THAT I STILL HAVE URGES TOWARDS ENDING YOUR LIFE--
--SUGGESTS THERE'S SOME RESIDUAL MEASURE OF MY RIGHTFUL INHERITANCE STILL IN YOU.
OR YOUR BLOODY URGES MIGHT SIMPLY BE LEARNED BEHAVIOR. AND THE SECOND REASON?
CALL IT ELEMENTARY PRUDENCE. IF I LET YOU LIVE, HOW CAN I EVER BE SURE YOU WON'T SOMEDAY COME AFTER ME?

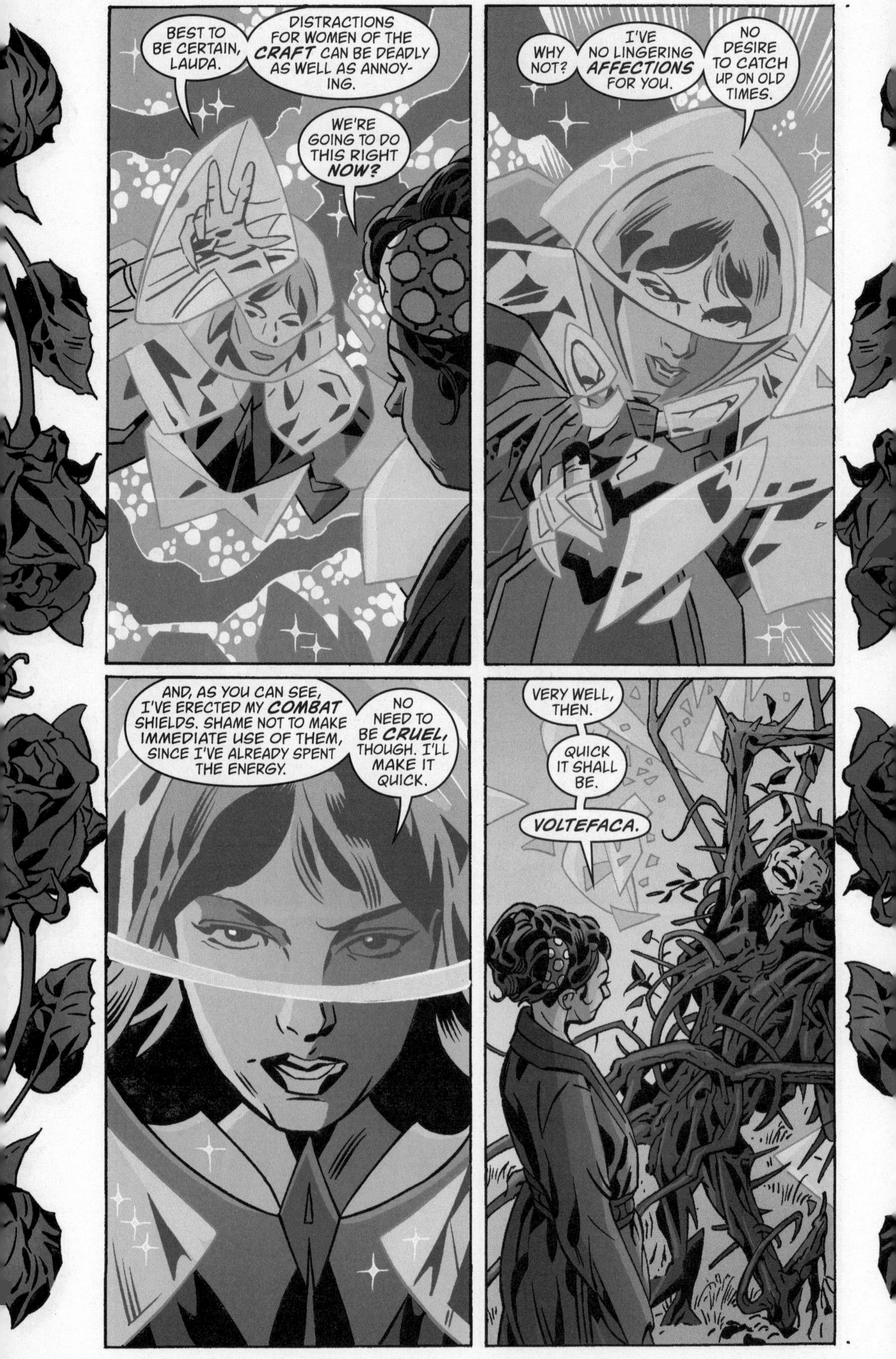
BEST TO BE CERTAIN, LAUDA.
DISTRACTIONS FOR WOMEN OF THE CRAFT CAN BE DEADLY AS WELL AS ANNOY-ING.
WE'RE GOING TO DO THIS RIGHT NOW?
WHY NOT?
I'VE NO LINGERING AFFECTIONS FOR YOU.
NO DESIRE TO CATCH UP ON OLD TIMES.
AND, AS YOU CAN SEE, I'VE ERECTED MY COMBAT SHIELDS. SHAME NOT TO MAKE IMMEDIATE USE OF THEM, SINCE I'VE ALREADY SPENT THE ENERGY.
NO NEED TO BE CRUEL, THOUGH. I'LL MAKE IT QUICK.
VERY WELL, THEN.
QUICK IT SHALL BE.
VOLTEFACA.

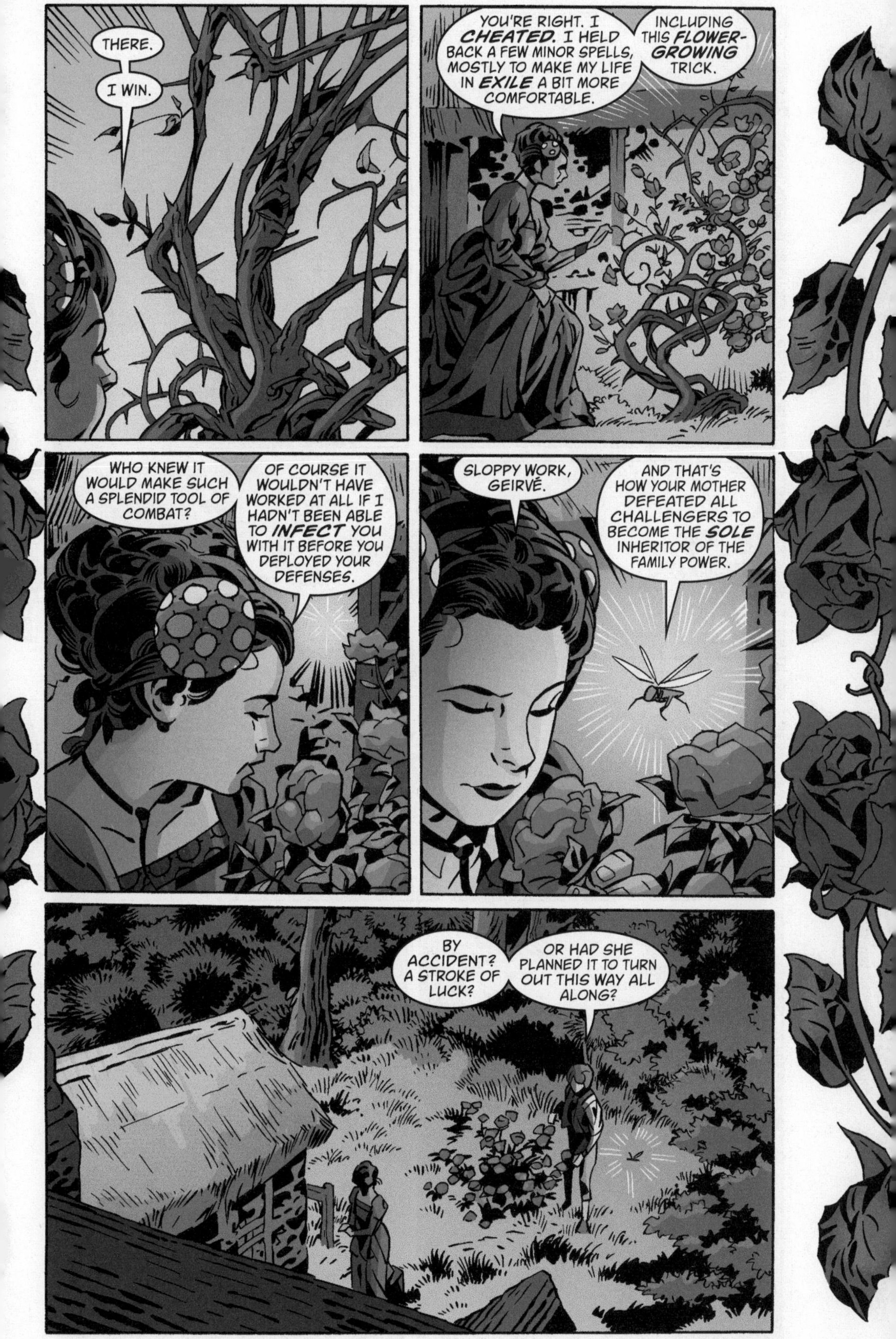
THERE.
I WIN.
YOU'RE RIGHT. I CHEATED. I HELD BACK A FEW MINOR SPELLS, MOSTLY TO MAKE MY LIFE IN EXILE A BIT MORE COMFORTABLE.
INCLUDING THIS FLOWER-GROWING TRICK.
WHO KNEW IT WOULD MAKE SUCH A SPLENDID TOOL OF COMBAT?
OF COURSE IT WOULDN'T HAVE WORKED AT ALL IF I HADN'T BEEN ABLE TO INFECT YOU WITH IT BEFORE YOU DEPLOYED YOUR DEFENSES.
SLOPPY WORK, GEIRVÉ.
AND THAT'S HOW YOUR MOTHER DEFEATED ALL CHALLENGERS TO BECOME THE SOLE INHERITOR OF THE FAMILY POWER.
BY ACCIDENT? A STROKE OF LUCK?
OR HAD SHE PLANNED IT TO TURN OUT THIS WAY ALL ALONG?

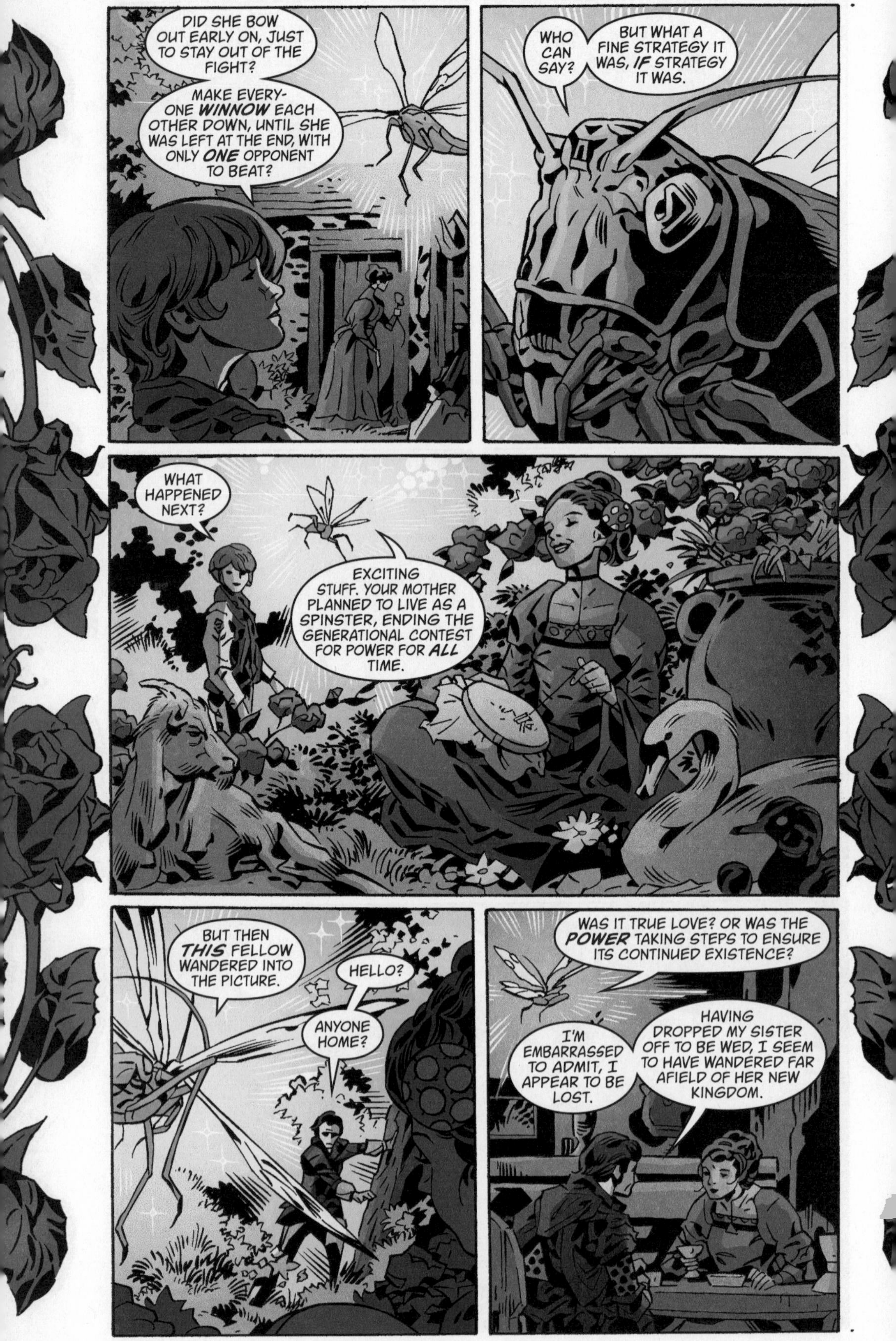

DID SHE BOW OUT EARLY ON, JUST TO STAY OUT OF THE FIGHT?
MAKE EVERY-ONE WINNOW EACH OTHER DOWN, UNTIL SHE WAS LEFT AT THE END, WITH ONLY ONE OPPONENT TO BEAT?
WHO CAN SAY?
BUT WHAT A FINE STRATEGY IT WAS, IF STRATEGY IT WAS.
WHAT HAPPENED NEXT?
EXCITING STUFF. YOUR MOTHER PLANNED TO LIVE AS A SPINSTER, ENDING THE GENERATIONAL CONTEST FOR POWER FOR ALL TIME.
BUT THEN THIS FELLOW WANDERED INTO THE PICTURE.
HELLO?
ANYONE HOME?
WAS IT TRUE LOVE? OR WAS THE POWER TAKING STEPS TO ENSURE ITS CONTINUED EXISTENCE?
I'M EMBARRASSED TO ADMIT, I APPEAR TO BE LOST.
HAVING DROPPED MY SISTER OFF TO BE WED, I SEEM TO HAVE WANDERED FAR AFIELD OF HER NEW KINGDOM.

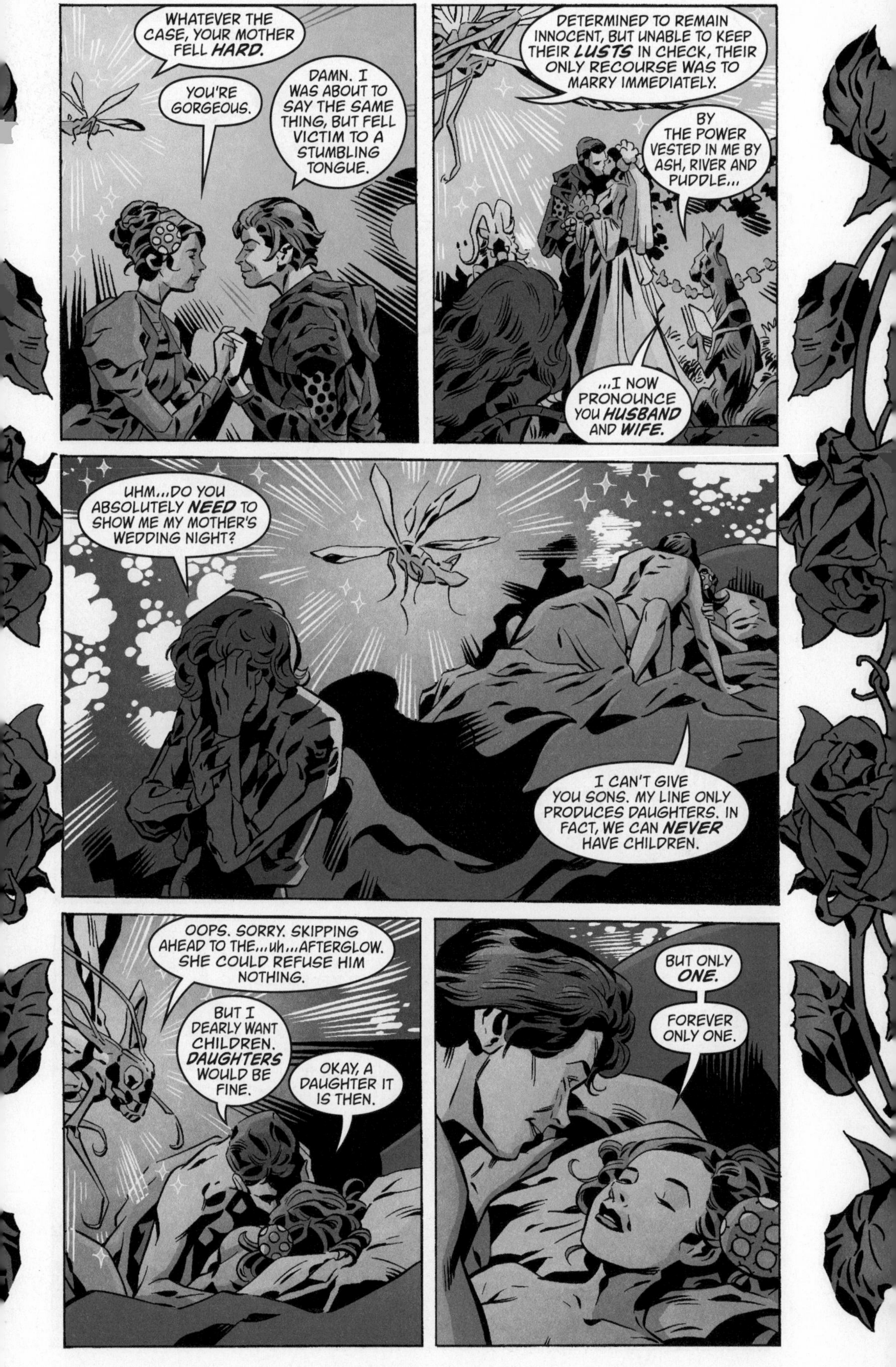
WHATEVER THE CASE, YOUR MOTHER FELL HARD.
YOU'RE GORGEOUS.
DAMN. I WAS ABOUT TO SAY THE SAME THING, BUT FELL VICTIM TO A STUMBLING TONGUE.
DETERMINED TO REMAIN INNOCENT, BUT UNABLE TO KEEP THEIR LUSTS IN CHECK, THEIR ONLY RECOURSE WAS TO MARRY IMMEDIATELY.
BY THE POWER VESTED IN ME BY ASH, RIVER AND PUDDLE...
...I NOW PRONOUNCE YOU HUSBAND AND WIFE.
UHM...DO YOU ABSOLUTELY NEED TO SHOW ME MY MOTHER'S WEDDING NIGHT?
I CAN'T GIVE YOU SONS. MY LINE ONLY PRODUCES DAUGHTERS. IN FACT, WE CAN NEVER HAVE CHILDREN.
OOPS. SORRY. SKIPPING AHEAD TO THE...uh...AFTERGLOW. SHE COULD REFUSE HIM NOTHING.
BUT I DEARLY WANT CHILDREN. DAUGHTERS WOULD BE FINE.
OKAY, A DAUGHTER IT IS THEN.
BUT ONLY ONE.
FOREVER ONLY ONE.

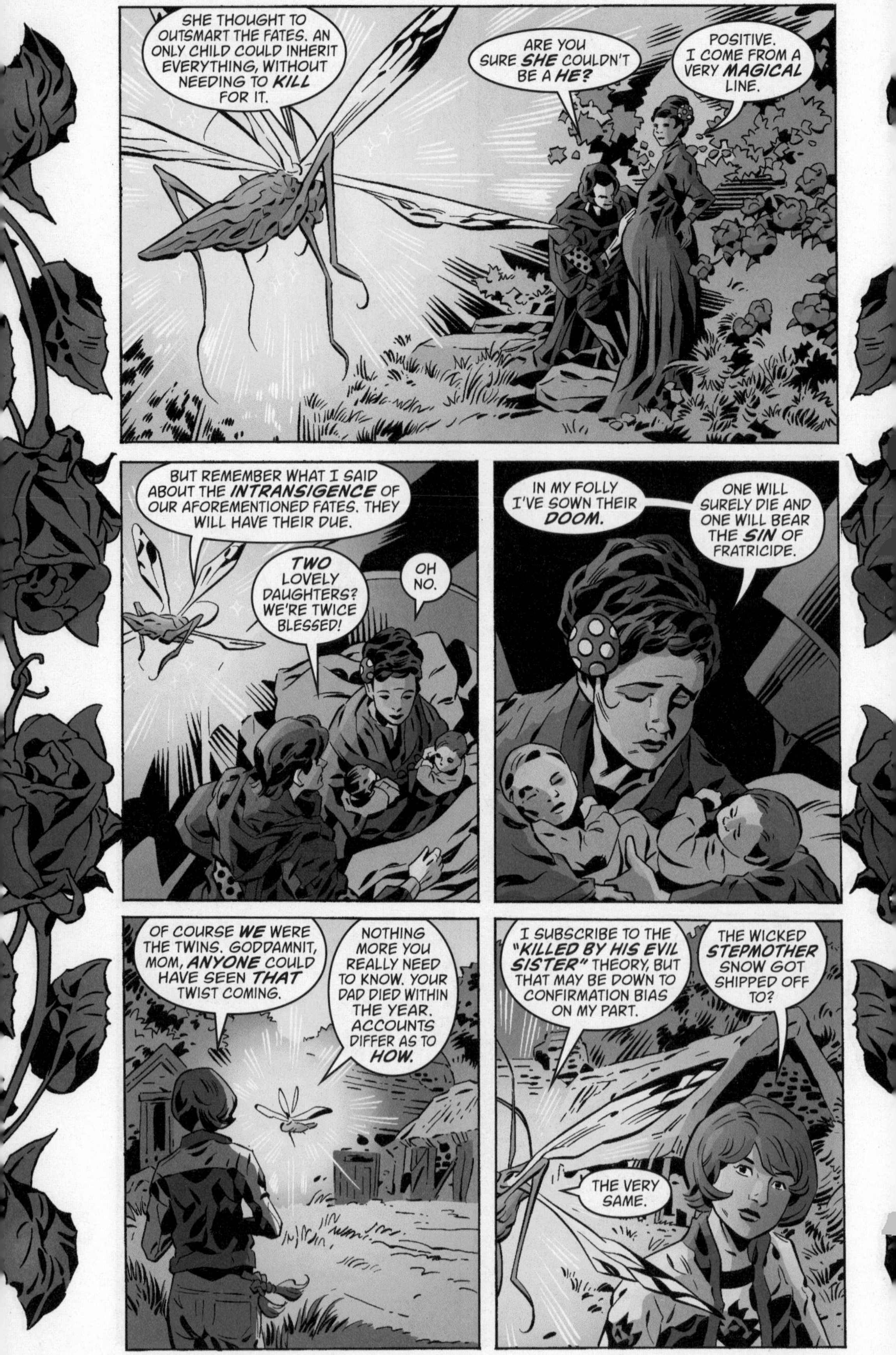
SHE THOUGHT TO OUTSMART THE FATES. AN ONLY CHILD COULD INHERIT EVERYTHING, WITHOUT NEEDING TO KILL FOR IT.
ARE YOU SURE SHE COULDN'T BE A HE?
POSITIVE. I COME FROM A VERY MAGICAL LINE.
BUT REMEMBER WHAT I SAID ABOUT THE INTRANSIGENCE OF OUR AFOREMENTIONED FATES. THEY WILL HAVE THEIR DUE.
TWO LOVELY DAUGHTERS? WE'RE TWICE BLESSED!
OH NO.
IN MY FOLLY I'VE SOWN THEIR DOOM.
ONE WILL SURELY DIE AND ONE WILL BEAR THE SIN OF FRATRICIDE.
OF COURSE WE WERE THE TWINS. GODDAMNIT, MOM, ANYONE COULD HAVE SEEN THAT TWIST COMING.
NOTHING MORE YOU REALLY NEED TO KNOW. YOUR DAD DIED WITHIN THE YEAR. ACCOUNTS DIFFER AS TO HOW.
I SUBSCRIBE TO THE "KILLED BY HIS EVIL SISTER" THEORY, BUT THAT MAY BE DOWN TO CONFIRMATION BIAS ON MY PART.
THE WICKED STEPMOTHER SNOW GOT SHIPPED OFF TO?
THE VERY SAME.

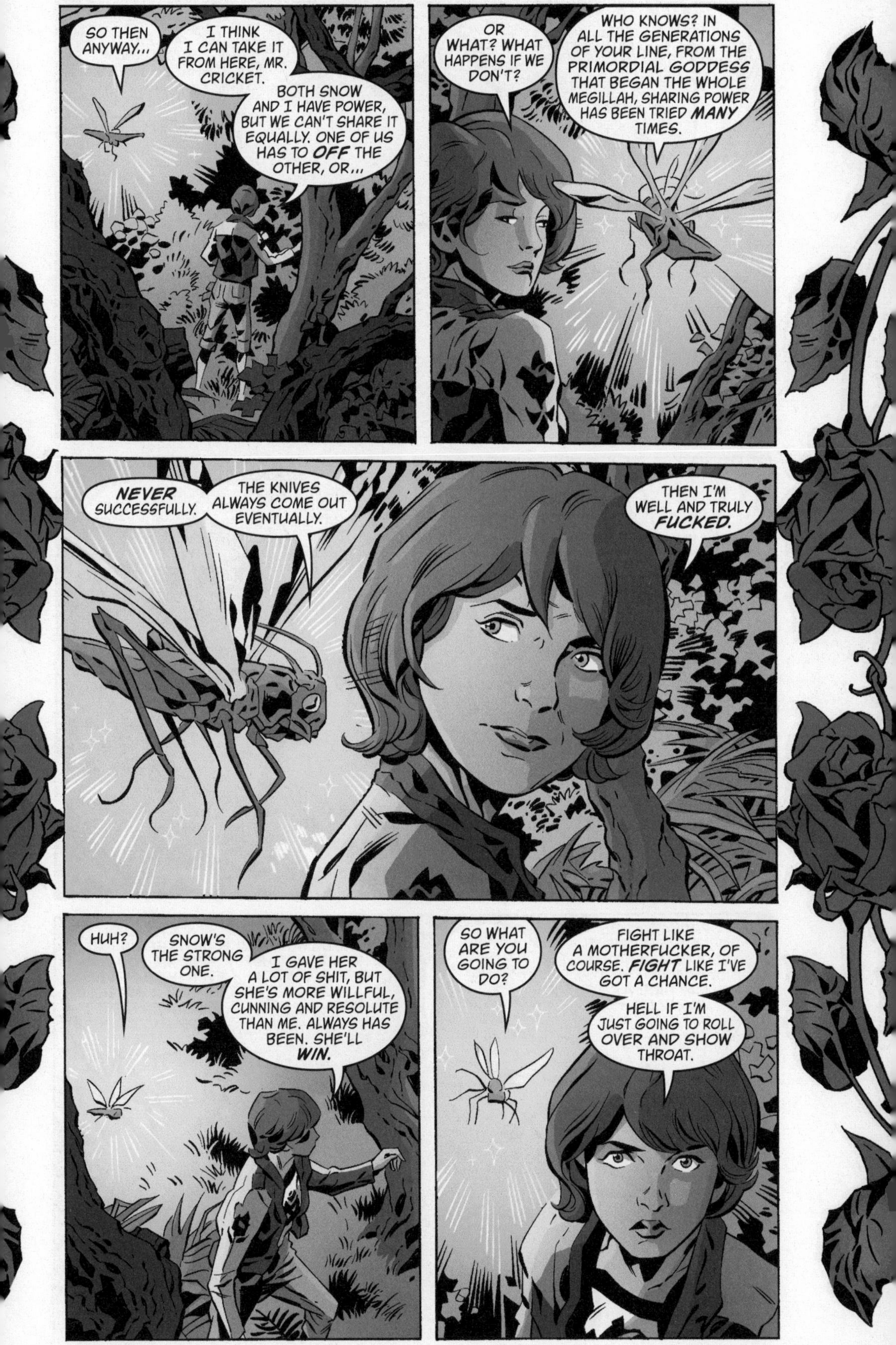
SO THEN ANYWAY...
I THINK I CAN TAKE IT FROM HERE, MR. CRICKET.
BOTH SNOW AND I HAVE POWER, BUT WE CAN'T SHARE IT EQUALLY. ONE OF US HAS TO OFF THE OTHER, OR...
OR WHAT? WHAT HAPPENS IF WE DON'T?
WHO KNOWS? IN ALL THE GENERATIONS OF YOUR LINE, FROM THE PRIMORDIAL GODDESS THAT BEGAN THE WHOLE MEGILLAH, SHARING POWER HAS BEEN TRIED MANY TIMES.
NEVER SUCCESSFULLY.
THE KNIVES ALWAYS COME OUT EVENTUALLY.
THEN I'M WELL AND TRULY FUCKED.
HUH?
SNOW'S THE STRONG ONE.
I GAVE HER A LOT OF SHIT, BUT SHE'S MORE WILLFUL, CUNNING AND RESOLUTE THAN ME. ALWAYS HAS BEEN. SHE'LL WIN.
SO WHAT ARE YOU GOING TO DO?
FIGHT LIKE A MOTHERFUCKER, OF COURSE. FIGHT LIKE I'VE GOT A CHANCE.
HELL IF I'M JUST GOING TO ROLL OVER AND SHOW THROAT.

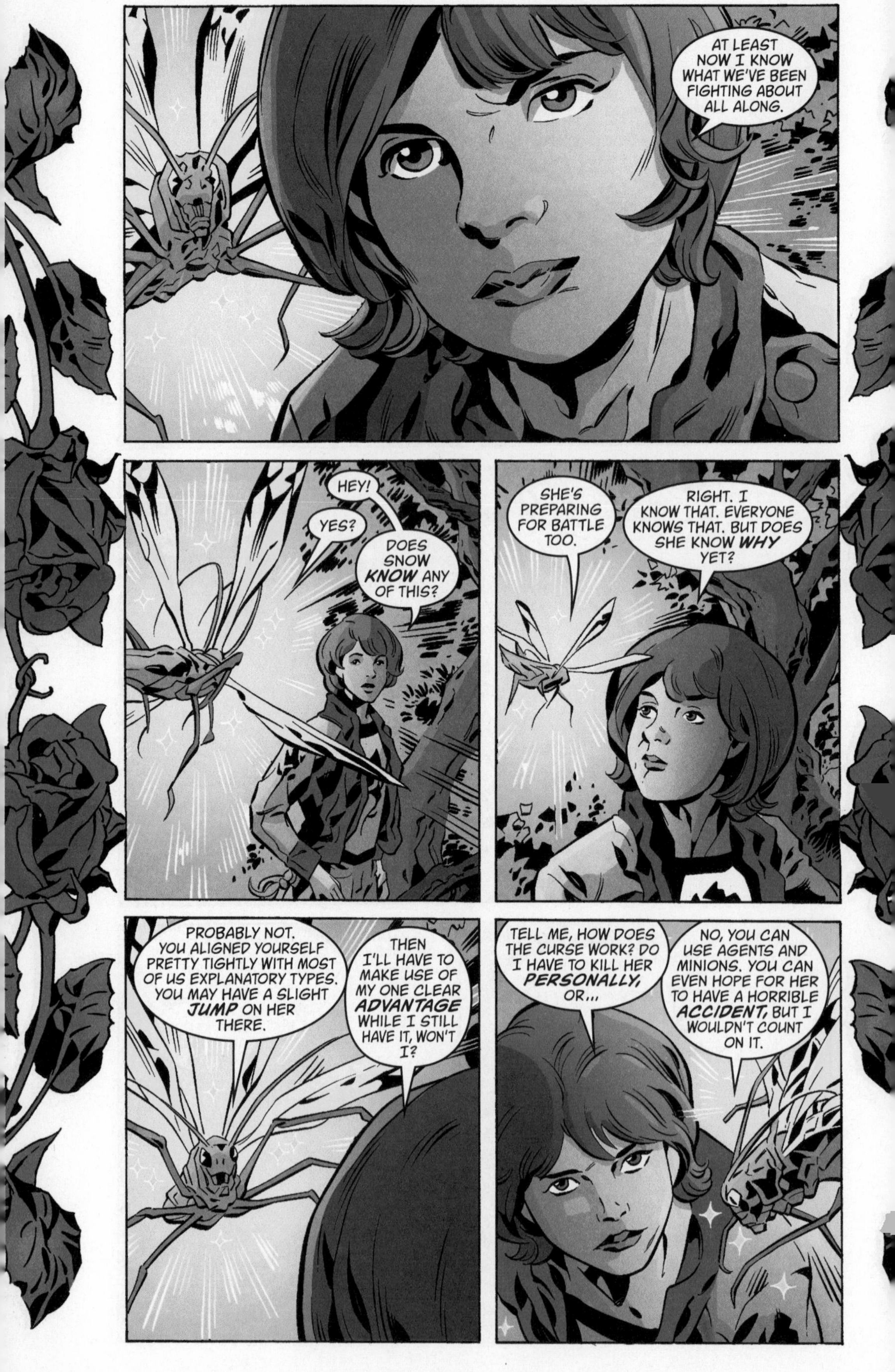
AT LEAST NOW I KNOW WHAT WE'VE BEEN FIGHTING ABOUT ALL ALONG.
HEY!
YES?
DOES SNOW KNOW ANY OF THIS?
SHE'S PREPARING FOR BATTLE TOO.
RIGHT. I KNOW THAT. EVERYONE KNOWS THAT. BUT DOES SHE KNOW WHY YET?
PROBABLY NOT. YOU ALIGNED YOURSELF PRETTY TIGHTLY WITH MOST OF US EXPLANATORY TYPES. YOU MAY HAVE A SLIGHT JUMP ON HER THERE.
THEN I'LL HAVE TO MAKE USE OF MY ONE CLEAR ADVANTAGE WHILE I STILL HAVE IT, WON'T I?
TELL ME, HOW DOES THE CURSE WORK? DO I HAVE TO KILL HER PERSONALLY, OR...
NO, YOU CAN USE AGENTS AND MINIONS. YOU CAN EVEN HOPE FOR HER TO HAVE A HORRIBLE ACCIDENT, BUT I WOULDN'T COUNT ON IT.

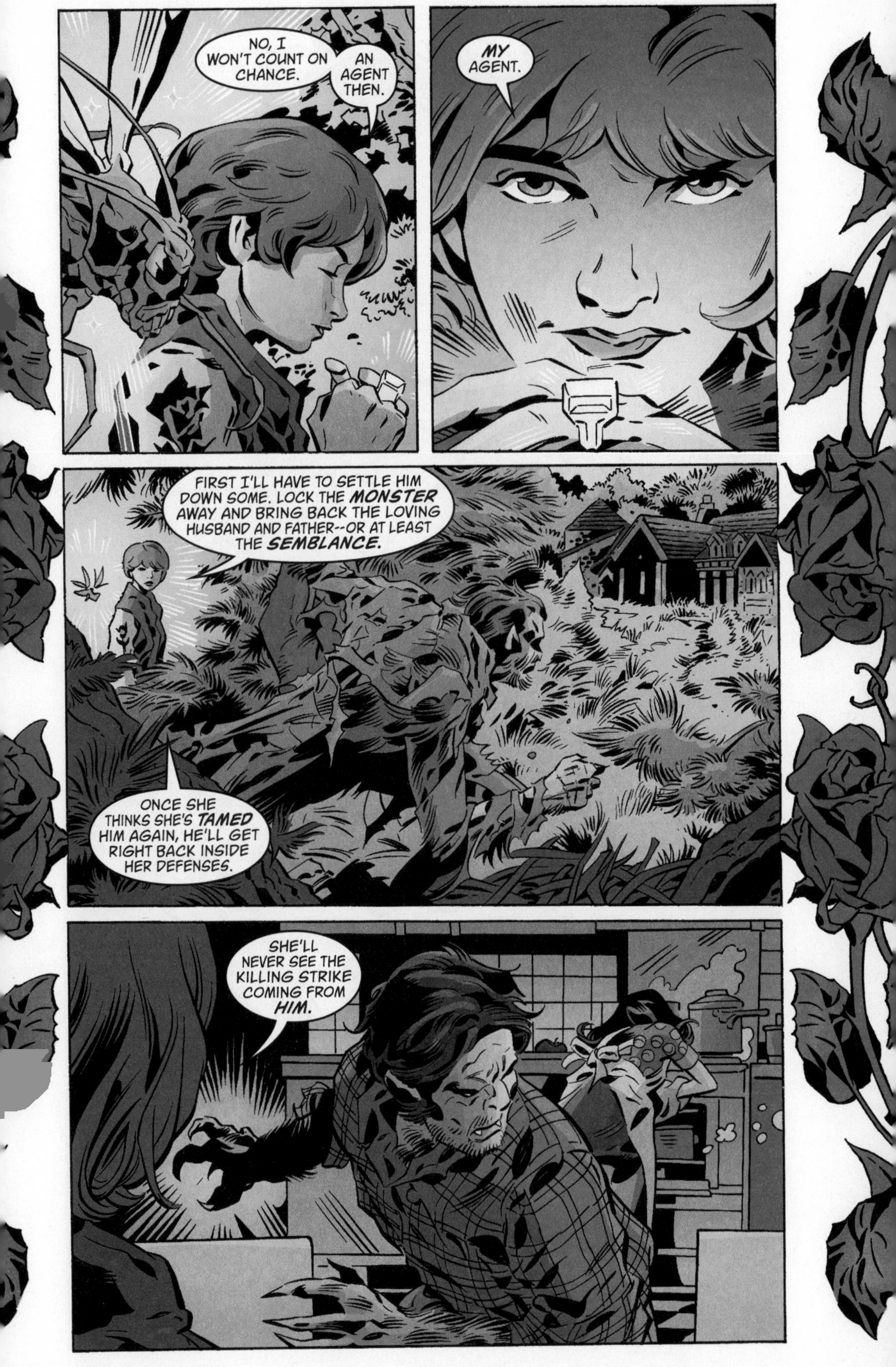
NO, I WON'T COUNT ON CHANCE.
AN AGENT THEN.
MY AGENT.
FIRST I'LL HAVE TO SETTLE HIM DOWN SOME. LOCK THE MONSTER AWAY AND BRING BACK THE LOVING HUSBAND AND FATHER--OR AT LEAST THE SEMBLANCE.
ONCE SHE THINKS SHE'S TAMED HIM AGAIN, HE'LL GET RIGHT BACK INSIDE HER DEFENSES.
SHE'LL NEVER SEE THE KILLING STRIKE COMING FROM HIM.

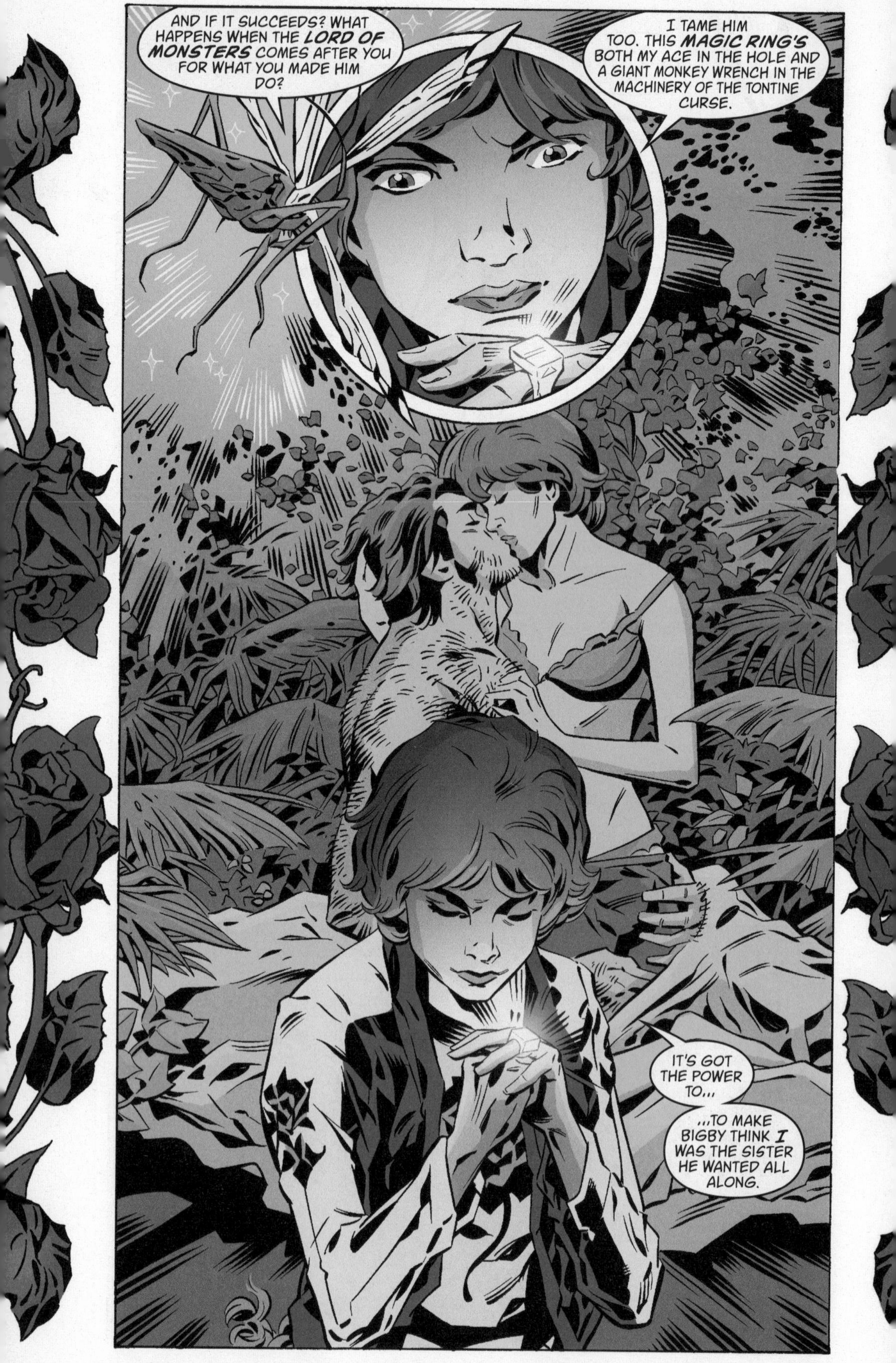
AND IF IT SUCCEEDS? WHAT HAPPENS WHEN THE LORD OF MONSTERS COMES AFTER YOU FOR WHAT YOU MADE HIM DO?
I TAME HIM TOO. THIS MAGIC RING'S BOTH MY ACE IN THE HOLE AND A GIANT MONKEY WRENCH IN THE MACHINERY OF THE TONTINE CURSE.
IT'S GOT THE POWER TO...
...TO MAKE BIGBY THINK I WAS THE SISTER HE WANTED ALL ALONG.

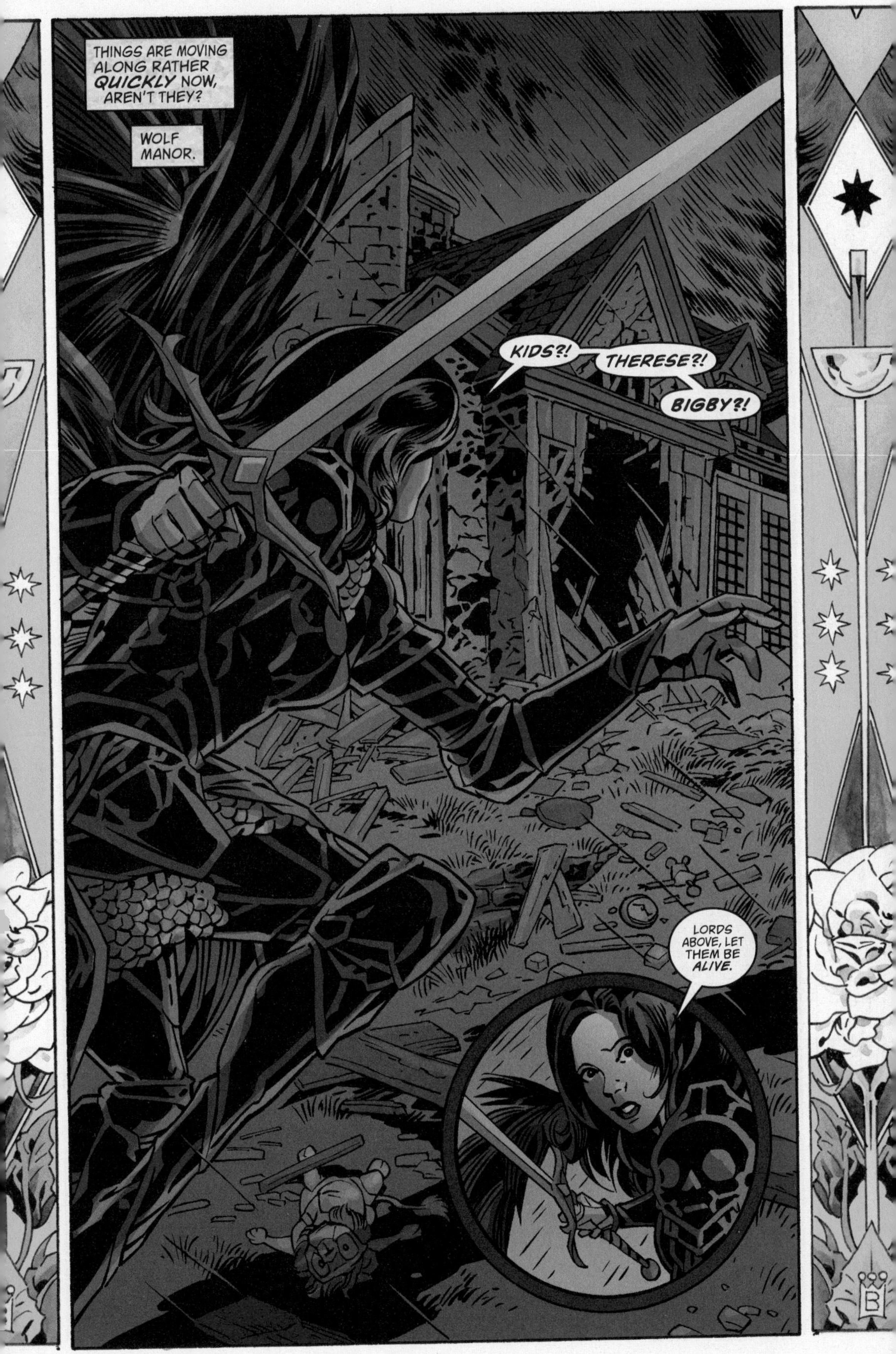
THINGS ARE MOVING ALONG RATHER QUICKLY NOW, AREN'T THEY?
WOLF MANOR.
KIDS?!
THERESE?!
BIGBY?!
LORDS ABOVE, LET THEM BE ALIVE.

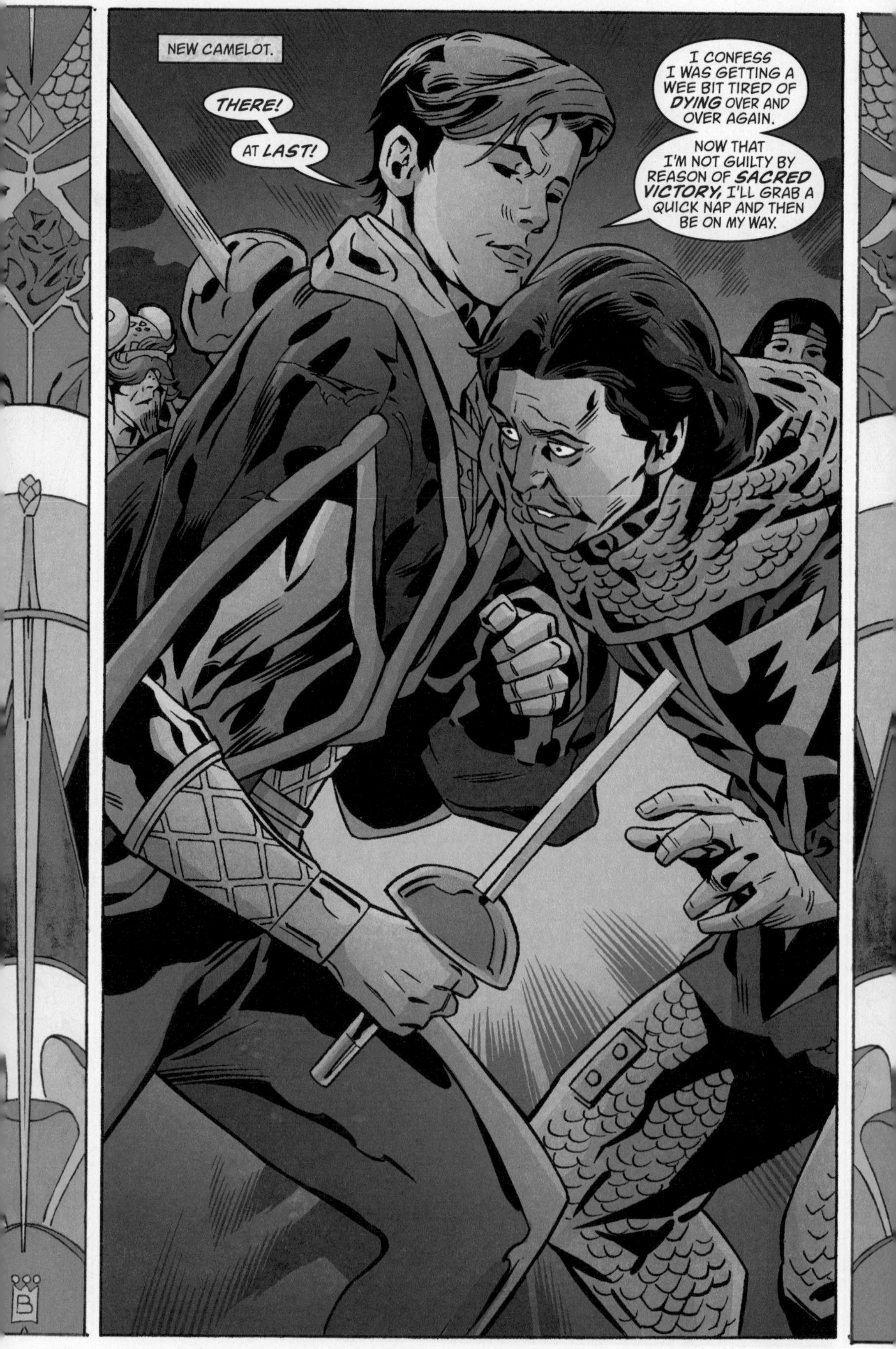
NEW CAMELOT.
THERE!
AT LAST!
I CONFESS I WAS GETTING A WEE BIT TIRED OF DYING OVER AND OVER AGAIN.
NOW THAT I'M NOT GUILTY BY REASON OF SACRED VICTORY, I'LL GRAB A QUICK NAP AND THEN BE ON MY WAY.

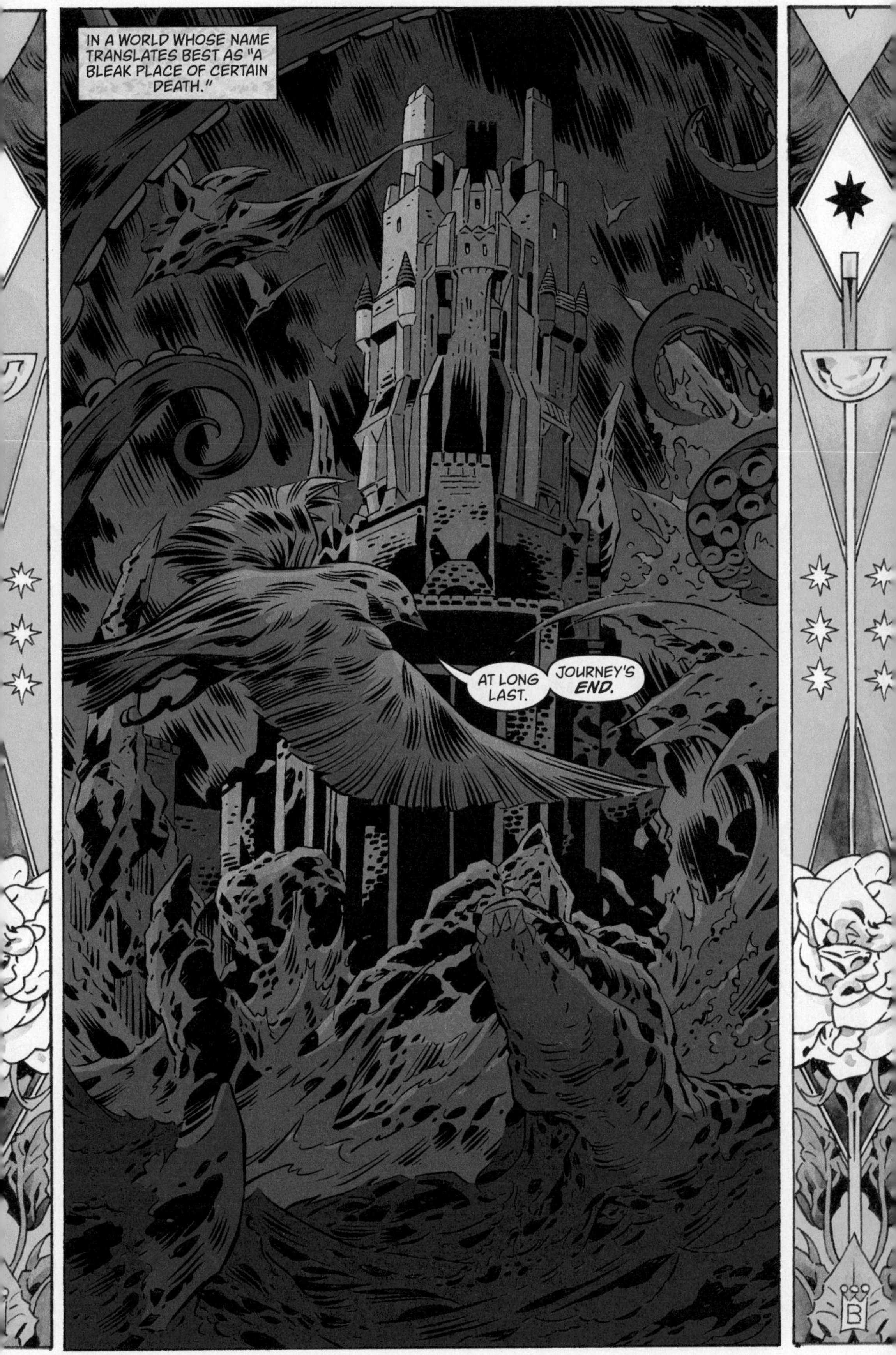
IN A WORLD WHOSE NAME TRANSLATES BEST AS "A BLEAK PLACE OF CERTAIN DEATH."
AT LONG LAST.
JOURNEY'S **END.**

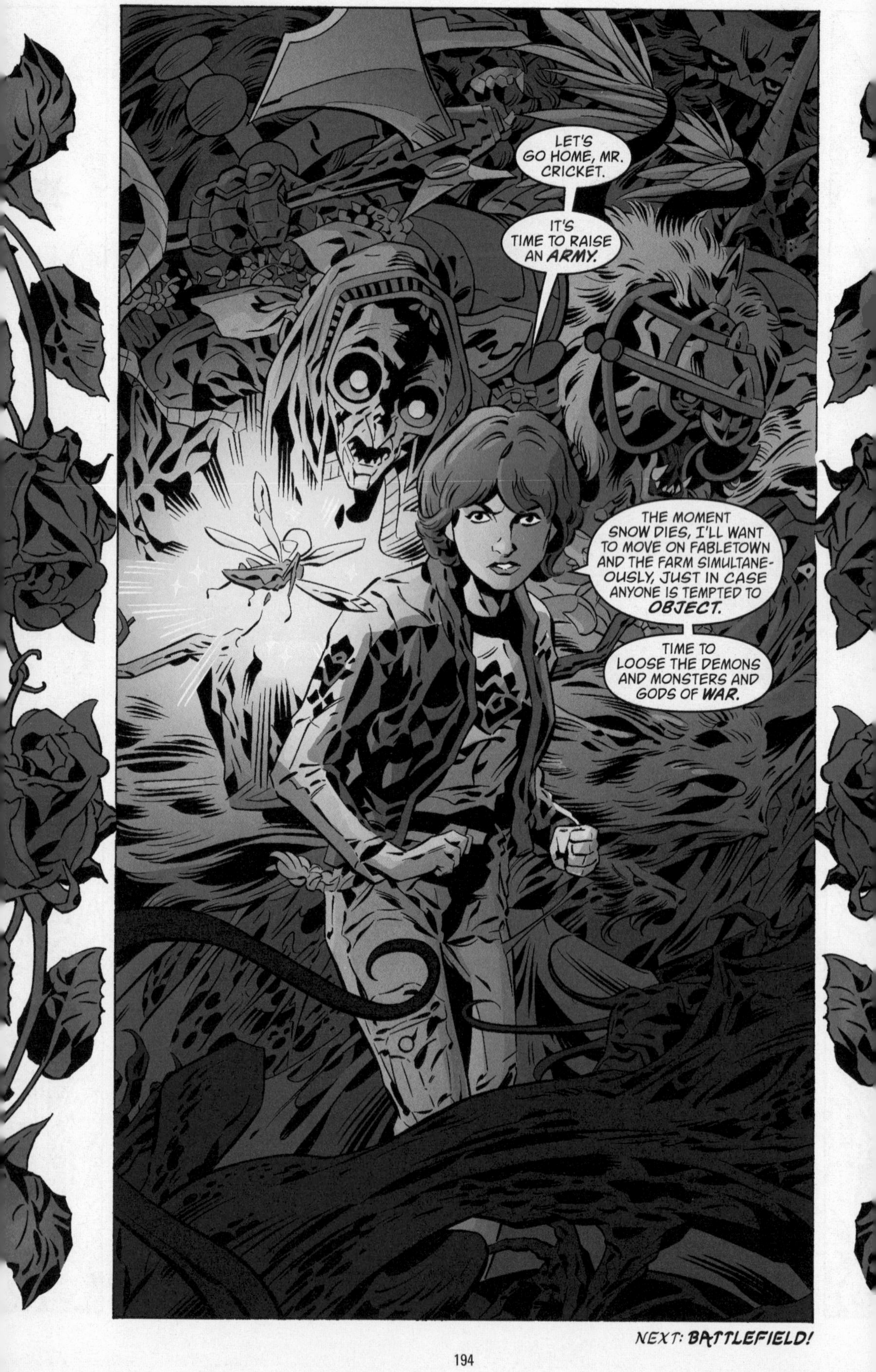
LET'S GO HOME, MR. CRICKET.
IT'S TIME TO RAISE AN ARMY.
THE MOMENT SNOW DIES, I'LL WANT TO MOVE ON FABLETOWN AND THE FARM SIMULTANE-OUSLY, JUST IN CASE ANYONE IS TEMPTED TO OBJECT.
TIME TO LOOSE THE DEMONS AND MONSTERS AND GODS OF WAR.

NEXT: **BATTLEFIELD!**

THE LAST BIG SLEEP

Being the last ever tale of Briar Rose, often known as the Sleeping Beauty, and of her demonic car Hadeon.

Bill Willingham writer/creator · Chrissie Zullo artist · Todd Klein letters · Rowena Yow assoc. editor · Shelly Bond editor

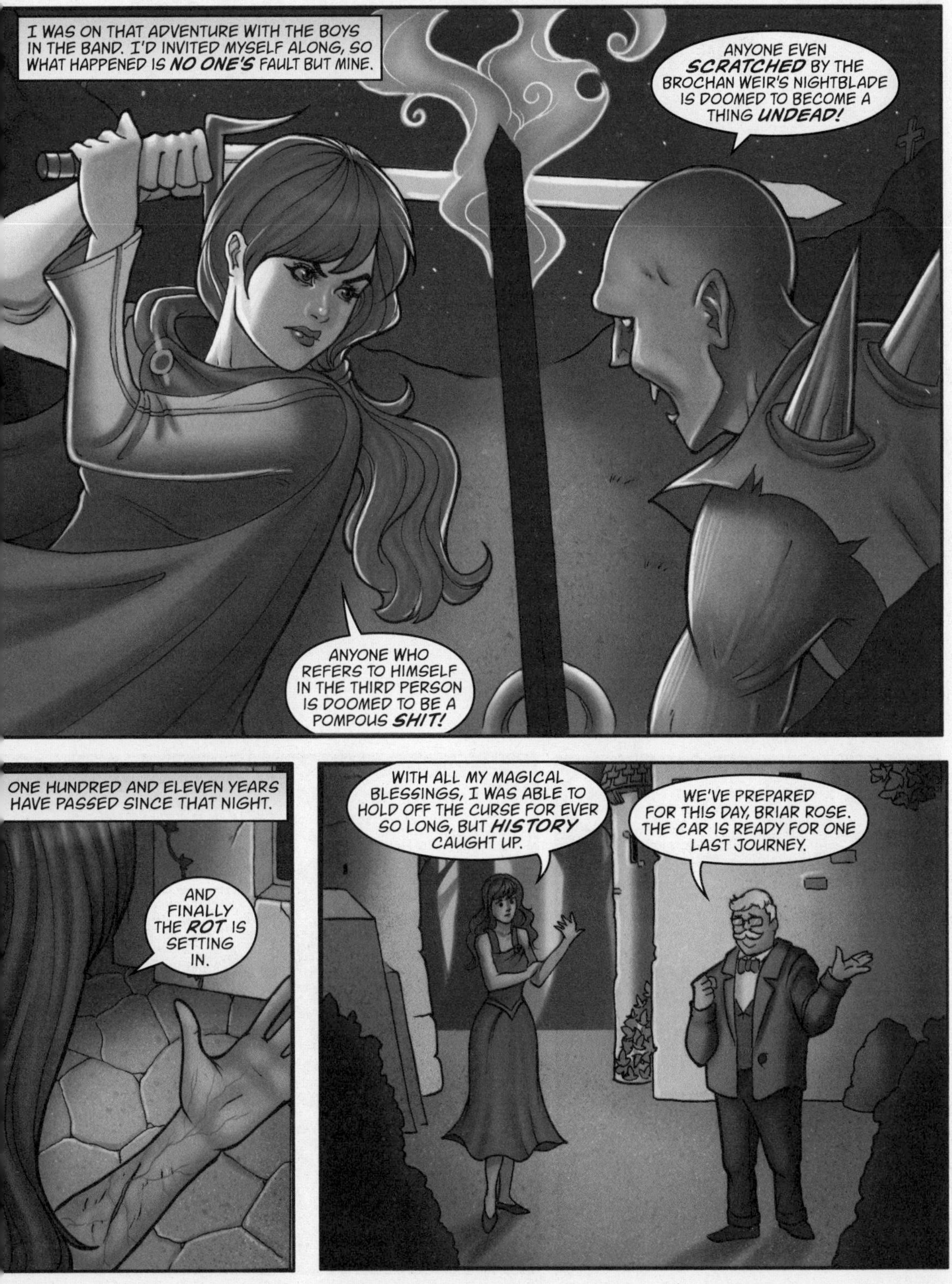
I WAS ON THAT ADVENTURE WITH THE BOYS IN THE BAND. I'D INVITED MYSELF ALONG, SO WHAT HAPPENED IS NO ONE'S FAULT BUT MINE.
ANYONE EVEN SCRATCHED BY THE BROCHAN WEIR'S NIGHTBLADE IS DOOMED TO BECOME A THING UNDEAD!
ANYONE WHO REFERS TO HIMSELF IN THE THIRD PERSON IS DOOMED TO BE A POMPOUS SHIT!
ONE HUNDRED AND ELEVEN YEARS HAVE PASSED SINCE THAT NIGHT.
AND FINALLY THE ROT IS SETTING IN.
WITH ALL MY MAGICAL BLESSINGS, I WAS ABLE TO HOLD OFF THE CURSE FOR EVER SO LONG, BUT HISTORY CAUGHT UP.
WE'VE PREPARED FOR THIS DAY, BRIAR ROSE. THE CAR IS READY FOR ONE LAST JOURNEY.

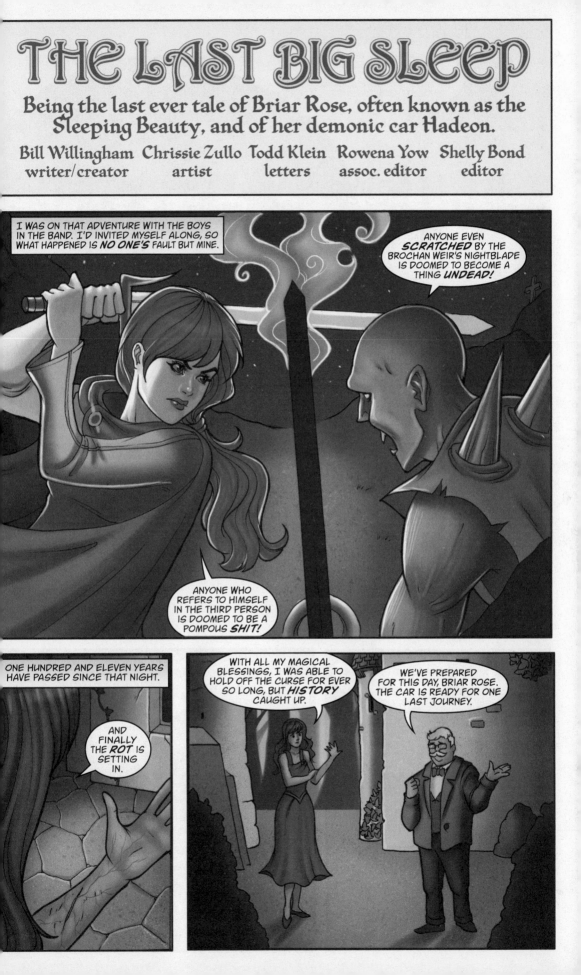

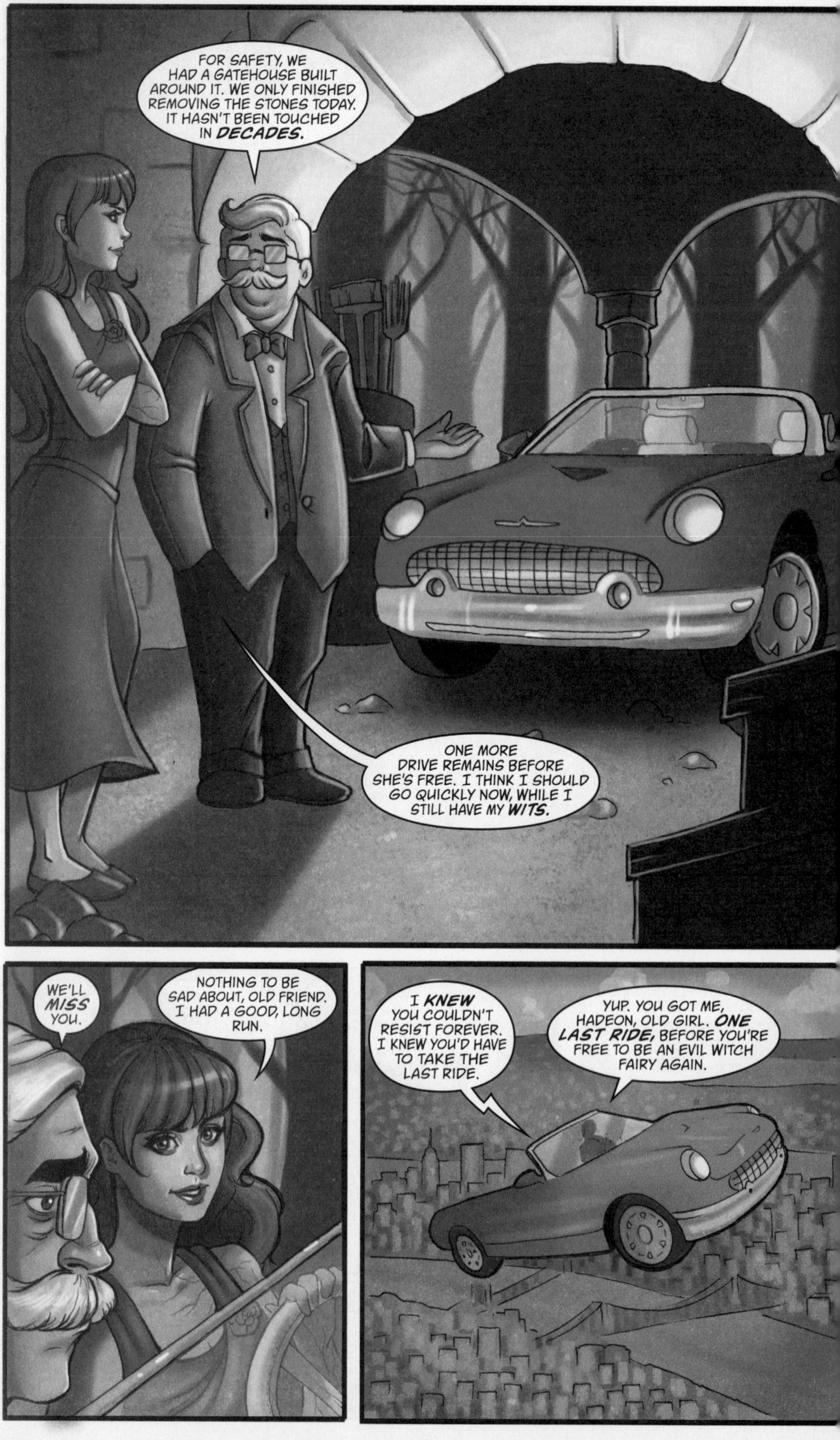
FOR SAFETY, WE HAD A GATEHOUSE BUILT AROUND IT. WE ONLY FINISHED REMOVING THE STONES TODAY. IT HASN'T BEEN TOUCHED IN ***DECADES.***
ONE MORE DRIVE REMAINS BEFORE SHE'S FREE. I THINK I SHOULD GO QUICKLY NOW, WHILE I STILL HAVE MY ***WITS.***
WE'LL *MISS* YOU.
NOTHING TO BE SAD ABOUT, OLD FRIEND. I HAD A GOOD, LONG RUN.
I ***KNEW*** YOU COULDN'T RESIST FOREVER. I KNEW YOU'D HAVE TO TAKE THE LAST RIDE.
YUP. YOU GOT ME, HADEON, OLD GIRL. ***ONE LAST RIDE,*** BEFORE YOU'RE FREE TO BE AN EVIL WITCH FAIRY AGAIN.

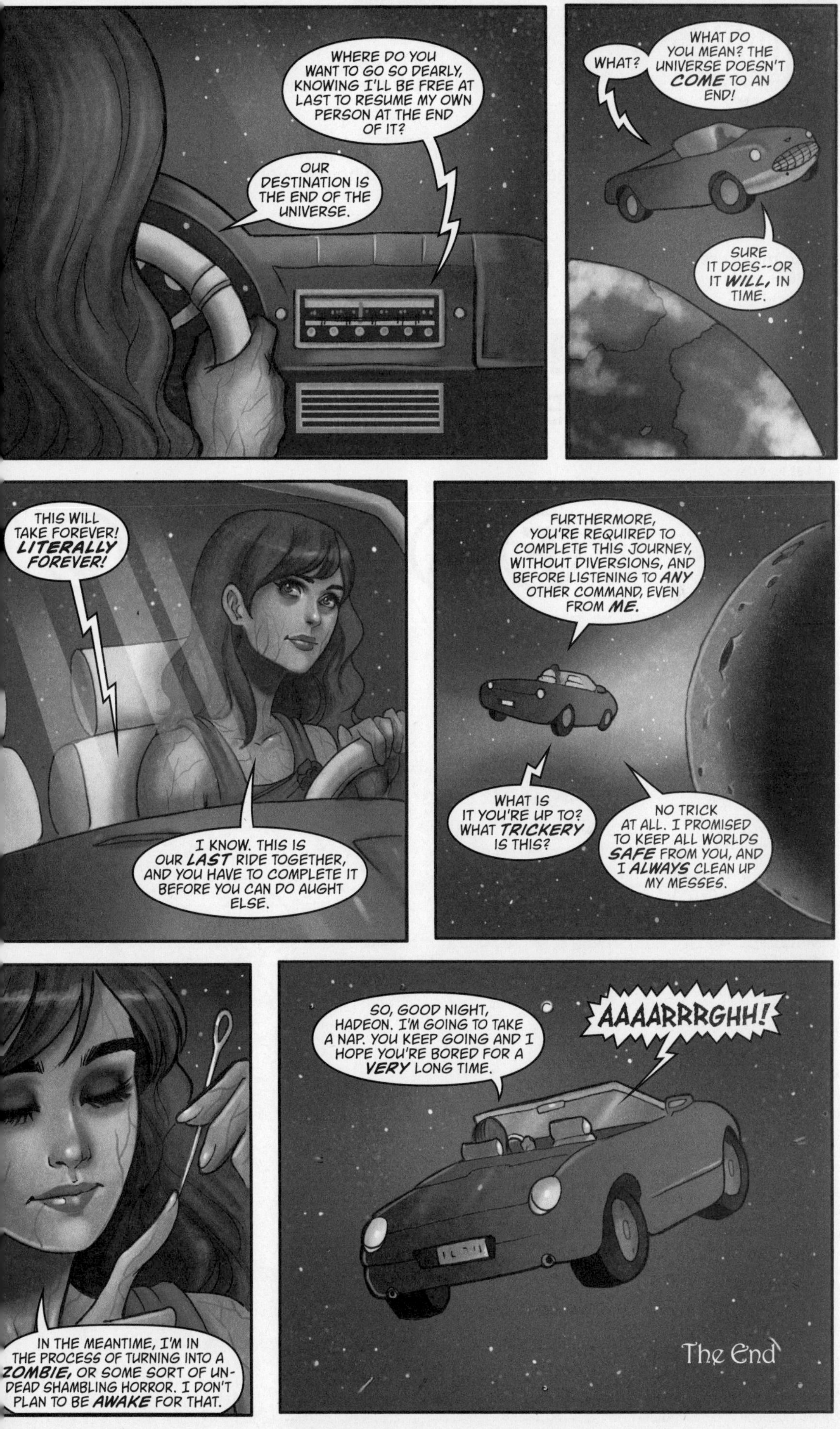
WHERE DO YOU WANT TO GO SO DEARLY, KNOWING I'LL BE FREE AT LAST TO RESUME MY OWN PERSON AT THE END OF IT?
OUR DESTINATION IS THE END OF THE UNIVERSE.
WHAT?
WHAT DO YOU MEAN? THE UNIVERSE DOESN'T *COME* TO AN END!
SURE IT DOES--OR IT *WILL,* IN TIME.
THIS WILL TAKE FOREVER! *LITERALLY FOREVER!*
I KNOW. THIS IS OUR *LAST* RIDE TOGETHER, AND YOU HAVE TO COMPLETE IT BEFORE YOU CAN DO AUGHT ELSE.
FURTHERMORE, YOU'RE REQUIRED TO COMPLETE THIS JOURNEY, WITHOUT DIVERSIONS, AND BEFORE LISTENING TO *ANY* OTHER COMMAND, EVEN FROM *ME.*
WHAT IS IT YOU'RE UP TO? WHAT *TRICKERY* IS THIS?
NO TRICK AT ALL. I PROMISED TO KEEP ALL WORLDS *SAFE* FROM YOU, AND I *ALWAYS* CLEAN UP MY MESSES.
IN THE MEANTIME, I'M IN THE PROCESS OF TURNING INTO A *ZOMBIE,* OR SOME SORT OF UN-DEAD SHAMBLING HORROR. I DON'T PLAN TO BE *AWAKE* FOR THAT.
SO, GOOD NIGHT, HADEON. I'M GOING TO TAKE A NAP. YOU KEEP GOING AND I HOPE YOU'RE BORED FOR A *VERY* LONG TIME.
AAAARRRGHH!
The End

VERTIGO

"FABLES is an excellent series in the tradition of SANDMAN, one that rewards careful attention and loyalty."
—PUBLISHERS WEEKLY

"[A] wonderfully twisted concept...features fairy tale characters banished to the noirish world of present-day New York."
—WASHINGTON POST

"Great fun." —BOOKLIST

READ THE ENTIRE SERIES!

FABLES VOL. 2: ANIMAL FARM

FABLES VOL. 3: STORYBOOK LOVE

FABLES VOL. 4: MARCH OF THE WOODEN SOLDIERS

FABLES VOL. 5: THE MEAN SEASONS

FABLES VOL. 6: HOMELANDS

FABLES VOL. 7: ARABIAN NIGHTS (AND DAYS)

FABLES VOL. 8: WOLVES

FABLES VOL. 9: SONS OF EMPIRE

FABLES VOL. 10: THE GOOD PRINCE

FABLES VOL. 11: WAR AND PIECES

FABLES VOL. 12: THE DARK AGES

FABLES VOL. 13: THE GREAT FABLES CROSSOVER

FABLES VOL. 14: WITCHES

FABLES VOL. 15: ROSE RED

FABLES VOL. 16: SUPER TEAM

FABLES VOL. 17: INHERIT THE WIND

FABLES VOL. 18: CUBS IN TOYLAND

FABLES VOL. 19: SNOW WHITE

FABLES: 1001 NIGHTS OF SNOWFALL

FABLES: WEREWOLVES OF THE HEARTLAND

PETER & MAX: A FABLES NOVEL

THE FABLES ENCYCLOPEDIA

BILL WILLINGHAM

FABLES VOL. 1: LEGENDS IN EXILE

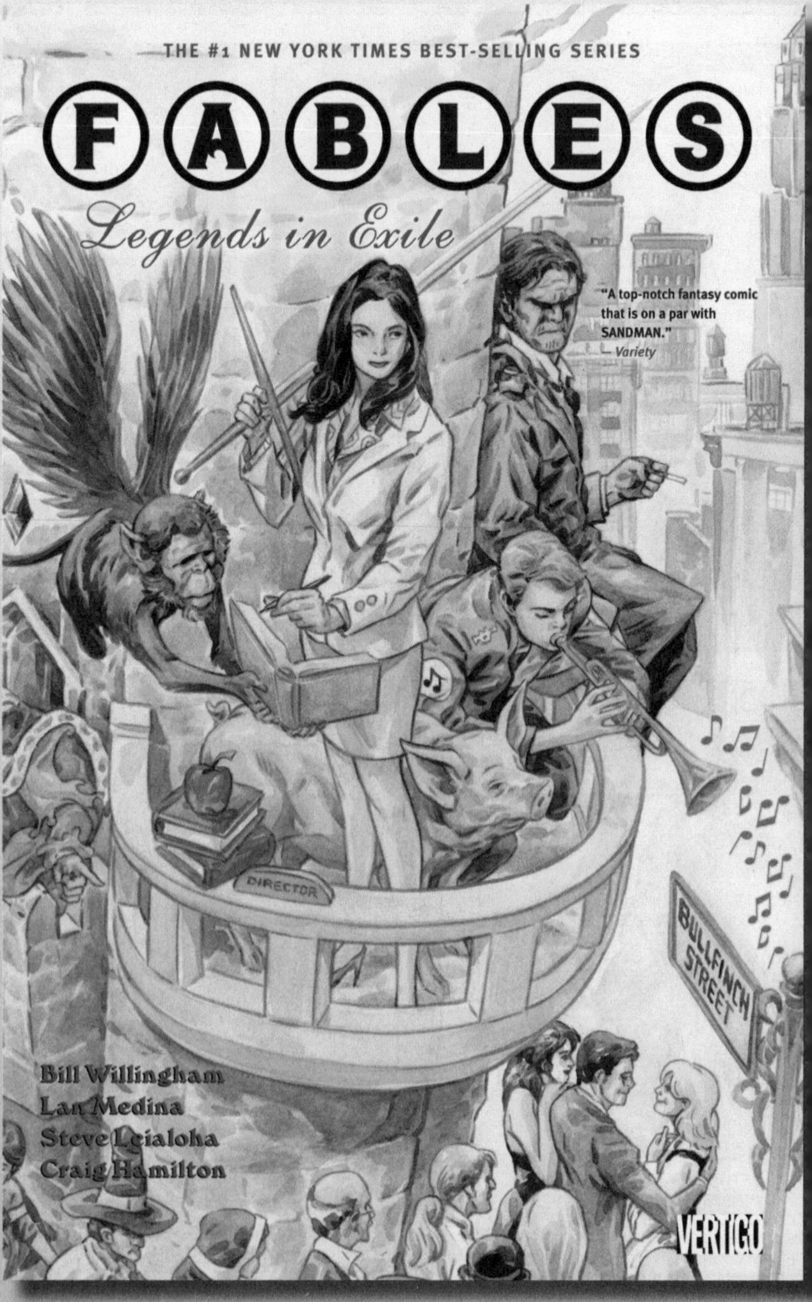

THE #1 NEW YORK TIMES BEST-SELLING SERIES
FABLES
Legends in Exile
"A top-notch fantasy comic that is on a par with SANDMAN." — Variety
DIRECTOR
BULLFINCH STREET
Bill Willingham
Lan Medina
Steve Leialoha
Craig Hamilton
VERTIGO